Frontispiece. Haddam, Connecticut.—The Birth-Place of David and John Brainerd.

THE LIFE

OF

JOHN BRAINERD,

THE BROTHER OF

DAVID BRAINERD,

AND HIS SUCCESSOR AS

MISSIONARY TO THE INDIANS OF NEW JERSEY.

Par Nobile Fratrum.

When reading such lives as those of Brainerd and Doddridge, I have often stood amazed, I could almost say envious of their power to sustain a real and spiritual intercourse with Heaven for large portions of a whole day.—*Thomas Chalmers, D.D.*

BY REV. THOMAS BRAINERD, D.D.

PASTOR OF "OLD PINE STREET CHURCH," PHILADELPHIA.

PHILADELPHIA:
PRESBYTERIAN PUBLICATION COMMITTEE,
1334 CHESTNUT STREET.
NEW YORK: A. D. F. RANDOLPH,
770 BROADWAY.

This Volume is Electrotyped by the liberality of
COLONEL H. S. McCOMB,
of the Central Presbyterian Church,
Wilmington, Delaware.

Electrotyped by L. Johnson & Co., Philadelphia.

JAS. B. RODGERS, PR.,
52 & 54 North Sixth Street, Phila.

PREFACE.

THE inclination of the author has heretofore led him to "hoe short rows" in the field of literature. He has edited a Child's Paper, a Youth's Magazine, a Religious Newspaper, and aided in a Quarterly. He has printed articles in Literary Monthlies, published Sermons and Tracts often; but this is his first attempt in making a *book*. If he have but imperfectly succeeded, there need be no alarm among his friends: he is not likely to repeat the offence. Dr. Livingstone, after escaping from sixteen years' travel and peril in Africa, said he "would rather repeat his journey than re-write his journal." We sympathize with him.

The author's full professional labors and incidental duties have so absorbed his time and taxed his energies, that leisurely, discriminating, and accurate authorship would imply a miracle of self-sacrificing ability. Failing to satisfy himself, he cannot hope to satisfy his critical friends.

In sending this volume into the world, the author has, however, some consolations:—

1. The work is finished, and off his hands.

2. His investigations have kept his eye on a pure and benevolent character, and led him into communion with a holy enterprise and the sainted fathers of the Church in the Middle States and New England.

3. Possessing the diary of his namesake and remote kinsman, and impressed by the holiness and consecration of his life, the author first projected this publication from family as well as public motives, with no expectation of gain or reputation; and, therefore, in any event he is not likely to be greatly disappointed.

4. His labor has been lightened and cheered by the ready aid of many friends, whose names it gives the author a grateful pleasure to record wherever he has appropriated their contributions.

5. By the ready insertion of such relevant documents as time has spared, and allowing John Brainerd to speak for himself by all the records

he has left of his life, the author has aimed to illustrate his subject rather than himself, even if thereby he subordinated the temporary popularity of the volume to its final utility.

6. As to the literary execution of his task, the author is satisfied that he has used all accessible materials fully, and that he has written intelligibly. He has furnished the historic facts set in plain English. If the critical ask for a better arrangement, higher coloring, and richer ornament, the world is wide, and they can employ a more skilful artist.

7. The book is sent into the world with a cheerful conviction that, if it accomplish no miraculous good, it certainly threatens no harm: for it attacks no religious denomination and stimulates no sectarian bitterness; but, like the "Life of David Brainerd by Jonathan Edwards," is adapted to those of all religious names, creeds, and forms, in all times and in all lands, "who love our Lord Jesus Christ in sincerity."

Besides the persons to whom we have given credit for their aid, we desire to add those of Rev. Charles Bliss, of Reading, Mass., James C.

Walkley, Esq., of Haddam, Conn., Cephas Brainerd, Esq., of New York, Rev. J. Addison Henry, O. H. Willard and George Young, Esqs., of Philadelphia. From our cousin, the Rev. Davis S. Brainerd, of Lyme, Conn., a native of Haddam and graduate of Yale College, and also at present one of its Corporators, we have had great sympathy in our labors. In a letter, under date of January 30, 1865, he says: "It affords me the truest gratification to learn that a living hand has lifted up the memory of an able and most estimable Christian minister from the almost complete oblivion under which it has so long lain. What there was of true eternal life in him will now be seen and profitably incorporated into the great Christian commonwealth of coming times."

Our anxiety is not lest our work should be undervalued and censured: in the secularities of the age and the excitements of the country, its great peril is that IT WILL NOT BE THOUGHT OF AT ALL.

THOMAS BRAINERD.

PHILADELPHIA, March, 1865.

CONTENTS.

CHAPTER XXVI.

CHAPTER XXVII.

CHAPTER XXVIII.

CHAPTER XXIX.

CHAPTER XXX.

CHAPTER XXXI.

CHAPTER XXXII.

CHAPTER XXXIII.

CHAPTER XXXIV.

CHAPTER XXXV.

CHAPTER XXXVI.

CHAPTER XXXVII.

CHAPTER XXXVIII.

CHAPTER XXXIX.

CHAPTER XL.

CHAPTER XLI.

CHAPTER XLII.

CHAPTER XLIII.

CHAPTER XLIV.

CHAPTER XLV.

APPENDIX.

INTRODUCTORY.

THE name of the Rev. David Brainerd is familiar and precious to the Church of God. Though more than one hundred years have elapsed since he died, his memory is still fresh and fragrant wherever Christianity has found a lodgment in any part of the earth. His holy life, his fervent prayers, his devout, tender, and earnest teachings, his apostolic labors, his martyr sacrifices and spiritual triumphs and successes, furnish models and motives to the ministry, and to the pious of every class, so precious and useful that the Church can never afford to let his name die.

As the great interests to which he gave his life and his energies were not of the day, nor the class, nor the place; as the great principles which he avowed are immutable and pertinent in all time and among all nations; as the great work he essayed is still unfinished; and as the concentrated vision of the Church for a century gone by has discovered in the martyr-missionary more of the image of his great Master, it is no wonder that the name of David Brainerd has constantly brightened, whilst more brilliant but less worthy names have faded from the memory of the Church.

In moving into the future, it is the destiny of man to move into relative darkness. Every individual human advance is an adventure in paths dim, difficult, and perilous, never yet trodden; an experiment of labors and perils not yet endured, of responsibilities yet to be discharged, and of aims and elevations yet to be surmounted. No wonder that in these circumstances man looks around him to inquire, "Has any one mapped out the way? Has any one successfully threaded the difficult and dreary paths? Has any one borne the labors and overcome the dangers? Has any one scaled the heights, and laid his hand on the proffered prize?"

The martial spirit is kept alive by the great names and achievements of its heroes; its Cæsars, Wellingtons, and Napoleons. Science renews its energy in communion with the names of its Galileos, Lockes, and Newtons. Men are brave to strike for human freedom under the shelter of the great examples of Hampden, Cromwell, and Washington! The biographies of the eminent dead not only furnish illustrations of what the living may be, and do, and dare; they not only lift men above the crowd to a higher estimate of human capacity and power; they do more, through the social principles by which one is set to imitate the good deeds which he contemplates in others. The Church of God has always availed itself of these principles of our nature; and, while war has cherished its heroes and science its devotees, Christianity has wisely embalmed the memory of her great teachers, her saints, and her martyrs. It is well it is so; for, however dwarfed may be the present age in any grace or attainment, the true and growing Christian can find solace, sympathy, and companionship with the more excellent men and things of the past.

No doubt Christian biography enrolls names more eminent for genius, learning, and eloquence than David Brainerd. No doubt hundreds, and perhaps thousands, have surpassed him in the wide-spread influence of their personal labors; for David Brainerd's ministry, like his great Master's, lasted but about three years. At his death he "began to be" only "thirty years old." He has not been remembered and famed as a man eminently great in intellect, though his biographer, President Edwards, says of him: "God sanctified and made meet for his own use that vessel (Brainerd), which he made of large capacity, having endowed him with very uncommon abilities and gifts of nature. He was a singular instance of ready invention, natural energy, ready flowing expression and sprightly apprehension, quick discerning, and a very strong memory; and yet of a very penetrating genius, clear thought and piercing judgment." This likeness was drawn by a master. The man of whom President Edwards could say all this had an intellect of the first order. But President

Edwards goes farther, to affirm that David Brainerd "had an exact taste; that his understanding was of a quick, strong, and distinguished scent; that his learning was very considerable, so that he was considered in college as one that excelled; that he had an extraordinary knowledge of men as well as things; that he excelled most that Edwards ever knew in a communicative faculty; that he had extraordinary gifts for the pulpit; being clear, instructive, moving, natural, nervous, forcible, and very searching and convincing;" that in private intercourse "he was of a sociable disposition," and had excellent talents for conversation, being entertaining and profitable. President Edwards sums up his estimate of Brainerd by declaring him "an extraordinary divine, unequalled, for one of his age, for clear, accurate notions of the power and nature of true religion;" and this superiority in David Brainerd he attributes "to the strength of his natural genius, his great opportunities of observation, and his own great experience."

We see from these extracts that President Edwards did not regard David Brainerd as simply a very remarkably pious and good sort of man, who had reached eminence and success by meaning well and industrious labor.

In the judgment of Edwards, David Brainerd was distinguished for an intellect of wonderful power; for gifts and graces that would have distinguished him in any profession, any age, or any land. His reputation as a great man intellectually has failed only in the greater brilliancy of his holy heart and martyr life.

But it is not David Brainerd, the man of genius and acute poetic sensibility; not the skilful metaphysician and dialectician; not the eloquent preacher and gifted and entertaining companion, whom the Church has embalmed in her memory and laid near her heart. She has had many other sons equally gifted and eminent in these regards. The David Brainerd who has stood before the Church for one hundred and twenty years, to stimulate successive generations to zeal, watchfulness, humility, prayer, and evangelical labor, is the missionary saint; his genius and attainments, his honor and wealth, his country, companionship, and home, all laid on the altar of God and humanity; the orphan-boy, struggling with doubt, fear, misapprehension, but led by truth and the Spirit into gradual light and peace in Jesus; the keenly-sensitive conscience and the lofty moral standard, that makes imperfection a crime to be overcome by prayers, penitence, and tears; the student, ambitious of learning and college-honors, but, for an indiscretion prompted by religious enthusiasm, banished from his *alma mater* and its doors forever barred against him; the candidate for the ministry, mastering in his studies alike the sublimest problems of theology and the hearts of his teachers, like Mills and Bellamy; the young and bold missionary to the Indians, alone with the savages in the howling wilderness, his dwelling a wigwam, his bed a blanket on the earth or gathered leaves, his food corn-cakes kneaded by his own hand and baked at his forest-fire; the missionary explorer, threading alone on horseback hundreds of miles of the wilderness, in the midst of tangled forest, swamps, ravines, and craggy precipices; surrounded by yelping wolves, and himself cold, weary, sick, and oppressed by the morbid depression so often the attribute of genius, so that literally, like his great Master, "he had nowhere to lay his head;" the shrewd, unwearied, skilful Christian teacher, bringing all the energies of his nature to render himself familiar first with one and then another Indian tongue, until he could speak without an interpreter the words of life; the parental sympathy and love, that made his people's joys and sorrows his own, by which he stole their hearts and opened their ears to truth; the unwearied assiduity by which, in season and out of season, he made truth to percolate through the dark minds around; the blameless and heavenly life he led, by which his Indians saw the gospel organized into a loving example of purity and charity; the earnest, lowly, and effective prayers by which he preserved in himself a heavenly spirit and brought to his aid the energy of the Holy Ghost; patient and unremitted labor and prayer while the revival-blessing was delayed, and the meek humility and quietude with which he bore himself when his labors were crowned with success; his pentecostal seasons of revival, his wonderful success in a few months of revolutionizing scores of savages into penitent, God-fearing, Christian men and women, and the simple eloquence and self-abandonment with which he recorded all this in reports to the Society that employed him; bearing to a considerable extent his own charges in all this work, and at the same time devoting his patrimony to aid in an education for the ministry of another young man to labor in the missionary work; literally, by labor, exposure, and religious anxiety, wearing himself out at thirty years, but brave, unfaltering, and submissive, seeking his own New England, to die in the presence of one that on earth he best loved; but not until he had summoned his own younger brother to enter the same field and bear the same burden in the great work of saving the poor Indians; this was the man whom the Church could not afford that humanity should forget.

But aside from his talents, his piety, and wonderful success, the fame of this distinguished man was not a little aided by the eminence and abilities of his greater biographer. Any man whose life Jonathan Edwards thought worthy to write would be certain of being remembered, as great and rapid streams impart motion to all things, great and small, thrown on the bosom of their waters.

There were some especial reasons why the great metaphysician and divine should throw his whole heart into his biography of the great missionary.

Brainerd was a protégé of Edwards, a martyr in college to his zeal for the Evangelical party, a type of that peculiar form of piety enjoined in the "Religious Affections," the accepted and betrothed lover of his daughter.

Brainerd's whole mental constitution and training, his moral characteristics and developments, prepared him to look up to Edwards with the profoundest reverence, and to regard him as a model of all that is sublime in wisdom or commendable in piety. It was natural that the heart of Edwards should be touched by the admiration and love of such a saint-like and gifted young man, and that he should tax to the utmost his vast powers so to set him forth as to gain for him that elevation in the eyes of the Church which he held in the estimation of his biographer. This Edwards actually did, and thereby threw around the name and deeds of David Brainerd a moral radiance which the lapse of ages has no power to dim or extinguish.

The REV. JOHN BRAINERD, the younger brother of David, and his successor in missionary labor among the Indians of New Jersey, though of kindred spirit, and perhaps equal moral worth, had not the eminent talents, nor the large acquisitions, nor the marked success of his brother David. But the relative oblivion into which his name has fallen is not mainly to be ascribed to any deficiency in these respects. He not only had the destiny to essay a work concerning which the highest expectation had been raised, while its novelty before the world had been exhausted, but to assume this work at its most difficult point; that is, to train to fixed principles and abiding Christian rectitude the wandering savages whom his brother David, by the grace of God, had converted to the hopeful profession of Christianity. Which brother had the harder task, I leave the reader to decide.

It is true, the younger brother had the advantage resulting from the experience and labors of his predecessor, and the prestige of his good name, and all the influence of the Church's approbation. These were benefits not to be undervalued. But even these did not so counterbalance the facts before stated as to give him or his mission any great prominence in the eyes of the Church. When we add to this the fact that his labors were signalized by no marked and extraordinary developments among either the Indians or his own countrymen, and that there was no President Edwards, with deep affection, patient toil, and consummate genius and skill, to give him a biography; we see how it is that, while the fame of David Brainerd has gone over the earth, his beloved brother and co-laborer has been almost overlooked and forgotten. One star has differed from the other star in glory. The greater brilliancy of the one has paled the mild but beautiful shining of the other.

Believing that the love of the Church in this and other lands for the memory of David Brainerd has created an interest which extends, in a certain degree, to his successor in the missionary work, and to the result of their united labors, the writer has been induced to undertake the preparation of the present volume. Representing their name, and sharing with them the great responsibilities of the ministerial office, claiming kindred with them according to the flesh, and humbled by the contemplation of their moral excellence, it seems pertinent that he should have great interest in their history, and be willing to give such information concerning them as he can furnish for the benefit of the Church of God. He has sought for information on the subject from every available source; but after the lapse of one hundred years, the materials for the biography of any man will in most cases be few and unsatisfactory. The Indian nations whom John Brainerd instructed in God's truth have faded and perished, and with them mostly the record of his toils for their welfare. But something still remains; and it has been the writer's responsibility to gather these fragments of a martyr-life, and, giving symmetry and completeness to the skeleton form, by linking "bone to its bone," to throw into it such a beating heart, and over it such a mantle of muscle and flesh, as would justify its introduction to the living generation of the nineteenth century.

Alone, the journal and biography of John Brainerd might lack interest, as the materials are scanty; but as a sequel to the memoir of his distinguished brother, it will, I trust, be regarded with satisfaction by the friends of Christ.

As the friend of Whitefield, the Tennents, Presidents Edwards, Burr, and Dickinson; as the trustee for twenty-six years of the College of Princeton; as the Moderator of the Old Synod of New York and Philadelphia; as one selected to fill the place of President Edwards at Stockbridge, on his transfer to Nassau Hall; as a chaplain in the Old French War on the frontiers of Canada; as the first domestic missionary of the Presbyterian Church in the United States; as a faithful missionary to the Indians for more than twenty years; and, above all, as a holy and consecrated man of God, I think there are materials in the life of John Brainerd to justify the tardy presentation of his journal and biography to the public. The author feels great satisfaction in being able to set a character so stainless and benevolent before the rising ministry of the land.

LIFE OF JOHN BRAINERD.

CHAPTER I.

JOHN BRAINERD'S PARENTAGE—HIS GRANDFATHER AND GRANDMOTHER—HIS FATHER AND MOTHER—HIS BROTHERS AND SISTERS—HIS STEP-BROTHER, JEREMIAH MASON—MAJOR-GENERAL JOSEPH SPENCER.

ABOUT the year 1649, there was brought, as is supposed from Exeter, in England, to Hartford, Conn., a little boy eight years of age, named Daniel Brainerd.* In what vessel he embarked, why he left home at such a tender age, by whom he was accompanied and cared for, we know not: we only know that this little boy came with the "Wyllis" family, one of the most affluent and respectable in Hartford, and that he remained in it until 1662, when he was twenty-one years of age.

* We have followed Dr. Field's "Brainerd Genealogy." In the Library of the Massachusetts Historical Society, at Worcester, we have lately seen a manuscript "Genealogy of the Brainerds," written in 1784, which states that Daniel Brainerd lived in the Wadsworth family, at Hartford, until he was of age, and then, after two years, removed to Haddam. We have no means of verifying the facts, as the whole matter rests on tradition.

What relation he sustained to the Wyllis family, whether he was a relative, or an orphan taken to be sheltered, or a bound boy, we have no knowledge. None of his name or blood have been clearly traced in Europe, nor outside of his descendants in America. Two hundred and twelve years ago, the boy of eight years put his little feet on the banks of the Connecticut; around him a great continent covered by a howling wilderness, and perilous from roaming savage tribes and beasts of prey. It is said that at least thirty-three thousand persons in these United States have looked back to that lone boy as the head of their family.*

Arrived at the age of twenty-one years, Daniel Brainerd, in company with twenty-seven others, young men of his own age, went about thirty miles below Hartford, and selected for settlement a tract of land twelve miles square, comprehending nearly equal portions on each side of the Connecticut River. Middletown, about nine miles above, and Saybrook, twenty miles below, had been already taken up and thinly peopled. *Haddam*, for

---

* The name *Brainerd* was variously spelled in the early records: sometimes we find it Bra*inard*, and again Bra*ynard*, but most commonly it was written Brai*nerd*. This was the mode of David and John, and has obtained most in the family.

However spelled, the name is identical, as all trace their origin to the common ancestor, Daniel Brainerd. The name is said to be of Norman origin. Tradition has it that the name was originally Brainwood, or Braidwood. This has some probability, as the name *Brainerd* is not now found in England.

this was the name given to the new settlement, comprehended one of the wildest and most picturesque portions of the State. Here the Connecticut River breaks through the mountain-range which terminates in the East Rock at New Haven. The broad, beautiful stream, the fine island opposite the town, the level fertile meadows reaching half a mile from the river, the terrace-like elevations by which the hills rise from the plain, the frowning and rocky bluffs which here and there force themselves to the water's edge, the deep lateral vales through which the smaller streams rush to meet the great river, and the dark shade of the semi-mountains, hundreds of feet high, looming everywhere in the little distance,—all these give to the scenery of Haddam a grandeur and beauty rarely to be equalled.

Brainerd selected his estate about two miles above the present village of Haddam, and one mile below the present village of Higganum, a great part of which was originally owned by some branches of the family. His farm, gently sloping down to the river from a considerable elevation, looking west on craggy hills, commanded a view of the Connecticut for miles up and down the river. Here, on land reclaimed by his own industry from the forest, John Brainerd's grandfather planted his family; and his property remained with his descendants nearly two hundred years, to the present generation.

The poet J. G. Brainerd, Esq., of New London, thus apostrophizes the beautiful Connecticut, on the banks of which his fathers had been settled for nearly two centuries:—

"Stream of my sleeping fathers! When the sound
Of coming war* echoed thy hills around,
How did thy sons start forth from every glade,
Snatching the musket where they left the spade!
How did their mothers urge them to the fight,—
Their sisters tell them to defend the right!
How bravely did they stand,—how nobly fall,—
The earth their coffin, and the turf their pall!
How did the aged pastor light his eye,
When to his flock he read the purpose high
And stern resolve, whate'er the toil may be,
To pledge life, name, fame, all—for liberty!
Bold river! better suited are thy waves
To nurse the laurels clust'ring round their graves
Than many a distant stream, that soaks the mud
Where thy brave sons have shed their gallant blood;
And felt, beyond all other mortal pain,
They ne'er should see their happy home again."

Of Daniel, the grandfather of David and John Brainerd, the Rev. D. D. Field, D.D., says, "The ancestor became the proprietor and settler of Haddam about 1662, and was a prosperous, influential, and very respectable man; a justice of peace in the town, a deacon in the church. He became the greatest landholder in Haddam, owning, besides

* Eleven of the Brainerd family served in the Old French War and in the War of the Revolution, four of whom fell martyrs to their country. In the present war to put down rebellion, the family has furnished many more soldiers and will mourn more victims. May their blood not be shed in vain!

rights in other places in the township, about a mile in the northeast part, on the Connecticut River, including what is covered by the present village of Higganum." As Brainerd aided to found the first church of Haddam almost the first year of the settlement, and served it as deacon, it appears that he was early and consistently pious, and wisely laid the foundation of his family hopes in the fear of God.

About the year 1664 he married Hannah Spencer, daughter of Jared Spencer, first of Lynn, Mass., and afterwards of Haddam. Of his wife's family the Rev. Dr. Samuel Miller, in his article* on the Rev. Elihu Spencer, D.D., of Trenton, N.J., says,—

"The ancestors of the family from whom this eminent man descended were five brothers, who emigrated from England to Massachusetts early in the seventeenth century. The eldest, John Spencer, appears to have been a large landholder, a magistrate, a member of the General Court, and a high military officer in Watertown, now Cambridge, from 1634 to 1638, when he returned to England, leaving no descendants on this side the Atlantic. William Spencer, the second brother, also settled in Cambridge, where he was a member of the General Court and a landed proprietor. He afterwards removed to Connecticut, where he died, leaving a numerous family. He was the ancestor of the late Ambrose Spencer, Chief Justice of New York. Thomas Spencer, the third brother, died in Haddam, the residence of his family, in 1685.

---

* Sprague's Annals, vol. iii. p. 165.

"Ichabod S. Spencer, D.D., late pastor of the First Presbyterian Church in Brooklyn, N. Y., and Hon. Joshua A. Spencer, late of Utica, are among his descendants. The fourth brother, Jared Spencer, originally settled with his brother in Cambridge, and came not long afterwards to Connecticut, when he became one of the first settlers of the town of Haddam. He died in 1685, leaving a numerous posterity. The Rev. Elihu Spencer, D.D., the subject of this article, and Major-General Joseph Spencer, a distinguished and active military officer during the Revolutionary War, were among his descendants."

Jared Spencer, alluded to in this article, was the maternal grandfather of John Brainerd; and, consequently, Rev. Dr. Elihu Spencer, of Trenton, was a cousin of the missionary.

Daniel Brainerd, the paternal grandfather of John, was the father of eight children. Seven of these were sons, all of whom settled in life, raised large families, and lived to advanced years.*

* It may interest a certain class of our readers to follow Dr. Field in a sketch of the descendants of these seven sons. Their names were,—1. Daniel; 2. James; 3. Joshua; 4. William; 5. Caleb; 6. Elijah; 7. Hezekiah, the father of David and John.

1. Daniel Brainerd was the ancestor of Dr. Daniel Brainerd, of Tremont, Ohio, Hon. Jeremiah Gates Brainerd, Hon. William F. Brainerd, J. G. Brainerd the poet, Dr. Dyer Throop Brainerd, of New London.

2. James Brainerd was the ancestor of the Rev. Eliezer Brainerd, late of Ohio, Rev. Davis S. Brainerd, of Lyme, Conn., Rev. Thomas Brainerd, of Philadelphia, Dr. Austin Brainerd, late of New York, Cephas Brainerd, Esq., of New York, Norman L. Brainerd, Esq., of Brooklyn, N. Y., Erastus and Silas Brainerd, of Middletown, Conn., and Leonard W. Brainerd, of New York.

It is believed they were all hopefully pious, and most of them officers in the Church. Their descendants, to the fifth and sixth generations, have inherited and illustrated to a great extent the religious faith and pure morals of their fathers.

Hezekiah Brainerd, the youngest son of Daniel Brainerd, Esq., and father of David and John, was the most prominent and influential of the family; a gentleman of education, means, and high official position. President Edwards calls him "the worshipful Mr. Brainerd, one of his majesty's council." Dr. Field says "he acquired much more education than was obtained by respectable young men generally in his day, and became a man of great dis-

---

3. Joshua Brainerd was the ancestor of Hon. John Brainerd, Representative in the Assembly in the Revolutionary War, &c.

4. William Brainerd was the ancestor of Rev. Chiliab Brainerd, of Eastbury, Conn., Roswell Colt Brainerd, Esq., of Middletown, Conn., Hon. Ezra Brainerd, late of Haddam, Lawrence R. Brainerd, of St. Albans, Vt., Hon. Lawrence Brainerd, late United States Senator at Washington, Rev. Israel Brainerd, late of Verona, N. Y., Hon. Joseph Hungerford Brainerd, of Vermont, Rev. Timothy G. Brainerd, of Halifax, Mass.

5. Caleb Brainerd was the ancestor of Dr. Daniel Brainerd, of Chicago, Ill.

6. Elijah Brainerd was the ancestor of the Rev. Elijah Brainerd, of South Carolina, Rev. Carolus C. Brainerd, of Warrenton, N. C., Almon Brainerd, Esq., Greenfield, Mass., John Brainerd, Esq., late of New Orleans, Rev. John Brainerd, of Maryland.

7. Hezekiah Brainerd being the father of David and John, we shall speak of his family in the body of this memoir.

"*Contributions to the Ecclesiastical History of Connecticut*," p. 401, gives the names of ten ministers of the name of Brainerd raised up by the Church in Haddam. As many more have entered the ministry elsewhere, all descended from Deacon Daniel Brainerd.

tinction and influence. He was Representative to the General Assembly and Speaker of the House of Representatives, a member of the Council, or Senate, who intrusted him with many public concerns. In consideration of extra public services, the Legislature gave him a farm of three hundred acres in Goshen, Conn." He died in the Capitol, while attending in his place as Senator, May 24, 1727, when his son David was nine and John seven years old. His tombstone is in the grounds of the First Church, Hartford, in the rear of the church-edifice.

Hezekiah Brainerd married Dorothy, daughter of the Rev. Jeremiah Hobart, pastor of the church in Haddam, October 1, 1707.

Mrs. Brainerd's family affinities are very fully drawn by President Edwards, to which the reader is referred. She was of an excellent stock, and, it is believed, a woman of fine intellect and ardent piety. The lapse of one hundred and thirty years has thrown the deep veil of oblivion over her person, her talents, her maternal modes and characteristics, her counsels, and her yearning prayers.*

How much David and John Brainerd owed of

---

* Dorothy Hobart was the young widow of Daniel Mason, grandson of the famed Captain John Mason, the hero of the Indian Wars. She had one son, Jeremiah Mason, the grandfather of Hon. Jeremiah Mason, the great rival of Daniel Webster, of Boston.

"Jeremiah Mason, the step-son of Hon. Hezekiah Brainerd, and step-brother of David and John, was born March 4, 1705, and married, May 24, 1727, Mary, daughter of Thomas Clark, of Haddam.

their peculiar piety and usefulness to the early lessons, example, and prayers of their excellent

---

Jeremiah at the time of his father's death was six months old, so that from his early infancy he was a step-child, and was brought up 'after the most straitest sect of our religion,' by a rigid Puritan, his step-father, who, as the family tradition tells us, 'looked after the boys.' It tells us also that Jeremiah, when a man, once coming in late at night, Mr. Brainerd asked him, 'Where have you been so late at night?'

"'I have been,' said he, 'to see Mary Clark.'

"'Oh! very well,' answered the step-father. 'Go to bed.'" [*Life of Mrs. Judge Boardman, of New Haven*, by Rev. Dr. Schrœder.]

The grandson before spoken of, the Hon. Jeremiah Mason, of Boston, died November 3, 1848.

Daniel Webster pronounced a eulogy upon him, November 4, 1848, before the Supreme Judicial Court of Massachusetts, at Boston; and presented to the court at the same time certain resolutions unanimously adopted a short time before at a meeting of the Bar of the county of Suffolk, on motion of the Hon. Rufus Choate.

On moving the resolutions, Mr. Choate said:—

"Mr. Mason was so extraordinary a person; his powers of mind were not only so vast, but so peculiar; his character and influence were so weighty, as well as good; he filled for so many years so conspicuous a place in the profession of the law, in public life, and in intercourse with those who gave immediate direction to public affairs, that it appears most fit, if it were practicable, that we should attempt to record somewhat permanently and completely our appreciation of him, and to convey it to others, who knew him less perfectly and less recently than ourselves. It seems to me that *one of the very few greatest men* whom this country has produced; a statesman among the foremost in a senate of which King and Giles, in the fulness of their strength and fame, were members; a jurist who would have filled the seat of Marshall as Marshall filled it; of whom it may be said that, without ever holding a judicial station, he was the author and finisher of the jurisprudence of a state; one whose intellect, wisdom, and uprightness gave him a control over the opinions of all the circles in which he lived and acted, of which we shall scarcely see another example, and for which this generation and the country are the better to-day: such seems to me to have been the man who has just gone down to a timely grave. I rejoice to know that the mother will never be fully known on earth. But this woman, the daughter of a clergyman and child of the Church, who gave to the world among her descendants such men as David and John Brainerd for the pulpit, Jeremiah Mason for the bar, and Thomas Minor for the healing art, is in no danger of being forgotten.

In respect to the father of the missionaries, the Hon. Hezekiah Brainerd, tradition gives us some reliable information. He is said to have been of great personal dignity and self-restraint, of rigid notions of parental prerogatives and authority, of the strictest puritanical views as to religious ordinances, of unbending integrity as a man and a public officer, and of extreme scrupulousness in his Christian life. From their father, no doubt, David and John Brainerd inherited a constitutional tendency to that keen sensibility, that high conscientiousness, that self-dissatisfaction, that moral adhesiveness to fixed purposes, and that general religiousness which their whole history so prominently exhibits.

---

eighty-first year of his life found his marvellous faculties wholly unimpaired.

"'No pale gradations quenched that ray.'

"Down to the hour when the appointed shock, his first sickness, struck him, as it might seem, in a moment, from among the living, he was ever his great and former self.

"He is dead: and, though here and there a kindred mind—here and there, rarer still, a coeval mind—survives, he has left no one beyond his immediate blood and race who in the least degree resembles him."

But whatever personal influence these parents may have early exerted on David and John Brainerd, it was destined to be short. Their father died when they were respectively nine and seven. When they reached the ages of fourteen and twelve, they lost their excellent mother, and thenceforth were orphans, left to the care of relatives, who, providentially, had the disposition and ability to do them every kindness. Their immediate family consisted of nine brothers and sisters. As five of these were older than the two missionaries, and several of them well settled in life, the two orphan boys and a younger brother and sister were not without efficient advisers and protectors.

The names and birth of the children of the Hon. Hezekiah Brainerd were as follows:—

1. Hezekiah	Brainerd, Jr.,	born	1708
2. Dorothy	"	"	1710
3. Nehemiah	"	"	1712
4. Jerusha	"	"	1714
5. Martha	"	"	1716
6. David	"	"	1718
7. John	"	"	1720
8. Elizabeth	"	"	1722
9. Israel	"	"	1725

Hezekiah retained the homestead in Haddam. Dr. Field says he was deacon in the church, clerk of the town, justice of the peace, repeatedly member of the Assembly, and colonel of the militia.

Among his descendants were Thomas Minor, M.D., and the Hon. Hezekiah Brainerd, M.D., formerly of Haddam.

Dorothy Brainerd married Lieutenant David Smith. We have no knowledge of her family.

The third child of Hon. Hezekiah Brainerd, father of David, was *Rev. Nehemiah Brainerd*, a graduate of Yale College, and settled in the ministry at Glastenbury (Eastbury), Conn. He is often mentioned in Edwards' "Life of Brainerd."

Rev. Nehemiah Brainerd succeeded his cousin, Rev. Chilliab Brainerd, a graduate of Yale College, who was installed in 1736, and died, after two years' pastorship, January 1, 1739. The monument over his grave calls him "a zealous and faithful minister of Jesus Christ." Rev. Nehemiah Brainerd had a similar history. He graduated in 1732, settled in Eastbury in 1740, and died November 9, 1742, aged thirty-two years. The following letter, for which we are indebted to Rev. President Allen, of Northampton, Mass., is all we have ever seen from his pen. It was written in a great revival, when his health was failing. It breathes the spirit of David and John, or rather it illustrates the spirit they received from an elder brother. We give it *verbatim et literatim*:—

"*To ye Revd* MR. WHEELOCK, *of Lebanon.*

"Rev & Dear Sr.

"Ye Lambs of my Flock seem to entertain a great

Desire for y^r^ coming and preaching to 'em, and some others y^t^ are older I think joyn with 'em. I entreat of you y^t^ in Brotherly Love you would answer our request, and send me word when you intend to come y^t^ I may warn a meeting. If you cant come till ye week after next, probably our Friend Buel and my Brother [David] will be here, & next Wednesday I design to preach at Hock-anum, so that day must be excepted. I trust, my dear Brother, you'll come, if you possibly can, & joyn forces with mine, & help me under my weakness & infirmities, and help gather in X's [Christ's] chosen here. There is, I trust, a great & effectual door opened to me, but there are many adversaries, especially in ye Town, where, I suppose, ye major part are rather opposing, & some are daring, hardy Soldiers of Satan indeed! Let us never forget each other & ye Ch. of X at ye throne of Grace.

"I am y^r^ sincere Friend & B^r^,

"N. Brainerd.

"Glassenbury, Satur: July 17, or 18, 1741."

Among his descendants we find the Hon. Nehemiah Brainerd, A.M., repeatedly a representative in the General Assembly of Connecticut, and deacon in the church, and General John Brainerd, of Haddam, who, by a donation of some fifteen thousand dollars, founded the "Brainerd Academy" in Haddam, and left two thousand five hundred dollars to the Congregational Church.

Jerusha Brainerd, David's second sister, married Samuel Spencer, of Haddam, December 19, 1732. She died a little before her brother David, and the news was carried to him when he lay sick in Boston. President Edwards says, "She was a sister between whom and himself (David) had long subsisted a peculiarly dear affection. But he had this comfort together with the tidings,—a confidence of her being gone to heaven."

Martha Brainerd, third sister of David and John, married General Joseph Spencer, of East Haddam, a well-known major-general in the army of the Revolution.*

---

* Of General Joseph Spencer, the brother-in-law of David Brainerd, and also descended from Isaac Spencer, Brainerd's great-grandfather, Dr. Smith, recently President of Marietta College, now of Buffalo, N. Y., said, in an obituary of Mrs. Martha Brainerd Wilson, of Marietta:—

"Mrs. Wilson was the daughter of the late Dr. Joseph Spencer, of Vienna, Wood county, Va. He was the son of Major-General Joseph Spencer, who served with reputation with the rank of colonel in the Northern Army during the French War, was a brigadier-general in the Continental Army, and in 1776 was appointed a major-general of the American Army of the Revolution, which he resigned in 1778, and was elected a member of the Continental Congress,—a man whose character won an expression of high esteem from Washington, and whose deep-toned piety, with that of many of his compatriots, contributed much to throw around that fearful struggle the sacred sanction of religion.

"In 1794, Dr. Spencer, who had held the office of surgeon and aide to his father in the army, emigrated to the West, and, in company with the late Colonel Abner Lord, purchased a tract of land in Wood county, below Marietta, fronting five miles on the Ohio River. Dr. Spencer left a family of eleven children,—six sons and five daughters. Of these sons three still survive,—Messrs. William and Brainerd Spencer, of Vienna, and Mr. George Spencer, of Louisiana. Of the daughters only two—Mrs. General Cass, of Detroit, and Mrs. General Hunt, of Maumee—are still living. To the two deceased—Mrs. Wallace, wife of Rev. Matthew Wallace, of Indiana, and the late Mrs. Judge Nye, whose character and virtues are well remembered

David Brainerd's history is already known, and

John Brainerd's we are to give elsewhere.

Elizabeth Brainerd, the youngest sister of David, and only ten years old when left an orphan, was married to David Miller, of Middletown, July 21, 1743. Their descendants, mostly residing in Northern New York, are numerous, and generally distinguished for moral worth.

Israel Brainerd, David's youngest brother, shared in the piety of the family. He was a member of Yale College when summoned to Boston to see his suffering brother David. President Edwards says, "This visit was attended to Mr. Brainerd with joy, because he greatly desired an opportunity of some religious conversation with him before he died."

In this interview the dying missionary gave a solemn charge to this younger brother to live a life of self-denial and devotedness to God. Among other things, he told him: "When ministers feel these special gracious influences on their hearts, it wonderfully assists them to come at the consciences of men, and, as it were, to handle them; whereas without them, whatever reason and oratory we may make use of, we do but make use of *stumps* instead of *hands*."*

---

in this community—it is now our melancholy duty to add the name of Mrs. Wilson."

* Memoirs, pp. 243, 244.

But Israel was not allowed to preach the gospel. He died the following winter, 1748, at New Haven. President Edwards describes him as an "ingenious, serious, studious, and hopefully pious person."

The son of the writer, while in the Freshman class of Yale College in 1855, was sauntering through the graveyard of New Haven on a cold day in autumn, when his attention was attracted by a broken marble slab matted in the grass, with the inscription underneath. Some curiosity prompted him to lift the stone: and what was his surprise to read his own name of *Brainerd* upon it! He read the whole epitaph; "This stone was erected in memory of *Israel Brainerd*, a member of Yale College, who died January 6, 1748." It was the grave-stone of David Brainerd's youngest brother, Israel, above described.

CHAPTER II.

JOHN BRAINERD'S CHILDHOOD AND YOUTH.

JOHN BRAINERD was born at the paternal home, the residence of his father, in Haddam, February 28, 1720. Concerning his childhood and youth we have very little certain knowledge.* We may, however, consider the circumstances around him, and estimate their influence in forming his character. In his seventh year he lost his father, in his twelfth, his mother. But before his mother's death his eldest brother Hezekiah was married to Mary, the daughter of Rev. Phineas Fisk, the clergyman of Haddam, and was settled in the family mansion. His elder brother, Nehemiah Brainerd, of Glastenbury, married Elizabeth, another of the Rev. Mr. Fisk's daughters. Two of his sisters, in 1732 and 1738, married, the one Samuel and the other Joseph (Major-General) Spencer, of East Haddam. With some one of these families, connected with him by the closest ties of blood, and all of the highest respectability and eminently religious,

---

* Webster, in his "History of the Presbyterian Church," says John was born in East Haddam. This is a mistake: he was born in Old Haddam.

John Brainerd found doubtless a good home in his double orphanage.*

The Rev. Phineas Fisk, his pastor, and the father-in-law of his two brothers, is described by Dr. Field "as one of the best scholars in Connecticut, who had long been a prominent instructor in the literary institution which was afterwards established at New Haven, named Yale College."

How strict were the principles of Mr. Fisk is shown by his advice to David Brainerd when he was under serious impressions at twenty years of age. "I remember," says Brainerd, "that Mr. Fisk advised me wholly to abandon young company and associate myself with grave, elderly people, which counsel I followed."†

If John shared in such counsel and followed it, as we have no doubt he to some extent did, we learn the Puritan severity and strictness of his training, and whence both the brothers imbibed a type of piety fitting them for the high resolve and patient endurance exhibited in their after-lives.

The natural scenery of John Brainerd's native place, Haddam, its traditions and legends, its earthquakes and mysterious noises, all adapted to impress the imagination of the young and give a bent to character, are so truthfully and graphically sketched by the Rev. Professor Parke, of Andover,

---

* Brainerd Genealogy, p. 253.

† Dwight's "Life of Brainerd," p. 35.

in his Memoir of Dr. Emmons,* that we shall confer an obligation on the reader by a large quotation:—

"Although Dr. Emmons wrote but little concerning the place of his birth, he thought much of it. In his later age he visited and re-visited his old home, with a childlike joy that the lines had fallen to him in so pleasant a place. His character was doubtless affected in some degree by the natural scenery and the early traditions of the township in which he was trained. The rock-bound hills of his native parish seem well fitted to nurture his habit of digging among the hard-twisted themes of theology. For many years his father lived on the very verge of a precipice, near a high and sharp ledge of rocks, at the foot of which flowed a swift brook. The rising grounds covered with the cedar and the oak, the intervening meadows, through which flowed limpid and rapid streams, the 'grate river' which the early records of the town celebrate as enriching its borders, the thrilling legends in regard to the Indian tribes who were attracted to the fishing-brooks and hunting-forests of the town, were not without their effect upon him, schooled though he was in the stern processes of metaphysics. He knew what was meant by a slight dash of poetic superstition. He *felt* what an artist would have *expressed.* His mind was silently moulded by that which a man of more imaginative tendencies would have celebrated in song.

"The appropriate influence of the scenes in this 'hill

---

* Memoir of Dr. Emmons, by Prof. E. A. Parke, Boston, 1861, p. 2, *et passim.*

country' of Connecticut has been well developed by the poet Brainerd. It was with his eye on the romantic townships of Old Haddam and East Haddam that he indited his poem on the Connecticut River, 'the stream of his sleeping fathers,' along whose noble shores

> "'The tall steeple shines
> At mid-day higher than the "mountain pines."
>
> "'Dark as the frost-nipped leaves that strewed the ground,
> The Indian hunter here his shelter found,
> Here cut his bow and shaped his arrows true,
> Here built his wigwam and his bark canoe,
> Speared the quick salmon leaping up the fall,
> And slew the deer without the rifle-ball.'"*

"The Salmon River, so called from the fish that once abounded in it, enters into the Connecticut at East Haddam. It was a favorite retreat of the poet Brainerd, as its clear waters had been for ages the chosen resort of the angler and its wooded banks had been the home of the Indian huntsman. Brainerd sings of this river:—†

> "'There's much in its wild history that teems
> With all that's superstitious, and that seems
> To match our fancy and eke out our dreams,
> In that small brook.
>
> "'Here Philip came, and Miantonimo,
> And asked about their fortunes, long ago,
> As Saul to Endor, that her witch might show
> Old Samuel.
>
> "'Such are the tales they tell. 'Tis hard to rhyme
> About a little and unnoticed stream
> That few have heard of; but it is a theme
> I chance to love;

---

* Remains, p. 60. † Ibid. pp. 139, 141.

"'And one day I may tune my rye-straw reed,
And whistle to the note of many a deed
Done on this river,—which, if there be need,
I'll try to prove.'"

The poem of Brainerd on "The Black Fox of Salmon River," and also the one entitled "Matchit Moodus," give us fine specimens of the legends which in the young days of Emmons were familiar to the natives of East Haddam.* With regard to the Matchit Moodus, Rev. Dr. Field remarks:—

"A large tribe [of Indians] inhabited East Haddam, which they called Machemoodus, or the place of noises; from the noises or earthquakes which had been heard there, and which have continued to the present time. These Indians were of a fierce and wretched character, remarkable for *pawaws* and the worship of evil spirits. The noises from the earth, regarded as the voice of their god, confirmed them in their monstrous notions of religion. An old Indian being asked the reason of the noises, said, 'The Indian's God was very angry because the Englishman's God came there.'†

"Those noises in East Haddam which caught the attention of the natives were not disregarded by the first settlers and their associates, nor have they been disregarded by later generations. Seventy or eighty years ago, in consequence of their greater frequency and violence, they gained the attention of the neighboring towns,

* Brainerd's Literary Remains, pp. 141, 147.

† A History of the Towns of Haddam and East Haddam. By David D. Field, A.M., Pastor of the Church at Haddam. Printed in Middletown, 1814, p. 4.

and became the subject of inquiry and discussion among the learned and inquisitive throughout the State."

Professor Parke, in continuation, says:—

"The Gazetteers of the day notice the fisheries, the navigation, the manufacturing establishments, the granite-quarries, of the tract of country once called Haddam; but they fail to herald its real glory. Dr. Emmons was wont to rejoice that his native township was distinguished for its Puritan spirit. The hard soil, the bracing air, the pure waters of New England, have done much in forming its peculiar character; but the religious habits of its fathers have done more. They have started an influence which will continue to flow onward, and will be felt even where it is not recognized. The Old Haddam settlement may be regarded as a representative region. It represents that part of our land which, like ancient Numidia, may be called '*arida matrix leonum.*' It exhibits the power which has been exerted over this entire country by our small Puritan communities. It illustrates the importance of sustaining with augmented vigor the schools and churches in these rural districts which have sent forth such a penetrating energy through the world. It is estimated that Deacon Daniel Brainerd, the grandfather of David and one of the original proprietors of Haddam, has had more than thirty-three thousand descendants. Many of them have attained high distinction in Church and State. Among the natives of the region formerly called Haddam who have been liberally educated, are David Brainerd, who alone gives importance to a community; Nehemiah Brainerd, a pastor in Eastbury (Glastenbury), Connecticut, who was a classical instructor of David, his younger brother; John Brainerd, an eminent minister, who succeeded his brother David in the Indian Mission and was for twenty-six years a trustee of Princeton College; Nathaniel Emmons; Edward Dorr Griffin, Professor at Andover and President of Williams College; his brother also, George G. Griffin, a noted lawyer and theological writer in New York City; Jeremiah Gates Brainerd, a Judge of the Superior Court of Connecticut and the father of John Gardiner Calkins Brainerd, 'the gentle poet of the gentle stream;' James Brainerd Taylor, and other men of no inferior note among the living as well as the dead.*

"As the maternal grandfather of David Brainerd was the minister of Haddam for twenty-four years, as the brother-in-law of David Brainerd, Mr. Phineas Fisk, the eminent 'tutor,' was pastor of the same old church for the same number of years, as the father of David Brain-

---

* Since its settlement there have been raised up on the original territory of Haddam the following ministers:—

David Brainerd,	Davis S. Brainerd,
John Brainerd,	Daniel C. Tyler,
Hezekiah May,	Joseph Harvey, D.D.,
Elijah Brainerd,	Joseph Vail,
Jonathan Hubbard,	Jedediah Chapman,
Eleazar Brainerd,	Elihu Spencer, D.D.,
Charles Dickinson,	George Hall,
Henry M. Field,	Epaphras Chapman,
Chilliab Brainerd,	Robert D. Gardner,
Nehemiah Brainerd,	H. M. Parsons,
Israel Brainerd,	Henry Fuller,
Israel Brainerd (2),	Nathaniel Emmons, D.D.,
James Brainerd,	Edward Dorr Griffin, D.D.,
Israel Shailer,	Warren D. Jones,

George A. Beckwith.

[*Contributions to the Ecclesiastical History of Connecticut*, New Haven, 1861, pp. 401, 426.]

erd was a man eminent for his gifts, and as there have been numerous intermarriages between the Brainerds and the other ancient families of that region, it is reasonable to believe that the household to which this missionary belonged has left a deep, decided impress upon all the townships into which Old Haddam is now divided."

These descriptions from Professor Parke have as real an application to the case of John Brainerd as to that of Dr. Emmons. Haddam scenery was adapted to nourish that solitary musing, that confiding faith in the supernatural, that awe of God, and that spirit of adventure and hardihood developed by the missionary brothers.

We can form a very ready conception of the early life of John Brainerd. The writer's grandfather was his contemporary and a deacon in the church of Haddam, only twelve years his junior, being born in 1732, and died 1815, aged eighty-four. My own father was born in 1754, resided in Haddam fifty years, within three miles of John Brainerd's early home, and in possession of all his faculties died in Lewis county, N. Y., 1838, aged eighty-four.

We had enforced on us in early life—with too little effect, we fear—many of the principles which formed the characters of David and John Brainerd one hundred and fifty years ago.

A boy was early taught a profound respect for his parents, teachers, and guardians, and implicit, prompt obedience. If he undertook to rebel, "his will was broken" by persistent and adequate punishment. He was accustomed every morning and evening to bow at the family altar; and the Bible was his ordinary reading-book in school. He was never allowed to close his eyes in sleep without prayer on his pillow.

At a sufficient age, no caprice, slight illness, nor any condition of roads or weather, was allowed to detain him from church. In the sanctuary he was required to be grave, strictly attentive, and able on his return at least to give the text. From sundown Saturday evening until the Sabbath sunset his sports were all suspended, and all secular reading laid aside; while the Bible, New-England Primer, Bunyan's Pilgrim's Progress, Baxter's Saints' Rest, &c., were commended to his ready attention and cheerfully pored over.

He was taught that his blessings were abundant and undeserved, his evils relatively few and merited, and that he was not only bound to contentment, but gratitude. He was taught that time was a talent to be always improved; that industry was a cardinal virtue, and laziness the worst form of original sin. Hence he must rise early, and make himself useful before he went to school; must be diligent there in study, and be promptly home to do "*chores*" at evening. His whole time out of school must be filled up by some service,—such as bringing in fuel for the day, cutting potatoes for the sheep, feeding the swine, watering the horses, picking the berries, gathering the vegetables, spooling the yarn, and running all errands. He was expected never to be reluctant, and not often tired.

He was taught that it was a sin to find fault with his meals,* his apparel, his tasks, or his lot in life. Labor he was not allowed to regard as a burden, nor abstinence from any improper indulgence as a hardship.

His clothes, woolen and linen, for summer and winter, were mostly spun, woven, and made up by his mother and sisters at home; and, as he saw the whole laborious process of their fabrication, he was jubilant and grateful for two suits, with bright buttons, a year. Rents were carefully closed and holes patched in the "every-day" dress, and the Sabbath dress always kept new and fresh.

He was expected early to have the "stops and marks," the "abbreviations," the "multiplication table," the "ten commandments," the "Lord's Prayer," and the "Shorter Catechism," at his tongue's end.

Courtesy was enjoined as a duty. He must be silent among his superiors. If addressed by older persons, he must respond with a bow. He was to bow as he entered and left the school, and bow to every man or woman, old or young, rich or poor, black or white, whom he met on the road. Special

* When the writer complained of any thing at table, his father would say: "You don't like your mother's provision. You may *leave the table*."

punishment was visited on him if he failed to show respect to the aged, the poor, the colored, or to any persons whatever whom God had visited with infirmities. He was thus taught to stand in awe of the rights of humanity.

Honesty was urged as a religious duty, and unpaid debts were represented as infamy. He was allowed to be sharp at a bargain, to shudder at dependence, but still to prefer poverty to deception or fraud. His industry was not urged by poverty, but by duty. Those who imposed upon him early responsibility and restraint led the way by their example, and commended this example by the prosperity of their fortunes and the respectability of their position as the result of these virtues. He felt that they governed and restrained him for his good, and not their own.

He learned to identify himself with the interests he was set to promote. He claimed every acre of his father's ample farm, and every horse and ox and cow and sheep became constructively his, and he had a name for each. The waving harvests, the garnered sheaves, the gathered fruits, were all his own. And besides these, he had his individual treasures. He knew every trout-hole in the streams; he was great in building dams, snaring rabbits, trapping squirrels, and gathering chestnuts and walnuts for winter store. Days of election, training, thanksgiving, and school-intermissions, were bright spots in his life. His long winter evenings, made cheerful by sparkling fires within and cold clear skies and ice-crusted plains and frozen streams for his sled and skates, were full of enjoyment. And then he was loved by those whom he could respect, and cheered by that future for which he was being prepared. Religion he was taught to regard as a necessity and luxury, as well as a duty. He was daily brought into contemplation of the Infinite, and made to regard himself as ever on the brink of an endless being. With a deep sense of obligation, a keen, sensitive conscience, and a tender heart, the great truths of religion appeared in his eye as sublime, awful, practical realities, compared with which earth was nothing. Thus he was made brave before men for the right, while he lay in the dust before God.

Such was Haddam training one hundred years ago. Some may lift their hands in horror at this picture; but it was a process which made moral heroes. It exhibited a society in which wealth existed without idleness or profligacy; social elevation without arrogance; labor without degradation; and a piety which, by its energy and martyr-endurance, could shake the world.

We are not to suppose that the boyhood of John Brainerd under these influences was gloomy or joyless: far from it. Its activity was bliss; its growth was a spring of life; its achievements were victories. Each day garnered some benefit; and rising life, marked by successive accumulations, left a smile on the conscience and bright and reasonable hopes for the future.

We might have desired that this Puritan training had left childhood a little larger indulgence,—had looked with interest at present enjoyment as well as at future good,—had smiled a little more lovingly on the innocent gambols, the ringing laughter, the irrepressible mirth of boyhood; and had frowned less severely on imperfections clinging to human nature itself. We might think that, by insisting too much on obligation and too little on privilege,—too much on the law and too little on the gospel,—too much on the severity and too little on the goodness of the Deity,—the conscience may have been stimulated at the expense of the affections, and men fitted for another world at an unnecessary sacrifice of their amiability and happiness in the present life.

But in leaving this Puritan training, the world "has gone farther and fared worse." To repress the iniquity of the age and land, to save our young men for themselves, their country, and their God, I believe we shall gain most, not by humoring childhood's caprices and sneering at strict households, strict governments, and strict Sabbaths, but by going back to many of the modes which gave to the world such men as John Hampden, William Bradford, Jonathan Edwards, Timothy Dwight, and David and John Brainerd.

The son of a tolerably wealthy father, nurtured

and trained by a pious mother, the early playmate, schoolmate, and companion of his sensitive, talented, and conscientious brother David, John's childhood was spent under the best influences for the conservation of his morals and the development of his mind and heart. Probably he and his younger brothers and sisters remained at the paternal homestead, with the elder brother Hezekiah, whose marriage, in 1731, with the daughter of the clergyman of the parish, Rev. Mr. Fisk, as before stated, would be likely to furnish a good home for the orphans.

I have thought this rather detailed account of the family of the missionary Brainerds might be instructive, as illustrating the influences to which they were subjected in early life, and the home-circles in which they embalmed their early affections, and, above all, the general prosperity and blessedness of families trained conscientiously in the fear and love of God. In this case, at least, the benediction descended to children, and children's children,—even to the fourth and fifth generation. "Godliness is profitable—to the life that now is."

CHAPTER III.

JOHN BRAINERD IN YALE COLLEGE—HIS BROTHER'S EXPULSION—ITS INJUSTICE—EFFECT ON JOHN—ITS INFLUENCE IN FOUNDING PRINCETON COLLEGE—LETTERS, ETC.

NEHEMIAH graduated at Yale College in 1732, and settled in the ministry in 1740.

As the three younger brothers, David, John, and Israel, all successively entered Yale College, it is probable that they were influenced by the example of the older brother, and all, moreover, aided by him in their classical studies.

The early convictions and struggles of David Brainerd, which he has related so minutely, were doubtless shared to some extent by his brother, brought up under similar influences and only two years his junior. He entered the Freshman class in Yale College in 1742, and graduated in 1746, when he was twenty-six years of age. No record is preserved of his college life and standing. The confidence reposed in him by the wisest men of New England immediately after his graduation is evidence that his moral deportment was correct, and his scholarship at least respectable.

As he entered college the year his beloved brother fell into difficulties, and was, as is now believed, treated with great and unnecessary severity and finally expelled, the heart of John must have been most sorely tried.

Assuming that our readers are to some extent familiar with the Life of David Brainerd, by Edwards, it is not necessary to go into details of the fault and punishment of the eminent missionary. The story briefly told is this. Brainerd was sincerely attached to the revival party of the times, and wrought up to high excitement in favor of a religion of the heart rather than a religion of orthodoxy and cold forms. Not to the neglect of his studies or the corruption of his morals, but against the arbitrary laws of his teachers,* he had attended upon the preaching of men like the sainted Gilbert Tennent. This had, probably, excited prejudice against him. On a certain occasion, when Tutor Whittlesey had led in prayer, and had retired from the chapel with the crowd, leaving Brainerd with only two or three friends in the hall, a Freshman overheard Brainerd say: "He has no more grace than that chair." A hard judgment, truly, but excusable if the prayer of Whittlesey was as brief, pointless, and heartless as some which we have heard in colleges and schools from clerical professors. Brainerd was imprudent in saying this, and, probably, uncharitable in thinking it; but, as it was spoken in private chat among his friends, it

* Edwards's Life of Brainerd, pp. 65, 117, 255.

was beneath the dignity of the college authorities to pry into the matter and persecute the young offender. A Freshman heard him say it of somebody, he could not tell of whom. The Freshman told a woman, and she gossiped the matter so that the authorities were put on the scent. By intimidating Brainerd's young companions, they drew from them the fact that it was Tutor Whittlesey whom Brainerd had so severely judged. When called to account, he confessed that he had done wrong. He ought to have been forgiven at once; but the college authorities insisted that he should disgrace himself for this venial offence by a public confession before the whole body of students. Brainerd, with the spirit of a man, refused, and was not only expelled, but "afterwards found no place for repentance," when, by full confession of the wrong, and by the powerful intercession of President Edwards and others, he asked to be allowed to take his degree. No wonder "Brainerd thought himself very ill used in the management of this affair, and thought it was injuriously extorted from his friends, and then injuriously required of him, as if he had committed some open notorious crime, to humble himself before the whole college in the hall for what he had said in private conversation."* His subsequent efforts to regain admission show how deeply the

* Edwards's Life.

sense of injury was burned into his heart. But the authorities of Yale College allowed no candid discernment to discriminate between a courser and a plough-horse,—between a sensitive and high-spirited genius and plodding obstinacy,—and, by their persistence, obliterated the name of David Brainerd forever from their "Triennial Catalogues." Whether Brainerd or the college lost most by this omission, I think the world has long since decided.

We have no doubt that the life of David Brainerd was shortened by his college persecution. His manuscript journal at Kaunaumeek develops the most intense and overwhelming mental suffering from the stigma fastened on him. President Edwards bears testimony to his Christian spirit when the negotiation for reconciliation at New Haven failed. But the blow was too crushing even for Brainerd's meekness. In his private journal he says, with a natural and indignant spirit savoring a little of the temper of the world:—

"*New Haven*, *July* 9, 1743.—I was still occupied with some business depending on certain grandees for performance. Alas! how much men may lord and tyrannize over their fellow countrymen, yet pretend that all their treatment of them is full of lenity and kindness,—that they owe them some special regard,—that they would hardly treat another with so much tenderness, and the like. Like the Holy Court of Inquisition, when they put a poor innocent to the rack, they tell him that what they do is all for the benefit of his soul! Lord, deliver my soul from this temper!"

John Wesley, in his "Life of Brainerd," is equally severe. He says, "Do those college authorities call themselves *Christians?*" *

John Brainerd must have felt deeply this treatment of his elder and favorite brother.

David's class was the largest that had ever entered Yale College, and he stood at the head of it. College honors were then highly estimated. To be stricken down in his course and dismissed in disgrace was adapted not alone to cut him to the heart, but to overwhelm with disappointment and shame his younger brother, as yet a timid Freshman. Indeed, the meanness, severity, and persistent obstinacy of the authorities in this matter

---

* The writer would greatly regret, if the manner in which he has told this painful story should lead any to infer that he is not an advocate of order and subordination among college students. The reverse is the fact. But he may be allowed to intimate his conviction, that clerical professors in colleges should not sink themselves into mere literary instructors, substituting dignity, insulation, and cold, reckless, and indiscriminate punishment for pastoral visitation, sympathy, forbearance, and admonition. To tolerate irregularities through half a century, and then begin reformations by selecting the most orderly and sensitive among transgressors for punishment that the wicked may fear, strikes me as neither very wise nor very kind. If clerical professors do not exert a kind, Christian influence to prevent irregularities, why may not the whole business of college instruction and government be left to laymen? We think we have known some instances of "college infirmity" and injustice that resembled, if they failed to equal, the wrong inflicted on David Brainerd. But it is not our province to settle such questions here.

seem to have shocked the sensibilities of the whole evangelical party in New England, and to have extended an influence far into New York, New Jersey, and Pennsylvania. It is thought that Old Nassau Hall, or Princeton College, owed its existence and first form not a little to the sympathy of the revival party with David Brainerd in his wrongs at Yale College.

Dr. Field* says,—

> "I once heard the Hon. John Dickinson, son of the Rev. Mr. Dickinson, of Norwalk, say that 'the establishment of Princeton College was owing to the sympathy felt for David Brainerd because the authorities of Yale College would not give him his degree, and that the *plan of the college was drawn up in his father's house.*' "

In a notice of Dr. Field's remarks† on this subject, that able and reliable work, "The Princeton Repertory," admits that they are correct; "that the men who founded Princeton College were stimulated to act promptly and efficiently in the great work by sympathy with the exiled student of Yale."

We have testimony to the same effect from another and most reliable source. The Rev. Archibald Alexander, D.D., in his history of "The Log College," says:—

---

* See Princeton Review on "Brainerd Genealogy," 1857.

† Brainerd Genealogy, p. 26.

"Messrs. Dickinson and Burr, the former pastor of the Presbyterian Church in Elizabethtown, and the latter in Newark, took the lead in this enterprise. Both these distinguished divines were graduates of Yale College; but just at this time their minds probably experienced some alienation from their *alma mater* on account of the harsh treatment which Mr. David Brainerd had received from the officers of that college; for he had been expelled merely for a harsh word spoken in private company and overheard by a student who happened to be passing the door, who knew not to whom it referred.

* * * * * *

"The attachment of all the members of the New York Synod to Mr. Brainerd was warm, and deservedly so. This affair, it is probable, quickened the zeal of these excellent men to get up a college of their own. Some years ago the writer (Dr. Alexander) heard the relict of the late Dr. Scott, of New Brunswick, say that when she was a little girl she heard the Rev. Mr. Burr declare in her father's house in Newark, 'if it had not been for the treatment Mr. Brainerd received at Yale, New Jersey College would never have been erected.' How many influences are made to combine and operate when Providence has the design of giving existence to an institution which has affected, and will still affect, the happiness of thousands."

This testimony of the Rev. Dr. Alexander so corroborates the statements of the Rev. Dr. Field, that we may regard the question as settled, that the expulsion of David Brainerd from Yale led to the founding of Princeton College. If so, it was not only evidence of the wisdom of Him "who brings good out of evil," but creditable alike to Brainerd's worth and the heartiness of his Christian friends. They made a noble and enduring protest against his wrongs.

But whatever outward excitement may have arisen from the expulsion of David Brainerd from Yale College, or whatever mortification and anguish it may have occasioned his brother John, neither of the brothers seems to have allowed any feeling to blind his judgment or change his purposes. John went on steadily with his studies, as if nothing unpleasant had occurred. He did not admire the religious spirit of the faculty, and could not but feel the injustice to his beloved brother. But he had no complaint to make of the competence and fidelity of his instructors. Colleges were few, and their privileges precious, and he was too wise and considerate to abandon Yale from resentment of its despotism or his dislike of individual professors. He knew that the trial would be temporary and the benefits enduring. We find him, therefore, enrolled on the Catalogue as graduating at the end of a full four years' course in 1746. Not only this, but we find these older brothers willing to send their younger brother, Israel, to pursue his studies in the same institution. I cannot but regard their whole conduct throughout this matter as indicative of a most Christian temper, elevated above the spirit of the world.

In consulting the Triennial Catalogue of Yale

College for 1857, the reader will find that no less than twenty persons of the name and kindred of these brothers have received the honors of that institution. However infelicitous may have been the treatment of the warm-hearted and over-zealous missiorrary, no one will doubt that his immediate kindred and family connections owe a vast debt of gratitude to the noble institution in whose benefits they have so largely shared. May the blessing of God and the benedictions of good men abide with it for a thousand years to come!

The following letters addressed by David to his brother John, in college, are of deep interest, as marking the influence exerted by the elder upon the younger, the dignity and delicacy of their fraternal intercourse, and the confidence which they reposed in the godly sincerity and earnest piety of each other. In the purest and noblest sense they were "*par nobile fratrum.*"

"KAUNAUMEEK,* ALBANY CO., N. Y., April 30, 1743.

"DEAR BROTHER :—

"I should tell you 'I long to see you,' but my own experience has taught me that there is no happiness and

---

* It is now the site of a village about sixteen miles east of Albany, twenty-four from Troy, and twenty west from Stockbridge. The village is now called Brainerd's Bridge; not from the missionary, but from Jeremiah Brainerd, Esq., afterwards of Rome, Oneida county, N. Y., who early settled on the spot, and built the bridge over Kinderhook Creek. It contains a factory, a tavern, several stores, about forty houses, and a good Presbyterian church, with an able pastor. No remnants of the Indian occupants remain except the apple-trees which

plenary satisfaction to be enjoyed in *earthly friends*, though ever so near and dear, or in any other enjoyment, that is not in God himself. Therefore, if the God of *all grace* be pleased graciously to afford us each *his presence* and *grace*, that we may perform the work and endure the trials he calls us to in a most distressing, tiresome wilderness, till we arrive at our journey's end, the local distance at which we are held from each other at present is a matter of no great moment or importance to either of us. But, alas! the presence of God is what I want. I live in the most lonely, melancholy *desert*, about eighteen miles from Albany; for it was not thought best that I should go to Delaware River, as I believe I hinted to you in a letter from New York. I board with a poor Scotchman; his wife can scarcely talk any English. *My diet* consists mostly of hasty-pudding, boiled corn, bread baked in ashes, and sometimes a little meat and butter. *My lodging* is a little heap of straw laid upon some boards, a little way from the ground, for it is a log room, without any floor, that I lodge in. *My work* is exceedingly hard and difficult; I travel on foot a mile and a half, the worst of ways, almost daily, and back again, for I live so far from my Indians. I have not seen an English person this month. These, and many other circumstances equally

---

they planted, some of which measure *four feet in diameter*. On the plain, in a bend of the creek girdled all round by hills, tradition locates the cabin of the missionary. In the vicinity Indian graves, arrow-heads, and hatchets have been found, indicating the place as an Indian resort, for which the fertility of its soil and wild beauty of its scenery amply account. In Hopkins' "Memorial of Sergeant's Stockbridge Mission," published about 1760, it is said of Stockbridge, "that it had forty miles of wilderness on the east, twenty miles on the west, and on the north the great and terrible wilderness reaching to Canada." Such was the country in the time of Brainerd's mission.

uncomfortable, attend me; and yet my spiritual *conflicts* and *distresses* so far *exceed* all these, that I scarce think of them, or hardly observe that I am not entertained in the most sumptuous manner. The Lord grant that I may learn to 'endure hardness as a good soldier of Jesus Christ.'

"As to my success here, I cannot say much yet. The Indians seem generally kind and well disposed towards me, are mostly very attentive to my instructions, and seem willing to be taught further. Two or three, I hope, are under some *convictions*; but there seems to be little of the special workings of the Divine Spirit among them yet; which gives me many a heart-sinking hour. Sometimes I hope that God has abundant blessings in store for them and me, but at other times I have been so overwhelmed with distress that I cannot see how his dealings with me are consistent with covenant love and faithfulness; and I say, 'Surely his tender mercies are clean gone forever!' But, however, I see I *needed* all this *chastisement* already. It is good for me that I have endured these trials, and have had hitherto little or no apparent success. Do not be discouraged by my distress. I was under great distress at Mr. Pomroy's when I saw you last, but 'God has been with me of a truth' since that; he helped me sometimes sweetly at Long Island and elsewhere. But let us always remember that we must *through much tribulation* enter into God's eternal kingdom of rest and peace. The righteous are *scarcely* saved; it is an infinite wonder that we have well-grounded hopes of being saved at all. For my part, I feel the most vile of any creature living. Now all you can do for me is, to pray incessantly that God would make me humble, holy, resigned, and heavenly-minded, by all my trials. Be strong in the Lord and in the power of his might.

Let us *run*, *wrestle*, and *fight*, that we may win the *prize* and obtain that complete happiness, to be 'holy as God is holy.' So, wishing and praying that you may advance in learning and grace, and be fit for special service for God,

"I remain, your affectionate brother,

"DAVID BRAINERD."

The above letter savors of the phraseology of the times and the morbid temperament of the writer; but the appeal which he makes for a younger brother's prayers implies a respectful and affectionate confidence not often existing in such an intimate relation. It shows at least how David Brainerd estimated the moral worth and piety of his brother John.

In December of the same year David writes again, in a similar strain:—

"KAUNAUMEEK, ALBANY CO., N. Y., Dec. 27, 1743.

"DEAR BROTHER:—

"I long to see you, and to know how you fare in your journey through a world of inexpressible sorrow, where we are compassed about with 'vanity, confusion, and vexation of spirit.' I am more weary of life, I think, than I ever was. The whole *world* appears to me like a huge *vacuum*, a vast empty space, where nothing desirable or, at least, satisfactory can possibly be derived; and I long *daily* to *die* more and more to it, even though I obtain not that comfort from spiritual things which I earnestly desire. Worldly pleasures, such as flow from greatness, riches, and honors, and sensual gratifications, are infinitely worse than none. May the

Lord deliver us more and more from these *vanities.* I have spent most of the fall and winter hitherto in a very weak state of body, and sometimes under pressing inward trials and spiritual conflicts, but, 'having obtained help from God, I continue to this day,' and am now somewhat better in health than I was some time ago. I find nothing more conducive to a life of *Christianity* than a diligent, industrious, and faithful improvement of precious *time.* Let us then faithfully perform that business which is allotted to us by Divine Providence to the utmost of our bodily strength and mental vigor. Why should we sink and grow discouraged with any particular trials and perplexities which we are called to encounter in the world? *Death* and *eternity* are just before us: a few tossing billows more will waft us into the world of spirits, and, we hope, through infinite grace, into endless pleasures and uninterrupted rest and peace. Let us then 'run with patience the race that is set before us.' Hebrews xii. 1, 2. And oh! that we could depend more upon the *living* God, and less upon our own wisdom and strength! Dear brother, may the *God of all grace* comfort your heart and succeed your studies, and make you an instrument of good to his people in your day. This is the constant prayer of

"Your affectionate brother,

"DAVID BRAINERD."

When David wrote the following letter, John had nearly finished his college-course.

"CROSSWEEKSUNG (CROSSWICKS), N. J., Dec. 28, 1745.

"VERY DEAR BROTHER:—

"I am in one continual, perpetual, and uninterrupted hurry, and Divine Providence throws so much upon me that I do not know how it will ever be otherwise. May I obtain mercy of God to be faithful unto death. I cannot say that I am weary of my hurry; I only want strength and grace to do more for God than I have ever yet done.

"My dear brother, the Lord of heaven, who has carried me through so many trials, bless you for time and eternity, and fit you to do service for him in the church below and to enjoy his blissful presence in his church triumphant.

"My dear brother, the time is short. Oh, let us fill it up for God. Let us count the sufferings of this present time as nothing, if we can but run our race and finish our course with joy. Oh, let us strive to live for God. I bless the Lord I have nothing to do with earth, but only to labor honestly in it for God, till I shall accomplish 'as a hireling my day.' I think I do not desire to live a minute for any thing which earth can afford. Oh that I could live for none but God till my dying moment!

"I am your affectionate brother,

"David Brainerd."

In the absence of other and more direct testimony, may we not safely infer that a college student capable of appreciating such letters, and deemed worthy of them by one who knew him so well, must have been a young man of rare excellence? We naturally consult the character and taste of our friends in our epistles to them, so that our sentiments and style not only mirror ourselves, but our friends. As to John Brainerd's scholarship we have no testimony. He graduated in course in 1746; creditably, doubtless, but not distinguished. He numbered President Stiles, Elihu Spencer, D.D., and other eminent men, among his classmates.

CHAPTER IV.

JOHN BRAINERD'S ENTRANCE UPON THE MINISTRY.

WITH whom John Brainerd studied theology after his graduation is not certainly known. "He probably studied for a brief space with the Rev. Mr. Mills, of Ripton, or Rev. Mr. Bellamy, of Bethlehem."* It will be remembered that he was connected by marriage with the Rev. Mr. Fisk, pastor of the church in his native town. Precisely what time he occupied with any or all of these is not known.

It may be said of men trained under the influence of the better class of families in New England a century ago, that their whole youth was spent in a school of theology; and that, like Timothy, from "their youth they had known the Scriptures." This was especially the case with the Brainerds. Hence, when their literary course was finished, they went forth to preach the gospel.

The first we hear of John Brainerd after his graduation is, that the *Correspondents*† had de-

---

* Brainerd Genealogy, Dr. Field, p. 288.

† These gentlemen were the *correspondents*, in New York, New Jersey, and Pennsylvania, of "The Honorable Society in Scotland for Propagating Christian Knowledge."—*Edwards*, p. 78.

signated him to supply the place of his brother David, whose health had so failed that he was compelled to discontinue his labors.

There can be no doubt that this application for his services among the Indians had its origin in the recommendation of David Brainerd. This fact, so far from abating, is apt to increase our respect for the younger brother; for when we bear in mind the deep piety, the high moral standard, and the intense love to the poor Indians of David Brainerd, connected with his discrimination of character and perfect knowledge of John's qualifications, it was in the highest degree honorable to be selected as David's successor. It is not often that a prophet has honor in his own country.

The intimacy of brotherhood often abates mutual respect. The many minor shades of character which are likely to be obvious in the intercourse of brothers, often prompts them to look abroad for those to whom they are about to confide their weighty responsibilities. If no man is great to his *valet-de-chambre*, it is because all human greatness has its narrow bounds, which the dullest intellect can ascertain by constant intercourse. We ordinarily allow the imagination to throw a veil over the weaknesses, and a halo over the virtues, of those for whom we cherish reverence or admiration. Men are often great, not by what they reveal but by what they conceal. The world reveres not so much the reality of heroes, statesmen, and saints, as the drapery thrown over its idols by a partial fancy. Like their own shadows, great men often grow less as the sun rises higher and the daylight becomes clearer. Lapse of time, distance, and obscurity have magnified some of the ancients to demigods, until they seem very great,

"Looming through the mist."

To be held in the highest estimate by the wise and good associated with us in the family, the store, the workshop, the neighborhood, is the infallible test of moral weight and worth. This seems to have been the happy lot of John Brainerd. Looking at the high standard to which David Brainerd held himself responsible, at the really great difficulties of the Indian missionary-work, at the wonderful attainments and successes of David, we might have presumed that in the widest range among the wise and good martyr-spirits of earth he would hardly find a man so eminent in talents, piety, skill, and energy, that the mission could be safely committed to his hands.

Whom did he, in fact, select? His own brother John, the playmate of his childhood, the companion of his youth, the intimate associate of his early manhood. He knew every weakness and imperfection of this brother; but he also saw in him such a combination of talents and grace that, above all others, he prefers him for the work.

Considering the nature of the responsibility and the relation of the parties, there never has been higher confidence reposed by man in man than is here shown by David in his brother John. He implies that his brother, by purity of motive, holiness of heart, by industry, skill, and power, is worthy to be his successor; and this confidence was never disappointed.

We shall defer our remarks on the origin and history of the Indian Missions of New York and New Jersey to the next chapter.

Our first introduction to John Brainerd after his graduation is by the diary of his brother David, under the date of April 10, 1747. He says,—

> "Spent the forenoon in Presbyterial business. In the afternoon rode to Elizabethtown; *found my brother John there; spent some time in conversation with him.*"

CHAPTER V.

CONDITION OF THE INDIAN MISSIONS AT THE TIME THE REV. JOHN BRAINERD ENTERED UPON HIS LABORS.

FROM the first landing of the Pilgrims at Plymouth Rock, in 1620, the obligation to attempt the conversion of the Indians to Christianity was recognized and, to some extent, essayed. But the struggles of the colonists for sustenance gave them little leisure for the work, and the bitter hostility of the red men toward the whites led to wars, antipathies, and resentments, alike unfavorable to the missionary spirit of the colonists and the disposition of the Indians to receive instruction from those whom they regarded as invaders of their lands and heritage. But some good men rose above the general apathy and prejudice, and, with a martyr spirit, attempted the conversion of their Indian neighbors.

As early as 1646, the Rev. John Eliot formed a settlement of praying Indians at Newton, Mass.; and in 1661 organized a church of Indians at Natick. Like Paul, he travelled extensively, preaching to the sons of the forest on the capes and islands of Massachusetts Bay and Plymouth Plantations. He translated the Bible and other pious books into the Indian language. Of his Bible fifteen hundred copies were published in 1663, and two thousand in 1685. He died in 1690, aged eighty-five, and has ever since been honored with the title of the "Apostle to the Indians."

Still earlier than Eliot on the islands of Martha's Vineyard and Nantucket, Thomas Mayhew began to preach the gospel to the Indians in 1643; and for five generations, until the death of Zechariah Mayhew in 1813, the Mayhew family kept up these labors. As a result, at Gayhead, in the western part of Martha's Vineyard, there is still an Indian property of four thousand acres held, as tenants in common, by the descendants of Mayhew's Indians. The State of Massachusetts furnishes them with churches and schools.

In the Plymouth colony in 1673, there were twenty-four regular churches of Christian Indians, taught not only the gospel, but the men to farm, and the women to spin, weave, sew, knit, cook, and keep house.*

These missionary labors and successes, glowingly reported in England, stimulated there the formation of societies, with the collection of funds, to aid the good work in America. Among these societies one was formed in Edinburgh, Scotland, in 1709, called "*The Honorable Society for Propagating Christian Knowledge.*" In 1730 this

---

* Tracy's History of American Missions.

society appointed correspondents, or a commission, in the United States, to settle its fields of labor, designate its missionaries, and disburse its American charities. They employed a Rev. Mr. Horton, who labored with considerable success among the Narragansetts, Pequots, Nantics, Mohegans, and Montauks. In 1743 the Rev. John Sergeant left his tutorship in Yale College, commenced a mission at Stockbridge, in a howling wilderness, and labored there fifteen years, until his death in 1749. His house is still standing in the vicinity of that beautiful village. When he entered on his labors, he found on the spot only fifty wild savages. He left them two hundred and eighteen in number, with neat dwellings, cultivated farms, a church, and schools of about one hundred pupils. His church consisted of forty-two communicants. He was succeeded by the great Jonathan Edwards, the biographer of David Brainerd.

It is too common to censure the severity of the Pilgrims toward the Indians. From what we have stated, it will be seen that had succeeding generations imbibed their benevolence and charity toward the aborigines, and had their spirit spread over the land, we should not now be compelled to reproach ourselves at the sepulchres of so many dead nations. The fact that some few remnants of once powerful tribes now exist is to be attributed to no governmental care, no sympathy of poets or philanthropists outside the Church, but to the humane and protecting power of Christianity. Would that this influence had been more earnest, efficient, and universal!

We must not overlook, in this connection, the efforts of our Moravian brethren. As early as 1740, Christian Henry Bauch commenced a mission among the Indians in Eastern New York, near Sharon, Conn. He had great success; but causes which have proved fatal to most other missions among the aborigines compelled him to remove. Rum sellers, land speculators, and such other bad men as hang on the skirts of civilization and barbarism, conspired against him. These drew to their aid such legislative authority and such persecutions that the Moravians were obliged to retire to Bethlehem, in the deeper forests of Pennsylvania. They also had establishments at Gnadenhütten, above the present borough of Easton, where, as is well known, their converts suffered a dreadful massacre in 1755, by Indians in the French interest. The Moravian brethren retreated deeper and deeper into the forest. They had successively missions at Friedenhütten, on the Susquehanna, at Friedenstadt, on the Ohio, at Gnadenhütten, on the Muskinghum, and finally near Detroit, in Michigan. They first and last numbered hundreds of sincere converts; but, followed everywhere by the same bad men who broke up their first mission, and subjected to constant interruption by political jealousy and the wars of the period, they finally settled, in 1792, on twenty-five thousand acres of land assigned them by the British Government on the river Thames, in Canada.

"The Indian Apple Tree at Kannaumeek, now Brainerd, N. Y."—P. 75.

CHAPTER. VI.

DAVID BRAINERD IN KAUNAUMEEK.*

IN 1743, David Brainerd, then a young man twenty-five years of age, was selected by the Committee of the before-mentioned "Society for Propagating Christian Knowledge" to begin a mis-

---

* Since this chapter was written, we have received the following letter and the sketch from the Rev. Mr. Barbour, pastor of the Presbyterian church at Brainerd's Bridge, the site of the ancient Kaunaumeek. We can testify to its accuracy of detail. The old apple-tree, we have no doubt, was planted in the days of David Brainerd:—

"BRAINERD, June 25, 1864.

"REV. AND DEAR SIR:—

"Your short visit at our place nearly two years since, and our ramble through the neighborhood and fields in search of traditions and relics of the Kaunaumeek Indians who inhabited this beautiful valley one hundred and twenty years ago, will long be remembered with interest.

"You will readily recall, as I often do, the peculiar interest we felt in passing along the bank of the Kinderhook Creek, where tradition alone marks the Indian burying-ground, over which was waving a luxuriant growth of oats; and in pausing at the turn of the road, on the western margin of the valley, where tradition also points out the spot where David Brainerd built his house, and in which he lived for about one year while serving the Indians in missionary labors. That small house which stood upon that spot, a few foundation-stones of which only now remain, had cost the worthy missionary many days of weary toil; but it added not a little both to his temporal and his spiritual comfort, judging from an extract from his diary, July 30, 1743:—

sion among the Indians at Kaunaumeek, in Nassau township, N. Y., near the site of the town of

---

"'Just at night moved into my own house, and lodged there that night; found it much better spending the time alone, than in the wigwam where I was before.'

"There Brainerd 'boiled his corn,' made his 'hasty-pudding,' baked his 'corn-cakes,' ate his 'sour' and 'mouldy bread;' there he fasted, prayed, and humbled himself before God again and again; there he read his Bible, consecrated and re-consecrated himself to Christ and his missionary work; there he wrote his diary, studied his sermons, and taught rude savages the way of salvation; there he enjoyed that retirement for which his panting soul often longed.

"'*Diary, November* 29, 1743.—Was perplexed for want of more retirement. I love to live alone in my own little cottage, where I can spend much time in prayer.'

"It is no ordinary privilege to look upon even the foundation-stones of a house which once contained so devoted and self-sacrificing a Christian minister as was David Brainerd.

"But the last, though not the least, of those interesting objects we viewed that day, pointing back to the time when the Indians dwelt here, must not be overlooked. I refer to the huge old *apple-tree* standing in the rear of the ample farm-house, whose owner tills these classic fields to reap abundant harvests. Its massive trunk and giant limbs and towering top show that it has come up through many generations.

"At your request, I send you a rude sketch of this old *century plant*, which still continues not only to bud and blossom as in its youth, but also to bear a fair, sweet apple, some years in great abundance.

"You will remember its trunk measured thirteen feet and four inches in circumference. Since you were here I have met with the following tradition among some of the old inhabitants of the place respecting the name of the old Indian settlement.

"Kaunaumeek was a name given to a mountain about three-quarters of a mile southwest of the head of the valley where the village of Brainerd now stands. The Indians who dwelt in the valley on the east of this mountain would occasionally hear a noise, which they understood as saying, *Kau-nau-meek, Kau-nau-meek.* They imagined that this sound always proceeded from the top of this mountain, and that it was a warning to them that the deer were now around, and that the chase might be commenced with prospects of success. The Indians gave this name to the mountain on this

New Lebanon, Columbia county. His letter to his brother John in college, already quoted, describes his fare and his labors. He studied the language, composed simple forms of prayer, translated the Bible, taught the children to sing, set up a school, living in a hut erected by his own hands, and bringing his bread, when he had any, a distance of fifteen miles. He entered on his labors at Kaunaumeek April 1, 1743, and continued them until March, 1744. His Indians were then advised to go to Stockbridge and put themselves under the care of the Rev. Mr. Sergeant. Mr. Brainerd himself was instructed to found a new mission in North Jersey and Eastern Pennsylvania; making the Forks of the Delaware, the present site of Easton, Pa., the centre of his labors. May 9, 1744, he left New England, crossed the Hudson River at Fishkill, and went to Goshen; and from thence began his journey of one hundred miles from the Hudson to the Delaware "through a desolate and hideous country above Jersey." There were few settlements. He was alone in a strange wilderness, and was, he says, "considerably disconso-

---

account; afterwards the name was given to the Indians of the settlement. Our village now bears the name of the Indian missionary.

"And now, dear brother in Christ, may the savory influence of the several memoirs of David Brainerd, and that of his brother John, which you are about to add to them, permeate the whole membership of the Church, enlarged and extended, over the entire world.

"Yours, fraternally,

"P. BARBOUR."

late." May 13, he reached the Forks, and entered at once on his labors.

Then, as now, the region was one of great picturesque beauty. Indeed, in the wildness of nature the scenery around must have approached the sublime; but the missionary was too much absorbed in his work to note attractions of river, hill, or mountain.

These Forks of the Delaware Brainerd has made classical by his residence and labors. Travellers seek out the places associated with his name, and Easton has honored his memory by naming one of the sanctuaries there the "Brainerd Church." May his spirit ever characterize that congregation.*

---

* The term "Forks of the Delaware" was not applied exclusively to the point of junction of the rivers Delaware and Lehigh, but also designated the whole delta or triangle back to the Kittaning Mountain, the first range of the great Appalachian chain. Into this triangle a few Irish and German settlers had penetrated as early as 1730. The presence of these white settlers did something to mitigate the solitude and insulation of the early missionary. In the Historical Collections of Pennsylvania it is said: "With the aid of a poor interpreter he translated prayers into the Delaware language. He speaks of the Indians of this region as excessively given to idolatry, as having contracted strong prejudices against Christianity on account of the wicked lives of the whites with whom they had intercourse; as being extremely attached to the customs and fabulous notions of their fathers, one of which was, 'that it was not the same God made them who made the whites, but another god, who commanded them to live by hunting, &c.' Besides this, they were made mad by their *powaws*, who were supposed to have the power of enchanting them in a very distressing manner. Nevertheless, some converts were gathered, and among them his interpreter, Moses Finda Fatuary, and his wife.

In July, 1744, Brainerd made his way on horseback over the mountains to the Susquehanna, having been invited thither by some Indians whom he found at Kansesaushong (Catasauqua); and in May, 1745, he again visited that region, and followed the Susquehanna to Duncan's Island, where he had "some encouragement from the good attention of the Indians."

On June 19 of the same year, he began his labors at Crossweeksung, N. J., among the Jersey Indians, the field of his greatest successes. For a detailed account of the wonderful power of God which attended his labors here, we must refer the

---

"Brainerd built himself a cabin with his own hands, not far from Bethel Church, and on moving into it, having, as he says, 'a happy opportunity of being retired in a *house of his own*,' he set apart a day for secret prayer and fasting. This cabin was still standing in the memory of Mr. John Wilson. Brainerd frequently speaks of preaching to the white people of the 'Forks,' the Irish, the Low Dutch, the High Dutch; of preaching to them in the wilderness on the sunny side of a hill, when he had a considerable assembly, consisting of people who lived, many of them, more than thirty miles asunder."

The house of Brainerd was at Lower Mt. Bethel, in what was called the Forks North, to distinguish them from Forks South, now Allen township.

The traveller who glides up the valley of the Delaware in a railroad-car and visits Easton, thronged by its busy thousands, enriched by commerce, mineral resources, and manufacturing industry; furnished with its classic temples for the worship of the true God, its courts of justice, its rising college and abundant schools; its general intelligence, morality, and refinement, can hardly realize the fact that one hundred and twenty years ago David Brainerd, on the same spot, gathered in, under forest trees or in smoky wigwams, wild pagans to hear the first tidings of Jesus Christ.—*Historical Collections of Pennsylvania*, p. 522.

reader to his well-known memoir, published first by Jonathan Edwards, in 1749, at Boston. Editions of his Life and Labors were subsequently republished in the last century by the Rev. John Wesley, by the Rev. Philip Doddridge, and others. More recently they have been republished in this country by the Rev. S. E. Dwight, D.D., by the American Tract Society, and in Sparks' American Biography. Brainerd's memoir is a classic in the literature of the Church, and we need not transcribe any portion of it in this volume. But we may be allowed to quote the testimony of a man whose extreme apprehension of fanaticism in revivals of religion has been criticized, whose calm judgment the Church has greatly approved, and whose caution in language gives weight to his opinions. The Rev. Ashbel Green, D.D., of Philadelphia, in his book on American Missions, says:—

"*At Crossweeksung, his success was perhaps without a parallel in heathen missions since the days of the apostles.* For his exertions were made single-handed; he had no fellow-laborer beyond a little occasional assistance from two or three neighboring brethren in the ministry. In opposition to discouragements which would have subdued any ordinary mind, and which went near to vanquish his own, he long persevered, with no prospect of obtaining the object of his wishes and his agonizing prayers, in the conversion of those to whom he ministered." *

---

* Presbyterian Missions, p. 40.

Dr. Green's language is strong, but true.

Of the power of the Holy Ghost to open the ears of savages to the truth, to soften their hearts, bend their wills, curb their passions, and inspire them with meekness, gentleness, docility, reverence, watchfulness, faith, love, joy, and practical obedience, there has been no higher illustration since the day of Pentecost than in the case of the Indians of New Jersey, under the ministry of Brainerd. His frequent revivals, marked by cries of anxiety, tears of contrition, earnestness of prayer, fulness of transformation evinced in subsequent holiness, have encouraged for a hundred years past the whole Church of God. Henry Martyn, Claudius Buchanan, and their thousand successors in the missionary work, have been stimulated by Brainerd's example and successes. Pastors in every land for three generations have toiled in brighter hope, as they saw in the results of Brainerd's labors that God is able to make a short work of the world's conversion.

In the year 1746 he carried out a plan to establish the Indians at Cranberry, N. J. At these two places, Crossweeksung and Cranberry, in eleven months, he baptized thirty-eight adults and thirty-seven infants; and concerning the character of these converts Mr. McKnight, of Cranberry, testifies, they "may be proposed as examples of piety and godliness to all the white people around them."

That such results were not reached without great toil may well be believed. Under date of November 5, 1745, Brainerd says:—

"I have now rode (horseback) more than three thousand miles since March last, in my own proper business as a missionary. I have taken pains to look out for a companion or colleague to travel with me, but have not as yet found any person qualified or disposed for this good work.

"The several companies of Indians to whom I have preached live at great distances from each other. It is more than seventy miles from Crossweeksung, in New Jersey, to the Forks of the Delaware, in Pennsylvania; and thence, to the Indians I visited on the Susquehanna, one hundred and twenty miles."

With all the modern appliances of railroads and steam, a missionary travel in six months of three thousand miles over a field two hundred and twenty miles in extent would be thought marvellous. What must it have been to the young, pale, consumptive Brainerd, threading alone the mountain-wilds and tangled forests of Pennsylvania!

It will scarcely be credited that, in addition to all these burdens, Brainerd was followed by constant persecution and slander on the part of those whose profits had been lessened by the temperance of his converts, and of the greedy speculators who were anxious to grasp the lands of the Indians. But he went on with his work in spite of all hardships and opposition.

His life, however, was wearing out. April 11,

1747, far gone with consumption, yet still brave and enterprising, he undertook his last journey from Cranberry to the Susquehanna. To avoid the Lehigh Mountains, he determined to come to Philadelphia, go first to the river, and then follow it up to the field of his mission. The details of this journey are too painful to dwell upon.

August 19, he struck the river near Harrisburg. August 20, "having lain in a cold sweat all night, he coughed up much bloody matter in the morning." August 22.—"All night lodged in the open woods. Enjoyed some liberty in secret prayer, and was helped to remember dear friends, as well as my dear flock and the Church of God."

August 23.—"Arrived at Shamoking [now Sunbury], and the next day (being Sabbath) discoursed to the Indian king and others upon divine things. *Spent most of the day in those exercises.*"

September 1, he started for the great island, fifty miles farther up the river; and lodged at night in the woods.

September 6.—"Spent the day in a very weak state, coughing and spitting blood. Was asked to do very little, except to discourse a while on divine things to my own people." By his "own people" he means the six Indians who accompanied him as guides and protectors.

September 8, he began his return, reaching Philadelphia on the 17th, and his Indian congregation at Cranberry on the 20th.

He spent one month at Cranberry, struggling with disease which almost entirely unfitted him for labor. On the 20th of November he left his people, and with much difficulty made his way to Elizabethtown; and there, in the house of his hospitable friend, the Rev. Jonathan Dickinson, he lay sick most of the time until the middle of March. Then, by taking two days for the journey, he revisited Cranberry. It was for the last time. Remaining two days only, he returned to Elizabethtown. His missionary toils were ended. By his personal efforts he had done something. By his indomitable spirit, his entire consecration, by forcing himself on in the face of obstacles and sufferings at the call of duty, he has furnished a model, stimulated a zeal, and suggested an energy, by which his influence will tell on the Church of God in all time to come. "He still lives" in the increased devotion and endurance of thousands of sturdier and longer-lived men. It is a complete summer, however brief, that ripens a full harvest.

Convinced that all efforts to labor on were now in vain, he advised the Correspondents, and they had sent, by his consent, for his brother John, to take his place in this missionary field.

It would seem that David had not yet surrendered all hope of resuming, after a season of rest in New England, his labors in the field. He had become used to travel and preach under the pressure of pain and weakness. With all his ailments, he had, nevertheless, with difficulty gained his own consent to intermit labor. And there were ties binding him to life. He was a young man, but twenty-nine years of age. He had won the heart and promised hand of one of the most intelligent, pious, and lovely daughters of New England; he had gained the confidence and friendship of the best men of his age; he had had eminent success in his glorious work, so that his name was mentioned with love and veneration not only in the wigwams of the savages whom he had educated, but in the praying circles of London and Edinburgh. It is natural to suppose that a young man with such ties should cling to life, and be slow to admit that his work on earth was done. But if he hoped for life, it was "against hope." His entire physical prostration,—confining him to his chamber for months in the house of his friend, his hospitable friend,—his cough, his hæmorrhages, his night-sweats, were all fingers pointing to an early grave. They must have thrown over his mind a foreboding that he had taken his final leave of his beloved Indian church, and that he was going home to New England to die. But whatever pain or presentiment of death might do to sadden, they did not overwhelm him.

On the 7th of April he says: "In the afternoon I rode to Newark, to marry the Rev. Mr. Dickinson, and in the evening performed that service.* Afterwards rode home to Elizabethtown in a pleasant frame, full of compassion and sweetness."

April 9, he appears to have occupied himself in the Presbytery of New York, then holding its sessions in Newark. He spent also the forenoon of the 10th in Presbyterial business; and, in the afternoon of that day returning to Elizabethtown, he says: "I found my brother John there. Spent some time in conversation with him; was extremely weak and out-done."

The meeting and conversation of these brothers must, in truth, strike the reader as deeply solemn, —almost sublime. The elder had been an exile for Christ among savages, dwelt in a forest hovel,

---

* As the Rev. Jonathan Dickinson is often mentioned in these pages, a brief account of him may be interesting. He was born in Hatfield, Mass., April 22, 1688, was graduated at Yale in 1706, and ordained to the gospel ministry in Fairfield, Conn., September 20, 1709. He began to preach in New Jersey in 1707, and his field of labor embraced not only Elizabethtown, but Rahway, Westfield, Connecticut Farms, and Springfield. He had more agency in founding the College of Princeton than any other man. It is said that the first charter granted by Governor James Hamilton, afterwards renewed by Governor Belcher, was drawn up in Mr. Dickinson's house (see p. 56) in 1746. He was made the first President, but died October 7, 1747, two days before David Brainerd, aged fifty-nine. It was a second wife to whom he was married by Brainerd one year before. He and the Rev. Aaron Burr, of Newark, and Rev. Ebenezer Pemberton, of the city of New York, constituted the clerical correspondents of the "Society for Propagating Christian Knowledge" under which Brainerd labored. Dr. Bellamy speaks of him as the "great Mr. Dickinson." As a wise counsellor and warm friend of the Brainerd brothers, he deserves this notice in the account of their lives.

pillowed his head on the hard ground, fed often on parched corn, been lost sometimes in the wilderness, sometimes maligned and slandered by the enemies of God and man. He had toiled and suffered until the energies of nature itself failed, and he was sinking to an early grave. The younger brother, twenty-seven years of age, of good family, easy circumstances, and finished education, had been "sent for;" and, with a wonderful abnegation of self and the world, with a martyr-love to Christ and unwavering submission to duty, he had come to assume the labors which had crushed an elder brother.

"The Correspondents," says President Edwards, "had sent for John to take David's place." What a cool matter-of-fact mode of summoning a moral martyr to leave home, kindred, and comfort, and bury himself among Indians in the wilderness! They pay here a noble tribute to the piety and philanthropy of John Brainerd. They say, substantially, that he only needed a call of duty to any work, however obscure, difficult, and perilous, and he would say, as he did say, "Here am I." May I be permitted to suggest here that, in thus promptly responding to the call of duty, young Brainerd exhibited the true spirit of a gospel minister? In the Roman Church, and in some Protestant denominations, young men are sent to their fields of labor by authority. One element of the power by which Loyola almost subdued the world to the Papal yoke was found in the fact that he held the authority by which he could "say to this man, Go, and he goeth." He could distribute genius, talent, learning, physical and moral energy, where they would most tell for the glory and enlargement of the Church.

The Episcopal Methodist Church, in its annual assignment of men to fields of labor, has had the benefit of the same authority, and used it with great efficacy for noble purposes.

The Presbyterian and Congregational policy has been different. It has limited the authority and responsibility of the Church as a governing body over its ministry, and implied a higher confidence in the individual, while it imposed greater personal obligations to learn and follow duty.

In our religious economy we have honored our ministers, by assuming for them such a baptism of the Spirit of Christ as would lead them to all diligence in ascertaining their personal duty, and all needful self-denial and fidelity in performing it. We have assumed that the love of ease, comfort, popularity, wealth, and high literary and social advantages, has no controlling place in the purposes and determinations of men who have professedly consecrated their all to the service of God. Hence we have no outward directions or constraint; no episcopal authority to distribute the talent, learning, and piety of the ministry where it will be most effective. Our system is not like a vast machine moved by some central spring of mighty energy controlling its entire action. It finds a better illustration in the movements of the orbs of heaven, where each planet turns on its own axis and wheels in its own orbit by an inherent impulse imparted by the finger of God. In short, the Church assumes that her youthful sons, fresh from their sacred studies, with burnished intellects, with sanctified hearts, with manly courage, noble fortitude, and holy zeal, will not selfishly and coldly stipulate for eminent places, positions, and emoluments; will not hang idly around cities and seminaries, waiting for eligible churches; will not, in ambitious scholarship and social exquisiteness, imagine themselves too precious to be thrown away in quiet towns among plain people.

It is to be feared that the sons of the Church have often lacked those high endowments of the Holy Spirit which would have fitted them to select their appropriate field and work. Some secular motive, some vision of worldly advantage, some compromise with conscience, has with links of iron held them back from rugged fields, but fields to which they were adapted, and in which they might have reaped glorious harvests. The world owes a special obligation to the pioneer husbandman who makes the *desert* blossom.

The harder the soil, and the more abundant the weeds, the briers, and the thorns, the more needful the spade, the plough, and the strong hand of the laborer; and the more beautiful, by contrast, the waving grain over hill and valley.

We once introduced a young minister to a missionary congregation in the suburbs of a great city. The people were highly pleased with him, and invited him to settle among them. He came to consult me on the subject. As he was an unmarried man, he regarded the salary as adequate. He had no fault to find with the number, the attendance, the attention and interest, of the congregation. I urged him to give an affirmative answer. He hesitated. "*I am afraid,*" said he, "*it is not the place for me to develop myself,*"—alluding to the plainness of the people. I replied: "It is an excellent place to develop the gospel of the Lord Jesus Christ, but I know not whether it is the place for you to develop *yourself.*"

He left the field, and has since "developed himself" by giving up the ministry. "He that exalteth himself shall be abased."

The little congregation, under the patient labors of purer and better men, has also "developed itself" into one of the most numerous, intelligent, and affluent churches in the land. Are there not other young ministers corroding in idleness, rejecting difficult fields, and waiting for a place to "develop themselves"?

Exactly the opposite of this seems to have been the spirit of John Brainerd. He knew all that his dying brother had suffered in his hard field, but still volunteered, in the true spirit of a martyr, to take that brother's place. David's whole record of their interview, at this period, is the following:—

"April 10.—Found my brother John there, and spent some time in conversation with him. April 11.—Assisted in examining my brother, by the New York Presbytery, for licensure. April 14.—This day my brother went to my people."

We doubt whether an interview stirring such thoughts, involving such heart-yearnings, ever had a record more brief. Its brevity is suggestive.

To these brothers, duty was every thing; themselves, nothing. They met as soldiers meet on the battle-field. One who had fought in the front rank, long, bravely, and triumphantly, had fallen wounded, and was returning home to die. The other, still fresh, strong, hopeful, and urged by a spirit as daring and a fortitude as enduring, stood ready to take his dying brother's sword and shield, to fight in the same conflict, or fall, as God should ordain. Their interview may remind the reader of a scene at the battle of Marengo. Desaix, one of Napoleon's bravest and most trusted generals, had been mortally wounded, and lay dying on the plain. Napoleon, pressing the retreating Austrians, paused by the side of his fellow-officer, who was expiring, and said that he was sorry he could not stay longer to weep for him. "I am sorry," said Desaix, "that I have but one life to give for the glory of France."

The servants of a nobler Master, and engaged with a spirit as heroic in a better cause, the brothers at Newark and Elizabethtown held a similar interview. The one must leave his dying brother for the field of duty; the other was regretting weakness, pain, and approaching death, only as they cut short his pious labors.

The letter subsequently addressed by David to John may well be taken as an index of the "conversation" between the brothers. John, now but twenty-seven years old, without experience as a minister or missionary, unaccustomed to Indian life and forest-fare, ignorant of the language of the people and a stranger to the localities of their neighborhood, had a thousand queries to propose and a thousand perplexities to be solved. No man ever had a better apology for self-distrust and shrinking at the outset of a great enterprise. On the other hand, David would have a thousand things to tell concerning his Indians, and, with his high standard of life and labors, a thousand solemn charges to impose. We can all readily picture the interest of this brief interview.

As we know the keen, almost morbid, sensibility of these young men, their matter-of-fact arrangements for duty show how they had subordinated every human sympathy to the obedience of Christ. We now leave the elder brother to pursue his last journey to New England, while we accompany John to the field of his future labors.

CHAPTER VII.

JOHN BRAINERD'S ENTRANCE ON THE FIELD AS A MISSIONARY.

LICENSED as a preacher of the gospel by the Presbytery of New York, then in session at Elizabethtown, endorsed as a proper substitute for his brother by the Edinburgh Correspondents, who allowed forty pounds annually to the mission,* John Brainerd is now ready for his work. Grieved at parting with his beloved, sick brother; burdened by the untried responsibilities before him, yet cheered by the benedictions of the Rev. Jonathan Dickinson, Rev. Aaron Burr, and other good men of the day; buoyed up by youthful hope, enthusiasm, and the consciousness of pure and lofty aims; trusting in the God of his fathers, he sets his face toward his wild forest home.

We can see him. He is mounted on horseback. His little wardrobe, his few books, and his appliances for wigwam life, are stowed in his stuffed portmanteau. The scenery around him in its softness contrasts strongly with his own rugged New England. He left behind leafless forests, bleak

---

* David Brainerd's salary was two hundred dollars a year; obliging him to draw on his own funds for support.

fields, and wintry winds. But now he has borne himself "nearer to the sun." His cheek is fanned by gales from the south; the forests are beginning to enrobe themselves in summer beauty; wild flowers are springing up around his path; birds are singing in the branches. Every advance is marked by some novelty. The rising villages of Rahway, Brunswick, and Princeton, if he took these in his route, the splendid scenery of the Raritan, his first vision of the noble Delaware, all these were adapted to impress by some novelty or charm by some beauty the heart of a reflecting and highly-educated young man. Still, amid all these attractions, there would be likely to come over him, like the chill of his own winters, the thought that he was a stranger, in a strange land, on a strange errand. He would reflect that for him no mother, sister, or friend had prepared the well-arranged apartment, had smoothed his pillow, provided his repast, and was waiting with arms of love to welcome him. He had left such far behind him; but before him was no such home. He would be solitary; his labors would be in obscurity, and often unappreciated. He was to dwell among a people of a strange language,—thus, for a time, at least, as to social life, be practically both deaf and dumb. He might pine for society, and for his New-England enjoyments; but he would be chained to his post. He might long for a word of sympathy and cheer in vain. He might be sick, with no science or affection to supply skill, sympathy, tenderness, or support. He might die alone in the wilderness, with no kind friend near to wipe the death-damp from his brow, to treasure his last words of love to kindred or of faith in God. He might sleep in a forest-grave,

"Unwept, unhonored, and unsung,"

in a grave sheltered by no sod, marked by no stone, visited by no human feet, wet by no human tears.

Thoughts like these would not be unnatural in a young man travelling on horseback and alone in the sands, under the sombre shades of the deep pine-forests of New Jersey, to find a home among savage tribes. All that we have sketched, save death itself, had been endured by his martyr-brother;. and may well be supposed to have hung cloudily over his adventurous successor.

But I apprehend that, in his first journey as a missionary to his field (he made David a social visit at Cranberry, May 23, one year before*), John Brainerd had a still deeper source of anxiety. He was untried, and might fail in the work. David had more genius, greater learning, rich experience, eminent holiness, powerful friends, like Edwards and others. His success had been wonderful, almost miraculous, and his renown had

---

* Edwards' Life of Brainerd, p. 301.

already reached two hemispheres. John might well ask: "Am I fitted to take the place of such a man, and sustain a burden which has crushed my brother to the brink of the grave?" We can almost hear him crying out on his way: "Who is sufficient for these things?" A distrust of his own spiritual fitness for his work was, probably, the heaviest weight which pressed on the heart of the untried missionary. His other troubles, however severe, concerned himself and earth only: his moral deficiencies might hinder the glory of Christ in the salvation of souls. The former he had fortitude to dare and endure; the latter he lamented in dust and ashes. This is the proper spirit of a soldier of the Cross.

CHAPTER VIII.

JOHN BRAINERD'S INTRODUCTION TO HIS MISSIONARY FIELD AT CRANBERRY, N. J.

WE are not allowed to describe the emotions of the young missionary as he reaches Cranberry, N. J., and takes up his solitary abode in the rude cabin which had been erected by the labor of his brother David. David had before this built, with his own hands, four houses "to dwell in, by himself, among the Indians,"—one in Kaunaumeek, in the county of Albany, N. Y.; one at the Forks of the Delaware, Pa.; one at Crossweeksung, N. J.; and, finally, one at Cranberry, where John was now to be settled. These forest cabins, in more senses than one, were like the "three tabernacles" which Peter and John desired leave to erect on the Mount of Transfiguration, to be filled with heavenly occupants. Jesus had dwelt in them all. David Brainerd, in his journal of September 27, 1746, says:–

"I was able to ride over to my people two miles every day, and take some care of those who were then at work erecting a small house for me to reside in among the Indians."

His is anticipation was hardly realized. He was

soon summoned to a mansion in heaven, leaving his "small house" in the wilderness to be occupied by his beloved and equally devoted brother.

John Brainerd found a most enthusiastic and joyful welcome from the pious Indian congregation. As a minister of Jesus, and a brother of their beloved sick pastor, he was received with open arms. To him, fresh from college halls, and from the most intelligent society of the long-settled and best-cultivated district in New England, every thing would seem strangely wild in the place and people.

Though the village of Cranberry, near the scene of his labors, had been long settled by whites, yet his Indian neighborhood in the township was almost a wilderness. His brother David, desirous of collecting the scattered Indians into some locality where they would meet fewer temptations than at Crossweeksung, from contact with bad white men, and where they could have good farms, a school, and a church, had encouraged them to enter upon some wild lands which they claimed as their own in Cranberry township. The Indians, confiding in the judgment of their beloved and revered pastor, cordially entered into this plan. Leaving their homes at Crossweeksung, the men cheerfully shouldered their axes, and, led by their pastor, sought out their new field, and began to level the forest-trees, roll and burn the logs, clear the lands, and fence the fields. In the course of a year from that time, John Brainerd arrived among them: they had, with an industry and perseverance wonderful for aborigines, cleared eighty acres, built their own cabins, erected a "small house" for their pastor, and a school-house, which served them for a sanctuary on the Sabbath. This clearing, embracing an area half a mile in length, a quarter of a mile in breadth, scalloped out of the pine forest, was the site of their village of scattered cabins. To give them encouragement in their labors, their emaciated and worn-out missionary had often shared in their toils, swinging the axe with his own hands. In relating the causes and the history of their removal from Crossweeksung to Cranberry, David Brainerd says:—

"*August* 21, 1745.—Spent the forenoon in conversation with Mr. Dickinson (at Elizabethtown), contriving something for the settlement of the Indians together in a body, that they might be in better advantages for instruction. October 29.—Rode and viewed the Indian lands at Cranberry. Still at Crossweeksung."

March 24, 1746, David Brainerd says:—

"Numbered the Indians, to see how many souls God had gathered together here since my coming into these parts, and find them about one hundred and twenty, old and young, and about fifteen absent.

"My people were out this day with the design of clearing some of their land, about fifteen miles from this settlement, in order to their settling there in a compact form, where they might be under the advantages of attending the public worship of God, of having their children taught in a school, and at the same time have a conveniency for planting; their land in the place of our *present* residence being of little or no value for that purpose. The design of their settling thus in a body, and cultivating their lands, of which they have done very little in their pagan state, being of such necessity and importance to their religious interest as well as worldly comfort, I thought it proper to call them together and show them the duty of laboring with faithfulness and industry, and that they must not now be 'slothful in business,' as they had ever been in their pagan state. I endeavored to press the importance of their being laborious, diligent, and vigorous in the prosecution of their business, especially at the present juncture, the season of planting being now near, in order to their being in a capacity of living together, and enjoying the means of grace and instruction. Having given them directions for their work, which they very much wanted, as well as for their behavior in divers respects, I explained, sang, and endeavored to inculcate upon them the cxxviith Psalm, common metre, Dr. Watts' version; and having recommended them and the design of their going forth to God by prayer with them, I dismissed them to their business.

"After the Indians had gone to their work, to clear their lands, I retired by myself and poured out my soul to God, that he would smile on their feeble beginnings, and that he would settle an Indian town which might be a 'mountain of holiness.'

"*March* 31.—Called my people together, as I had done the Monday evening before, and discoursed to them again on the necessity and importance of laboring industriously in order to their living together and enjoying the means of grace, &c. Having engaged in a

solemn prayer to God among them for a blessing upon their attempts, I dismissed them to their work. Numbers of them, both men and women, seemed to offer themselves willingly to this service; and some appeared affectionately concerned that God might go with them, and begin their little town for them; that, by his blessing, it might be a place comfortable for them and theirs, with regard both to procuring the necessaries of life and to attending on the worship of God.

"Towards night I enjoyed some sweet meditations on these words:—'It is good for me to draw near to God.' My soul, I think, had some sweet sense of what is intended in these words.

"*Cranberry*, *May* 26.—Rode home to my people at Cranberry, whither they *now removed*, and where I hope God will settle them as a Christian congregation."

In order to render safe their new possession, he had already by order of the Correspondents paid the debts of the Indians, amounting to *eighty-two pounds five shillings*, to secure their lands, and that there might be no entanglement lying upon them. "It is hoped," he says, "God designs to establish a church for himself among them, and hand down true religion to their posterity."*

I have sketched the history of this migration of the Indians from Crossweeksung to Cranberry,

---

* It is hardly necessary to say that this hope of a good man was thwarted by land-graspers and rum-sellers. Even this movement to Cranberry "raised a terrible clamor." Numbers gave out hard words to terrify or threaten the Indians, pretending a claim on their lands. We shall see in the sequel that the malice and cupidity of ungodly men at last expelled these poor Indians from Cranberry.

fifteen miles, that the reader may the better sympathize with John Brainerd in entering on his missionary field.

We must here bear in mind that not two years have yet elapsed since David Brainerd found all these Indians wild, roaming, reckless, stupid savages. They have now, many of them, been transformed by God's truth and Spirit into humble, docile, and earnest Christian men and women. In the brief period of their Christian life they have had the most intelligent, patient, and faithful instruction. Their progress in Christian knowledge and grace has been wonderful, so that their holy and consistent lives, in the opinion of Mr. McKnight, of Cranberry, and his elders, "put to shame their white brethren in other churches." They have a simple and confiding faith, which is adapted to invite instruction and gladden the heart of their minister. They are prepared to look upon their young pastor with profound reverence as a man of God, and with deep affection as the brother of their spiritual father.

All this is delightful; but there is a shade in the picture. They have just emerged from savage life, without education or books, without any knowledge of science or the arts, without any skill in trade or agriculture, without any civilized ideas of taste or refinement, without any home-comforts of beds, chairs, tables, and separate apartments in their dwellings, without fixed habits of industry, definite aims, or any *beau-idéal* to stimulate their energy and elevate their social and pecuniary position. They are barbarians still.

They doze in their unpaved, unglazed, dark, smoky cabins; or they creep out unwashed, uncombed, and half dressed, to lie on the ground and bask in the sun. They tear their half-cooked meat with their fingers, and masticate it with almost the avidity of beasts of prey. Every hour of the day, in every circle, service, and occupation, by some rudeness, stupidity, or indecency, they violate the taste and shock the sensibilities of their young missionary; and what adds to his chagrin is the fact, that to him their chatter is an unintelligible jargon, and he a barbarian to them. Entirely alone as a missionary, with no wife or Christian family for companionship, we are not to be surprised if the gloom of which David so often complained throws its dark wing over John Brainerd in his Indian cabin. And in his efforts to preach the gospel he had many embarrassments and annoyances. Not only was he ignorant of the Indian language, but of their mental constitution, early associations, modes of thought. He was ignorant of their prejudices and antipathies. As his brother's journal had been but recently published, John Brainerd could have had only slight knowledge of the mode in which his Indians had been taught, or of the nature and extent of their religious attainments; and his church-edifice was but a miserable hut, devoid of all cheerfulness, taste, and convenience. His brother David says:—

"I have often been obliged to preach in their houses in cold and windy weather, when they have been full of smoke and cinders, as well as unspeakably filthy, which has thrown me many times into violent sick headaches."

He says, moreover:—

"While I have been preaching, their children have cried to such a degree, I could scarcely be heard; and their pagan mothers would take no manner of care to quiet them. At the same time, perhaps, some men have been laughing and mocking at divine truths, others playing with their dogs, whittling sticks; and this not from spite and prejudice, but for want of better manners."

Rather a forbidding prospect, this, for the young graduate of Yale, just entering on the ministry! Theological dandies, ambitious of style and good society, would hardly have accepted this "call" to the red men of Cranberry. There is no good library there; there is no appreciation of intellectual taste. The young missionary has no prospect of the smiles of beauty, or invitations to elegant soirées. If he be not sustained by his own good conscience, the joy of benevolence, and the grace and favor of God, the Lord have mercy on him!

He was, doubtless, thus sustained. He remembered the dying commands of his Saviour:—"Go ye into all the world, and preach the gospel to every creature." Brainerd had come to the Cranberry Indians to do the very work intrusted to him by his Divine Master; and if great trials and bereavements were before him, he would bear himself bravely in the thought that "The servant is not above his Lord."

Parting with a dying brother to find a home and field of labor among savages in the forest was but a fitting preparation for, and apprenticeship to, that moral martyrdom which, we shall show, characterized his whole life. "Mirthfulness" may be a very pleasant and profitable subject for eulogy by well-paid and well-fed literary lecturers in classic halls, or in great cities radiant with wealth, beauty, and fashion; but this "mirthfulness" has not been the ordinary characteristic of the ministers of Jesus, who, by lives of obscurity and self-denial, have "filled up the measure of the sufferings of Christ for the world's salvation." "No cross, no crown," has ever been their motto.

But perhaps we have done John Brainerd injustice in supposing that the shade of the wilderness threw any sadness over his spirit. He has left no record of gloom. His wild forest-home and wild companions may have occasioned a pleasant excitement, aided as they were by manly courage and elevated Christian purposes. He doubtless could say:—

"Sure, 'tis a glorious path,
  To tread where martyrs trod;
To disenthral mortality,
  And give a world to God."

CHAPTER IX.

JOHN BRAINERD'S FIRST YEAR AMONG THE INDIANS—THEIR NUMBER—CRANBERRY—BETHEL—THE REVIVAL—LETTER TO REV. MR. PEMBERTON.

WE must now look at young Brainerd as domesticated for life in New Jersey; for he never, except for brief visits, returned to his own New England. As already stated, the number of Indians who from regard to the gospel had rallied around Cranberry, had increased from fifteen or twenty, first found at Crossweeksung, to over one hundred and twenty; seventy-eight of whom had been baptized. The church embraced nearly forty. There were also about fifty on the Rancocas, near Mount Holly, and a few scattered families elsewhere in East Jersey. Besides these, Brainerd was expected to follow up, as he had time and opportunity, the labors of his brother in the Forks of the Delaware and the Valley of the Susquehanna.

The location of this Indian settlement near Cranberry has been ascertained with sufficient definiteness by the researches of the Rev. Mr. Symmes, of Cranberry Church, who, with the writer, carefully explored the region not long since. For particulars, we refer to the letter of Mr. Symmes.* The cut exhibits the old parsonage in which the Brainerds were often entertained over one hundred years ago.

Bethel was the name which they gave to their new erection of cabins. This place Bethel, from which John Brainerd dated his correspondence, is often spoken of by President Edwards as the "Indian town in New Jersey." As Bethel, in Hebrew, signifies the house of God, their piety suggested the name given to the new settlement.

John Brainerd began his labors, April 15, 1747. He says:—†

"It pleased the Lord greatly to smile on my brother's [David] endeavors, and in the most remarkable manner to open the eyes of the poor savages, and to turn them from Satan to God. The Indians had settled themselves on a tract of land near Cranberry, far better [than Crossweeksung] for cultivation and more commodious for such a number as were now gathered together. In this situation I found the Indians when I arrived among them at their new settlement, called Bethel, about the middle of April, 1747. And this summer officiated for my brother, who took a journey to the eastward, thinking it might possibly be a means of recovering his health. But his disease [consumption] had taken such hold of his vitals as not to be diverted or removed by medicine or means. He was, on his return from Boston to New Jersey, detained at Northampton by the increase of his disorder,

---

* See Appendix A.

† See letter in Sprague's Annals, vol. iii. p. 150.

and there made his exit out of a world of sin and sorrow, and, no doubt, entered upon a glorious and blessed immortality, in October, 1747."

He continues:—

"The work of Divine Grace still went on among the Indians, although those extraordinary influences that appeared for a time had begun some months before to abate, and still seemed gradually going off; but the good effects of them were abiding in numbers of instances."

We are to look at this statement more in grief than surprise, that the "extraordinary influences" had begun to abate. According to the journal of David Brainerd, the "extraordinary" revival influence first manifested itself at Crossweeksung, in August, 1745, nearly two years before. That among these poor, insulated, ignorant Indians the work should have been so continued, that in April, 1747, John Brainerd found it only "gradually going off," is evidence of its original purity and power. All revivals of religion marked by great power of the Holy Ghost, and attended, necessarily, with great excitement, have usually been, relatively, of brief continuance. We may regard this as almost a necessity, for it admits of a plain explanation. Where there is great energy of means, and a powerful influence of the Spirit, by which many are deeply moved and hopefully converted, one of two effects will be produced on the impenitent. They will either bow to the influence of the truth and Spirit, and be reckoned among the converts; or they will, by resisting truth, conscience, and the Holy Ghost, attain a moral hardihood which enables them to neutralize all efforts for their renovation. There may be, as there was in the case before us, a lingering of the good influence for a long time. New individuals may be brought under the influence of the revival from without; and time may change the moral attitude of some within, who at first resisted these influences. It is of the very nature of a powerful work of grace soon to exhaust the subjects on which it acts, and to cease as a result of its triumphs. We must not expect to load ourselves with abundant sheaves repetitiously on the field from which we have already gathered the rich harvest: the gleaning is all that is left us. These remarks, of course, must be restricted to localities and communities under the same influences; for outside, in the wide world, there will always be ample scope and subjects for the most powerful, widé-spread, and permanent revivals, until the last great harvest of souls is gathered in.

Are not thoughts like these adapted to give useful hints to some zealous and true-hearted, but not very discreet, pastors, who press revival means, exhortations, and reproofs after the revival power has waned, and thus disgust and alienate those who have placed themselves, for the time being, in resistance to such influences; but who, allowed to unbend, and led by various evangelical teachings to new angles of vision and new subjects of religious reflection, would be kept within the hearing of truth and become hopeful subjects of the next revival? Are not those pastors wise men who, instead of expecting always to reap, improve the time of sowing and watering, and thus in the "waning," from whatever cause, of one revival, "give diligence" to educate their people in sound Christian doctrine, in preparation and certain expectation of another?

While on this subject, which some may regard as excursive from our memoir, we may be allowed to say that there were peculiar reasons for the subsidence of the great work at Crossweeksung and Cranberry, among the Indians. Not only were they few in numbers, weak in understanding, fickle in habits, and strongly tempted by pagans of their own race and corrupt whites in the neighborhood, but the very characteristics of the Great Revival were not of a kind to promise permanence. Although the power of a great revival of religion is of God's sovereignty and rich grace, yet, as this power operates by human instruments and agents, its manifestations will put on a certain type under the impression received from these instruments or agents. As David Brainerd was a laborer and almost a martyr in the Great Awakening of 1740–41, so graphically described by Edwards; as he looked up to Edwards, Whitefield, Gilbert and William

Tennent, Aaron Burr, and Jonathan Dickinson with the most profound reverence; as William Tennent, of Freehold, was his near neighbor; as his Indians, some of them at least, must have had some observation of revival-scenes in the Christian congregations of New Jersey; and, above all, as God in this great and glorious work had been pleased, in this region, to signalize the presence of his Spirit by certain remarkable and uniform effects, we may not wonder that the revival at Crossweeksung among savages and pagans imitates in its characteristics and developments, while it excels in energy and excitement, the revivals in Freehold, N.J., Bethlehem, Conn., and Northampton, Mass.

In all these places there was, for the time being, the same solemn sense of God's awful presence, the same realization of a long eternity, the same regard to the worth of the soul, the same rushing together from widely-separated places as to a great sight, the same tendency to abide day and night under the preaching of the word and in prayer. The preaching was attended by crowds, all dissolved in tears, uttering bitter and distressing cries, horrified by the consciousness of guilt and peril, or beseeching God for clear and joyful evidence of a new heart wrought by the Spirit. In this "awakening," preachers, in the most intense enthusiasm of gospel benevolence, everywhere ran to and fro, yearning for souls; preaching in season and out of season, and giving no stint to their prayers; acting like men who believed that the great day of God's mercy had dawned, and that they were the appointed leaders in the work of salvation. None will wonder that in some cases this heaven-inspired enthusiasm was carried into rank and baneful fanaticism, so that they saw unearthly visions and had miraculous dreams.

While Brainerd carefully protected his people from fanaticism, he nevertheless tolerated that high religious excitement and those natural demonstrations of deep feeling which have usually attended great outpourings of the Spirit of God.*

* "Few Christians appear to have enjoyed such abounding, even overwhelming, manifestations of the Divine Presence and favor as fell to the share of the heavenly-hearted Brainerd. In youth he would pass whole days in the wild solitudes of the forest, in a state of ecstasy, in which he was insensible to the flight of time, to hunger, and every impression of an outward kind; and during the whole course of his ardent, evangelic life there were seasons not unfrequent in which, through the abundance of the revelations, he might have said, with the apostle, that whether they were passed in the body or out of the body was known, not to him, but to God. Yet it is recorded that 'there was no sight of heaven in his imagination, with gates of pearl and golden streets, and a vast multitude with shining garments; no vision of the book of life opened with his name written in it; no sudden suggestions of words or promise of Scripture, as then immediately spoken or sent to him; no new revelations, or strong suggestions of secret facts.' But the way he was satisfied of his own good estate was by feeling within himself the lively actings of a holy temper and heavenly disposition, the vigorous exercise of that Divine Love which 'casts out fear.' Also on the subject of his missionary labors he says: 'I look upon it as one of the glories of this work of grace among the Indians, and a special evidence of its being from a divine influence, that there have been till now no visionary notions, trances, and imaginations intermixed with those rational

The bodily exercises which marked the Great Revival in Western Pennsylvania, Kentucky, Virginia, and Tennessee in the beginning of the present century, so graphically described by the late Rev. Dr. Baxter, of Virginia, the faintings and prostrations attending the great Irish Revival of 1858–59, were transcripts of the popular enthusiasm and impression in the Revival of 1742; so well described, and alternately lauded and condemned, by Jonathan Edwards.

This last revival, into the spirit of which David Brainerd had so deeply drank, was produced in all its main characteristics under his own labors at Crossweeksung and Cranberry.

Thus, under date of August 8, 1745, at Crossweeksung, he says:—

"The power of God seemed to descend upon the Indians especially, '*like a mighty rushing wind*,' and with an astonishing energy bore down all before it. I stood amazed at the influence which seized the audience almost universally, and could compare it to nothing more aptly than the irresistible force of a mighty torrent or swelling deluge, that with its insupportable weight and pressure bears down and sweeps before it whatever comes in its way. Almost all persons of all ages were bowed down with concern together, and scarcely one was able to stand the shock of this surprising operation. Old men

---

convictions of sin and solid consolations which numbers have experienced; *and might I have had my desire, there had been no appearance of any thing of this nature at all.'* "—*A Present Heaven.* Ticknor & Fields, Boston, 1863.

and women who had been drunken wretches for many years, and some little children not more than six or seven years of age, appeared in distress for their souls. The most stubborn hearts were now compelled to bow.

"They were almost universally praying and crying for mercy in every part of the house, and many out of doors, and numbers could neither go nor stand. Their concern was so great, each one for himself, that none seemed to take any notice of those about him, but each prayed freely for himself. I must say I never saw any day like it in all respects.

"*Sabbath afternoon*, *Aug.* 9.—Though I had not spoken a word of terror, a divine influence caused several persons to cry out in anguish of soul.

"*August* 16.—I never saw the work of God so independent of means as at this time. I seemed to do nothing, and, indeed, to have nothing to do but stand still and see the salvation of God; and found myself obliged and delighted to say, 'Not unto us,' as instruments and means, 'but to thy name be glory!'"

The scene was Pentecostal. Indeed, considering the numbers impressed, compared with the whole number present, it transcended in results the glorious day of Pentecost itself.

"A young Indian woman, who had on her way to the meeting laughed and mocked, was so concerned for her soul, that she seemed like one pierced through with a dart, and cried out in the assembly. After public service was over, she lay flat on the ground. She could neither go, nor stand, nor sit in her seat without being held up.

"I hearkened to her prayer. It was: '*Guttummaukalummeh wechaumeh kmeleh nolah!*' that is, '*Have mercy on me, and help me to give you my heart!*'"

Remember that David Brainerd spoke by an interpreter of ordinary capacity and attainments, sincere but illiterate, and you will see there was no opportunity for passionate rhetoric. It is also well known that Brainerd always held a strong rein on his imagination. In modern days he would be regarded as scholastic, biblical, theological; almost prosaic. In preaching, he relied more on the love of Christ than on the terrors of the law and the fear of perdition.

The effects following the preaching of such a man to such a people indicate the presence of a Divine Power, which we regard with awe and reverence.

Under this power savages became civilized, murderers relented, drunkards reformed, adulterers became chaste, scoffers reverential. Among these pagans marriages were solemnized, families organized, altars set up in wigwams, dwellings erected, farms cleared and cultivated, schools patronized, the Sabbath consecrated, and the public worship of God attended. This wonderful scene advises the Church what may be hoped for the whole pagan world, when men like David Brainerd go everywhere to pray and preach, and the Holy Ghost descends to help. A nation will be born in a day.

But, as we have said, such excitements among one hundred and twenty Indians, two-thirds of whom had become hopeful Christians, could not be long continued.

With the waning novelty of gospel truth, the frequent and long absences of the pastor, and the natural tendency of even the converted heart to re-act from great excitements, it is matter of gratitude that two years after the revival began John Brainerd could say, "the work of Divine Grace still went on among the Indians."

Happily we have fallen on a letter, giving a very brief but distinct outline of the Mission in 1747. We extract the letter from the Appendix of Dr. Philip Doddridge's "Life of David Brainerd:"—*

"For the Rev'd Mr. EBENEZER PEMBERTON, of New York.

"Since you are pleased to require me to give an account of the present situation of affairs among those *Indians* which, at this present time, I have the more immediate care of, I shall endeavor to do it in as brief but just a manner as I can. And,

"1st. There are now belonging to the Society of Indians something upward of one hundred and sixty persons, old and young, who, I think, may properly be

---

* Dr. Philip Doddridge, in his "Abridgment of the Life of David Brainerd," published in London, 1748, says, p. 13:—

"The Honorable Society in Scotland for Propagating Christian Knowledge have very lately received letters from their corresponding members at New York, dated in February last, 'giving an account of the much-to-be-lamented death of Mr. David Brainerd, who (as they express it) *was much honored by God in life and death!*' And that his brother, Mr. John Brainerd, succeeds in the honorable employment of missionary at the new Indian town, which they have properly enough named Bethel, where he bids fair to follow the footsteps of his deceased brother, not only in his piety, but in his abilities, activity, and zeal for the kingdom of God; and that he meets with great encouragement and acceptance among the Indians, whose congregation and English school continue to prosper and increase by new-comers from other Indian countries."

The above shows the estimate in which Rev. John Brainerd was held, at that early day, by the able men who employed him.

called inhabitants of the town. 2dly. Among these there are thirty-seven who have been admitted to the Sacraments of Baptism and the Lord's Supper, and who, in a judgment of charity, appear to have experienced a work of saving grace in their hearts. There are also several others who, as I have reason to think, are truly religious, and stand as proper candidates for those gospel ordinances.

"3dly. Out of the number first mentioned there are about thirty persons who came to this place since my arrival here, which was the 15th of April last. About ten of these are adults. I have reason to think all rationally convinced of the truth of the Christian religion, and under some degree of concern; and most of them appear to be much concerned, and their convictions seem to be permanent and genuine.

"The next thing I shall mention is the school, which consists of fifty-three children, who properly belong to it and generally attend upon it; twenty-seven of these read in the Testament, and most of them can say the Assembly's Shorter Catechism throughout by heart. Others read in Psalters, Spelling-books, and Primers, and many of them can say the Catechism half through. These children are many of them under religious impressions, and seem to be earnestly inquiring the way to Zion; and some, even of the new-comers, are much concerned for the salvation of their souls, and all that are grown to any considerable bigness (so far as we can know by observing and inquiring of their parents, and of one concerning another) do live in the constant performance of secret duties.

"As touching their secular affairs, they are much more comfortable than they were. They have upwards of forty acres of English grain in the ground, and near about so much Indian corn; and they do, I think, in general follow their secular business as well as can be expected, considering they have all their days been used to sloth and idleness. Thus, sir, I have given a very brief answer to your demands, but, I think, just account of the present condition of these Indians; and am,

"Rev. sir, yours, &c.,

"JOHN BRAINERD.

"From Bethel, the Indian Town
in New Jersey, June 23, 1747."

CHAPTER X.

JOHN BRAINERD MEETS AFFLICTION IN THE OUTSET—SICKNESS AMONG THE INDIANS—SLANDERS FROM THOSE WITHOUT—SENT FOR TO ATTEND HIS DYING BROTHER DAVID.

JOHN BRAINERD had hardly settled himself at Cranberry before he began to experience great and unanticipated trials. He says:—

"About this time a mortal sickness prevailed among the Indians, and carried off a considerable number, and especially of those who had been religiously wrought upon; which made some infidels say, as in the days of Constantine, that it was because they had forsaken the old Indian ways and become Christians."

Such a pestilence in the forest must have been a painful spectacle to the young pastor. Swarthy, stout-limbed hunters writhing in death on the earth floor of their cabins; Indian mothers suffering, but tearless and firm, bidding farewell to their homeless, penniless, and almost friendless children; young men, maidens, and little children, but slightly educated in gospel truths, were compelled to face the awful mystery of death!

Without a full shelter from the cold, the heat, the wintry storm or summer rain, without a soft resting-place or friendly attendant, without proper diet or medical skill, without materials for pleasant reflection, or hope as an anchor to the soul, the wigwam of a dying savage seems almost an appropriate vestibule to the dark world of woe itself.

Brainerd doubtless mourned the fact, that his Christian people were mainly the victims; but he must have drawn some relief from the hope which cheered them in dying, and the gospel beams which illumined their dark cabins and softened their hard pillows. It would give him a sustaining joy to know that so many of those who had wept with his brother were going to triumph with him in heaven.

But this was not all. He was not only doomed to an early bereavement by the loss of his dear people, but compelled to endure the taunts of the wicked; as if Christianity were a crime to be visited with Divine judgments. When the good suffer affliction, infidels are likely for the time to affect piety and see the hand of God in his providence.

Brainerd does not say so in words; but we gather from his remarks that the afflictions of his people were seized upon by hardened opposers as an occasion to prejudice the yet unconverted Indians still more against Christianity, and "to add affliction to his bonds." No wonder Brainerd says: "This seemed to me a mysterious frown of Divine Providence." We hope he did not forget that,

> "Behind a frowning Providence
> God hides a smiling face."

Of Brainerd's first labors, from April to September, 1747, we have few details. He seems to have prosecuted his work in the very spirit of his brother, with zeal, assiduity, wisdom, and success. In the memoirs of President Edwards and of David Brainerd we have a few hints throwing light on the young missionary's first endeavors.

David Brainerd, after parting with John at Elizabethtown, set out on his final journey to New England, April 21. Travelling slowly on horseback, he reached his friends in Haddam, Conn., about the 1st of May. From thence, by easy journeys up the valley of the Connecticut, he made his way, May 28, to Northampton, the residence of Dr. Edwards. Tarrying there until June 9, he then started for Boston.

He was accompanied in this final journey by Jerusha Edwards, a young lady in her eighteenth year, the second daughter of President Edwards.

The relation of David Brainerd to this young lady constitutes one of the most romantic incidents of his personal history. Though it is not so affirmed directly by her father in his memoir of Brainerd, yet it is believed that the young lady had given her heart and plighted her hand to the martyr missionary. The Rev. Dr. Field, of Stockbridge, says:—

"They had anticipated great happiness in married life in this world, surrounded by pious relatives and friends, and engaged with them in acts of piety and devotion;

but they have enjoyed more in connection with each other in heaven already, and their happiness is only begun."

The two on horseback, every thing to each other, wending their way over hills and valleys for one hundred miles to Boston, would be a fine subject for the poet's pen or the painter's pencil. The tall, attenuated, yet striking form of the missionary, his brilliant eye but blanched cheek, his worn features, on which labor and suffering had put at the age of twenty-nine the stamp of years; his hallowed reveries, his deep spiritual communion, his pensiveness, often interrupted, checked, and humanized by the conscious presence, the blooming cheek and radiant eye, the musical voice and cheerful bearing of the healthful, hopeful, and affectionate being at his side,—what a scene for canvas,—what a theme for poetry! But perhaps poet and painter have shrunk back in despair at their inability to depict earth's highest hopes paling and dying under the brighter gleamings of Heaven's nearing glory. Earth's deepest affections and softest emotions still living and glowing, but absorbed in the richer love of Christ!

We shall allude again to this companion of Brainerd, and only quote here the language of Peabody:—

"She said, when dying, that for years she had not seen the time when she had the least desire to live one moment longer, except for the sake of doing good and filling up the measure of her duty: such a being, though no warmer sentiment mingled with her admiration of his character and her delight in his conversation, was a fit companion of his dying hours." *

Her offer to accompany Brainerd, as his sole companion and nurse, is evidence of her brave and generous love. That no parental prudence detained her, and no breath of scandal ever lighted upon her, is a proof that her moral worth was equal to her great heroism.

The interesting travellers reached Boston in three days. Instead of mending, Brainerd grew rapidly worse. "My friends," he says, "divers times gathered around my bed to see me breathe my last, which they expected every moment, as I myself also did."

Retaining unimpaired his intellectual powers, watching in the fear of God his frame and temper of mind, and stimulated by the most vivid and penetrating apprehensions of an opening eternity, he not only from day to day, as a little returning strength permitted, recorded his own dying experience, but indited and transmitted to his missionary-brother John, in New Jersey, and others, his dying thoughts and counsels.

We regard the following letter as one of the most remarkable ever written. It was addressed to his own absent, well-beloved, and trusted bro-

---

* Sparks' Biography, vol. viii.

ther as a final message, but it hardly alludes to the fraternal relation of the parties. The writer seems like one who has already insulated himself from earthly ties and become like an angel of God. He writes like one so lifted above earth that its cords were sundered and time lost in a broad vision and deep penetration of eternity.

We quote from President Edwards:—

"*David's final letter to John, at Bethel, the Town of Christian Indians in New Jersey.*

"DEAR BROTHER:—

"I am now just on the verge of *eternity*, expecting very speedily to appear in the unseen world. I feel myself no more an inhabitant of earth, and sometimes earnestly long to 'depart and be with Christ.' I bless God he has for some *years* given me an abiding conviction, that it is impossible for any rational creature to enjoy true *happiness* without being entirely 'devoted to him.' Under the influence of this conviction I have, in some measure, acted. Oh that I had done more so! I saw both the excellency and necessity of *holiness* in life; but never in such a manner as now, when I am just brought from the sides of the grave. O my brother, pursue after *holiness*,—press towards this blessed mark; and let your thirsty soul continually say, 'I shall never be satisfied till I awake in thy likeness.' Although there has been a great deal of *selfishness* in my views, of which I am ashamed, and for which my soul is humbled at every view, yet, blessed be God, I find I have really had, for the most part, such a concern *for his glory* and the advancement of *his kingdom* in the world, that it is a satisfaction to me to reflect upon *these years*.

"And now, my dear brother, as I must press you to pursue after *personal* holiness, to be as much in *fasting* and *prayer* as your health will allow, and to live above the rate of *common Christians*, so I must entreat you solemnly to attend to your *public* work: labor to distinguish between *true* and *false* religion, and to that end watch the motions of God's *Spirit* upon your heart. Look to *him* for help, and impartially compare your experiences with his *word.* Value religious *joys* according to the *subject-matter* of them: there are many who rejoice in their supposed justification; but what do these joys argue, but only that they *love themselves?* Whereas, in *true* spiritual joys, the soul rejoices in God for what he is *in himself;* blesses God for his holiness, sovereignty, power, faithfulness, and all his perfections; adores God, that he is what he is, that he is unchangeably possessed of infinite glory and happiness. Now, when men thus rejoice in the *perfections of God*, and in the *infinite excellency of the way of salvation by Christ*, and in the holy *commands* of God, which are a transcript of his holy nature, these *joys* are divine and spiritual. Our joys will stand by us at the hour of *death*, if we can be then satisfied that we have thus acted above *self*, and in a disinterested manner, if I may so express it, rejoiced in the *glory* of the blessed God. I fear you are not sufficiently aware how much *false* religion there is in the world: many serious Christians and valuable ministers are too easily imposed upon by this false blaze. I likewise fear you are not sensible of the dreadful effects and consequences of this false religion. Set yourself, my brother, to crush all appearances of this nature among the Indians, and never encourage any degree of heat without light. Charge my people in the name of their *dying minister*, yea, in the name of *Him who was dead, and is alive*, to live and walk as becomes the gospel. Tell them how great the expectations of God and his people are from them, and how awfully they will wound God's cause if they fall into vice, as well as fatally prejudice other poor Indians. Always insist that their experiences are *rotten*, that their joys are *delusive*, although they may have been rapt up in the *third heavens* in their own conceit by them, unless the main tenor of their lives be spiritual, watchful, and holy. In pressing these things, 'thou shalt both save thyself and those that hear thee.'

"God knows I was heartily willing to have served him *longer* in the work of the ministry, although it had still been attended with all the labors and hardships of past years, if he had seen fit that it should be so; but, as his will now appears otherwise, I am fully content, and can, with the utmost freedom, say, 'The will of the Lord be done.' It affects me to think of leaving you in a world of sin; my heart pities you, that those storms and tempests are yet before you from which, I trust, through grace, I am almost delivered. But 'God lives, and, blessed be my Rock!' he is the same Almighty Friend; and will, I trust, be your Guide and Helper, as he has been mine.

"And now, my dear brother, I commend you to God, and to the word of his grace, 'which is able to build you up, and give you inheritance among all them that are sanctified.' May you enjoy the Divine Presence both in private and public; and may 'the arms of your hands be made strong by the right hand of the mighty God of Jacob.' Which are the passionate desires and prayers of

"Your affectionate, dying brother,

"DAVID BRAINERD."

The emotions stirred by reading in his lone Indian cabin such a letter from a dying brother, we leave the reader to imagine.

But it was the will of God that David Brainerd should not die in Boston. By going there he had accomplished a great work. He had illustrated in his own person the martyr-spirit of Christianity and the beauty of holiness. He had originated a deep and practical sympathy for missions, which has survived to the present hour. He had by his counsel influenced the selection of two young men, Job Strong, of Northampton (Brainerd's cousin), and Elihu Spencer, of Haddam, to go as missionaries to the Six Nations of Indians. He had a work to do of laboring and suffering in Boston: "he finished the work" there given him to do.

When his brother Israel, from Yale College, reached Boston, David had revived. The young brother brought to him "the sorrowful tidings of his sister Spencer's* death in Haddam."

She was a dear sister. Her house in Haddam, save his Indian cabin, had been his only earthly home. But he was comforted by confidence in her true piety, which inspired a hope of soon meeting her in heaven. She had crossed the cold river:

---

* The Rev. Dr. Hall, in his History of the Presbyterian Church, Trenton, N. J., supposes the sister Spencer above referred to was the wife of General Joseph Spencer, of the Revolution. This is a mistake. Two of Brainerd's sisters, Jerusha and Martha, married Spencers. Jerusha married Samuel Spencer, of East Haddam; Martha was the wife of the general.

See Dr. Field. Brainerd Genealogy, p. 252.

his own feet began to touch the stream. He could say:—

"My gentle sister crossed the flood,
And I am crossing now

July 20, David Brainerd had so far recovered that he started for Northampton. The company now consisted of Jerusha Edwards, David Brainerd, and his young brother Israel. Averaging sixteen miles a day, the little, stricken, but religiously peaceful group reached Northampton in a few days. The ages of the party were respectively twenty-nine, twenty-three, and eighteen: all highly educated and devoutly pious, but all destined to die in less than one year.

They arrived at Northampton, July 25. Brainerd had been stimulated by his journey; but now "he gradually decayed, becoming weaker." September 2, "for the last time he went out of our gate alive," in a final visit to the house of God.

His brother John, advised of his increased sickness, had left Cranberry to meet David at Northampton. To the dying missionary this was an unexpected pleasure. He had not suggested it, though he desired it. President Edwards says:—

"He was much refreshed by this visit, for his brother was peculiarly dear to him; and he seemed to rejoice in a devout and solemn manner to see him, and to hear the comfortable tidings he brought concerning the state of his dear congregation of Christian Indians. John also brought some of his private writings, particularly his diary, which he had kept for several years past."

This *diary*, so considerately brought to him, gave him intense satisfaction. He lived his life over, and comforted the weakness of his dying hours by the recollection of honest and earnest labor in the past.

John remained one week, and then, being compelled to return to New Jersey on urgent business, intrusted the invalid to the care of his younger brother Israel, who reached Northampton on the 17th of September.

That John could leave a brother in this state at the call of duty is evidence of great conscientiousness; that he hastened his return from the long journey proves his deep fraternal love. No human passion was allowed to control conscience, and no pretence of religious obligation was urged as an apology for the absence of natural affection. In these brothers the conscience and the fine sentiments of humanity seemed to have a most beautiful and symmetrical blending.

In the temporary absence of his brother, David employed his fleeting hours in carrying out, by painfully-written epistles, his missionary plans. He counselled his young brother; he wrote to the Rev. Mr. Bryan, of New Jersey, a letter for the benefit of his church; he gave repeated exhortations to friends around his bedside, and especially to the younger children of his distinguished friend, President Edwards.

But he especially occupied himself in correcting

his *diary*.* He seems to have been conscious of the power and eloquence of his sublime religious experience, and expecting to live, as he has lived, in the Church's memory.

On the 27th of September, he said:—

"I am almost in eternity. I long to be there; my work is done! I am willing to part with all. I am willing to part with my dear brother John, and never see him again, to go and be forever with the Lord."

---

* We have before us one hundred and twenty pages of this *diary in the author's own* hand. He wrote in small duodecimo books, about four by six inches in size, comprehending from forty to one hundred pages each. Each little manuscript volume was neatly bound in strong paper or parchment. We have two of these volumes entire. The first contains only his religious experience, a great part of which was copied verbatim by Edwards. It is bound with parchment. On the first page is only written, "*David Brainerd's Book.*" The other volume is his journal at Kaunaumeek (or, as he spells it, "Cannaumuck"), from May to November, 1743. It includes the entire history of his conflict with Yale College, his confession in full, and his remarks on his treatment. Of this journal, Edwards published not more than a fourth part: we may yet give it entire, just as Brainerd wrote it. It is justly severe on the college authorities: they broke his heart.

This "Cannaumuck" diary is marked "V. VOL.," showing how early and carefully he recorded his daily life.

In the diary of his experience, on the margin of page 30, he says: "*I can correct no farther.*—D. B." David Brainerd's initials are inserted at the close of his corrections. It was probably the last he wrote, as on the next page we read: "*The author's own corrections by another hand,*"—that is, by the hand of his brother Israel. It may interest some to know that the lines in Brainerd's Diary were about the sixth of an inch apart; the chirography neat, clear, and tasteful, and scarce an interline or blot in two hundred pages. As he wrote while journeying in the forest, and in smoky Indian wigwams, this is an evidence of exceeding care in such minor matters. I know some of my friends will think the *present writer* might profit by such an example.

There seems to have been a mysterious, almost unearthly, bond linking the hearts of these brothers. They loved as brothers by blood, and as angels love who discern in each other "the beauty of holiness."

John was still absent,—detained against his will in New Jersey. David had expressed a desire, if it might be the will of God, to live till his brother returned. John's delay and absence threw a shade over the heaven-lit raptures of the dying saint. But he submitted to the will of God.

Probably his longing for John's presence was not wholly from his natural affection, but from his great interest in the Indian mission.

> "When he spoke of his own congregation of Christian Indians in New Jersey, it was with peculiar tenderness, so that his speech would be *presently interrupted and drowned in tears.*"

His beloved brother, his affianced bride, his earthly friends, were precious; but dearer than all was his Master's work. His glazing eyes moistened only as flitted before his mental vision the Indian converts, for whose salvation he had sacrificed his life. October 2, he says:—

> "I felt sweetly disposed to commit all to God,—even my dearest friends, my dearest flock, my absent brother, and all my concerns for time and eternity. Oh that his kingdom might come in this world; that all might love and glorify him for what he is in himself! O come, Lord Jesus! come quickly! Amen!"

These are the last words, dictated to Israel, in David's diary. Was any diary or any life ever better ended since the Great Martyr cried, "It is finished"?

But the scene does not close here. On the Sabbath, October 4, he looked on Jerusha Edwards pleasantly, and said:—

> "Dear Jerusha, are you willing to part with me? I am quite willing to part with you. I am willing to part with all my friends. I am willing to part *with my dear brother John*, although I love him the best of any creature living. Though if I thought I should not see you and be happy with you in another world, I could not even part with you. But we shall spend a happy eternity together."

At first sight, this seems to be a strange declaration. That a young man of twenty-nine years of age should aver to an affectionate, faithful, comely maiden of eighteen, to whom he had pledged his hand and heart, and who with martyr-love had clung to his weakness day and night for weeks and months; who had almost overstepped the proprieties of her sex to soothe his dying pillow, who now stood in anguish and tears at his bedside to catch and embalm his words of tenderness as life-treasures; that Brainerd should say to such an one that he "preferred his brother John to all creatures living," seems at first blush to be unnatural, almost unkind, and inconsistent with his character. Some have inferred that the love of the parties was unmingled with sentiments more tender than general admiration and Christian regard.

We do not draw this inference; nor do we infer any want of tenderness in the dying martyr. In his holy affections he had so sublimated every sympathy of his nature, that he judged and estimated those around him as a spirit of another sphere alighting on the earth might have done. His brother John he had known from childhood. He had prayed deliberately and specially for him, with fasting, in his wigwam, at Kaunaumeek.* He had imparted to him the most deliberate and searching counsels. That brother was dear to him as a kinsman; but doubly dear when, sanctified by grace, he had undertaken to carry out the life-aims of David, and was then actually folding the dying martyr's little flock in the wilderness. This seems the key to explain the mysterious declaration.

Jerusha Edwards was his own peculiar treasure, which he could surrender for a time to reclaim and enjoy in heaven. His brother John was not only his treasure, but the ambassador of God, appointed to a holy labor, on which David would gaze with interest from the skies. In this view, Jerusha did not infer that she possessed less love than her

---

* In David Brainerd's manuscript journal, under date of May 6, 1743, he says: "I was somewhat drawn out in prayer for a certain friend, *meo fratri juniori*, that God would make him a blessing in his day." He says the same elsewhere.

heart claimed, but that her dying friend subordinated even his deepest earthly affection to one more elevated and holy. Her own father, by recording this declaration with apparent approval, seems to have understood it in this sense. In returning from this episode, may we not ask if the man whom David Brainerd "loved better than any other creature on earth" is not worthy of this biography, that he might to the end of time be loved by the whole Church of God?

We have alluded to the submissive, but strong desire of David to see John once more. He was gratified. True to his promise and fraternal impulses, John, after many hindrances in New Jersey and a long journey, nevertheless reached Northampton, October 7, before David died.

John had been detained by a "mortal sickness among the Indians." Duty first. His heart yearned to be with his sick brother; but he subjects his feelings to his conscience, and the comfort and solace of one man, even his own brother, to the pastoral duty of sustaining and comforting the hearts of such of his Indian flock as were dying under the dark wing of a fatal pestilence. He was worthy to be David's brother and successor.

So David regarded the matter. He was affected and refreshed by seeing him, and fully satisfied with the reasons of his delay, *when the interests of religion and the souls of his people required it.* Pastors! missionaries! In looking at these brothers, may we not "put our shoes from off our feet. The ground on which we tread is holy."

With David, life was fast ebbing. In the latter part of the night preceding the morning of his death, he besought prayers for support under his agonies. He said "it was impossible to conceive the distress which he felt in his breast." In these circumstances, "when it was very late at night, he had much profitable discourse with his brother John concerning his congregation in New Jersey, and the *interests of religion among the Indians.*"

This scene occurs in one of the most beautiful villages on the banks of the Connecticut, and in the dwelling of one of the greatest metaphysicians and divines of that or any other age. The whole family is gathered. The grave father and mother are there. The heart-stricken Jerusha, almost afraid to give vent to her sorrow, stands at his pillow. The little children of the household, to whom Brainerd was dear, are struggling between the weight of drowsiness and the wakeful awe of approaching death. A neighboring minister has kindly come in to relieve the hour of agony.

David feels the ice-chill of death stealing over him, and knows that he has but an hour or two to live. How does he employ this hour? In selfish complaints? He utters none. In pathetic and repetitious leave-takings? He had done this already. In messages of love to friends? They needed no assurances of his affection. In dread apprehensions of an opening eternity? He felt no fear. Amid his wasting and dying agonies, his mind is with his poor Indians in New Jersey. Here was a love literally "stronger than death."

These brothers, holding such discourse at such an hour, in such circumstances, and in such a circle, would be central figures to stand out sublimely and honorably on any painting, even though an angel's hand held the pencil. It was no doubt limned on memories in earth and in heaven, in colors which eternity will never efface.

At six o'clock, Tuesday morning, October 9, 1747, the curtain fell. David Brainerd entered into that holy temple in whose vestibule he had so submissively waited. His body rests in the old graveyard at Northampton, marked by a plain monumental slab. A well-worn pathway to his grave shows it to be the shrine of many a pious pilgrimage. Some years since, during a session of the General Association of Massachusetts, a long procession was formed, and went up to his monument. Rev. Justin Edwards, D.D., delivered an appropriate address.

Jerusha Edwards survived Brainerd but six months. "They were lovely" and loving "in their lives, and in death not divided."*

It is grateful to think that David Brainerd sleeps, awaiting the last trumpet, in a most beautiful neighborhood, on the banks of the noble river by which

---

* Brainerd Genealogy, p. 283.

he was born, and in the bosom of the old Commonwealth of Massachusetts, where the missionary heart beats warmest, and where, by a diffused religious intelligence and sympathy, all are prepared to appreciate the early missionary martyr. Massachusetts is willing and worthy to cherish Brainerd's ashes, and Brainerd was worthy to die and be buried in the State where the great American Board of Foreign Missions was to have its origin and expansion.

CHAPTER XI.

JOHN BRAINERD'S LABORS AFTER THE DEATH OF DAVID—HIS APPOINTMENT—HIS ORDINATION—HIS REPORT TO THE SCOTCH SOCIETY—HIS COMPANIONS IN THE WINTER OF 1747-48—REV. ELIHU SPENCER, D.D.—FIRST CONCERT OF PRAYER.

HITHERTO John Brainerd has been but a satellite in the orbit of his more eminent brother. Now we must regard him as the principal in the missionary work. His trial in the loss of his brother was severe. He reciprocated David's intense affection, and cherished profound reverence for his character and admiration of his talents. John had lost his companion, mentor, and model, and turned with a heavy heart from Northampton to seek his forest home. He had until now regarded himself only as a substitute or *locum tenens* for David. He was employed as such by the "American Correspondents," having had no regular appointment from the Society in Scotland, which had employed and paid his brother. Nor had he been ordained. He seems at once to have returned from Northampton to his work at Cranberry; but we have no details of his labors from October, 1747, to February, 1748.

He says:—

"In February, 1748, I was ordained, and soon after

had the Society's commission sent me from Scotland, and continued in their service several years."

By the kindness of my friend, the late Hugh Elliott, Esq., of this city, of the old firm of Grigg & Elliott, I have been able to obtain from Edinburgh the manuscript records of the "*Society for Propagating Christian Knowledge.*" They make the following minute of the appointment of Rev. John Brainerd in place of his brother. These manuscript records have never before been published:—

Extract from Minutes of date Edinburgh, November 5, 1747.

"Received a letter from Mr. Pemberton, Preses of the Correspondents at New York, dated the 21st day of July thereafter, bearing testimony that the converted Indians evidence the sincerity of their change by a conversation becoming the gospel, and their numbers are lately increased by considerable additions from several places, who all live together in a regular society. That an English schoolmaster is maintained amongst them by private contributions in these parts, and many of their children make great progress in reading and learning the Catechism. That Mr. Brainerd has been confined by sickness for a long time, and is yet in a low and dangerous state of health, occasioned by his excessive fatigues and travels in the prosecution of his mission; but, lest the Indian service should suffer, he has procured his brother, Mr. John Brainerd (a pious and ingenious youth, a candidate for the ministry), to reside among the Indians, who meets with great acceptance among them. Mr. David Brainerd sends word that he has materials for a large journal, but the state of his health prevented his being able to methodize and transcribe it. Mr. Pemberton transmits hither a letter, dated 23d of June last, from the said Mr. John Brainerd, containing an account of the situation of affairs among the Indians. That in the Indian town in New Jersey, called Bethel, there are one hundred and sixty persons, old and young, inhabitants thereof; among these are thirty-seven who have been admitted to the Sacraments of Baptism and the Lord's Supper, and appear to have experienced a work of saving grace in their hearts; and several others are wisely religious and proper candidates for these gospel ordinances. That in the school are fifty-three children, who learn and read the Testament and repeat the Shorter Catechism."

Extract from Minutes of date Edinburgh, 2d June, 1748.

"The Committee reported that there are lately come to hand letters from the Correspondents in New York. That the Rev. David Brainerd, the other missionary minister among the Indians, died in the month of October last, very much regretted, and that a printed copy of the funeral sermon preached on that occasion by the Rev. Mr. Edwards is also transmitted hither. That the said Correspondents had ordained Mr. John Brainerd, brother to the said Mr. David, to the office of the holy ministry among the Indians; and they transmit hither a letter from him, containing a brief account of his diligence and success in his mission since the death of his said brother. The Correspondents further mention that the school under his inspection flourishes exceedingly, though it has no settled fund for its support other than the contributions of some charitable persons and sometimes a public collection at the church-doors in and about New York; and the Committee is of opinion that this General Meeting do order a commission to the said Mr. John Brainerd, to supply as missionary minister in room of his deceased brother, and do report that a certain gentleman in England had taken the trouble to make an abridgment of the large journals of the said Mr. David Brainerd, now deceased, which abridgment is now publishing at London, with a *preface* by the Rev. Doctor Philip Doddridge. The Committee had directed Mr. Anderson to purchase one hundred copies thereof, to be sent hither for the use of the members of this Society, and authorized him to purchase as many more copies as shall be found proper to be distributed among the correspondent members and other charitably disposed persons at London; and it appearing by the transcript of a letter from Mr. Pemberton, at New York, that a charter is granted for the erection of a college or seminary for learning in that province [College of New Jersey], where some encouragement is now wanting for purchasing books, the Committee have recommended to members and other well-disposed persons to contribute for this purpose, and have ordered that a copy of the Society's letter, dated 23d February, 1747, bearing their agreement to have one young man educated at the Society's expense, and to be sent to Mr. Pemberton, with a letter acquainting him that this Society will heartily concur to encourage this new-erected seminary of learning for educating of youth, and desiring to know what books they have already got, and what kind are mostly wanted. The General Meeting having heard the said report, and considered the several particulars above set forth, approved of their Committee's opinion thereupon, and resolved accordingly that Mr. John Brainerd have *commission to be one of the Society's missionary-ministers in place of the aforesaid Mr. David Brainerd*, *deceased*, and that all encouragement competent be granted by this Society to the aforesaid College and Seminary of Learning in New Jersey."

It will be remembered that David Brainerd had made arrangements in Boston for the support of two missionaries among the Six Nations* of Indians in Western New York. He had selected two young men for the work,—Rev. Elihu Spencer, of Haddam, and Rev. Job Strong, of Northampton. Of these young men, President Edwards says:—

* These Six Nations were called Iroquois, embracing the Mohawks, the Oneidas, the Onondagas, the Cayugas, the Senecas, and the Tuscaroras. The Mohawks were northeasterly on the Mohawk River, below the present *Little Falls*, number 420. The Oneidas came next, extending over the region of Utica and Rome, number 600. Next to the Oneidas, and forty miles distant westerly, were the Onondagas, numbering 800. The Cayugas, amounting to one thousand and forty, were forty miles southwest of the Onondagas. The Senecas, forty miles northwest of the Cayugas, were in number 4000. The Tuscaroras numbered 1000.—(Documentary History of New York, vol. iv. p. 1093.) This was in the year 1771. In 1796 the numbers had fallen: the Mohawks to 300; the Oneidas, 628; Cayugas, 500; Onondagas, 450; Senecas, 1780; Tuscaroras, 400. At present only a few hundreds of the Senecas and Tuscaroras remain in New York, preserved by missionary care.

The Mohawks and Cayugas, having taken part with the British, mostly migrated to Canada, where a few fragments remain. Some of the others have remnants in the far West, under government protection. But it is sad to think that the great Iroquois race, the noblest of Indian blood in the land, inhabiting the beautiful and fertile district of Western New York, with its charming lakes and streams, have perished from the earth. They protected the early English from French aggression, and aided to give this land to Protestant Christianity, but could not protect themselves from the destiny of the red man. Had the early missionaries been seconded properly, the case might have been different.

"They were, undoubtedly, well-qualified persons, of good abilities and learning, and pious dispositions. The Commissioners did not think proper *to send them immediately to the Six Nations;* but ordered them to 'go and live during the winter [1747–48] with Mr. John Brainerd, in New Jersey, among the Christian Indians; there to follow their studies, and get acquainted with the manners and customs of the Indians.' "*

This arrangement was carried out, greatly, we have no doubt, to the satisfaction of all parties. It must have cheered the heart of John Brainerd to welcome to his log cabin, in Bethel, two young men of his own age, early friends, of classic education and of congenial spirit and aims. We can readily imagine them by their evening fire, keeping "bachelor's hall," holding frequent counsel as to the missionary work, praying together, laboring together among the Indians, settling many a knotty point in theology and science, calling up many a reminiscence of college-life and their New-England homes, and relieving the burdens of serious toil by noting the amusing peculiarities of their Indian neighbors and by many a feat of gymnastic exercise. This was natural in young men thus separated from the world; and we have no doubt they spent many a happy hour in their smoky cabin.

But their letters to distant friends say nothing of all this. With them duty, not pleasure, was life. We have one of these letters, which throws

---

* Life of President Edwards, p. 29.

light on the spiritual condition of the Indian congregation and the employment of their teachers.

This letter is as follows:—

"BETHEL, NEW JERSEY, Jan. 14, 1748.

"HONORED AND DEAR PARENTS:—

"After a long and uncomfortable journey, by reason of bad weather, I arrived at Mr. Brainerd's the sixth instant, where I design to stay this winter; and as yet, upon many accounts, am well satisfied with my coming hither. The state and circumstances of the Indians, spiritual and temporal, much exceed what I expected. Notwithstanding my expectations were very much raised from Mr. David Brainerd's journal, and from particular information from him, yet I must confess that, in many respects, they are not equal to that which now appears to me to be true concerning the glorious work of Divine Grace among the Indians.

"Religious conversation seems to be very pleasing and delightful to many, and especially that which relates to the action of the heart. And many here do not seem to be real Christians only, but growing Christians also,—as well in doctrinal as in experimental knowledge. Beside my conversation with particular persons, I have had opportunity to attend upon one of Mr. Brainerd's catechetical lectures, where I was surprised at their readiness in answering questions to which they had not been used; although Mr. Brainerd complained much of their uncommon deficiency. It is surprising to see this people who, not long since, were led captive by Satan at his will, and living in the practice of all manner of abominations, without the least sense even of moral honesty, yet now living soberly and regularly, and not seeking every man his own, but every man, in some sense, his neighbor's good; and to see those who, but a little while past, knew nothing of the true God, now worshipping him in a solemn and devout manner, not only in public, but in their families and in secret,—which is manifestly the case, it being a difficult thing to walk into the woods in the morning without disturbing persons with secret devotions. It seems wonderful that this should be the case not only with adult persons, but with children also. It is observable here, that many children (if not the children in general) retire into secret places to pray. And, as far as at present I can judge, this is not the effect of custom and fashion, but of real seriousness and thoughtfulness about their souls.

"I have frequently gone into the school, and have spent considerable time there amongst the children, and have been surprised to see not only their diligent attention upon the business of the school, but also the proficiency they have made in it, in reading and writing, and in their catechisms of divers sorts. It seems to be as pleasing and as natural to these children to have books in their hands as it does for many others to be at play. I have gone into a house where there has been a number of children accidentally gathered together, and observed that every one had his book in his hand and was diligently studying it. About thirty of these children can answer all the questions in the Assembly's Catechism, and the greater part of them with the proofs to the fourth commandment. I wish there were many such schools: I confess that I never was acquainted with such an one, in many respects. Oh that what God has done here may prove to be the beginning of a far more glorious and extensive work of grace among the heathen!

"I am your obedient and dutiful son,

"JOB STRONG."

The gravity and spiritual discrimination of this letter mark the writer as one of kindred spirit to the Brainerds.

President Edwards had warmly commended Brainerd and his two friends to Governor Belcher, of New Jersey. Governor Belcher says in response, in a letter dated at Burlington (then the capital), February 5, 1748:—*

"You will be sure, sir, of me as a friend and father to the missionaries this way, and all my might and encouragement for the spreading the everlasting gospel of God our Saviour in all parts and places where God shall honor me with any power and influence.

"As to myself, sir, it is impossible to express the warm sentiments of my heart for the mercies without number with which I have been loaded by the God who has fed me all my life long to this day."

These would be noble sentiments from the lips of any man. From the chief magistrate of the commonwealth they are the more beautiful as they are eminently rare. The friendship and patronage of such a man would be most valuable to young Brainerd, and fully appreciated.†

---

* Edwards' Life, p. 266.

† No life of John Brainerd would be perfect that did not pay a tribute to the memory of Governor Belcher.

He was a native of New England, and inherited an ample fortune, by which he received the advantages of the best education and of foreign travel. For a time he was the Royal Governor of Massachusetts. When appointed Governor of New Jersey, in 1747, he was advanced in years and infirm in health.

It had been the purpose of the "Correspondents" that, after spending the winter at Bethel, Messrs. Strong and Spencer should make an excursion with Brainerd to the Indians on the Susquehanna River; but, as the Susquehanna tribes were subject to the Six Nations, they dared not receive the missionaries without the consent of these nations. Governor Belcher (we shall often mention the good man's name) wrote President Edwards that in this visit to the Susquehanna the young men "should have all his assistance and encouragement, by letters to the king's governors [in Pennsylvania and New York] and his letters to the Sachem of those tribes."

The journey, for the cause mentioned, failed. Messrs. Strong and Spencer in the spring, instead of going to the Susquehanna, returned to New England, and spent the summer in Northampton in study with President Edwards. Mr. Strong's health soon after so failed, that he renounced the missionary work and settled in the ministry at Portsmouth, N. H., June, 1749. President Edwards preached his ordination sermon.

Not distinguished for great intellect, and perhaps rather self-complacent and fond of show, pomp, and ceremony even for that age, he still had a large, genial, pious heart, which made him a friend of good men and of every good work. He was a firm champion of gospel truth in the most orthodox forms, and the hater of all error and iniquity. He enlarged and confirmed the charter of Princeton College, and until his death was a fast friend of the institution. President Burr pronounced an earnest, elaborate, and beautiful eulogy at his death, to which we refer the reader.

Mr. Elihu Spencer, Brainerd's other companion, was ordained by a Council in Boston, September, 1748, and sent to establish a mission among the Six Nations, "at a place called by the Indians Onohanquanga, about one hundred and eighty miles west of Albany," in the Oneida tribe. His mission was a failure, but by no fault of his own. His interpreter was the wife of a fanatic Englishman who opposed Spencer's views, and the woman herself was too indolent and obstinate to aid him in conversing with the Indians. After six months Spencer came away, in the spring of 1749, discouraged; and an enterprise which had commanded the dying regards of David Brainerd, and the charity of the purest and best men of the age, was relinquished. It is a specimen of the difficulties met in the early Indian missions.

Rev. Elihu Spencer, probably attracted by the vicinity of Brainerd and his own acquaintances in New Jersey, came to Elizabethtown, and was settled there as the successor of the Rev. Jonathan Dickinson, February 7, 1750, in his twenty-ninth year.*

* As the Rev. Elihu Spencer was intimately associated with John Brainerd during his life, and his intimate friend, a brief sketch of him seems appropriate in the outset. He was the son of Isaac Spencer, of Haddam, and second cousin to David and John Brainerd. As natives of the same town, they were playmates in childhood. He graduated at Yale College in 1746, a classmate of John Brainerd. He was pastor at Elizabethtown six years. He held the office of Trustee of Princeton College from 1752 to his death, in 1784. In 1756 he removed from Elizabethtown to Jamaica, L. I., and occupied

John Brainerd's general fidelity and success in his first labors are vouched by President Edwards. Writing in 1749, he speaks of John's succeeding his brother "in a like spirit, and under whose prudent and faithful care the congregation had flourished and been happy, and probably could not have been so well provided for otherwise." This is good testimony, and from a competent source.

July 26, 1746, twelve clergymen of Scotland in a memorial proposed a United Concert of Prayer to the Churches of America. They addressed their letter to President Edwards, who eagerly caught

---

a church there two years. He was a chaplain in the army during the French War. He then came back to New Jersey, and labored some time in the congregations of Shrewsbury, Middletown Point, Shark River, and Amboy. In 1764 the Synod of New York and Philadelphia sent him, with the Rev. Alexander McWhorter, on a mission to North Carolina. Soon after his return he settled at St. George's, Delaware, as successor to the Rev. Dr. Rodgers, transferred to New York. He remained five years, and then accepted a call to Trenton. In the Revolutionary struggle he took an active part. Congress sent him to conciliate the wavering in North Carolina; and he performed his extraordinary mission. The Tories hated him, and once burnt a part of his library. The University of Pennsylvania conferred on him the title of D.D. in 1782. He seems to have deserved it. He peaceably ended life at Trenton, December 27, 1784, in the sixty-fourth year of his age. His epitaph in the grounds of the First Presbyterian Church says: "He possessed fine genius, great vivacity, and eminent, active piety." If not greatly studious and scholarly, he was, doubtless, a man of great energy and executive power. Among his grandchildren were reckoned the wife of the late Rev. Dr. Samuel Miller, of Princeton, N. J., and the late John and Thomas Sergeant, of Philadelphia. Our readers will see that the young men who sat by the log-cabin fire in Cranberry, in the winter of 1747–48, "have left deep footprints on the sands of time." We shall often meet Elihu Spencer in this memoir, and our readers will now know him.

the idea, and published an Appeal with this long title, viz.:—

"An Humble Attempt to promote Explicit Agreement and Visible Union among God's People in Extraordinary Prayer for the Revival of Religion and the Advancement of Christ's Kingdom on Earth, pursuant to Scripture Promises and Prophecies concerning the Last Time."

The work was as elaborate as the title; and it doubtless laid the foundation for that *Monthly Concert of Prayer* which is now observed over the earth. Edwards proposed a Quarterly Concert, and he urged it with great success not only among the New England churches, but the Indian missions. The Brainerds entered heartily into its spirit.

David expressed "his wonder that there was no more forwardness in promoting *united extraordinary prayer* according to the Scotch proposal," and sent his dying advice to his own congregation that "they should practise that proposal."*

How well they took this advice, and how heartily John Brainerd entered into the matter, we learn from President Edwards' letter to Rev. Mr. McCulloch, of Scotland under date of May 23, 1779. He says:—

"I sent another copy into New Jersey, to Mr. John Brainerd, missionary to the Indians there, with a desire that he would communicate it to others, as he thought would be most serviceable.

---

* Brainerd's Life, p. 400.

"He writes in answer, March 4, 1748, as follows:—'I received yours of January 12 on Sabbath morning, February 5; and desire to acknowledge your kindness with much thankfulness and gratitude. It was a great resuscitant as well as encouragement to me, and, I trust, has been so to many others in these parts, who are concerned for the prosperity of Zion. The next Thursday after (as perhaps, sir, you may remember) was the quarterly day appointed for extraordinary prayer; upon which I called my people together, and gave information of the most notable things contained in your letter. And since I have endeavored to communicate the same to several of my neighboring ministers and sundry private Christians, as I had opportunity. I have also thought it my duty to send an extract, or rather a copy of it, to Governor Belcher. I have likewise (for want of time to transcribe) sent the original to Philadelphia by a careful hand, that the Rev. Mr. Gilbert Tennent might have the perusal of it; where a copy was taken, and the original safely returned to me again. I cannot but hope that this letter, as it contains many things wherein the power and goodness of God do appear in a most conspicuous manner, will be greatly serviceable in stirring up the people of God in these parts, and encouraging their hearts to seek his face and favor, and to cry mightily to him for the further outpouring of a gracious Spirit upon his Church in the world. For my part, I think the remarkable things which your letter contains might be sufficient to put new life into any one who is not past feeling, and as a means to excite a spirit of prayer and praise in all those who are not buried in ignorance or under the power of a lethargic stupor. And it is looked upon by those whom I have had an opportunity to converse with, whether ministers or private Christians, that what God has done is matter of great thankfulness and praise, and might well encourage his people to lift up the hand of prayer, and be instant therein.' "

The little Indian church of Cranberry gathered to pray, "Thy kingdom come," presents a novel spectacle.

Writing under the same date to Mr. Robe, of Scotland, President Edwards says:—

"We have had accounts from time to time of religion being in a flourishing state in the Indian congregation of New Jersey, under the care of Mr. John Brainerd; of the congregation's increasing by the access of Indians from distant parts; of a work of awakening carried on among the unconverted, and additions made to the number of the hopefully converted; and the Christian behavior of professors there. Mr. Brainerd was at my house a little while ago, and represented this to be the present state of things in that congregation."

CHAPTER XII.

JOHN BRAINERD'S INDIANS DISTURBED AT BETHEL—CHARACTER OF CHIEF-JUSTICE R. H. MORRIS—HIS TRAGIC DEATH—THE INDIANS LOSE THEIR LANDS.

JOHN BRAINERD has now been nearly two years at his work, and with eminent success. David, his brother, was a hard man to equal; but it seems that John approximated his predecessor in fidelity and usefulness.

But dark clouds began to lower over the pathway of the young missionary. We have seen with what sacrifices and with what hopes the poor Indians had been removed from Crossweeksung to Cranberry. David had paid their debts. They supposed the land was their own. They had made their clearings, built their cabins, erected their church and school-house, and their pastor had, with his own hands, aided in finishing the rude parsonage. They had called the place Bethel. It had been sanctified by Christian labor, prayers, and tears. In the desert of Indian paganism and barbarity it was *the first oasis.* Can we believe that any could be found vile enough to break up this Christian community, to wring the heart of this young pastor, and to crush the hopes of Christians abroad by exiling these Indians from their homes?

There were men wicked enough to plan all this, and powerful enough to accomplish it. We get the first intimation of the coming storm in a letter of President Edwards to Mr. Erskine, of Scotland, dated June 20, 1749. He says:—

"As to the mission in New Jersey, we have from time to time had comfortable accounts of it; and Mr. John Brainerd, who has the care of the congregation of Christian Indians there, was about three weeks ago at my house, and informed me of the increase of his congregation, and of their being added to from time to time by the coming of Indians from distant places and settling in the Indian town at Cranberry, for the sake of hearing the gospel; and of something of a work of awakening being all along carried on among the Indians to this day, and of some of the new-comers being awakened, and of there being instances from time to time of hopeful conversions among them, and of a general good and pious behavior of the professing Indians. But he gave an account also of some trouble the Indians meet with from some of the white people, and particularly from Mr. Morris, the chief justice of the province, a professed deist, who is suing them for their lands under pretext of a will made by their former king, which was undoubtedly forged. However, he is a man of such craft and influence that it is not known how the matter will issue." *

* The opinion here expressed of Robert Hunter Morris, Chief Justice of New Jersey from 1738 to 1764, was doubtless too true. He was the second son of Lewis Morris, Governor of New Jersey, and uncle of Gouverneur Morris, whose life has been written by Sparks. In 1749 he visited England, and by intrigue got himself appointed Governor of Pennsylvania, retaining at the same time his judgeship

This is a song of "mercy and judgment." Internally the mission was blessed, but outwardly foes were plotting and combining for its ruin.

The Indians seemed doomed to perish; and one grand instrument of their ruin was the spirit of avarice.

New Jersey had two classes of land titles: one from the original proprietors, the other from the Indian occupants. Up to the time of Judge Morris, Indian titles were respected; but he and his associates having obtained from the proprietors a title to a considerable part of New Jersey, and

---

in New Jersey. In 1756 he resigned the Governorship of Pennsylvania, but retained his office of Chief Justice of New Jersey successfully, resisting in 1759 the claims of Nathaniel Jones, who had been appointed to the office by the crown.

His aristocratic connections, his great talents and legal acuteness, his restless and generally successful ambition, his grasping avarice and utter moral unscrupulousness in using his judicial influence for his own self-emolument,—all these, with the absence of any religious faith or generous sentiments of humanity, made him a hard antagonist for the Indians of Bethel. He claimed their land as his own under a dreamy title, and finally exiled them from their homes.

There is a God in heaven. Sometimes, as in the case of Herod, the wicked soar only to make their fall more terribly and instructively sublime.

On the morning of 27th of January, 1764, Morris left Morrisiana in fine health on a visit to Shrewsbury, where he had a cousin residing, the wife of the clergyman of the parish. "In the evening there was a dance. The chief justice made one of the gay throng, and entered heartily, as was his habit, into the festivities of the occasion. He had led out the parson's wife, opened the ball, danced down six couples, and then, without a word, or a groan, or a sigh, *fell dead upon the floor!*

"What, then, were those things that he had provided" at the expense of justice and the Bethel Indians?—*Mr. Smith's letter. New York Historical Society.*

either trumping up some Indian conveyance, or treating Indian titles as a nullity, began actions of ejectment against a large number of occupants resting securely on their farms.* This was for a time resisted by popular violence, which often and for a long period protected justice at the expense of the technicalities of law and the decisions of interested judges. But the chief justice, sheltering his designs under legal pretensions, finally triumphed; and, as a consequence, a large number of New Jersey farmers, and the Indians of Bethel among the rest, were driven from the fields they had cleared and the houses they had erected. In "Smith's History of New Jersey," now a rare but most instructive book, is a full account of these land conflicts and of Judge Morris. To that book we refer the reader.

That our readers may have all we can glean of Brainerd's history at this period, we close this chapter with another extract from the archives of the "Society for Propagating Christian Knowledge" at Edinburgh. It gives collateral facts of interest:—

---

* A large quantity of East Jersey lands under the Carteret title had gotten into the hands of Robert Hunter Morris and James Alexander, Esquires, who held important offices in the province,—the one being chief justice, the other, secretary, and both at times were in the Council. These gentlemen, with other extensive proprietors, during the life of Governor Morris and toward the close of his administration, commenced actions of ejectment, and suits for the recovery of quit-rent, against many of the settlers.—*Gordon's History of New Jersey*, p. 109.

Extract from Minutes, Edinburgh, 23d March, 1749.

"The Committee reported, that by a letter from Mr. Pemberton, in name of the Correspondents in New York, it appears that the missionaries employed by this Society among the Indians continue diligent in the business of their mission; that the Indians under the care of Mr. Brainerd are not only incorporated in a church, but dwell together in a regular civil society; that the school, which is supported by contributions in these parts, is greatly increased, and an additional allowance is made for the encouragement of one or two well-qualified young Indians who assist in the instruction of the rest; that by the charity of well-disposed persons they have got spinning-wheels, that Indian women may be trained up to industry and diligence, which was unknown until Christianity was introduced among them."

Extract from Minutes, Edinburgh, 2d November, 1749.

"The Committee reported, that having received letters from their Correspondents at New York, mentioning the erection of a College at New Jersey for the education of youth intended principally for training up for the ministry, the Committee had agreed for encouragement of such a seminary of learning that a parcel of good books be purchased, at an expense not exceeding thirty pounds of the Society's funds, to be sent to the said new-erected college, and transmitted to the Rev'd Mr. John McLaurin, one of the ministers of Glasgow, a short account they had laid before them of the said college, to the end that from thence, and a more full account thereof in his hands, a narrative be drawn up and transmitted hither in order to be printed, after being revised by the Committee; that the Correspondents at

New York had likeways sent hither journals of the Rev'd Mr. John Brainerd, from the 1st May, 1748, to 7th September, 1749, and of Azariah Horton, from the 26th August, 1748, to the 9th April, 1749, as missionary ministers employed by this Society for the conversion of the infidel Indian natives living upon the borders of the Provinces of New York, New Jersey, and Pennsylvania, bearing their diligence and success in their mission. That the Indians under the charge of Mr. Brainerd are forming themselves into a civilized and orderly society; the men cultivate their lands, and the women learn to spin, so that they have in a great measure abandoned their slothful course of life; and a difficulty arising about the property of the land now possessed by the Indians in New Jersey, which is claimed by one Mr. Morris, Chief Justice, on pretence of a will made many years ago by one of the Indian kings, the Correspondents are to bring the cause to a trial at law.

"The General Meeting, having heard the above report, approved of the Resolution above mentioned, for purchasing books for the said new-erected college, and also of publishing an abridgment of the journals of the aforesaid missionaries, and likewise an account of the College of New Jersey, and remit the Committee to see the same done accordingly."

CHAPTER XIII.

DIARY OF JOHN BRAINERD AMONG THE INDIANS—HOW PRESERVED—HIS SPIRIT OF DEVOTION—HIS INDUSTRY—HIS SELF-DENIAL.

WE are now allowed to let Mr. Brainerd speak for himself. The following diary we received from Mrs. John C. Sims, of Philadelphia, a great-granddaughter of Mr. Brainerd. It is a small duodecimo manuscript book, of seventy-seven pages, written closely and legibly, after the manner of the day, but inferior in artistic execution to the diary of his brother David. It was retained as a keepsake by a remote relative of the family when the remainder of his papers were innocently, but most unthinkingly, committed to the flames about thirty years ago.

In deciphering its time-stained pages, we confess to a feeling of profound awe and veneration. We seem to be holding communion with a spirit of holiness over the lapse of more than a hundred years. It will be remembered that when Brainerd began this diary he was only twenty-nine years of age. Obviously, it was not designed for publication, but as a kind of thermometer by which he could estimate his own religious state, and enrich his mind by his own recorded experience and observations.

The language is perfectly unstudied, devoid of grace, sometimes tame and repetitious, and, in respect to taste and spirit, is not equal to his brother's. He sees nothing which has not a bearing on religious duty. It is monotonous, like David's; but we say of it, as a record of evangelical labor, what Dr. Thomas Chalmers says of David's journal, "it is the monotony of sublimity."

We could greatly enliven this diary by alterations and abbreviations, but in doing this we should throw a veil over the real spirit and character of the man. By giving it in his own language, we show more fully the missionary as he was; and no defects of style nor simplicity of narration will conceal that "beauty of holiness" with which the diary is filled. It was probably but one of a series of similar journals covering his life; but, excepting this fragment, all are lost. It begins abruptly, and extends through half a year. At its commencement, as he had been on the field two years already, the diary may be regarded as a fair specimen of his life and labors.

Journal of Rev. John Brainerd among the Indians at Bethel, near Cranberry, N. J.

Tuesday, Aug. 15, 1749.—Was something comforted in the duties of the morning, blessed be the Lord! I spent a considerable part of the forenoon in discoursing with sundry of my people, who came to see me. Afterwards had a little time to read.

After dinner visited a poor young woman, whom I

apprehend to be near her end. Prayed with her, but could have no conversation with her, she being not able to converse.

Visited another sick person, and then returned home.

Spent the remainder of the afternoon chiefly in reading. In my evening devotions had considerable freedom and comfort.

O Lord, I humbly thank thee for all thy kindness and goodness unto me, most unworthy!

Wednesday, *Aug.* 16.—Had some comfortable freedom this morning in prayer. Took care of some secular business. In the afternoon was called to attend the funeral of the young woman mentioned yesterday, and had considerable freedom in prayer at the sorrowful procession; afterwards spent some time in secret prayer, and a little before sundown called my people together, and explained the fifth and sixth commandments to them, concluding with some practical improvement and exhortation. Then returned home and attended family and secret duties, in which it pleased God to give me much freedom and comfort. Blessed be his holy name!

Thursday, *Aug.* 17.—Was comfortable this morning in holy duties. Spent most of the forenoon in taking care of, and attending upon, one of the Indians, who was very sick.

In the afternoon attended upon the funeral of one of my neighbors, the same mentioned in my journal of Lord's day and Monday.* A great number of people was present, to whom Mr. McKnight preached with freedom and earnestness. May the gracious Lord bless

---

* This refers to a previous diary, now lost.

the same to the lasting benefit of all the hearers! Made it evening before I came home, and had time only to read a portion of Scripture and to attend religious duties.

O Lord, sanctify to me the opportunity of repeatedly attending on funerals for my spiritual and lasting good!

Friday, *Aug.* 18.—Went to take care of the Indian mentioned yesterday; spent most of the day with him, and joined in prayer with him. Then rode out a little way to see a sick neighbor among the whites. People tarried some time at the house, and I had considerable discourse upon things of religion, and some in particular with the sick man: at his desire and the desire of his wife, prayed with him, and, taking leave of them, returned home. Went to see the sick Indian, tarried a while with him, and gave orders how he was to be tended; but felt much indisposed in body myself, and so, returning home, attended family and secret duties, in which, I hope, I had some taste of divine things. Blessed be the Lord!

Saturday, *Aug.* 19.—Was very much indisposed in body this morning, yet something comfortable in mind. Attended religious duties with comfortable composure, but no special enlargement.

Took some care of the sick man in the forepart of the day, but towards noon felt so poorly I was obliged to lie down; continued unwell all day. Towards evening thought it my duty to take an emetic. Endeavored to commit myself to God in a few petitions. The Lord graciously accept of me in and through Christ.

Lord's day, *Aug.* 20.—Was very weak this day; not able to attend the public worship in the forenoon, and very poorly able to attend even family and secret duties; but in the afternoon, feeling a little better, I went to meeting, and had considerable freedom in the various parts of divine service. The worship of God was also attended upon with much seriousness both by the white people and the Indians.

In the evening visited the sick man mentioned yesterday, &c.; found him unable to converse, so I prayed with him, and returned home. Blessed be the name of the Lord! *

Monday, Aug. 21.—Attended religious duties. Was very poorly in body; notwithstanding, went to see the sick man several times, and had some discourse with him; but his senses were so disordered that it was to little purpose. Visited him about two o'clock, and prayed with him. Then took leave of him, thinking it my duty to ride out for my health; and, commending myself and my people to God by prayer, I set out, and rode first to Mr. Tennent's,† and then to Dr. Le Count's,

---

* Sick himself, he forgets his weakness in care of his flock. How like his brother David in this energy of duty!

† This was the Rev. William Tennent (2), of Freehold, about six miles from Bethel. He was the second son of the Rev. William Tennent, of Neshaminy, Pa., father of Gilbert, William, John, and Charles, all preachers of note in their day. William Tennent (2) was settled in Freehold, as successor to his brother John, by the Philadelphia Presbytery, October 25, 1733, and remained pastor until 1777, forty-four years. His wonderful trance, his marvellous answers to prayer, and hair-breadth escapes from enemies, have made him famous. He was a near neighbor and warm friend of the Brainerds, and often took the care of the Indian Church in their absence. He was a holy, active, warm-hearted man, of large—almost superstitious—faith, and just the man to cheer and comfort John Brainerd in his sadness and depression. Dr. Le Count was a pious parishioner of Tennent's. His name is still fragrant in New Jersey.

and tarried there all night; was very kindly entertained, and had considerable refreshment in conversation. Attended family prayers and secret devotions, in which I had comfortable composure of mind and something of freedom. Praised be the Lord!

Tuesday, Aug. 22.—Attended religious duties, and after some time took leave of Dr. Le Count and his spouse, and rode about three miles to a medicinal spring, where were a number of my people, who came there to drink the waters; with these I spent considerable time in conversation and prayer. Took leave of them, and went to several houses in Freehold, where I had business, and in the evening came to Mr. Tennent's; after some conversation with him, attended to religious duties and went to rest.

Wednesday, Aug. 23.—Took leave of Mr. Tennent and his spouse, and returned home. Visited the sick man mentioned the day before yesterday, and found him still very low, but yet, I hope, something better. In the evening called my people together, and explained to them the four last commandments, concluding with some spiritual improvement.

Returned home; visited the poor sick man again, &c. Spent some time in reading, and attended religious duties with some comfortable freedom. The Lord's name be praised!

The simplicity of this diary may strike some as almost puerile; but, as a transcript of a real life one hundred years ago, it will be of interest.

We see from it the regularity and specialty of Brainerd's devotions. How constantly he watched for the Divine Presence in his prayers, and how gratefully he acknowledged any special influence of the Spirit on his own heart! Every hour had its duty, and every duty was assigned to its appropriate hour. This entire absorption in his work; his readiness to sympathize with the poor, to bear their burdens, and improve their character and condition; his humility, prayerfulness, and earnest fidelity to every obligation, marked him as a model missionary and a fit disciple of Him who "fulfilled all righteousness."

CHAPTER XIV.

A JOURNEY OVER THE DELAWARE—VISITS PRINCETON—HOPEWELL—CROSSES THE RIVER—FINDS SOME INDIANS, AND PREACHES TO THEM—HIS INTERPRETER RETURNS HOME WITH THREE SQUAWS—REV. CHARLES BEATTY, SAMUEL HAZARD, ESQ., REV. RICHARD TREAT.

THURSDAY, *Aug*. 24.—Visited the sick man; found him considerably better, and had some discourse with him. Blessed be the gracious Lord for his kindness to him!

Visited the sick Indian again, and prayed with him; took leave of him and several others of my people, and set out on a journey about three o'clock in the afternoon. Called at Mr. Wales' as I passed along; tarried a little while, and then came to Princeton. Went to Justice Stockton's,* and tarried there. I spent the evening mostly in conversation, and afterwards attended family and secret duties, in which I was favored with some comfortable composure of mind, but had no special enlargement.

* By Justice Stockton, Mr. Brainerd refers to John Stockton, Esq., of Princeton, father of the Hon. Richard Stockton, of Revolutionary memory. The grandfather of Richard Stockton purchased some five thousand or six thousand acres of land at an early day, and, leaving it to his heirs, founded one of the most affluent families in the State. We believe the present Commodore R. H. Stockton, a lineal descendant of John, still retains a portion of the first purchase. John Stockton was an elder of the church, a gentleman of fortune and influence, a most liberal friend of the College of New Jersey and its early presidents, and a presiding judge in the county court. His house was a frequent home for both the Brainerds. His memory is blessed!

Friday, *Aug.* 25.—Attended religious duties. Took leave of Mr. Stockton and the family, and proceeded on my journey, but felt very unwell; it being very hot, I could not travel far. Stopped at two or three places, and spent some time with my friends. Came a little after sundown to Mr. Paine's, at Hopewell,* and there tarried all night. Was much indisposed; notwithstanding, had considerable discourse on divine subjects, and, I trust, some real taste of divine things in family and secret duties.

Saturday, *Aug.* 26.—Set out with my interpreter towards Delaware. Travelled about twelve miles up the stream, and crossed the river; then rode about eight or nine miles, and found the Indians I was in quest of. Spent the remainder of the day with them, mostly in private conversation and prayer. In the evening went to a house about a mile off, where I was courteously entertained. Was much indisposed, and had no special freedom in holy duties. The Lord graciously quicken me by his Holy Spirit!

Lord's day, *Aug.* 27.—Had some taste of divine things

---

* Hopewell was the ancient name of Pennington, in Mercer county. The church was founded in 1709, and is yet flourishing. It is eight miles north of Trenton, and on Brainerd's course from Princeton to Neshaminy, Pa. In 1744, what was termed a "New Light Church" was erected, by persons who seceded from the Presbyterian Church under the labors of Whitefield, Tennent, and others. (Webster's History.) The last preacher of this church was the famous Rev. James Davenport, who died there in 1757, aged forty years. After his death, his congregation, having perhaps accomplished its mission as a witness for holy zeal and eminent earnestness in religion, returned to the old church. The two parties may have been necessary to each other. Mr. Paine doubtless belonged to the new church.

in holy duties this morning; was still very unwell. However, I visited the Indians again, and spent the forenoon with them.

Attended public worship, and had some divine aid in prayer and preaching. One or two persons were considerably affected; the rest attended with commendable decency. In the afternoon I preached to a large number of white persons, who gathered together; and it pleased God to give me very comfortable freedom in speaking to them, and sundry persons seemed to be much affected with divine truths. Afterwards spent some time with the Indians, conversing with them privately.

Felt very poorly;* not able to sit up long; but it pleased God to give me comfortable freedom of soul in family and secret duties. Forever praised be his holy name!

Monday, Aug. 28.—Visited the Indians again, and spent the forenoon with them. Conversed privately with them some time, and afterwards preached to them. The word was attended unto with decency and much seriousness; and, as they were about to remove, I endeavored to per-

---

* These frequent allusions to *ill health* are remarkable and painful in a young man of twenty-eight. He shared, we fear, in the feeble constitution that carried his brother David to the grave at twenty-nine, Nehemiah at thirty-two, Israel at twenty-three, and his sister, Jerusha Spencer, at thirty-four. Though he himself reached sixty, his whole life seems to have been a struggle with physical infirmity. It must, however, be confessed that in the whole Brainerd family for two hundred years there has been a tendency to a morbid depression, akin to hypochondria. They have been generally, in fact, long-lived, and in health relatively better in old age than in youth. But their nervous sensibility, restless activity, and impaired digestion, either as a cause or effect of peculiar temperament, have made them often in imagination "die daily." *Quorum pars fui.*

suade them to come to the Indian town* in New Jersey; but they seemed not willing, and desired that I would come up to the place where they were going, about thirty or forty miles above the Forks of Delaware, and they would be willing to hear me. So I took leave of them, and they went their way. My interpreter also left me by agreement, and returned into the Jerseys with two or three squaws who came here from the Indian town to see these Indians; and I proceeded on my journey, and rode to Mr. Beatty's,† at Neshaminy, and tarried there all night. Attended family and secret duties with some comfortable composure of mind. The Lord be praised for all his goodness and kindness to the most unworthy of all creatures!

---

* Bethel.

† The Brainerd brothers had no friend more intimate, more reliable and valued than Rev. Charles Beatty, of Neshaminy, Pa. In David's journal, October 28, 1746, he makes a touching allusion to the kindness of Mr. Beatty and others, who had taken pains to ride thirty or forty miles to see him at Princeton. Mr. Beatty was born in Ireland in 1714, came to America in 1729, was licensed by New Brunswick Presbytery in 1742, and settled at the Forks of Neshaminy (now Hartsville, Bucks county, Pa.), May 26, 1743, and continued pastor until he died at Bridgeton, in the island of Barbadoes, in 1782. His fervent piety and apostolic zeal endeared the Brainerds to him, and him to them. He was one of the master-minds of his day. As a missionary to North Carolina for a season, and to the Indians at Muskingum with Dr. Duffield in 1766, as the successful agent for a public charity to England, as moderator to the Synod in 1764, as chaplain in the army and evangelist among the churches, as the faithful pastor at Neshaminy for forty years, his name occurs everywhere in the annals of the period, and always with honor. His grandson, the Rev. C. C. Beatty, D.D., Steubenville, Ohio, has made the name precious to another generation. I am happy by this brief note to pay this little tribute to a man so cherished by the subject of this memoir.

Tuesday, *Aug.* 29.—Took leave of Mrs. Beatty, and proceeded on my journey. Visited Mr. Treat* on my way to Philadelphia. Dined with him, and spent some time in conversation with him; then set forward, and came to Philadelphia a little after sundown. Went to Mr. Hazard's,† and tarried there. Spent some time at a singing meeting, and afterwards attended family and secret duties, but with very little freedom or enlargement. The Lord forgive, and graciously quicken me by his Holy Spirit!

---

* The Rev. Richard Treat, of Abington, Bucks county, Pa. He was born at Milford, Conn., in 1708, graduated at Yale in 1725, and settled at Abington in 1731. In 1734, after having preached six years, he was converted, or re-converted, under the preaching of Whitefield. Becoming a zealous revivalist according to the mode of the "New Side," he was "excluded" by the Philadelphia Presbytery, and attached himself to the Presbytery of New Brunswick. He was a most useful man in his day, and survived until 1778.

† This was, no doubt, Samuel Hazard, formerly a respectable merchant of this city, and father of the late Ebenezer Hazard, an early Postmaster-General under the old Congress. Samuel Hazard took a very active part in the religious and benevolent institutions of the day. He was one of the founders of the Second Presbyterian Church under Rev. Gilbert Tennent, then worshipping in the "new building" erected by Rev. G. Whitefield, on Fourth, below Arch Street, and also an elder. When the congregation was obliged to remove from thence, a sale of the building having been made to the Trustees of the Academy in 1749–50, he was one of a committee to purchase a new lot for the church and burial-ground at the corner of Arch and Third, as well as superintend the erection. He continued, it is believed, elder, treasurer, or trustee, till the time of his death, which occurred July 19, 1758; and he was also one of the early contributors to the foundation of the Pennsylvania Hospital, and was at the first election chosen a manager, and as such served for three years, from 1751 to 1753. In many other respects he was considered a very excellent and useful man.

CHAPTER XV.

ENDEAVORS TO BENEFIT A QUAKER—RANCOCAS INDIANS—AN INDIAN FUNERAL—AN INDIAN GOD—SATURDAY SERMONS—MUCH DISTURBED BY WHITE PEOPLE—A LITTLE INDIAN BOY CRIES TO GO HOME WITH MR. BRAINERD—IS TAKEN ALONG.

WEDNESDAY, *Aug.* 30.—Attended family and secret devotions; visited a friend or two, and then, taking leave at Mr. Hazard's, crossed the ferry, and came to a number of Indians near Rancocas,* where I had appointed my interpreter to meet me. I spent some time in private conversation with them, and afterwards called them all together, being about twenty-two in number, and preached to them. They attended on divine worship with seriousness and considerable decency. I spent the remainder of the day in private discourse with them, and about sundown went to my lodgings. May the Lord follow what has been spoken with his blessing!

* Rancocas is the name of a river which rises in Burlington county, N. J., and after a course of some twenty miles empties into the Delaware, about sixteen miles above Philadelphia. It is navigable to Harrisport, about ten miles up from the Delaware. The village of Rancocas is on the south side of the stream, about six miles up the river. Many Indians lingered about this stream until their final removal from the State. Their principal settlement was about a mile west of Vincenttown, on Quakeson Creek. At a later period, when Mr Brainerd removed to Mount Holly (or Bridgetown), on the Rancocas, he had a log church, in which he preached to these Indians many years. It was afterwards occupied by the whites. A schoolhouse about two miles from Vincenttown is said to have in it some of the timbers of the old Rancocas Indian sanctuary built by Brainerd.

I spent some time in conversation with the man of the house, whom I found to be a Quaker. Endeavored to convince him of the reasonableness and duty of family religion, such as asking a blessing and giving thanks at table, family prayer, &c. He had nothing to object against these things, but yet was not willing to comply. After some time, returned to my lodging-room; spent some time in reading and prayer, and then went to bed.

Friday, Sept. 1.—Visited the Indians again. Spent some time in private discourse with them, and then gathered them all together and preached to them. They attended on the several parts of divine worship with seriousness and decency, and one or two seemed to be affected with divine truths. Blessed be the Lord! Oh that it might please a gracious God to bring them to a saving acquaintance with himself! Spent some time in discoursing with them, and then returned to my lodgings; took some refreshment, and came back to the Indians again; found a great number of white people with them, who came to attend the funeral of an old Indian who died the day before. The old man, it seemed, had been an honest creature, and had gained the respect of all the neighbors.

I called the Indians together in one place, and, after prayer, discoursed to them, suiting my discourse to their understanding and the occasion as well as I could; and when I had done speaking to the Indians, turned to the white people, a great number of whom were present,—I believe at least one hundred and fifty or two hundred of all sorts,—and gave them a solemn word of exhortation (may the Lord follow it with his blessing!). After public worship was ended, attended the funeral of the old man. The Indians were generally sober; but one or two had too much drink, notwithstanding all the pains I had taken the day before and in the forenoon. After the funeral was over and the white people gone, I spent some time discoursing with the Indians, and, upon their desire, determined to tarry with them the Sabbath over. A little after came my interpreter and two more, an Indian and a squaw, with whom I had some discourse, and, to my comfort, found them well inclined.

The woman after the meeting in the forenoon came to me, and told me that she had an aunt about eight or nine miles off who kept an idol image, which, indeed, partly belonged to her, and that she had a mind to go and fetch her aunt and the image, that it might be burnt; but when she went to the place she found nobody at home, and the image also was taken away. After this I spent some time in reading the Bible, and in my evening devotions had something of freedom and comfort. The Lord's name be praised for all his kindness to me!

Saturday, *Sept.* 2.—Had, I hope, some real desire after God this morning in secret prayer for precious souls, especially of the poor Indians. Spent some time in reading; then waited on a friend who came from New England, and spent some time in conversation with him. Afterwards visited the Indians, had considerable conversation with them in a more private manner; then retired a little while for prayer, and afterwards called the Indians all together and carried on public worship; prayed, and gave them some instruction from the word of God; after meeting discoursed more privately to several of them, and then retired to my quarters. Took some refreshment, and came again to the Indians. Spent about an hour in more private conversation with them, and then called them all together and preached to them again.

These Indians (being near twenty in number) seem to be generally convinced of the truth of the Christian religion, and one or two seem to be concerned for their souls, and desire to go where they can have opportunity to hear the gospel. I encouraged their going to Bethel, the Christian Indian town, which I suspect a number will do; but others seem inclined to go over towards Susquehanna. May the Lord follow them, wherever they go, with his blessing, and make them savingly acquainted with his dear Son!

Spent some time in conversation with the people of the house, and afterwards in reading and meditation; and attended secret devotions, in which I had some freedom and, I hope, a real sense of divine things. Praised be the Lord!

Lord's day, Sept. 3.—Spent some time in meditation, and afterwards had some conversation with the man of the house. Observing that he talked about worldly things, endeavored to show him the evil of the same, and that the Sabbath ought to be kept holy in both word and deed. Went to the Indians about nine in the morning; attended divine worship with them, there being now about thirty persons more able to attend on religious worship.

After meeting, went about half a mile to preach to a number of white people, at their desire (many of the Indians attending there also); and it pleased God to grant me very comfortable freedom in preaching. May the Lord set home the word upon their hearts for their saving good!

After I had some refreshment, returned again to the Indians. Gathered them all together, and attended divine worship with them, in which it pleased a gracious

God to give some freedom and an ardent desire for their souls.

They attended again with seriousness and solemnity, although there were many white people present who behaved very badly, going from place to place and talking loud, so that I was obliged to speak to them and desire them to be still. Took some refreshment, and had some discourse with several persons who came in. Afterwards attended secret devotions, in which it pleased God to give me some freedom and comfort. Blessed be his holy name!

Monday, *Sept.* 4.—Rose early this morning. Soon after bid farewell to the honest old man and his wife, who were so kind they would take nothing of me for my keeping. Then went to the Indians; spent some time in conversation, and then called them together and attended public worship; prayed, preached, &c., and after I had done, gave them a more particular account of the state of affairs among the Indians at Bethel, where I live, and advised them to come there.

Just as I was about to take leave of them, there came a little boy of about ten or eleven years old, and hung about me and began to cry, upon which I inquired what he wanted. I soon understood that he wanted to go with me; so I asked his parents if they were willing. They said, "yes." So I sent him along with an Indian who belonged to the place where I live.* Another showed a very great desire to go, and cried heartily enough because he could not go then; and when I took my leave of them the most of them seemed to be sorrowful. May

* The fate of this little volunteer we know not. We hope his choice of God's people led him to Christ. It was a scene which must have cheered the heart of the earnest missionary.

the Lord bless what has been spoken to them, and grant that the good impressions made on their minds may never wear off till they are brought to a saving acquaintance with himself!

Travelled to Maidenhead,* and was kindly welcomed by a friend there.

Tuesday, Sept. 5.—Attended family and secret duties, and then took leave of my friends and came on my way. Went to visit a number of Indians as I passed along, and spent considerable time with them in prayer, singing, and conversation; visited also several Christian friends. Took leave of the Indians, etc., and came up to Justice Stockton's, at Princeton, with whom I tarried all night.

Wednesday, Sept. 6.—Attended religious duties, and then took leave of Mr. Stockton, etc., and came on my way homeward. Visited Mr. Wales,† and spent some hours with him, and came home about four o'clock in the afternoon. Spent the remainder of the day and evening mostly in conversation with my people, who came to see me, and was considerably refreshed. Praised be the Lord for all his kindness and goodness to me on this

---

* Maidenhead was the ancient name of the present village of Lawrenceville. It is about five miles from Trenton, and the same distance from Princeton. It is a place of historic Revolutionary interest, and at the present time distinguished for its excellent male and female academies. James Brainerd Taylor was here prepared for college.

† The Rev. Eleazer Wales graduated at Yale College in 1727, and is said to have been settled at Allentown, N. J., in 1730. David Brainerd assisted him at a communion at Kingston, near Princeton, June 15, 1746. As John Brainerd found him at Allentown, on the way from Princeton to Bethel, we are inclined to believe he occupied both Kingston (Milestown anciently) and Allentown. He died in 1749, shortly after this visit from John Brainerd.

journey, and that he has been graciously pleased to bring me home in safety to my family and people! Oh, may I live as well as speak his praise!

Thursday, *Sept.* 7.—Conversed with two or three of my people, who came in to see me. Afterwards began to transcribe my journal, but felt so exceedingly poorly in body that I was not able to write; so I spent some time in reading. Felt something dejected, but yet not altogether uncomfortable in mind.

After dinner, spent some time in prayer, in which I found considerable freedom. Blessed be God! All the world appeared like nothing to me, and God seemed like all in all; and it was the earnest desire of my soul to glorify him in heart and life. After this I read a little, and in the evening called my people together and worshipped in my usual manner, and afterwards made some practical improvement of the subject. It pleased God to give me considerable freedom this evening, especially in prayer. Returned home; spent some time with a Christian friend, and afterwards attended family and secret duties, in which also I had some outgoings of soul to God. Blessed be his holy name!

Friday, *Sept.* 8.—Took care of a temporal affair belonging to the Indians. After dinner, spent two or three hours with a couple of Indians about some particular business; afterwards occupied some time in reading, and the evening was wholly spent in reading and prayer. O Lord, grant me the quickening influence of thy grace and Holy Spirit, I humbly beseech thee!

CHAPTER XVI.

JOHN BRAINERD FOLLOWS THE INDIANS TO A MINERAL SPRING—INDIAN MISTRESS ATTENDING TO PRAYERS—REV. MR. DAVENPORT—BRAINERD MAKES ANOTHER JOURNEY—ELIZABETHTOWN—NEWARK—REV. AARON BURR—THANKSGIVING—LEAVES HOME AGAIN—AMWELL—BRUNSWICK—REV. MR. ARTHUR.

SATURDAY, *Sept.* 9.—Attended morning devotions in the family and secret, but had not much life; yet I had some real desire to love and glorify God. May the blessed Lord increase the same! Spent a little time in reading the Bible; afterwards rode about fifteen miles to visit a number of my people, who were gone to a medicinal spring, being valetudinary. Conversed with them, and then prayed with them, and, taking leave of them, called at Rev. Mr. Tennent's, and then came home. Found the mistress and the Indians attending on divine service, as usual, this evening. Had thoughts of going to join with them, but, going into the house, found Rev. Mr. Davenport * within, much indisposed and not able

* The Rev. James Davenport, the great-grandson of the Rev. John Davenport, founder of the colony of New Haven, Conn., was born in Stamford, Conn., in 1716; he graduated at Yale College under President Williams. Whitefield met him in May, 1740, and calls him "one of the ministers whom God has lately sent out; a sweet, zealous soul." He caught fire in the Great Revival, and was among its most zealous promoters. Whitefield said of him: "He knew no man keep so close a walk with God." Twenty Niantic Indians were converted under his preaching at East Lyme. With talents, piety, and zeal, fitting him for vast influence and usefulness, he fell into

to attend the meeting. Attended family and secret duties, and had, I hope, some real sense of divine things. Praised be the Lord for any favor vouchsafed to an unworthy creature!

Lord's day, Sept. 10.—Had some comfort this morning in holy duties. O Lord, pardon and quicken me by thy Holy Spirit! Attended the public worship at the usual time, and was favored with something of freedom in the various parts of divine service. Preached from the Parable of the Supper. In the afternoon Mr. Davenport preached, without an interpreter, from Matt. xi. 23, in which he seemed to have considerable freedom, and several of the Indians were much affected with divine truths; and the whole assembly attended with seriousness, there being also many white people present.

Toward the close of the day attended a third meeting; Mr. Davenport being unable to go. Repeated the heads and substance of his discourse, and concluded with some exhortations which seemed to have a desirable effect on the minds of the audience, and several appeared to be much affected. Blessed be the Lord! Oh, may those efforts be productive of good effects! Returned home; it being something after sundown. Spent some time in religious conversation, and attended family and secret du-

---

fanaticism. His excesses at one period, attended, as they were, by a "long fever" and "cankery humor," with "inflammatory ulcerations," raise a presumption of insanity; and he was a better subject for a lunatic asylum or hospital than the jail to which bigotry consigned him. He recovered physically and mentally, repented of his extravagance, removed to New Jersey, and was installed, October 27, 1754, over the congregations of Maidenhead (Lawrenceville) and Hopewell, where he died in 1757, and was buried about a mile from Pennington, towards the Delaware.

ties, and had, I hope, some comfortable desires and outgoings toward God. Praised be thy holy name, O Lord!

Monday, Sept. 11.—Spent some time with Mr. Davenport, and, after he was gone, attended upon some business relating to the Indians, which occupied me till noon. In the evening called my people together; spent some time in discoursing to them on a divine subject and prayer, which was attended to with much seriousness and affection in some. Returned home; read a portion of Holy Scripture, and attended secret devotions with some enlargement of heart.

Tuesday, Sept. 12.—Set out on a journey to Newark. Had some comfortable meditations on the way. Went no farther than Elizabethtown this day. Tarried at Mr. Woodruff's; after some conversation, attended to family and secret devotions, but had no special freedom therein. The Lord pardon my deadness, and quicken me by his Holy Spirit.

Wednesday, Sept. 13.—After family and secret devotions, set out for Newark. Visited a friend on the way, and came to Mr. Burr's about ten o'clock. Spent some time at his house; after dinner rode with him to the Mountains,* to Mr. Smith's; tarried with him two or

* Newark Mountains embrace the region now called Orange, north of Newark, N. J. The Rev. Caleb Smith was born in Brookhaven, L. I., in 1723; graduated at Yale in 1743. In common with Brainerd, he was a warm friend and trustee of the College of New Jersey. He married a daughter of President Dickinson. His sermon on the death of the Rev. President Aaron Burr is highly creditable to his intellect and taste. He died in 1762, aged thirty-nine. His descendants are highly respectable.

three hours, and then returned to Mr. Burr's. Visited a dear Christian friend in the evening, and returned to Mr. Burr's again. Spent the remainder of the evening mostly in conversation.

Thursday, *Sept.* 14.—Set out with Mr. Burr for Shrewsbury, upon some business relating to the college. Came as far as Dr. Le Count's, and lodged there. Spent the evening chiefly in religious conversation; and had some refreshment in holy duties, especially in secret prayer.

Friday, *Sept.* 15.—Rode with Mr. Burr to Shrewsbury, intending (after the business was accomplished) to ride a considerable part if not all of the way home on the same day; but, it growing very stormy in the afternoon, was obliged to tarry there. Was comfortable in mind and, I think, resigned to the disposal of Providence, though I exceedingly wanted to be at home. In my evening devotions had comfortable freedom and enlargement. For-ever blessed be thy holy name, O Lord!

Saturday, *Sept.* 16.—Attended holy duties, &c., and then set out with Mr. Burr on my journey home. Came to Dr. Le Count's, and there parted; he turning to the right hand, and I to the left. Reached home a little after noon. After some short time, convened my people together, and entertained them with a discourse from Matt. xxv. 6, in which it pleased the Lord to give me very comfortable freedom. Sundry of the Indians also were much affected with divine truths, and attended with much seriousness. After sermon we spent some considerable time in prayer, and then returned home. Spent the evening mostly in reading, meditation, and prayer, and had, I hope, some real sense of divine things and some desires to be devoted to God. Praised be the name of the Lord!

Lord's day, Sept. 17.—Spent a considerable part of the morning in secret prayer, in which, I hope, I had a real sense of divine things, but no special enlargement. Attended public worship at the usual time, and it pleased God to give me some aid in the various parts of divine service. Preached from Isa. liii. 5, and several persons were much affected. When the exercise was concluded, I administered the Lord's Supper, in which it pleased the gracious God to give me a comfortable sense of spiritual and divine things. Forever praised be his holy name! The Indians also were, many of them, sweetly affected while at the table.

After a short intermission, again preached from Isa. lv. 5, and it pleased the gracious Lord to give me freedom in speaking and, I trust, some real assistance, and much comfort in every part of divine service. It seemed also to be a refreshing season among the dear Indians. The Lord's name be praised! Returned home, being much spent in body, but, through the grace of God, comfortable in mind. Afterwards visited several of my people, and found, to my great satisfaction, it had been a refreshing season to their souls. After this returned home, and attended secret prayer, in which I was favored with very comfortable outgoings of soul to God.

Monday, Sept. 18.—Attended family and secret duties, and was very comfortable therein. Had some discourse with one of my people, who came to see me. About nine o'clock called my people together, and entertained them with a discourse from Titus iii. 8, in which I had comfortable freedom, as also in the other parts of divine service; the Indians seemed also greatly affected. After public worship, had some discourse more privately with sundry persons, and found it had been a refreshing season to their souls. O Lord, I humbly thank thee for all thy kindness and goodness to me and the dear people thou hast committed to my charge, especially on this solemn and sacramental occasion! May there be lasting good effects from it on all our souls!

After I came home, spent considerable time with one and another of my people, who came to my house; then wrote a letter to a friend, and afterwards had a little time to read; but in the evening came Mr. Davenport and Justice Stockton, who had been at Mr. Tennent's sacrament. With these I spent the evening, and after some time attended family and secret duties. I hope I had some real sense of spiritual things. O Lord, increase my view of and love to thee, and let me ever live to thy glory!

Tuesday, Sept. 19.—Having occasion to go to Amwell* on some business for the Indians, after attending religious duties, set out with Mr. Davenport and Mr. Stockton, their road and mine being the same for about ten miles. Called to see Mr. Wales, and dined with him; then proceeded on our journey. Parted with my two companions and rode the rest of the way alone, being something more than twenty miles, and arrived there early in the evening. Lodged at the house of an old honest Dutchman, and was kindly entertained. After some conversation with him, retired to my lodging-room; attended to secret devotions, and went to rest.

---

* Amwell was a township of Hunterdon county. It embraced the territory in which are now situated Flemington, Sergeantville, Ringoes, Prattsville, and Lambertsville.

Wednesday, *Sept.* 20.—Arose early; attended to secret duties; took leave of the honest man and his family, and came on my way towards Brunswick, being obliged to go that way because I could not accomplish the business at Amwell that I went upon. Arrived there about one of the clock, being about thirty miles. Dined at Rev. Mr. Arthur's;* tarried some time in town, but could not accomplish the business I aimed at. Left the town about five o'clock, and came home in the beginning of the evening. Read a little, but felt tired with my journey; so, after attending family and secret duties, went to rest. Blessed be the Lord for all his goodness in carrying me forth and returning me home in safety! Oh, may I speak and live his praises!

Thursday, *Sept.* 21.—Spent the forenoon in writing. In the afternoon, called my people together and preached to them from Eccl. xii. 5, giving a particular view to the young people and children. After sermon, catechized the children, and concluded with some exhortation. Spent the remainder of the day and evening mostly in writing.

Friday, *Sept.* 22.—Attended religious duties, and sat down to write. Spent most of the day in transcribing my journal. Attended family and secret prayers, and, blessed be the Lord, had some freedom and comfort in both!

Saturday, *Sept.* 23.—Spent some time with the Indians, discoursing with them, and especially with one of them,

* This was Rev. Thomas Arthur, pastor of the church of New Brunswick. He graduated at Yale in 1743, and was an original trustee of New Jersey College. His obituary says: "He was a good scholar, a graceful orator, an excellent Christian." He died at the early age of twenty-seven.

on a matter of difficulty and prejudice. Set out on a journey for Shrewsbury,* and came to Justice Little's after sundown. Felt very poorly in body, and not very comfortable in mind. Attended family prayer, and spent some time in private meditation and prayer, but had very little freedom. The Lord pardon and quicken me for his mercy's sake.

Lord's day, Sept. 24.—Spent the morning mostly in meditation. Attended divine worship in public, but had no special freedom in the forenoon service; in the afternoon had considerable enlargement, both in prayer and preaching. Oh that it might be set home upon their hearts for spiritual good! Spent the evening mostly in conversation and singing psalms, and had something of freedom in holy duties, especially in secret prayer.

Monday, Sept. 25.—Spent the forenoon at Mr. Eaton's (it being rainy), partly in reading and partly in conversation. In the afternoon came to Dr. Le Count's, but, it being very stormy, could proceed no farther.

Tuesday, Sept. 26.—After family and secret duties, took leave of the doctor and his spouse, and came to Rev. Mr. Tennent's, and then returned home. Called my people together; exhorted as usual, and afterwards made some practical reflections.

---

* Shrewsbury is a village of Monmouth county, N. J., twelve miles east from Freehold, and fifty southeast from Trenton. It is a seaport town. Shrewsbury township embraces Long Branch, the famous watering-place. Visitors of the present day can hardly picture the country as, in its wildness, it met the eyes of Brainerd in 1749.

CHAPTER XVII.

NEW JERSEY COLLEGE COMMENCEMENT—JOHN BRAINERD TAKES HIS MASTER'S DEGREE—HIS GRATITUDE—THE REV. MR. POMROY—REV. SAMUEL FINLEY.

WEDNESDAY, *Sept.* 27.—Set out with Mr. Tennent for Brunswick, it being the day of college commencement there. Had opportunity of seeing and conversing with many of my friends and acquaintances, which was very comfortable and refreshing. The Lord make me truly thankful, and graciously pardon any thing that may have been amiss in me, or wherein I may have misimproved the opportunity!

About two o'clock, attended upon the commencement exercises, and, after the disputations were over, took my Master's degree with Mr. Davenport, Mr. Finley,* and Mr. Green,† which was given me gratis. Oh that I

---

* The Rev. Samuel Finley was born in Ireland in 1715, prepared for the ministry at the Log College, and was licensed by the Presbytery of New Brunswick August 5, 1740. He was a zealous revivalist; was prosecuted for irregular preaching in New Haven, Conn., put in jail, and sent out of the colony as a vagrant. He was settled in Nottingham, Md., in June, 1744, and remained pastor seventeen years. He there established a famous school, and counted among its pupils Governor Martin, of North Carolina, Benjamin Rush, of Philadelphia, Rev. Dr. Alexander McWhorter, of Newark, and Rev. James Waddell, of Virginia. He was elected President of New Jersey College at the death of President Davis.

† The Rev. Mr. Green, who took his Master's degree with Brainerd, was the Rev. Jacob Green, father of the Rev. Ashbel Green, D.D., late of Philadelphia. He was born at Malden, Mass., in 1722,

may have grace to improve this and every advantage I am favored with to the praise and glory of Him who is the giver of all!

After meeting, spent some time in conversation with one and another of my dear friends, and then attended an evening lecture, and heard the Rev. Mr. Pomroy, of Hebron, in Connecticut, from Exod. xxxii. 10; but, before he had proceeded far in his discourse, I was called out to wait on the Correspondents and to give them some account of the circumstances and affairs of the Indians I have the pastoral charge of; which being done and their meeting broke up, I soon returned to my lodgings, and there spent the remainder of the evening in company with Mr. Pomroy, Mr. Davenport, and Mr. Spencer, and after some conversation attended family and secret prayers, but was very cold and lifeless. O Lord, forgive and graciously quicken me for thy mercy's sake!

Thursday, *Sept.* 28.—Waited on the Governor, having some particular business with him. Spent the day with the ministers and other gentlemen of my acquaintance. Towards night took leave of them, and came home;

---

graduated at Harvard in 1744, and ordained pastor of the church at South Hanover (now Madison), N. J., in 1746. He was a faithful minister and warm patriot. Against his will he was elected to the Provincial Congress. As a decided abolitionist, he provoked the malice of slaveholders around him. Dissatisfied with strict Presbyterianism, he separated himself from the Synod and organized Morris Presbytery, of which he was the head. In short, he was as remarkable for ultraism as his distinguished son Ashbel was for conservatism in Church and State. But, if one moved in an eccentric and the other in a regular orbit, both were equally shining orbs, leaving in their track a broad train of light on the world. The memory of both father and son is blessed.

was informed by the Mistress that several Indians had been drunk, and that one family had gone to the Moravians,* which things were a great exercise to me. Oh, how distressing it is to have the charge of such a people! How much need have I of Divine support! O Lord, I design to depend on thee alone; I am not able to bear this people,—it is too heavy for me! Oh, grant me Divine help and support, suitable to bear all the distressing difficulties thou knowest I labor under, and let me have grace and wisdom from above so to behave under all my trials that I may be an honor to the holy religion I profess and the character I sustain among these poor people. Attended family and secret prayers, and found some relief and comfort therein. Blessed be the Lord!

Friday, Sept. 29.—Had some discourse with two persons who had lately come into town. In the afternoon

* As this is the first allusion which Brainerd makes to the Moravians, it may be proper to caution the reader on a few points. One class of Whitefield's disciples, in their enthusiastic reliance upon the teaching of the Spirit and distrust of dead orthodoxy and cold forms, had assimilated to the Moravian modes and adopted their name. Whitefield himself was supposed to lean in that direction. His friends and the friends of truth and order became alarmed, and filled the country with pamphlets and exhortations against the errors and moral effects of the Moravian communities. Imbued with the spirit of these warnings, Brainerd approached the Moravian settlements. As he had no confidence in their orthodoxy or order, but regarded them as perverters of his brother's Indian converts, and as he was entirely ignorant of their language and early training, it is no wonder that he thought "no good could come out of Nazareth," or the Moravian Bethlehem itself. There was, doubtless, much that was puerile, fanciful, and fanatical among the early Moravians; but, at the same time, they have evinced a godly sincerity, a Christian earnestness and benevolence, which for more than one hundred years have made them models of piety and martyrs in spreading the gospel. In noting their defects, we must not overlook their virtues.

had a little time to write, but was diverted by a Christian friend who came in to see me.

As I came into the town from a visit, I heard the noise of a drunken Indian, which was affecting to me. Took care that he should not be able to hurt anybody, and, when I had seen him tied, returned home.

Saturday, *Sept.* 30.—Attended morning devotions, and spent some time in discoursing with several Indians, especially with him who was drunk last night. In the afternoon rode out and visited a poor woman who had lately lost her husband. Found her very sorrowful, and endeavored to administer some comfort to her. Returned home and spent some time in studying, and in the evening attended a religious meeting with my people; read and explained thirteen verses in the beginning of the eighth chapter of Matthew, and made some practical improvement of the same, concluding with some exhortation. The Indians attended with seriousness, and one or two discovered considerable feeling. Returned home; attended family and secret duties, but had no special enlargement.

Lord's day, *Oct.* 1.—Arose something later than usual this morning, and first of all endeavored to commend myself to God in secret, and beg his gracious presence and assistance in the holy duties of the day. Then attended family prayer, and retired again to my study, and spent a considerable part of the morning in prayer. In the forenoon preached from Isa. i. 18, but had no great freedom in any part of divine service. Notwithstanding, one or two persons were considerably affected. In the afternoon preached without an interpreter. Very diligent and solemn attention was given to the word, but nothing else remarkable appeared in the assembly. Returned home; took some refreshment, and again convened my people together, and preached to them from Isa. i. 19, 20; sundry of the people were much affected. After meeting discoursed with a stranger who had lately come, being one of that company of Indians to whom I preached September 1st, 2d, 3d, and 4th. Two more also of that company are come to town, and as yet behave well, and seem to be rationally convinced of the truth of the Christian religion. May the Lord graciously carry on this work in their hearts! Returned home, and spent some time in conversation with a *negro*, who came in to see me, and was pleased to hear him express so much of the life of religion, and with so much simplicity.

Read several chapters in the Bible, and afterwards attended secret devotions with some freedom and comfort. Praised be the Lord for all his goodness to me!

Monday, Oct. 2.—Attended family and secret devotions, and after a little while called my people together, and entertained them with a discourse from Luke vii. 43, intending the next day to set out on a journey to visit a number of Indians about forty miles above the Forks of the Delaware; and after I had explained the word, and showed that it was my duty to preach the gospel to other poor Indians as well as to them, I gave them some directions how to behave and conduct in my absence, and earnestly exhorted them to behave seriously and to live like Christians one with another, and concluded the meeting with prayer. They all attended very seriously, and several persons were much affected with what they heard.

Spent the remainder of the forenoon with the Indians. In the afternoon came the Rev. Mr. Gilbert and William Tennent to my house, with whom I spent some time, and then set out with them for Princeton. Went with Mr. W. Tennent to Mr. Hall's, and tarried there all night. Spent the evening in conversation, particularly endeavoring to make up a breach that subsisted between him and his father-in-law, Mr. Bainbridge, and we were so intent upon it that we sat up till after midnight. I felt something poorly in body, but it pleased God to give me some comfortable sense of divine things, especially in secret devotions. Praised be his holy name!

Tuesday, *Oct.* 3.—Arose pretty early this morning; attended family and secret devotions, then took leave of Mr. Hall and his spouse, and proceeded on my journey with Mr. Tennent. Called at Justice Stockton's, but did not tarry there, but went forward to Maidenhead (Lawrenceville). Came to Mr. Bainbridge's, hoping to make up the difference between him and his son-in-law. Was kindly received, and treated with courtesy. Had a long discourse, and some encouragement that the breach might be healed.

Took leave of Mr. Bainbridge and his wife, and went forward to Trenton, and, after taking some refreshment, attended the Presbytery, and spent the afternoon in business. Rode with Mr. McKnight * to see a relation of his, and tarried there all night. Was very poorly in

---

* This was the Rev. Charles McKnight, pastor of the church of Cranberry and Allentown. He was licensed by New Brunswick Presbytery, June 23, 1741, and installed October 16, 1744. April 21, 1767, he accepted a call to Middletown Point, Shark River, and Shrewsbury, Monmouth county.

He was captured by the British and his church burned in the Revolution. He died in 1778, and his church at Shark River became extinct. He was Brainerd's nearest clerical neighbor and firm friend.

body, and not well able to sit up long. Attended family and secret prayers, and went to rest.

Wednesday, *Oct.* 4.—Returned to town again, and sat in Presbytery all the forenoon; felt sick, but was able most of the time to sit in Presbytery. In the afternoon the commission of the two Synods of York and Philadelphia met, to endeavor an agreement of the two Synods. Spent the evening with the commission of York Synod, but felt very poorly.

Thursday, *Oct.* 5.—Felt much out of health this morning; notwithstanding, being appointed to preach at Amwell, on my way to the Forks, I took leave of the ministers, and arrived at Amwell meeting-house about two o'clock. Found the people generally gathered together, and it pleased the Lord to give me some freedom in the various parts of divine service. Forever blessed be his holy name!

After service, being invited by Colonel Reading, I went home with him five miles, and tarried there all night. Was treated with much kindness and respect, and was well pleased with my entertainment. Attended family prayers. Retired to my lodging-room, and spent some time in reading, meditation, and secret devotion, and had, I hope, some real sense of divine things.

Friday, *Oct.* 6.—After attending family and secret duties, took leave of Mr. Reading and his family, and came to Mr. Lewis', at Bethlehem.* Spent some time

* Bethlehem was a township on the east of the Delaware, now called Alexandria. The Rev. Thomas Lewis, referred to in the journal, was a fellow-student of David Brainerd, graduating at Yale College in 1741.

in conversation with him and his spouse; and he, having a lecture appointed this day, urged me to tarry and preach it, which I did, but was considerably straitened in the several parts of divine service. After meeting, returned to Mr. Lewis'; spent the evening mostly in conversation with him and several neighbors who came in, and afterwards attended family and secret prayers. O Lord, pardon and quicken me for thy mercy's sake.

Being a zealous friend of the Great Revival, like Davenport, Symmes, Allen, and others, he sought to escape the persecutions of Connecticut in the more peaceful borders of New Jersey. He was settled in Bethlehem October 14, 1747. Subsequently he labored at Oxford, Hopewell, N. J., Smithtown, L. I., and finally settled at Mendham, N. J., where he died May, 1778.

CHAPTER XVIII.

PREACHES AT THE FORKS—IRISH SETTLEMENT—THE CRAIGS—GNADENHUTTEN—HIS IMPRESSIONS OF THE MORAVIANS.

SATURDAY, *Oct.* 7.—Took leave of Mr. Lewis and his spouse, and came on my journey to the Forks; but, being hindered several hours at the ferry,* did not arrive at Mr. Hunter's till after sundown. Was very much fatigued; but it pleased the blessed Lord to make me comfortable in mind, and to give me much freedom in family and secret duties. Forever praised be his holy name!

Lord's day, *Oct.* 8.—Spent the morning mostly in meditation and prayer; and having inquired concerning the Indians that used to live here, and finding that they were gone, and that no congregation of them could possibly be had, I preached to the white people both parts of the day. In the afternoon, especially, it pleased the Lord to give me very comfortable freedom and enable me to press home divine truths upon the hearers. May the Lord bless the same to them for spiritual and saving good!

After meeting, spent some time in prayer to God. Afterwards attended family duties, and spent some time in conversation with Mr. Hunter and others; but felt poorly, and so retired to my lodging-room,† the same that

* He crossed the river, probably, at a place called Achen's Ferry, in Upper Mt. Bethel, about fifteen miles from Easton.

† This room was said to be an addition, probably of logs, to the

my *dear brother* David used to lodge in when he preached to the Indians in the Forks. Read several chapters in the Bible, and attended secret devotions, in which I hope I had some real sense of eternal things.*

Monday, *Oct.* 9.—Attended morning devotions, and spent some time in conversation concerning the Indians, designing to prosecute my journey among them as soon as I could; but, it being stormy, was obliged to tarry here to-day. Was much indisposed, especially in the afternoon; but in the evening felt something better, and spent some time in prayer, and wrote a little.

Tuesday, *Oct.* 10.—Took leave of Mr. Hunter and his family, and proceeded on my journey. Called at one of the Moravian settlements.† Spent some time in conversation with them, especially with one of their ministers. Tarried and dined with him, and was treated with courtesy. After dinner, took leave of them, and came forward to Mr. Lawrence's settlement, but found him not at home. Went to Captain Craig's,‡ and tarried all

---

house of the good Mr. Hunter, of Easton, Pa. It was standing within the memory of aged persons who died a few years ago.

* We insert in the Appendix, marked B, a communication prepared at our request by Matthew Henry, of Easton, author of the "History of the Lehigh Valley." He was fifty years with the Moravians at Bethlehem, and has spent his whole life in the vicinity of the Forks. It is adapted to help modern readers to follow the journeys of the Brainerds in their early explorations of that region.

† In the opinion of Mr. Henry, the historian of Lehigh Valley, this Moravian settlement was Nazareth.

‡ Craig's Settlement and the Irish Settlement are identical. It was a name derived from the number of Irish families who settled in the vicinity, the principal of whom was the Craig family. The settlement was, it is supposed, at the Lehigh Water-Gap, in Allen township, where a village still exists, and where General Craig, of

night. Visited the Justice, his father, in the evening. Returned to the captain's; spent some time in reading, attended family prayers, and retired to my lodging-room.

Wednesday, Oct. 11.—Took leave of Mr. Craig and his spouse (having been treated with much kindness by them), and came forward on my journey, and, by good providence, found a man who lived not far from the Indian settlement and was returning home. Joined myself to him, and came forward. Spent the whole day in riding about twenty miles, it being, I think, the worst road I ever saw in my life.* Came to his house, as I judged, about sundown, it being rainy, as it had been most of the afternoon. Was uncomfortable, it having been a cold, raw day. Was kindly treated by the man and his wife, and, after I had taken some refreshment, was more comfortable. Spent some time in reading and conversation, and concluded the business of the day with family and secret duties.

Thursday, Oct. 12.—Attended family and secret devotions. Took leave of the honest man and his wife, and proceeded on my way towards the Indians, and, when I came to them, found they lived in the same town with the Moravians, and were entirely brought into their scheme of religion, which inwardly grieved me and greatly sunk my spirits, especially when, in conversation with some of them, I saw how erroneous and enthusi-

---

Revolutionary memory, died in 1832, at the advanced age of ninety-two. He must often have heard the Brainerds preach. The settlement was the starting-point for their Susquehanna journeys.

* He crossed the first range of the Appalachian chain. Its height is from twelve to sixteen hundred feet, rough and rocky, and, being narrow on the top, the sides are very steep and precipitous.

astic they were in some of their tenets. However, I spent the day in this place, which the Moravians call *Canatanheat*,* partly in conversation with them and partly with the Indians. Visited all that were at home, going from house to house, but had very little satisfaction, fearing that they were—many of them—poor deceived creatures. Discoursed with some of the white people as well as the Indians, and observed their manners and behavior, and found they set very lightly by verbal prayer, either private or public, saying that they always prayed in heart, that they very little saw the necessity of informing the understanding in the doctrines of religion, dehorting from sin, or exhorting to the observation of the divine commands and the practice of godliness, saying that persons must be told to believe in and love [our Saviour], as their expression always is, "to look to and keep close to him, and then there would be no danger, but they would certainly be directed and inclined to do every thing right;" and I observed farther, as far as I could learn, that the spring and foundation of their love to the *Saviour* was because he suffered and died for sinners, and them in particular, which I endeavored to detect and show that that was not the only foundation or the prime cause of a true believer's love to God and Jesus Christ, &c. &c. I also, in my discourse with one who bears the character of a minister, endeavored to convince and impress upon him the danger of deceiving the poor Indians and making them believe that they had an interest in Christ's merits when they have never experienced a change of heart, for I observed that they made

* This was, doubtless, Gnadenhütten, founded by the Moravians in 1746. It was situated on the Mahoning Creek, near the Lehigh River, about three miles below Mauch Chunk (Indian Bear Mountain), and about thirty above Easton.

no account of a previous work of the law, and some of the Indians told me they had not been under any special concern, but, after they were baptized, their hearts began to love *our Saviour*, and one of them told me his heart was *quite good*, *quite good enough*. And this I found to be the case, that the Moravians would tell the Indians how Christ died and suffered, and ask them whether they loved him and were willing to be baptized, and, if they assented, would proceed to administer the ordinance to them, and admit them, if adults, to the Lord's Supper. When the evening was come, the bell was rung, and the whole society called together to attend divine worship, upon which I also attended. They first sung one or two short hymns in the German language, then one of them took a text of Scripture and spoke upon it perhaps near a quarter of an hour; after this they sung a hymn, and concluded with a very short prayer; and this I found was all they pretended to do, either public or private. I could not but be affected at the slight these people put upon prayer to God, and felt an inward desire to retire alone and pour out my soul to him; which I did, and it pleased the gracious Lord to give me considerable freedom and enlargement. Blessed be his holy name! After this, had some further conversation, and concluded the day.

Friday, *Oct.* 13.—Arose early this morning, and retired for secret devotion; it pleased the Lord to give me some freedom at the throne of grace. Not long after, the whole society was again called together by the ring of the bell, and the service of this morning consisted only in singing a short hymn or two, and a few words spoken to the people, which I understood was the more usual way, and that they rarely joined prayer with them. After this, was invited to breakfast, at which there was no appearance of a blessing asked or thanks returned, even so much as in a mental way. Soon after breakfast was over I took leave of the Moravian Brethren, and proceeded on my journey; rode up the west branch of the Delaware * a little way, and came to two Indian wigwams, in which were several Indians, though some were gone from home. Some of the Indians were turned to the Moravians, but three or four of them were not yet brought over. With these I spent considerable time, discoursing with them in the best manner I could, and got the promise of one or two of them to come and see me at our Indian settlement in the Jerseys, and then took leave of them, leaving them to the mercy and goodness of God. Then I proceeded on my journey. Rode between fifteen and twenty miles to visit a number of Indians that lived near a great hill, called the Blue Mountain.† Spent some time in conversation with such of them as I found at home, and found that the most of them were baptized by the Moravians, and brought into their interest. This made me despair of doing any considerable good among them; so, after some conversation, I took leave of them for the present (it being now evening), and went to the house of a High-Dutchman, being the nearest and best I could find, and there lodged. The man could speak a little broken English, but his wife did not know one word. Their not being able to understand English rendered my circumstances very difficult, and, besides, they were extremely poor. After I had made the best provision I could for my horse, &c., I retired for secret

---

* Brainerd means the Lehigh River. Lehigh in Indian means Fork. The river was so called as the Fork of the Delaware.

† This was the Kittany Mountain, called still in the neighborhood the Blue Mountain from its appearance in the distance, looking from the east upon it.

prayer, in which it pleased the Lord to give me some encouragement in the midst of my difficulties; then I came into the house and got something for my refreshment, and after some time returned again and prayed. Then came into the house, and, when we had sat some time, endeavored to make the man understand something about God and the propriety of family prayer before we lay down to sleep, but could not, by all the signs I could make, give him to understand any thing of it. So, endeavoring to commit myself to God, lay down on some straw that I had provided, and it pleased the Lord to grant me considerable refreshment by sleep. Praised be his holy name for all his kindness toward me!

CHAPTER XIX.

CROSSES THE BLUE MOUNTAIN—MR. LAWRENCE VISITS BETHLEHEM—MR. BRAINERD'S DISCUSSIONS.

SATURDAY, Oct. 14.—Arose early in the morning, and, when I had taken my breakfast, bid farewell to the family, and visited the Indians again, and spent some time with them. Found two of the Moravian Brethren, who came the evening before and had been with them all night; after some time spent with them and the Indians, took leave of them all except one of the Brethren, who came forward with me. With some difficulty passed over the great mountain yesterday, on horse, which is by far the highest and most difficult I ever crossed. From thence I came to the Irish Settlement, on the west branch of the Delaware. Went to Mr. Craig's, and there found Mr. Lawrence,* he being just returned from his journey. Spent some time in conversation with him.

---

* The Rev. Daniel Lawrence was born in Long Island, in 1718, studied at the Log College, and was licensed at Philadelphia, May 28, 1745. He began his labors at the Forks of Delaware (Easton), May, 1746, and was installed the third Sabbath in June, 1747. The Forks north and the Forks west, fifteen miles apart and embracing the country between, was the field of his labors. His health failed, and in 1751 he removed to Cape May, but was not installed before 1754. He died April 13, 1766.

Being of the same age and similar sentiments, his presence in that wild region must have greatly cheered his friend Brainerd.

Lord's day, Oct. 15.—Soon after I arose, retired for secret prayer, and it pleased the Lord to give some considerable freedom therein. Blessed be his holy name! Spent the morning partly in conversation with Mr. Lawrence, and partly in meditation. About eleven o'clock attended public worship, and, at Mr. Lawrence's discretion, carried on divine service. Had some freedom in prayer, but not so much in preaching, especially in the first part of my discourse; but towards the close, especially in the applicable part, it pleased the Lord to give me some deep feeling of divine truths, and some assistance in pressing the great and solemn truths of the gospel on the minds of the audience. May the Lord set home his word upon their conscience with divine power! In the afternoon, heard Mr. Lawrence from John xiv. 19, in which he seemed to speak with some life and power. After meeting, came to Mr. Craig's with Mr. Lawrence.

Monday, Oct. 16.—Spent some time with a number of people who came from home (Bethel) about the same time with me, with a design to hunt in those parts; and had I been seconded in my undertakings, and found any number of persons together who were not brought into the Moravian scheme, they (the Bethel Indians) would have been with me. But, my design being frustrated, most of my other people (being about fifteen in number) went no farther than Mr. Lawrence's upper settlement, and were there when I returned from my journey above. With those I spent most of the forenoon, conversing with them and instructing them as I thought proper, and so took leave of them for the present; and in the afternoon rode with Mr. Lawrence to Bethlehem,* having a

* Bethlehem was founded by the Moravian Brethren in 1741. It

desire to get some further acquaintance with the Moravians. When we came there, we were received with kindness and treated respectfully. Had considerable conversation with two or three of them, though several of their principal men happened to be out of town. After some time, with as much decency and candor as I could, touched upon some matters of faith; but they seemed much to dislike speaking in a way of dispute, and when any thing was proposed would handsomely wave it, and endeavor to say as little as possibly they could. However, from what they did say I was abundantly confirmed that they held those errors referred to in my journal of Thursday last, and from their discourse I could not but fear they worshipped the human nature of Christ, for I never heard the name of God once mentioned among them, and that they did not really believe the morality of the Sabbath. For, as I discoursed with them concerning the day to be kept, they said they looked upon the seventh day to be the proper day; upon which I said

---

comprised five hundred acres. Its schools have obtained a high reputation, and the entire Moravian community sustain an excellent character for industry, neatness, probity, and true religion. It must also be said that in their records they have spoken kindly of both the missionary Brainerds. In Heckwelder's Narrative, under date of 1747, he says:—

"About this time the Brethren [Moravian] also paid a visit to the Rev'd David Brainerd, missionary to the Indians in New Jersey, and rejoiced at the success with which that faithful servant of God had been blessed in preaching the gospel to the Indians; and some time after this, that worthy man, accompanied by some of his converts, visited both Bethlehem and Gnadenhutten, much to his satisfaction."

We have also received from the records of the Moravian Community at Bethlehem the following notice of this visit of Brainerd and Lawrence:—

"*October* 27, 1749.—Mr. John Brainerd arrived here to-day, in company with Mr. Lawrence, the Irish minister who lives in the Forks. Mr. Brainerd has been at Gnadenhutten and Meniolagomikok, visiting the Indians. He also examined them in religious matters.

"*October* 28.—Mr. Brainerd left; and he showed himself very friendly, and was cordial in his manner."—*Bethlehem Diary*, 1749.

I thought it was not essential to religion which, but that one ought to be kept holy, and no work ought to be done upon it but what was of absolute necessity; and I thought we ought every day, and in all our actions, aim at the glory of God; yet if God had reserved one day in seven peculiarly for himself, it should be devoted more to his immediate service? To this they made no reply.

When the evening was come, I retired for secret prayer, and it pleased the Lord to comfort and refresh my soul in this holy duty. Blessed be his holy name! After some time I attended on their evening service, which consisted in singing hymns* and speaking about five or six minutes to the people. When we came to the house where we

---

* The Germans are poetic and musical, and in the early days of the Moravian Community they employed hymns in worship which they would not tolerate at the present day. We have in our possession a book, entitled "A Collection of Hymns, compiled chiefly from the German. London. Printed for James Hutton, Bookseller, in Fetter Lane. MDCCXLIX." It purports to be a standard Moravian hymn-book. The first article of the Augsburg Confession in rhyme, with a prayer attached, we give:—

HYMN I.

Tune—The Saviour's Blood and Righteousness.

ARTICLE I.

1 I do believe, that in Heaven's throne Dwells one Divine being alone!
Who's called (as he himself explains), And truly is, God, and remains
2 Of like duration of pow'r one, As God our Father, God the Son,
And God the Holy Ghost likewise. This three one Divine being is,
3 Which is eternal, without parts, Immense, Almighty Pow'r exerts;
His Mission ne'er can measured be, Nor fathom'd his Benignity.
4 Maker, Preserver of as well Things unseen as the visible,
By the word Person is expressed, No piece divided from the rest,
5 Nor some mere property, which may Itself in different kind display,
The Church by Person understands, What by itself subsisting stands.

PRAYER.

O holy, blessed Trinity! God Father! Warring under thee!
God the Holy Ghost! Thou being guide, I with God's Son go, side by side.

We give also the thirty-sixth hymn entire:—

were to lodge, I questioned those who came with me why they did not pray at their meeting, inasmuch as we receive all from God, and entirely depend on him, why they did not acknowledge him? The answer was, that they did pray publicly sometimes, when it was the mind of our Saviour. I questioned them further, but had no satisfaction. Afterwards, in discourse, one gave me to understand that they believed assurance to be the essence of faith, or, that there was no true believer but knew that he was so. I took occasion to let him know that I did not believe what he said, but another replied that they did not incline to dispute the point. Several other things were proposed to them in way of discourse, which they waved; so it was difficult to know what their sentiments were in many points. Thus we spent the evening, and finally were shown our lodging-room.

Thursday, Oct. 17.—Arose early this morning, and endeavored to commit myself to God by prayer, and was

---

HYMN XXXVI.

Tune—Elder of thy Train.

1 Dear Church, art thou well, In the side Hole's cell?
Art thou other places scorning, At thy rising in the morning?
Hid within the Shrine Of this wound divine?

2 Dost thou know the hand Of thy dear husband?
Hast thou been so well all over, That thy eyes the bliss discover,
And this day by day? Canst thou Amen say?

3 Really that Hole dear, Open'd by the spear,
Always Room enough is given, That we all may there be living;
And who will be well Must come in this cell.

4 Husband of Thy She (Banished once from Thee),
But, through Thy most holy Passion, Purchas'd out of every Nation,
From all curse and fear, Stand her Husband dear!

I think intelligent readers of the nineteenth century will decide that the Rev. John Brainerd was affected by the prejudices of his age and party in his criticism on the Bethlehem Brethren; but, from the specimen we have given of Moravian hymns, it must be admitted that there was much in the Brethren to deserve criticism.

going with Mr. Lawrence to attend the Moravian service; but, as we were going towards the house, we perceived that worship was over. Upon which we returned to the house again, and had some further conversation with two or three of them. After breakfast, we took a walk with one who conducted us into the town to view the buildings, &c. Went into their place of worship, viewed the organs that were played there, and several other things. Among the rest saw a writing, in very large letters, placed over the minister's seat, which was written in the German language. I desired him who conducted us to explain it, which he did, as near as I can remember, to this effect: "*O wounds* (meaning the wounds of our Saviour), *preserve us*, *thy people*, *and me*, *in particular!*" So, after we had viewed every thing that was curious, we returned to the house where we had lodged; and, hearing of a number of Indians who lived about three miles down the river,* I had a mind to make them a visit. We rode to see them. I found they were Indians whom I had some time ago been acquainted with, for several of them had lived a considerable time at our Indian town in Cranberry, and went from thence because one of the men had a mind to put away his own wife and take another woman, and I could by no means allow it, and reproved him because he would leave his wife and go and lodge in the same house where this other woman lived. Finally they went off together, and several more, near relations, with them. With these I had considerable discourse, and found they were all baptized by the Moravians, although they appeared to me to be the same poor, carnal creatures that they were when they went from the Indian town.

* This place is now called Skinnersville, near Freemansburg.

In discourse with them, I found the Moravians had changed their names, although all except one had Scripture names before. I asked them why they changed their names; and one of them said that the Moravians said they had those names in sin, and they would not have them now when they were come to be Christians, and that Jesus Christ gave them a new name. After this, I asked them if they came also to the Lord's table. They said, "Yes." I inquired if they understood the nature of the ordinance. They were light and vain even while I was speaking of this most solemn institution of Christ, which surprised and much affected me. However, I found by what they said that they were taught to believe the real Presence of Christ in the sacrament, that they did absolutely eat and drink Christ's body and blood. I endeavored to show them the absurdity and impossibility of it, and observed that these elements were only a sign or representation of Christ's body and blood, and not really and substantially so; and, withal, they had need take care how they approached that holy ordinance, for such as come unworthy eat and drink their own damnation; or, in other words, that it would be much worse for them than if they had stayed away. So, after I had discoursed some considerable time, I invited them to come and see me, which they promised they would do, at Cranberry, and so took leave of them; being in heart affected at their miserable, blinded condition. May the Lord have mercy on them for Christ's sake!

Returned to the Moravian town, called and took leave of the Brethren, and returned with Mr. Lawrence to Mr. Craig's.* Took some refreshment, and then, according

---

* Craig's Settlement was about seven miles from Bethlehem north, and three miles from the present town of Catasauqua.

to my appointment, went to see a number of my people mentioned yesterday, proposing the next morning to set out on a journey homeward; but they proposed to tarry a while longer in these parts, and it pleased the Lord to give me very comfortable freedom in speaking to them from Phil. i. 27, and in other parts of the divine service. Many of the white people were present.

After the meeting was over, took leave of the Indians, it being now considerably in the evening, and returned to Mr. Craig's with Mr. Lawrence, and had very comfortable freedom in private and family devotions. Praised be the Lord for all his goodness of this day!

Wednesday, Oct. 18.—Spent the forenoon with Mr. Lawrence, the weather being stormy; but in the afternoon, the storm having abated, took leave of him and other friends, and came to Mr. Hunter's,* upon the north branch of the Delaware, in the evening.

Thursday, Oct. 19.—After attending religious duties, took leave of Mr. Hunter's family, and came, in company with him, to Mr. Henry's, at Greenwich.† Dined there, and then proceeded on my journey, and came to Mr. Lewis', at Bethlehem. Spent an evening with him, and attended family and secret prayers, but had no special freedom.

---

* At Aken's Ferry. Mr. Alexander Hunter was a native of the North of Ireland, a sound Presbyterian. He settled at Upper Mt. Bethel in October, 1730. Being an educated man, he was made one of the first magistrates of the county in 1747 or 1748. He was a man of large influence in his day.

† Greenwich township lies opposite Easton. The church was about three miles from the river. There is still a flourishing Presbyterian congregation on the spot. Its present edifice is the third one.

Friday, Oct. 20.—After duties of the morning were attended, took leave of Mr. Lewis and his spouse, and came on my journey to Hopewell. Went to Mr. Paine's, and, it being near night, lodged there. Spent the evening mostly in religious conversation, and had very comfortable outgoings of soul in family and secret duties. Blessed be the Lord!

Saturday, Oct. 21.—Arose early this morning. Took leave of Mr. Paine (his family not being up), and came to Mr. Alling's. Attended family duties, and took breakfast with him, and then proceeded on my journey. Dined at Mr. Stockton's, in Princeton. Came home a little before sundown, and found my people generally well, though two or three were sick. The Lord be praised for all his goodness to me on my journey, and to my people in my absence!

Called them all together, and, after friendly salutation, carried on divine service among them, in which it pleased the Lord to give me very comfortable freedom. Explained a part of the ninth chapter of Matthew from the beginning. The Indians were, many of them, much affected.

Lord's day, Oct. 22.—Attended secret and family devotions, and then retired again, and spent the remainder of the morning in meditation and prayer. Attended public worship at special time, but had no considerable enlargement in any part of divine service. Preached from Matt. ix. 12, 13; yet two or three persons seemed to be much affected and really concerned for their souls. Oh that God would carry on the work which he has so graciously begun in their hearts till they become lovingly acquainted with himself!

In the afternoon, preached without an interpreter, and it pleased the Lord to give me freedom in the several parts of divine service. There seemed to be a very solemn and devout attendance on the worship of God, and considerable concern in one or two interpreters.

Monday, Oct. 23.—Visited one of my people who had been taken ill the day before. Spent some time in conversing with him, and afterwards prayed with him; then came home. Spent some time in writing and praying, and did some business of a secular nature.

Tuesday, Oct. 24.—Arose early this morning, and attended family and secret duties. Spent some time in the forenoon in particular business; afterwards had a little time to write. In the afternoon, spent some time with a Christian friend who came to see me. After him, came in a woman of my congregation, who seemed to be much oppressed in mind. I inquired into the reason of it, and found it was because she had been out of temper and even angry at something that occurred in my absence, which she confessed with as much sorrow and brokenness of heart as I think I ever saw in my life. It was very affecting to hear her speak of what she had been guilty of, and to see the distress and anguish of her soul: I think I never saw any person more deeply affected with the death of the dearest relation than she seemed to be at this time and on the account before mentioned. She desired me to pray with and for her, which I did, and, after some further discourse, dismissed her. Then visited a sick man, and endeavored to have some discourse with him, but could get him to say but little. After this, visited a poor woman who has been in a low condition for a long time; had some discourse with her and her husband, keeping them in mind of the dispensations of Providence towards them, and that they should labor to be resigned to his holy will and to have a sanctified hope of the effective dispensations of God. Afterwards spent some time in writing, and concluded the business of the day with prayer.

Wednesday, Oct. 25.—Attended to some secular business, and spent the remainder of the forenoon mostly in writing. In the afternoon, visited the sick man mentioned yesterday; had some considerable discourse with him, although he was not now so free to talk as I could have desired; then prayed with him, in which it pleased the Lord to give me some comfortable enlargement.

Spent the remainder of the day and part of the evening in removing my household goods from the place where I had lived hitherto, about half a mile, to a place which the Master and I bought to commode the mission; it being dangerous to live on the Indian land, by reason of the proprietors who lay claim to it, and we having now a little house built outside.

Thursday, Oct. 26.—Went on with the business I had begun last night, and spent the whole day in fitting up the house and setting the things in order. In the evening, convened my people, and, after prayer and singing, entertained them with a discourse from Isa. xlix. 15, 16, in which it pleased the Lord to give me good freedom, and it was also, I trust, a comfortable season to some of my hearers.

CHAPTER XX.

GOVERNOR BELCHER AND HIS LADY VISIT MR. BRAINERD—HIS SERMON ON THE OCCASION.*

FRIDAY, *Oct.* 27.—Governor Belcher having sundry times manifested a desire of coming and seeing the Indians, and his purpose of doing it upon his return from Amboy to Burlington,† at the rising of the Assembly, I thought it my duty to wait upon his Excellency, and, hearing that he desired to leave Amboy this day, after family and secret devotions, set out for that place, and met the governor about a mile on this side of the town. As soon as I had opportunity to speak with him, I found he desired to be at Rev. Mr. W. Tennent's that night, and the next day visit the Indians, and I must wait upon him the round; which I did, and arrived at Mr. Tennent's a little after sundown. Spent the evening mostly in conversation, but felt poorly in body, having a pain in my head, and yet comfortable in mind.

Saturday, *Oct.* 28.—Attended family and secret devotions, and tarried till after two o'clock; it being very stormy, spent the time mostly in conversation with the governor, Mr. Tennent, etc., and then, the storm being

---

* This visit of the governor was a great event in the life of the secluded missionary, and he marks his estimate of the honor by the seriousness and particularity of his description.

† Burlington was at this time the seat of government of New Jersey.

something abated, set out for home. But, the weather being so uncomfortable, did not attend a religious meeting as usual, but spent the evening mostly in reading, meditation, and prayer.

Lord's day, Oct. 29.—Attended the religious duties of the morning, and then spent some time in my study, but had not much freedom in private devotions. At the usual time attended divine worship in public, and preached both parts of the day from Matt. viii. 35. The Indians as well as the white people attended seriously, but nothing remarkable appeared in the assembly.

After meeting, visited a woman that seemed to be near her end; conversed with her as much as I could by reason of her weakness, and prayed with her. Then, taking leave of her, returned home, took some refreshment, and then visited another sick person. Conversed some time, and prayed with her; and, after we had sung a hymn, returned home, and attended family and secret prayers, in which it pleased the Lord to give me some comfortable freedom and refreshment. Blessed be the Lord!

Monday, Oct. 30.—Took care to make some provision to receive the governor, he having appointed this day to make a visit to the Indians. After I had put things in some order, sat down to study, being expected to preach to the Indians before the governor. About twelve o'clock, waited upon his Excellency and Madam Belcher, his consort. Mr. Tennent and his spouse, and many others, attended the governor; and, after a little time, I called the Indians all together, and preached by an interpreter from Matt. xi. 23, in which I had comfortable freedom; and when I had a little explained the words, raised these two propositions:—1. *That those who enjoy the means of grace and the ordinances of the gospel are highly honored and privileged of God;* 2. That those who abuse or misimprove such precious privileges *make themselves awfully guilty before God, and procure to themselves the most sore and dreadful judgments;* viz., "*Those who enjoy,*" etc. 1st. I observed it was a great honor, because ordained and sent by the most honorable Being, viz., by the great God; 2d. Because the proposals are most honorable in their own nature. It was a great privilege, because thereby we were taught to know God and how to love and glorify him; (2) because we are taught our perishing condition, and how we may obtain deliverance and recovery therefrom; (3) because we are thereby taught those things, and the way to make ourselves happy in this world; (4) we are taught those things which make us comfortable in death and completely and eternally happy in the next world.

And as to the second proposition, viz.: "*That those who abuse,*" etc., I inquired when persons might be said to improve the gospel aright, and when to abuse it. (1) When they don't accept of the Lord as he is offered in the gospel; (2) when they don't square their lives according to the rules of the gospel; (3) when, instead of being humble and thoughtful for such blessed privileges, they are lifted up with pride and forgetful of their duty to devote themselves to God. When it is thus with the people, the means of grace and ordinances of the gospel are abused, but rightly improved when the contrary is true.

And as to the punishment inflicted on those who abuse the means of grace, it would be as near as it could be to conform to the dignity of the Being offering and the greatness of the mercy offered, and, consequently, unspeakable and eternal. Then I proceeded to some improvement. (1) A use of examination,—that all should examine how they had improved the gospel, etc.; (2) of exhortation to all to make a wise and faithful improvement of the precious privileges they were favored with; and of the honor done them by God, and by man also, with relation *to the governor's visit* among them. The Indians, and many friends, were much affected; and after meeting, taking some refreshments, the governor, his lady, etc. walked through the town, to visit the Indians and see their town and dwellings. I waited upon them, and returned a little after sundown. Spent the remainder of the evening in conversation with the governor and others, and had something of freedom in holy duties. O Lord, I thank thee for all thy goodness to me! *

Tuesday, *Oct.* 31.—Arose early this morning, and attended religious duties. Waited on the governor, with Mr. McKnight and sundry others, about twenty miles. Dined with his Excellency, and waited upon him and his lady till they had mounted a chaise to go to Burlington. Took leave of them, and returned home in the evening; then, after having attended family prayer, retired to my lodging-room, attended secret devotion, and went to rest.

Wednesday, *Nov.* 1.—Arose early; wrote a little, and in the afternoon attended the funeral of a woman, and had, I hope, some sense of divine things in speaking to the people and in prayer. May the Lord bless what was

---

* Mr. Brainerd's sermon before the governor, which, from the importance of the occasion, he saw proper to record, is certainly not remarkable for either originality, point, or power; but it had the grand excellence of faithfulness and truth. It is the simple gospel. His use of the governor's visit as a motive to honor the gospel is a little strained, but with the Indians might be telling.

spoken to the benefit of the hearers! Returned home, and spent the evening mostly in settling accounts with the Master and some other secular business.

Thursday, *Nov.* 2.—Attended religious duties in family and secret. Spent the day in transcribing my journal for Scotland; in the evening attended a religious meeting, designing to have catechized as usual, but, my interpreter being absent, I could not proceed; so I spent the time in giving them some familiar and easy instructions, concluding with exhortation and prayer. Visited also, this evening, two sick persons.

Saturday, *Nov.* 4.—Attended holy duties this morning, but was in a great measure lifeless. The Lord mercifully guide and quicken me by his Holy Spirit!

Spent most of the day in writing my journal; but in the evening attended a religious meeting with my people, and explained part of the ninth chapter of Matthew, concluding with some exhortations. It pleased the Lord to give me something of freedom, but no special enlargement.

Lord's day, *Nov.* 5.—Spent the time before meeting mostly in prayer and meditation; attended public worship at the usual time. Blessed be the Lord, had freedom in the several parts of the divine service! Preached both parts of the day from John xiv. 19. Extraordinary attention was given to the word by the white people as well as the Indians, and several persons were greatly affected with divine truths. Toward evening, met again. Requoted some of the words of my preceding discourse, and had considerable enlargement. I have reason to think that, through the grace of God, it has been a refreshing season to some of God's dear people; and to his holy and blessed name be all the glory!

Returned home, and spent some time in writing. Attended family and secret duties.

Monday, *Nov.* 6.—Attended morning devotions, and spent the remainder of the day in writing my journal for Scotland. In the evening was troubled with evil thoughts, and in my attendance on holy duties, especially in secret, I was something broken and distracted. The Lord pardon and graciously deliver me for Christ's sake!

Tuesday, *Nov.* 7.—Between eleven and twelve o'clock called my people together, it being the Quarterly Day of Prayer,* and, when I had reminded them of the greatness and solemnity of the business we were come upon, made one prayer. I preached a discourse from Gal. vi. 9; after which we spent some time in prayer. Several of the Indians prayed, who seemed to be much affected; but nothing remarkable appeared in the assembly.

* Quarterly Concert of Prayer on the plan of President Edwards.

CHAPTER XXI.

VISITS ELIZABETHTOWN—HIS LABORS THERE.

WEDNESDAY, Nov. 8.—Set out on a journey to Elizabethtown. Visited Mr. Arthur, at Brunswick, and Mr. Richards,* of Rahway, and arrived at Mr. Woodruff's in the evening. After a little while, I went with him and Mr. Spencer to see a man who was truly supposed to be near his end. Had some discourse with him, though he was not able to say much, and afterwards prayed with him. Returned to Mr. Woodruff's, and spent the rest of the evening in conversation with Mr. Spencer.

Thursday, Nov. 9.—Spent the day mostly in transcribing my journal for Scotland. Attended on evening service, and preached from John xii. 26, but had very little sense of divine things, which was exceeding distressing to me; but in the last prayer was more comfortable.

Returned to Mr. Woodruff's, and felt very poorly in soul and body; afterwards had some relief by secret prayer. Blessed be God!

Friday, Nov. 10.—Went with Mr. Spencer to Newark, to see Mr. Burr, with whom I had considerable business.

* The Rev. Aaron Richards, of Rahway, graduated at Yale in 1743, and was ordained by the New York Presbytery in 1749. Throughout his life he was harassed by hypochondria: still, he was a good man, and ended his life peaceably, May 16, 1793, in the forty-fifth year of his ministry and the seventy-fifth year of his age.

Tarried with him till about one o'clock, and then came to Elizabethtown and attended the funeral of the man mentioned yesterday, at which I felt very solemn and impressed.

Lord's day, Nov. 12.—Was something composed in morning duties, but had no special enlargement; was also poorly in body, and felt faint.

Attended public worship at the stated time, and it pleased the Lord to give me freedom and, I trust, some real sense of divine things. Preached on a funeral subject, and endeavored to suit my discourse in some measure to the circumstances of the sorrowful widow the funeral of whose husband I had lately attended. After some intermission, attended divine worship again, and it pleased the gracious Lord to give me much enlargement in preaching his dear and blessed gospel, and in other parts of divine service. Baptized a child, and had much freedom in prayer previous to that holy ordinance. May God sanctify the opportunity of this holy day to the living good and benefit of his people!

After meeting, came to Mr. Woodruff's, and endeavored to pour out my soul to God for a blessing on his word in this and other places, and that he would mercifully please to make and keep me humble.

In the evening, visited a dear friend; then went, with Mr. Woodruff, to see the sorrowful widow mentioned in the forenoon, and found her in a sweet, comfortable, and Christian frame. Was much refreshed in conversation.

Returned to Mr. Woodruff's, and transcribed a letter to Dr. Philip Doddridge. The Lord has made this day comfortable to my soul. Forever blessed be his holy name! My people were supplied by Mr. Spencer, who tarried with them Sabbath over in my stead.

Monday, Nov 13.—Attended religious duties; then took pains to gather some money among my friends to help a poor Indian who was cast into prison for debt. Had some success. Afterwards took leave of my friends, and came out of the town.

Dined at Mr Pierson's, and proceeded on my journey. Visited the poor Indian above mentioned in prison, and gave him some good advice, and so came forward; but, being hindered at the ferry, did not get home till some time in the evening. Some time after I came, was informed by the Master that several of the Indians had been drunk in my absence, and had fought to such a degree that one, in all likelihood, would have been killed had he not been rescued. This greatly sunk my spirits. Alas! it seemed to me as if all would come to nothing; and my heart was discouraged within me. I fell down before the Lord, and it pleased him to help me to open my cause to him; and, blessed be his name, I found some relief.

CHAPTER XXII.

JOHN BRAINERD'S PASTORAL LABORS—HIS TRIALS—HIS CONSECRATION —END OF DIARY—ITS CHARACTER.

TUESDAY, *Nov.* 14.—Attended holy duties this morning with something of freedom; afterwards had opportunity to discourse with two of the Indians who had lately been drunk. They seemed to be convinced of their folly, and discovered considerable sorrow for it, but, I have reason to fear, will do the same again the first opportunity. The Lord grant it may be otherwise!

Spent some time in taking care of temporal business, and, towards the close of the day, rode to Freehold, designing to visit a number of my people who were still at the medicinal springs. Went to Dr. Le Count's, and there spent the evening in pleasant and edifying conversation and in family and secret duties.

Wednesday, *Nov.* 15.—After the performance of holy duties, took leave of the doctor and his spouse, and came to the place where the Indians lived. Found one in a low condition, and had little expectation that she would ever recover. Had considerable discourse with her, but found that she was under some darkness, although I trust she is truly gracious; then prayed, in which it pleased the Lord to give me freedom.

Took leave of them for that time, and rode to the court-house, having some business in the court relating to the Indians, but could not accomplish it. Came to

Mr. Tennent's, and tarried with him all night. Spent the evening mostly in conversation, but was exceeding low in spirits and had little freedom in holy duties. The ill circumstances and ill behavior of some of my poor people, and the difficulties that living among them is attended with, are often very painful and depressing, and were so this evening. May the Lord help me to behave like a Christian under all afflictions and difficulties!

Thursday, Nov. 16.—Spent the forenoon with Mr. Tennent, it being rainy and uncomfortable weather. In the afternoon set out for home. Did some business of a temporal nature on the way, and came home in the evening. Spent some time in reading, and was more comfortable than I had been in family and secret duties. May the Lord's holy name be forever praised!

Friday, Nov. 17.—Was obliged to spend much time in temporal affairs; but in the afternoon, the Master having permission to ride out, I kept the school.

Saturday, Nov. 18.—Attended family and secret duties this morning, but had no special enlargement. Oh that the Lord would help me, and graciously quicken me by his Holy Spirit, that I might always live and act for him!

Visited one of my poor people (a professor) who had been out of the way with drink, and found him in great distress on that account. Discoursed with him a considerable time, and could not but be deeply affected with his condition, and yet could not but inwardly rejoice to see him sensible of the wrong he had done to God and the reproach he had brought upon religion.

There are two or three Indians who make a profession of religion who, alas! have of late been overtaken with drink, which has given me awful apprehension concerning them, and God only knows the event; but, oh, may the Lord save his cause from reproach and them from finally falling away! It has been sometimes like death to me; I know not how to bear up under the weight of it. But God (forever adored be his holy name) has hitherto helped me, and will, I trust, still be my helper. As to the rest, their behavior has been comfortable, although there have been some slips among some. I have often thought of the apostle's words, and, I trust, felt the weight of them, 1 Thess. iii. 8: "*For now we live, if ye stand fast in the Lord.*" It has been life to me to see their good behavior; and the contrary has sometimes seemed more bitter than death.

Spent the remainder of the forenoon in conversing and discoursing with my people. In the afternoon, spent some time in endeavoring to inform myself concerning the foundation of the Indian language, intending to learn it. Had considerable discourse with a young man about eighteen years old, and could not but entertain some hope that he had undergone a saving change. In the evening called my people together, and explained and applied a portion of Holy Scripture that I thought was suited and adapted to the circumstances we were under. There was serious attention.

Returned home, and *spent the remainder of the evening in reading my brother's Life* (*having lately obtained the book*), and God, I trust, made it profitable to me. Attended family prayers, and afterwards sat up till twelve o'clock. Spent the time in reading, meditation, and prayer; had longing desires after holiness, and inwardly covenanted to be devoted to the service of the blessed God. Oh, when shall it once be! Come, dear Lord Jesus! come quickly!

Lord's day, *Nov.* 19.—Had, I hope, some real sense of God and divine things in holy duties. Oh that God would daily increase the same!

Attended public worship, and it pleased the Lord, I humbly trust, to give me some assistance in the various parts of it. Preached in the forenoon from Psalm cxix. 136; in the afternoon, without an interpreter, from John xiv. 19. The Indians as well as the white people (a number of whom were present) gave good attention to the word spoken, but nothing very special appeared in the assembly. I had much sweetness and comfort in my soul this day, especially in the afternoon. Blessed be the gracious Giver!

After I came home, felt much sweetness and calmness in my soul, and so through the evening earnestly desired to be wholly devoted to God and perfectly free from sin. Oh, how sweet is such a feeling! Oh, how much does it surpass all that the world can possibly afford! May I ever live with and for the blessed God! May I wholly die to all sublunary things, and be wholly wrapt up in the joy that is unspeakable and full of glory. May I live upon those glimpses that I have of Christ, or, rather, on Christ himself while I have but, as it were, a glimpse of him, till I shall come to the beatific vision and full fruition of him in the blessed heavenly world!

Monday, *Nov.* 20.—Felt some earnest desire to give away myself to God, if the Lord would graciously accept of me, abundantly qualify me for his service, and make me an instrument of his praise and glory.

Spent the forenoon in reading and writing; in the afternoon was obliged to ride out upon some temporal business, which took me till some time in the evening. Felt much indisposed after I came home, but in an hour or two was much better. Attended family prayer, and afterwards read in the Bible, in which I had considerable comfort, as also in secret duties. Blessed be the Lord! Oh that I could wholly and forever be devoted to his service!

Tuesday, *Nov.* 21.—Attended holy duties in family and secret. Oh, how apt is my poor heart to warp off and wander from the blessed God! Oh, 'tis most affecting that I should wander from him, who is in himself the best good and only satisfying portion of my soul! Oh, when shall I be delivered from this body of death, and drop this world's earthly chains and fetters!

Was obliged to spend this day in hard labor, excepting that I read a little in the Bible in the morning, and in the evening composed a letter to a friend. My little affairs of a temporal nature being much out of order by reason of my being absent, and being exceedingly crowded with other business since my return, I had no time to do any thing, scarcely, as a preparation for the winter; and having tried to procure some help, but being unsuccessful, I am obliged to do it myself.

I was exceedingly troubled for a little while this day with evil thoughts, for which I desire to be humbled before God, and even to hate and abhor myself; but soon had some deliverance. Blessed be God! Though I had no realizing sense of the wrong done to God, or of his goodness to me, till the evening, then it pleased the Lord to give me an humbling sense of it, and an earnest desire to be free from this body of sin and death. The Lord help me to keep a more strict watch over my heart for the future, and mercifully strengthen me against all temptations!

Spent the evening partly in reading the Bible, and partly

in *reading my brother's Life, and could not but be affected at my own extreme barrenness* and nonconformity to God. I saw that, although he was an imperfect man, I was very short of being what he was and doing what he did, which made me ashamed to look up.* However, I trust I had some real desire to devote my all to God, and both in family and secret devotions had comfortable outgoings of the soul to God. Blessed be his holy name! Oh that the same might be increased day by day!

End of Diary, November 21, 1749.

Thus ends the daily journal of this eminently pious young man. It is but a fragment; it was written only for his own eye, and barely escaped destruction with his other papers. It is often repetitious and tedious in detail. But we could not consent to pass it over, nor even abridge it; for, with all its imperfections, there is something in it which will deeply interest every true Christian heart longing for holiness and communion with God. It presents a most perfect exhibition of the hidden life of a devout and holy missionary of the Cross. It confirms a saying common in Haddam, the native town of the two brothers, that, "*although not so great a man, John Brainerd was as holy as his brother David.*" In each there was the same profound humility, prayerfulness, activity, self-denial, and longing for Christian perfection.

* The marked influence of David's biography on the heart of John indicates how entirely they sympathized in their aspirations for holiness and in their zeal to do good.

If David's journal develops a wider range of thought and a more graphic power of language, it is also shaded with a deeper sadness, from which the diary of his brother is relatively free. I think our missionaries in the field will see much in John Brainerd's diary to remind them of their own experiences and to stimulate their self-denying labors. He speaks to them over a lapse of one hundred and twenty years as a pioneer in their great work; and in communion with his spirit they will realize that, by his example, he is still with them as an elder brother.

CHAPTER XXIII.

EXTRACT FROM THE MINUTES OF THE SCOTCH SOCIETY—MR. BRAINERD'S FULL REPORT—HIS EVENTFUL JOURNEY—HIS LABORS, PERILS, AND OBSERVATIONS.

THE difficulty of constructing a continuous narrative of Mr. Brainerd's life and labors has induced us to prefix the date of each successive year, and throw under it such fragments concerning him as time has left. In this way we shall glean up many insulated facts which would otherwise be lost.

1750.

In this year we have no other record of Mr. Brainerd's life than a few hints in the reports of the Society in Edinburgh. They say:—

"At a meeting held in Edinburgh, on 22d March, 1750, letters were read from the New York Correspondents, in which the Society was recommended to augment Mr. Brainerd's salary, on account of his frequent and long journeys. This recommendation the Society at its next meeting declined, on account of the low state of the funds."

Extract from the Minutes of date Edinburgh, 5th January, 1751.

"The Committee reported, that they have received letters from the Society's correspondents at New York, and from Azariah Horton, one of the missionaries among the infidel Indian natives upon the borders of that and neighboring province, with journals of the said Mr. Horton from to and of Mr. John Brainerd from to , which journals are put into the hands of members for their perusal, and thereafter to be put into some proper hand in order to compose a short narrative of the progress of the gospel in those foreign parts. That the Committee have, for the encouragement of these foreign missionaries, allowed them to draw for their salaries each half-year, and have ordered the payment of six pounds, the half-year's allowance for boarding and educating one of the young Indians at the new-erected College of New Jersey. In the said letter from the Correspondents at New York, they renew their request for an augmentation of the salary of Mr. Brainerd, and propose an application to be made to the General Assembly for a national collection for the benefit of the said new college. The General Meeting, having heard the said report, approved of the above-mentioned order for payment of the foreign missionaries' salaries each half-year, as also of the above allowance for the young Indian, and remit to the Committee to do with respect to the augmenting Mr. Brainerd's salary as they see cause."

Minutes of 2d November, 1752.

"The Society, upon the recommendation from London in respect of Mr. Brainerd's great fatigue and expense in his mission, augmented his salary from £40 to £50."

The death of Rev. David Brainerd is noted in the Records of the Presbyterian Church for 1748. The name of John Brainerd is entered the same year, and the Rev. Elihu Spencer allowed to sit as a correspondent. In 1749 and 1750, Brainerd seems to have been absent from the Synod.

1751.

This year Mr. Brainerd was enrolled as a member of the Presbytery of New York,* at the Synod meeting in Newark; and was henceforth until late in life seldom absent.

We have procured from Edinburgh the following letter, which will show how Mr. Brainerd was employing himself:—

To the Reverend Ebenezer Pemberton, President of the Correspondent Commissioners from the Honorable Society in Scotland for Propagating Christian Knowledge.

Journey to Wyoming.

REV'D SIR:—

After the account given in my last, which concluded with April 22d, I continued with the people of my charge residing at Bethel, in New Jersey, one Sabbath, and carried on the worship of God among them as usual. The Wednesday following I convened them together again for divine worship, and, being about to take a long journey, entertained them with such instructions and exhortations as I thought would be most for their benefit and edification. The next day, having visited some of my people, and being visited by them in general, I took leave of them, and set out in the afternoon with a design to visit the Indians living on Susquehanna and parts adjacent.

* Minutes of the Synod of New York, pp. 236, 244.

Leaving my people to the care of the schoolmaster, who was to reside constantly on the spot, and expecting also to have my place supplied most if not all the time by the neighboring ministers, on Saturday evening following I arrived at the Forks of Delaware; being much retarded in my journey by having a horse to lead, that was much laden with provisions for the journey.

At this place I tarried three days, partly to procure some more provisions for my journey, in which I proposed to be out about three months, and partly to visit a number of my people who for some time past have lived in these parts and attended the ministry of the Rev. Mr. Lawrence, among whom I hoped to procure one to go with me as an interpreter.

On Wednesday, May the 7th, I set out with my interpreter for Susquehanna, and the next Saturday evening we arrived at an Indian town on that river, called Whawomung, the same mentioned in my journal last year. I had a very fatiguing journey to this place, being obliged to travel almost the whole day on foot by reason of the almost impassable mountains, and the horses being deeply laden with provisions for our long-intended journey. When I came to the town, the people generally came together, seeming glad to see me, and treated me with more courtesy and kindness than I expected, which was a great comfort to me after my tiresome and tedious travel. I had not been in town long before I understood that there was an army from the Six Nations, who were upon a march with a design to fight the Catawba Indians, who live on the borders of South Carolina.*

* These people have been at war one with another for many years together, and frequently commit the most cruel barbarities one upon another; but at a late treaty between the Governor of York and Commissioners from several provinces on the continent and the Six

An Indian Dance—Frightful Gestures.

In the evening, these Indians gathered to one place, where they held a martial dance, and such an one as indeed was almost terrible to behold. The manner of the dance was as follows. There was a post set up, about seven or eight feet high, painted in spots with red, and on the top of it was fixed a bunch of feathers. Near by it was a fire, and not far off sat two Indians, one with a small drum and the other with a gourd of rattles in each hand, with which they made a continual noise. The Indians placed themselves in a great circle round them all, and jumped round with great swiftness as one man, or as though they had been framed together; sometimes erect, sometimes half bent, and sometimes seeming to let or rest themselves on the strength of their knees, but still going round in the same order, making a most hideous noise, and seeming to try to look as fierce and furious as they could. Indeed, their countenances were rueful to behold; they appeared rather like creatures come from the infernal regions than inhabiters of the earth. This horrid dance they held, I suppose, the most of the night; and the dolorous noise of them was the last thing I heard before I dropped asleep. The next morning, which was the Lord's day, they went off early, and were so intent upon their journey that to try to detain them for any time was utterly in vain.

Divine Worship evaded.

After they were gone, I visited the principal men of

United Nations, at which a number of these Catawbas were present, a cessation of arms was concluded upon; and there is a prospect of a firm and, we hope, lasting peace between them, which will very much prepare the way for the spreading of the gospel among the Indians in general.—*J. B.*

the town, and, having informed them of my design in making them a visit, asked them if they would call the people together and attend upon divine worship, that I would instruct them in those things that would be for their good, etc. They told me, that the next day the Indians up and down the river were to meet together at their town (as, indeed, I had heard before), that the young men must all go a-hunting in order to get some provisions for their brethren, and the women also had much to do to make ready for their coming. I urged, that the old people and such as could be spared might attend, and pressed the matter as much as I thought it would bear; but they seemed to be so much taken up with their expected meeting that they had no ears to hear about any thing else. Besides, a grand objection was that the interpreter was gone.* When I saw that no meeting could be obtained, I visited the people at their own houses, and discoursed with them in the best manner I could upon religious subjects.

Indian Council—Indian Poison.

The next day the Indians, generally, came together, according to appointment. They came, up and down the river, to this as a central place, near thirty miles. Their meeting was not on the account of my coming, but to consult about some affairs of their own, and, as I understood, particularly with a view to a revelation lately made to a young squaw in a trance. What the particulars of this revelation were, I am not able to say; I

---

* It must be observed that, though I had an interpreter with me, yet he could not serve as such in this place, because they speak a dialect entirely different from him, and there is but one in the town that can speak English well, though sundry others can do considerable at it, and the most of them understood some.—*J. B.*

made some inquiry, but the Indians seemed somewhat backward to tell. But this much I learned, that it was a confirmation of some revelations they had had before, and particularly that it was the mind of the Great Power that they should destroy the poison from among them.* Soon after the Indians were met together, I sent a message to them, desiring to be admitted into their Council, and, withal, letting them know that I had something of importance to propose to them; and, when they had sat one day, they sent me word that I might come. Accordingly I went, and, when all was ready, I informed them of the errand and design I was come upon, how and by what authority I was sent, and that I had a sincere desire to instruct them and their children in those things that would be greatly for their benefit both in this and the future world. By their answer, I perceived that some of their old and leading men especially had imbibed some late prejudices against Christianity, which, I afterwards understood, were occasioned by the false reports of some ill-minded persons who had been trading among them.

The Indians' Theory of Races.

They told me that the great God first made three men and three women, viz.: the Indian, the negro, and the white man. That the white man was the youngest bro-

* 'Tis said that the Indians keep poison among them, and that it is of such a nature that if any one takes it in his breath it will cause him, in a few months, to pine away and die. And this is supposed to be in the keeping of their old and principal men, and by this means they keep the people in continual dread of them. And some of the Indians seem to be so sottish as to imagine that they can poison them by only speaking the word though they are at the distance of twenty or thirty miles, and, consequently, are afraid to displease them in any point.—*J. B.*

ther, and therefore the white people ought not to think themselves better than the Indians. That God gave the white man a book, and told him that he must worship him by that; but gave none either to the Indian or negro, and therefore it could not be right for them to have a book, or be any way concerned with that way of worship. And, furthermore, they understood that the white people were contriving a method to deprive them of their country in those parts, as they had done by the sea-side, and to make slaves of them and their children as they did of the negroes; that I was sent on purpose to accomplish that design, and, if I succeeded and managed my business well, I was to be chief ruler in those parts, or, as they termed it, king of all their country, etc. They made all the objections they could, and raked up all the ill treatment they could think of that ever their brethren had received from the white people; and two or three of them seemed to have resentment enough to have slain me on the spot.

I answered all their objections against Christianity, and likewise the many grievous allegations laid to my charge, and whatever was spoken by any of them. But, when I had done, they told me that I had been learning a great while, and 'twas no wonder if I could out-talk them; but this did not at all convince them that I was not upon a bad design, and therefore they would give me no liberty to preach to their people, but charged me not to come any more upon such an errand.

Mr. Brainerd discouraged.

When I saw the Indians so much prejudiced against Christianity, I did not think it prudent to urge the matter any further at this time, but to wait till an opportunity should present for the removal of their groundless prejudices; therefore I did not attempt to gather any number of them together, but visited them at their several houses, and had much opportunity of conversing with them at my own, and of showing them kindness, having good store of provisions, of several sorts. which they much wanted and were very glad of.

Indians pump the Interpreter.

After some time, they sent for my interpreter, and discoursed with him on the subject of Christianity. They desired him to give them the reasons why he forsook the Indian ways and became a Christian, which he freely and readily did. And when he had done, and answered to many questions, they told him they should be glad if the Christian Indians should come and live there; that they should take their choice of all the uninhabited land on Susquehanna, and should have liberty to worship God as they thought right, and that the young people in those parts should have liberty also to join with them, if they desired it.

The interpreter told them that the Christian Indians could not come to live there unless their minister came with them. They replied, the minister must not come, because he was a white man; that, if one white man came, another would desire it, etc., and so by-and-by they should lose their country. But the minister might live on the nearest land belonging to the white people, and visit them as often as he would. This, the interpreter insisted upon, would not do, but the minister must come with them and live on the spot. The result of the conversation was this: the interpreter, upon his return home, should inform the Christian Indians that the king and the principal Indians on Susquehanna desired to see them (or at least a number of them), and would have them make them a visit as soon as they could conveniently. Accordingly, soon after his return to the Forks of Delaware, he made the Indians in this place a visit, and faithfully delivered his message; and, as sundry of the Indians in those parts desired the same of me, and as I cannot but hope, through the blessing of Heaven, it may be a means of removing some of their unjust prejudices against the Christian religion, I have encouraged the matter, and propose to send a number of the most judicious of my people, so soon as their circumstances will permit.

Mr. Brainerd loses his Horses.

When I had tarried some time at this town, and used the best endeavors I could with the inhabitants to bring them to a good thought of Christianity, I determined to cross the river and go over the mountains to the West Branch, upon which I proposed to travel two hundred miles or more, but was unhappily prevented by losing my horses, which, I have abundant reason to think, were taken by an Indian trader who was there at the time of my first arrival in the place. So, when I had made thorough search for my horses (employing Indians day after day for a week together), and found all my endeavors unsuccessful, I was obliged to give away the remainder of my provisions, and make the best of my way home, which, indeed, I did not accomplish without great difficulty and much fatigue.

My interpreter, the first day that my horses were missing, as he was looking for them, unhappily so lamed himself that he was capable of being no further help to me, but rather stood in need of being tended upon. He was utterly unable to walk; nor was it possible that I could travel with such a load as was necessary to be taken with me. I used my best endeavors to procure a horse among the Indians, but all to no purpose, and finally was obliged to purchase a canoe and come down the river, expecting to have gone near one hundred miles by water to the first white inhabitants. But, having proceeded about thirty miles, I stopped at an Indian town, where I tarried a day or two; and finding myself much fatigued with coming thus far, and having little expectation of help in my farther progress down the river, I renewed my endeavors at this place also to get a horse, which, through a kind providence, I at last obtained. Accordingly, the same day, taking leave of the Indians, I set out through the woods alone, being obliged to leave my interpreter behind; and having, through the goodness of God, been preserved from many dangers in crossing the mountains until I arrived among the inhabitants.

Mr. Brainerd buys a new Horse, and gets home.

I had the good fortune soon to purchase a horse, whereby I was enabled to proceed further on my journey, and the next day came to the Forks of Delaware, from whence I sent back an Indian with my horse to convey my interpreter home; and there expected his coming, which was not many days after, to our mutual comfort and satisfaction.

After some small tarry here, in which I preached several times to those of my people who reside at this place, and sundry others that were providentially with them, I proceeded on my journey home, and on Saturday, the 8th of June, arrived at the Indian town in New Jersey, having been gone six weeks wanting four days.

On the Lord's day, June the 9th, I attended and carried on the worship of God with my people, as heretofore. The next day I set out on a journey to New

York, proposing to have a meeting of the Correspondents in order to consult about some affairs relating to my mission among the Indians, particularly what measures were to be taken to remove those prejudices above mentioned; but two of the members being out of town, and those in the country not having been before apprized of it, I was not able at this time to accomplish my design.

The Indians afraid of Slavery—Ministry disrespected.

The reason why I was so speedy in my endeavors to obtain a meeting was this. There was a treaty appointed at Albany, and to begin within a few days, between several of the governors on the continent, or their commissioners, and the chiefs of the Six United Nations; and I could not but think that this presented us with a fair opportunity of doing something for the removal of sundry obstacles that lie in the way of propagating the gospel among the Indians, especially on Susquehanna. Particularly the Indians there object that they have not leave from the chiefs of the Six Nations, whom they own as their heads, to allow ministers to come and preach the gospel to them; and, till that be obtained, they can give no encouragement. Another thing is, the false and malicious stories of such as trade among the Indians, which are to this effect: That the great men in York, Philadelphia, etc. have laid a scheme to deprive the Indians of all their lands in those parts, and to enslave them and their posterity; that the ministers are sent among them purely to accomplish that design; that they are knowing to the whole matter, and can assure them of the truth of it, etc.; and one thing more that is a great hindrance to the propagation of Christianity among them is the carrying of strong liquors.

Now, the commissioners at their treaty would be under

special advantages to remove these several obstructions out of the way, and so open a door in some measure for the spreading of the gospel in those parts; and, though I could not obtain a meeting of the Correspondents, yet I had opportunity to converse with several of the members upon these and sundry other points relating to the Indians. I likewise had opportunity with the Rev. Mr. Pierson, of Woodbridge, to wait on Governor Belcher, and to acquaint him with these things; and, at our desire, the governor wrote to the commissioners on this head.

Bigotry illustrated.

I had farther an opportunity to converse with a gentleman, the commissioner from South Carolina, who appeared forward to do any thing that might subserve the propagation of the gospel among the Indians; and, when the commissioners came together at Albany, this was proposed as one thing to be treated upon, but, as I have been since informed, was opposed and flung out principally by the New York commissioners, because no missionaries of the Established Church appeared to go among the Indians on Susquehanna and parts adjacent. But, as it is well known that the French are using many artful endeavors to bring the Indians over to their interest, and there is much danger of it if some speedy care is not taken, how impolitic, as well as fraught with bigotry, this was, I leave others to judge.

Mr. Brainerd home again.

I returned to my charge the same week, and on the Sabbath ensuing carried on public worship as usual; the next Sabbath I administered the Sacrament of the Lord's Supper, which seemed to be a time of revival, especially to the communicants; since which time I have been steadily with my people, attending divine services among them, except that I have supplied two destitute congregations once, and was absent one Sabbath by reason of attending a meeting of the Correspondents.

And as to the state of the Indian congregation, I think there is considerable encouragement. The Indians have been, in general, more healthy of late than they used to be, and some of them much more disposed to industry than heretofore.

There has not, indeed, been for some months, that I know of, any work of saving conversion among them; but there is a number that appear to be under some degree of spiritual concern, especially at times, and the people in general attend the public worship in a serious and consistent manner.

Some of those likewise that make a profession of religion, and who have not heretofore lived so agreeable to their profession as could have been desired, have behaved well of late, and I cannot but hope will continue so to do; and the children make desirable proficiency in reading, learning their Catechisms, etc. In a word, the circumstances of these people appear with a more encouraging aspect this summer than for some time past, and we cannot but hope that He who has so graciously begun will perfect his goodness among them.

As to the Indians on Susquehanna, the account I have given of my late journey there, and the treatment I met with among them, seems to hold forth some discouragement. 'Tis true, indeed, there are at present some obstacles in the way; but these, I doubt not, with some prudent care and pains, might in a great measure be removed. But no undertaking of this nature can possibly be managed without a very considerable expense, which at present there is no provision for. For instance: the chiefs of the Six Nations might be treated with upon the affair above mentioned in their own country; and doubtless those could be found that would freely go upon such an errand.

Better Support required.

But there is nothing to support the charge that would necessarily attend such an action, and consequently the matter must rest where it is. And many things of the like nature might be done which would greatly prepare the way for the spreading of the gospel, and be matter of encouragement to missionaries to use endeavors for the same. But for want of this they must be obliged to encounter many unnecessary difficulties and discouragements, which ought by no means to be added to those that are unavoidable in Christianizing a heathen pagan people. This mission, ever since I have been concerned in it, has greatly suffered for want of a more liberal support; and I have constantly looked upon myself as one sent out to fight with his hands tied. I am sensible the goodness of God is to be acknowledged for the provision that has been made, not to mention the great kindness of that honorable and worthy Society that has been the instrument of conveyance to us; but yet the medium is much too short to support and carry on such an undertaking.

Disadvantages of his late Journey.

When I took my late journey, I was obliged to go under the utmost disadvantages. Instead of having a fellow-missionary with me and a number of Indians, I was obliged to go alone, with one Indian only; and had not wherewithal so much as to pay his wages, and bear the expense of his travel. Now, the benefit of a number of Indians, besides the help they would afford a missionary on the way by hunting, etc., is very apparent. Their presence and conversation with their pagan brethren would greatly tend to remove their jealousies, and convince them that the missionary had a real design for their good; and though finally the missionary should be denied the liberty of preaching, yet, having the advantage of carrying on divine worship and preaching to his own company, numbers of the pagans would out of curiosity come to hear, and so be in the way of receiving some good.

But such a thing as this cannot be done without something to bear the expense of it. The Christian Indians in this place would, any of them, cheerfully go upon such an expedition if any thing could be done for the support of their families the meantime, and a small matter could be allowed them so that they might be able to support themselves. But so low are their circumstances that, without some help, they cannot afford much assistance without exposing their families to extreme want.

These Indians, when they first embraced Christianity, were inexpressibly poor, vastly involved in debt, and, notwithstanding the help they have received from the white people, are still poor and indigent. They are not able to work upon their land so much as I could desire, being many of them obliged, while they should be planting, sowing, etc., to do something to supply their present exigencies, or, perhaps, to pay some debt that they are sued for, as has often been the case since I have been among them, which has made me frequently reflect on the words of the wise man: "*The destruction of the poor is their poverty.*" And though they do apparently gain upon it in respect of their outward condition, yet nothing is to be expected from them that is any way chargeable and expensive.

Brainerd's want of Funds to enable him to succeed.

When I went to Susquehanna last year, I was obliged to find my interpreter's family a considerable part of their eatables while he was gone, as well as bear his expenses and give him considerable beside.

And, though the Correspondents were pleased to make the addition of £10 York currency to my salary, yet that was so far from being sufficient to support my extraordinary expenses in such a journey, that it would not make my salary competent at home, much less enable me to hire an interpreter and bear his expenses through the journey. It is scarce possible for any one who has not made trial to conceive what is necessary to support a missionary among a number of indigent Indians, especially where there is much sickness and the poor creatures frequently reduced to the last extremity, as has been much the case here; and likewise where pagan strangers are frequently coming to the place, who are yet (if possible) more needy, and want something of a temporal nature to encourage them at their first coming. What would be counted a plentiful salary among the English will by no means support a missionary among the Indians.

The Correspondents this year also, at one of their meetings a little before I set out on my journey, were pleased to vote me £12 York currency, and to bear the expenses of an interpreter, the most of which I have received since my return (there being then little or no money in the treasury), which has been a considerable help to me: but still my necessary expenses far exceed my incomes.

I do not mention these things by way of complaint. I have often thought that if the Society should please to continue me in their service, and I should see any prospect of being further useful among the Indians, I should continue in the business till I had spent what little substance God has put into my hands, and then nothing further can be expected or desired of me. But what has led me to speak of this, is because I find myself much cramped in the business I am employed in, my designs crossed, and my endeavors to convert the heathen in a great measure rendered abortive, for want of something more liberal to support such an undertaking.

Why his Susquehanna journey failed.

My last journey to Susquehanna (as I have already observed) was under the most abject circumstances, whereby I was not only exposed much more to dangers and hardships, but my endeavors in a great measure rendered useless.

I likewise proposed to the Correspondents at a late meeting to take a journey into Alagana, a large country near five hundred miles from Susquehanna, where, I am informed, there are great numbers of Indians, and that some have manifested a considerable desire to have a minister come among them. I have for some time been desirous of making them a visit, and proposed in my late journey to have gone at least two hundred miles that way, and was not without hopes, if I should then enjoy a comfortable degree of health and be smiled upon by Divine Providence, to have gone through and made an entrance among them; but, meeting with an unhappy disappointment, I was obliged soon to return, as related above.

Then I proposed in my own mind, and afterwards in

a meeting of the Correspondents, to take a journey into that country next spring; but this proposal was immediately rejected, because there was no money to defray the expense that must necessarily attend such a journey.

Brainerd's reason for taking long Journeys.

If it should be wondered why I incline to take such journeys, so remote from the people of my more peculiar charge, and looked upon as desiring to run before I am sent, I answer: These people among whom I chiefly reside are but a handful in comparison with those that live remote from the white inhabitants. They are gathered together in a collect body, and, with the help of a schoolmaster residing constantly among them, and the neighboring ministers, who can with ease visit and preach to them once in a while, they may be under comfortable circumstances, the worship of God may be kept up among them, and they may be without a constant ministry for some time without any great detriment to the cause of religion among them.

Reason for sending Missionaries to places where the Gospel was never Preached.

Indeed, if there were a sufficient number of missionaries among the pagan inhabitants of this land, if the Society for Propagating the Gospel in heathen and infidel parts, instead of sending the missionaries where the gospel is universally preached already, and bestowing their bounties upon a wealthy, opulent people who are sufficiently able to maintain the gospel themselves,—if, instead of this, they would send them into the heathenish and benighted parts of this land, where the people are *perishing for lack of vision*, so that they might be generally supplied,—if this was the case, a missionary might well be employed wholly among these people, and doubtless to better purpose than many of our English missionaries who are sent under a pretence of gospelizing the heathen. But, as the Indians are universally involved in darkness, and under the most wretched and deplorable circumstances, there is no one, I believe, who has seriously thought upon it, and especially been an eye-witness to their sad and perishing condition, that would not be earnestly desirous to afford them some relief, and be ready to use any lawful means to that end. Nor could he content himself to be confined to one little spot, when whole countries are dying for want of knowledge. It has been matter of sorrow to me that I could do no more towards spreading of the gospel among the heathen as well as promoting the work of God in my own congregation; and truly no small trial to find myself so much pinched and unable to take those measures which, I have been satisfied, would be of special service to the cause I am engaged in, for want of that which is so much abused by the most of mankind, and serves them only to gratify their lusts and accomplish their lawless desires.

A Female School desirable.

And here I cannot but mention one thing in particular that has been much upon my mind for some time, and which, I doubt not, would be of singular service to the cause we are endeavoring to promote in this place; and that is the setting-up of a female school,—a school for the benefit more especially of the younger sort of women and girls, at which they might be instructed in the several sorts of business that the white women are employed in.

The female inhabitants of this place are much better inclined in all respects than the men. They are better, in general, as to their morals, and much more industrious, but, in the latter respect, not under half the advantage. The men have plenty of land to work upon; but the principal means that the women have to get any money is by making baskets and brooms; and, as we have lived long in this place, they have pillaged the country round about, so that there is now no suitable wood within a great distance whereof to make these wares, and, consequently, many of them are obliged to be almost idle at home, or else scatter abroad where suitable stuff can be found, which is attended with great inconvenience.

These women would gladly come into an English way of living, if they were able; but, being unable to purchase wool, flax, etc., they are obliged to keep on in their old track, and so to buy all their clothing at the ready penny. And this still keeps them low, and renders them unable to procure those materials by the benefit of which they might get into a better way.

Brainerd buys Spinning-wheels for the Indian women.

I have indeed, some time ago, bought them several spinning-wheels with some money that I begged for that purpose, hoping that this might be some encouragement to them, and some have done a small matter at spinning linen; but, having nobody to instruct them, and especially being unable to purchase flax, it has in a great measure dropped. Now, if there could be a small fund raised whereby a Mistress could be supported for a year or two, a few more wheels and other materials procured, I doubt not but in a little time they would get into a way of making their own clothing, which they have hitherto bought at a dear rate by brooming, basketing, and the like. This, it appears to me, would be of unspeakable advantage to the cause, for by this means they might not only clothe themselves at a much cheaper rate, but would be more constantly at home to attend public services, and their children to attend the school; whereas they are now obliged to be much absent from our exercises of divine worship, and frequently to take their children with them. And truly 'tis in vain to pretend to keep these people together without bringing them into an English method of living. In order to make them a Christian people, considered as a body, and to keep up a Christian church among them, they must even in temporal respects conform to the manners of the Christian world.

Indians waiting to see the Result of Christianity.

Many of these people are sensible of this, and are using endeavors to get into such a way. Several of late have discovered an inclination to put out their children to learn trades, and some have actually done it,—a thing that heretofore they have shown a great aversion to. And in sundry other respects they have manifested a disposition to conform to the English; and I cannot but think if we could be at a little more expense with them, they would soon be brought into a better way of living. And the better circumstances these people are under, the more encouragement there would be for the remote Indians to embrace Christianity. They are now, many of them, waiting to see how it fares with their brethren who are become Christians, and whether they are in a better condition than themselves who remain heathen; and doubtless would be much influenced one way or the other, either to reject or embrace the Christian religion, —I mean, as to the outward and external part of it. I am sensible that for a person or people heartily to embrace this religion and become truly Christian, there is absolute need that the power of Almighty God be exerted, and that nothing short of the irresistible operations of his Holy Spirit will produce such an effect,—which may the Lord grant as an attendant of his gospel throughout the whole world!

Thus I have, after some sort, represented the state of the Indian affairs here and elsewhere, and what appears to me necessary to the further propagating the gospel and carrying on the work of God among them, secretly hoping that, through the blessing of Heaven, it may some way or other be a means of strengthening our hands and helping us forward in so good a work.

May the Lord open the hearts of his people as opportunity shall present to contribute liberally to such a pious and charitable design. May many faithful instruments be raised up and sent forth, who shall be willing to *spend and be spent* in so good a cause; and may the effectual operations of the Divine Spirit attend a preached gospel to the most distant parts of the world, till the *knowledge of the Lord shall cover the earth as the waters cover the sea, and all flesh shall see the salvation of God* through Jesus Christ, to whom be glory forever. Amen.

(Signed) JOHN BRAINERD.

BETHEL, August 30, 1751.

CHAPTER XXIV.

MR. BRAINERD'S SALARY—HIS LONDON LETTER.

1752.

THE salary of David Brainerd, as we have said, was forty pounds (two hundred dollars) a year. He says that, in addition to this, he had spent in less than three years fifteen hundred dollars of his own means to carry on his mission,—all this in addition to his support of a candidate for the ministry in Yale College. John Brainerd probably had less means, and, as he was about to marry and settle in life, and was subjected otherwise to extraordinary expenses in his labors, it is no wonder he felt pinched and sought an "augmentation of stipend." His first application failed, but he succeeded to a moderate extent the next year. We quote again from the records of the Scotch Society in Edinburgh:—

Extract from the Minutes, dated Edinburgh, 21*st September,* 1752.

"Read the minutes of the correspondent members at London, at their meeting held the sixth day of August; that he had paid twenty pounds, as a half-year's salary, to Mr. John Brainerd, from the fifteenth day of September, one thousand seven hundred and fifty-one years, to the fifteenth day of March last, as missionary-minister abroad, whereby there is a balance in Mr. Johnston their cashier's hands of one hundred and eighty-five pounds, nine shillings, and nine pence; that the said Correspondents at London have recommended to this Society to augment the salary of the said Mr. John Brainerd, in respect of his very great fatigue and expense in his missions. The Committee, after reasoning, resolved that the said Mr. Brainerd have ten pounds of augmentation to his salary, commencing from the fifteenth day of September instant."

To whom the following letter is addressed we have no certain knowledge.

Brainerd corresponded with the Rev. Philip Doddridge, the Marquis of Lothian, and many others in England. As the prefix "Rev." is attached, I am inclined to think it was sent to Dr. Doddridge, who in his "Life of David Brainerd" says he had invited John Brainerd's correspondence. The letter lies before us in a neat pamphlet. An extract from it has been often republished,* but the entire letter has never been reprinted in this country. We give the title verbatim:—

* See Gillies' Collection, Glasgow, 1754, p. 448; "Dwight's Life of Brainerd," 449, and elsewhere.

A Genuine

L E T T E R

FROM

Mr. JOHN BRAINERD,

Employed by the

SCOTCH SOCIETY for Propagating the GOSPEL,

A MISSIONARY to the *Indians* in *America*, and MINISTER to a Congregation of *Indians*, at *Bethel* in *East Jersey*,

To his FRIEND in *ENGLAND*.

Giving an Account of the Success of his Labours, as well as the Difficulties and Discouragements that attend his MISSION among those Savages.

LONDON:

Printed for J. WARD, at the *King's-Arms* in *Cornhill*.
M.DCC.LIII.

(Price 2 *d*. or 18 *d*. *per* Dozen.)

BETHEL in NEW JERSEY, October 4, 1752.

REVEREND AND HONORED SIR:—

When your courteous and obliging letter by Captain Grant arrived, I was in New England, using endeavors to procure some assistance for carrying on the good work among the Indians, the people of my charge; and since my return have been in such a low state of health, and withal so crowded with a throng of business, that I have not been able to send you an answer so soon by months as I could have desired. This, I hope, will in some measure apologize for me, and that you will be so good as to overlook my deficiency.

And now, dear sir, what shall I say? I cannot but admire the goodness of God, that he should put it into the hearts of his servants at so great a distance to think of these poor people, and to show any regard to me, who am *less than the least of all saints.* But God does his sovereign pleasure, and it is the great happiness of his children that he rules and governs the world.

I accept your generosity with much thankfulness, and, I hope, some degree of gratitude to the bountiful Author of all our mercies, as well as the instrument he is pleased to employ, and shall see that your orders are punctually fulfilled; your request, likewise, respecting some account of the Indian affairs, I shall endeavor to comply with, though I am exceedingly crowded for time.

I have been employed as a missionary among these Indians for above four years and a half, besides officiating for my brother several months during his last sickness. In this space of time the number has considerably increased, though for more than two years after I came we were visited with much sickness and great mortality.

Condition of the Mission.

We have now near forty families belonging to our society, and our church consists of thirty-seven communicants, besides two or three more that stand as candidates for admission. Our school has sometimes consisted of above fifty children, but the number at present is not altogether so great. The children in general seem to be as apt to learn as English children, and some are very forward considering the opportunity they have had. Not less than twenty, I believe, are able to read pretty distinctly in the Bible and repeat most of the Assembly's Short Catechism; and some are able to repeat it through, together with the proofs, giving chapter and verse; and sundry of them can write a decent legible hand. We have one training up for the ministry, in a great measure at the expense of the Society in Scotland: he is a very promising young man, makes good proficiency in his learning, and is, I hope, truly pious. May the Lord continue his life, and make him a rich blessing to his pagan brethren!

I have spent the most of my time, since I have been employed as a missionary, among these people, but not wholly confined myself to them. I have taken several journeys out among the remote Indians, and some to those at a great distance. By this means, with the blessing of God on my labors, I have persuaded sundry to come from distant parts and settle here, where they and their children have the advantages of instruction, which, I trust, have been blest to the saving conversion of some. May the Lord daily increase the number!

These people, thus settled on this spot, do universally do something more or less at husbandry; but they have been brought up in such an idle, wandering manner that it is very difficult to keep them steady to any business, and indeed it is not without difficulty that they learn to do the several sorts of work that belong to tillage of land, etc. But I find they gain upon it in both these respects, and I hope in some time will come to live like Christian people.

I am getting some of the boys put out to learn trades, and propose shortly to set up a working-school for the girls, at which they must be taught to spin, knit, etc. I have had my mind upon this for some time, and have made one or two attempts before, but have been unable to support the expense of it; but having of late obtained some assistance from New England and elsewhere, I hope to be able to carry on the affair to some good purpose. And I cannot but think, with the blessing of Heaven, it will be of excellent use to the cause I am engaged in, serve abundantly to civilize and bring them into a more comfortable way of living. I propose another school of the like nature for the boys, such as are not put out to trades, at which they may be learned to work, and from their very childhood inured and trained up to the business of husbandry. This might be another excellent help to our cause, if it could be obtained. I have no provision for it yet, saving that, at a very considerable expense, I have secured a large tract of land suitable for the business to be managed upon, and hope before a great while, by some means or other, to accomplish my design, and for the blessing of Heaven to succeed my endeavors.

Facilities, Discouragements, and Obstacles.

You desire me, sir, in your letter, to let you know "my encouraging experiences and prospects, my discouragements and obstructions." Some of these I have occasionally hinted at already, and shall further observe that, as the number of inhabitants in this place has increased, notwithstanding the great mortality among us, so our church is enlarged, although we lost at least a third part of those that were members of it when I came. And although some that were most hopeful and gave the fairest prospect of being a blessing among us were removed, yet the Lord hath mercifully raised up others who in some measure fill up their places; some that not long since were the basest drunkards are now become sober, and live a regular Christian life. We have a very considerable number of serious regular Christians, who are an ornament to religion; although some that make a profession have grievously backslidden. The Lord has preserved and continued a Christian congregation together, though many attempts have been made by Satan and his instruments to disperse and destroy it. And there are sundry persons besides professors that are under serious impressions and thoughtfulness about the great concerns of their souls, and one at least hopefully converted of late, whom I propose shortly to admit into the church. And though we have many careless, unconcerned souls, that seem to have little thoughtfulness about the things of another world, yet it is evident the congregation in general make proficiency in knowledge both as to spiritual and temporal things, and are abundantly more and more civilized as to their dress, behavior, and manner of living. These things give me some encouragement, and cause me to hope that the Lord will place his name here and delight to build us up, that he will glorify the riches of his grace in establishing his church in this place, spread the saving knowledge of his gospel far among the poor Indians, and cause his grace to be made known even to their most distant tribes.

As for the difficulties I meet with, they are best

known to God and my own soul. But any one that considers the education of barbarous, uncultivated heathens will easily see that it must be attended with no small difficulty to bring such to a civilized, Christian manner of life. My exercises among these people, I must needs say, have been very pressing indeed; but, *having obtained help from God, I yet live.*

The Great Evil—Intemperance.

The great and almost universal propensity in the whole nation of Indians to strong drink is a great obstacle in the way of their being brought to Christianity. This, above all others, is the sin that easily besets them, and has been the greatest blemish to the cause of religion among them in this place.

This sin of drunkenness and the effects of it have given me inexpressible trouble and anxiety of soul since I have been employed in this business; and although I have done my utmost, and even summoned all the powers of my soul to represent the evil of it, yet with some it is still prevalent.

Bad Whites—Grog-sellers.

And our neighbors the white people are not a little accessory to the commission of this evil. There is scarce one of them that has strong liquor to dispose of but what will sell to the Indians, although I have set the evil before them and earnestly besought them not to do it; and some, I have been told, will buy drink in taverns and public houses, and give them, to see if they cannot make Christian Indians drunk as well as others. Some likewise have endeavored to asperse my character to the Indians, and represent me as a vagrant, wandering fellow, that wanted to pick up something among the Indians for a living; but, blessed be God! their malicious and groundless aspersions have not had the desired effect. The poor Indians are conscious to themselves that I am their good friend, and sincerely engaged to promote their best good.

Indolent, wandering Habits.

Another thing that renders it exceeding difficult to bring the Indians into a Christian method of living is an indolent, wandering, unsteady disposition, which greatly prevails among them. In this manner they have been educated, and it seems to be so riveted into their natures that it is almost as difficult to reform them upon this point as to change their color. This has been a sore trial to me ever since I entered upon the business. I have preached one lecture after another upon this subject, and used my utmost endeavors in a more private manner to reform them, and have reason to bless God my labors in that respect have not been altogether in vain, though I have yet much exercise on that head.

His Susquehanna Tour.

In my journeyings abroad, especially over Susquehanna River, I have met with many difficulties and obstructions. The bodily fatigues of such journeys I need not say much about, though they are not so small to any one who makes the experiment. That road and the difficulties attending it are the same that my brother has given an account of in his printed journal. In my last journey there, I travelled three days without a house of any sort whatsoever, and, by reason of the extreme badness of the way, and my horse being deeply laden with provisions for the journey, I was obliged to go almost the whole on foot. But my greatest difficulty was the disappointment I met with after I came there. I found my way hedged up, and an immovable bar laid in my path, and that principally by the instrumentality of wicked men, emissaries of Satan, who trade among the Indians: these had persuaded them that I was sent by crafty men with a view to bring them into a snare, and finally deprive them of their country and liberties. Upon which the principal sachems would not suffer me to preach; but the common sort of people, being not so credulous of these false and groundless stories, would freely have heard me. With these people I tarried near a fortnight, and, visiting from house to house, endeavored in a more private manner to refute the malicious aspersions of the traders and bring them into a good opinion of Christianity.

Want of Pecuniary Means.

But, among other difficulties, the want of a more liberal support has been a great discouragement to me. Such undertakings as this are very chargeable, and cannot be pursued to any good purpose but at a great expense. I have been by no means able to take the most likely measures to convert the heathen, for want of wherewithal to support the expense that must necessarily accrue. For instance: in my last journey to Susquehanna I was obliged to go with one Indian only, and, indeed, had not a farthing for his encouragement, but was obliged to pass my word that I would pay him when I could get money. Soon after our arrival there, he accidentally lamed himself, so that I had him to tend, instead of receiving any help from him. And, to complete our misfortune, we lost our horses (which we supposed were stolen by an Indian trader who was there at that time), and found them no more during our tarrying in those parts, although I employed Indians at least a week to look for them, and, consequently, were put to unspeakable difficulty in our return home.

Now, if I had had a few pounds for the support of about half a dozen of my Christian Indians to have gone along with me, it would not only have saved me much fatigue, but, what is vastly more, would in all probability have made my journey prosperous. For these Christian Indians could have contradicted and refuted the false and groundless aspersions of the Indian traders; and, besides, I could certainly have had liberty to preach to my own company, and then, in all probability, had the whole town to hear me out of curiosity, as was once the case in a former journey there. But the want of this rendered my journey, with all its toil and fatigue, almost fruitless; and this may serve as a specimen of instances too numerous to mention in this place. On this account I have labored under great discouragement; but I hope and trust that, as this work of grace among the Indians comes to be more generally known and spread abroad, there will be greater plenty of provision for the promotion of the same; and may the Lord hasten the blissful time! Upon the whole, although I am feelingly sensible of many difficulties and discouragements in Christianizing the Indians, yet I cannot but think there has been and still is as much encouragement as could rationally be expected before any attempts of this kind were made, and that which is sufficient for us still to act upon and to make further attempts of this nature. There is ground to hope that within these seven years last past there have been at least forty persons savingly converted to God even in this small place, which at most does not contain above two hundred souls, old and young, of all sorts; and were there any spirited to go unto the more remote parts, where there are greater numbers of these miserable savages, who can tell what the Lord will do? What a glorious prospect might soon open! What numbers might we hope would quit the service of the grand impostor, and embrace the offers of the blessed gospel!

But, in order to this, proper measures must be taken, and suitable provision made. This work, in an ordinary way, cannot be accomplished but at great expense; and would to God it were a thing of more general concern among Christians! It is affecting, indeed, to see these poor, benighted souls groping in darkness and perishing for lack of vision while the light of the glorious gospel is at their next door; to see them led captive by the prince of darkness while the glorious victory of the all-conquering Jesus, and redemption by him, are proclaimed almost within their hearing! This is very affecting, indeed, and I may well say with the poet: *Quis talia fando temparet alacrymis;* and further, *Qæque ipse miserima vidi.* Oh, may the time soon come when the Lord will send out many faithful laborers, especially into the highways and hedges, that the poor, lost, deluded heathen might be gathered in! And may the set time to favor Zion in general draw near. May the harvest be great, and the laborers be plenteous, and you, reverend and honored sir, share largely in the comforts and glories of it in your own soul and in your dear congregation. My heart has long wished for the revival of religion in Great Britain, as well as in our American parts; and sometimes I entertain hopes that the Lord's time is near. May the latter-day glory be hastened, and the British realms and plantations share largely in the same.

Concert of Prayer among Indians.

The Quarterly Days of Prayer for the prosperity of

Zion are observed by some in these parts, and have been very constantly attended in my congregation; and some of my people have appeared very affectionate and warmly engaged at such times. May the Lord hear and answer the supplications of his people, and cause his church to arise and flourish, and even become a praise in the whole earth.

Gratitude for the Past.

I humbly thank you, dear sir, for your pious endeavors by letter to animate and strengthen me in my arduous and difficult work; I hope I shall also be favored with an interest in your prayers that I may be faithful to my trust and successful in my undertaking. You was pleased to encourage me likewise about using some endeavors to afford me further assistance as to outward things, and desire me to let you know whether it would be best sent in money or goods. I thankfully acknowledge your kindness, and must beg leave to submit it to yourself, to do that which you can with the greater convenience; either will be very acceptable, and, if nothing, still I shall be under great obligations for what is past. I bless God I am not in pinching necessity, and yet, I must needs say, my income is much too small, and I cannot well carry on my business without a more liberal supply. My people are most of them extremely indigent, and, instead of affording me any help, I am obliged continually to be assisting them in money, provision, etc. Nor is it possible for any one, who has either any bowels of compassion or concern for the promotion of the cause, to live among them without. My annual allowance from the Society is no more than forty pounds* sterling, whereas sundry of our mis-

---

* It was increased to fifty pounds this year.

sionaries from the Society for Propagating the Gospel in Foreign Parts have sixty, and some seventy, besides something very considerable from their people, I believe near half as much more. And, by the way, whether that money be improved in the best manner, while it is employed to maintain missionaries in a populous and plentiful country,—as New England, in particular, where, I believe, there are not less than four hundred regular well-settled ministers, and the people universally able to maintain the gospel among themselves,—whether it was the design of the first founders of that Society, and of the present donors to it, to sink thousands of pounds annually only to gratify a few *sticklers for a party*,* I leave others of more wisdom and knowledge in that affair to determine. But I am sure it has been no small grief and exercise of mind to me to see such sums of money expended in that manner, while our poor heathen neighbors lie almost utterly neglected; Satan, the prince of darkness, suffered to reign in triumph among them, without let or molestation, whole nations being subjected to him, and perishing by thousands for want of knowledge. This appears to me one of the most affecting things that can be mentioned or thought of; and I bless the Father of Mercies that I am not left to spend his substance in such a way.

But I am sensible I have exceeded the bounds of a letter, and should not have so far presumed upon your patience had it not been for this clause in yours: "And let it be a long letter you write, giving me an account," etc. This, sir, I hope, will excuse me.

And now, dear sir, I conclude with acknowledging all

---

* Mr. Brainerd refers here to Episcopal missions in New England and New York, which he regarded as sectarian, as they disturbed existing Christian churches.

your kindness and goodness to me, and wishing that the best of blessings from above may descend upon your person, family, and flock; that the Lord would make your labors abundantly successful among them, and bless you with a glorious harvest. I would likewise desire a remembrance in your addresses to the throne of grace for me, my people, and the cause of God among the Indians. And, if you should have leisure, and think it worth while to write, please to direct for me at Bethel in New Jersey, to the care of Mr. William Grant, Merchant, in Second Street, Philadelphia, or to the care of Mr. Denny de Berdt, Merchant, in Artillery Court, Chiswell Street, London.

I am, with the greatest respect,
Reverend sir,
Your much obliged
And very humble servant,
JOHN BRAINERD.

This letter indicates an earnest and resolute life. It is marked also by a comprehensiveness of view and power of analysis and graphic description above his ordinary efforts, and rivalling his eminent brother.

In this year, 1752, Mr. Brainerd was united in marriage to Miss Experience Lyon, of New Haven, Conn. Of her past life, and where or in what style they set up housekeeping, we know nothing. If he took his young wife with him to Bethel, the Indian town, we may infer that

"Wedded love's first home"

had rude surroundings and appointments. We only know that the union was a happy one.

CHAPTER XXV.

VISIT FROM REV. SAMUEL DAVIS—LETTER TO SCOTLAND—CHANGE OF FIELD—LETTERS OF PRESIDENT EDWARDS—REV. GIDEON HAWLEY.

1753.

WE are allowed to catch a glimpse of Mr. Brainerd at home. President Davis, in his transit from Virginia to embark at New York for Europe as agent for the College of New Jersey, spent a little time in New Jersey. Under date of September, 1753, he says:—*

"Lodged at Mr. Brainerd's, the good missionary among the Indians, and was pleased with his account of the progress of religion among them, though now they are scattered by their land being fraudulently taken from them.

"*Tuesday.*—I took a view of the Indian town, and was pleased with the affection of the poor savages to their minister, and his condescension to them. Rode on towards Philadelphia, and spent the time in pleasing conversation, principally on the affairs of the Indians, with Messrs. Spencer, Brainerd, and Brown." †

---

* Davis' Journal, in Foote's "Sketches of Virginia," p. 230.

† The Mr. Brown here mentioned was probably the Rev. John Brown, of Fagg's Manor, Pa. He removed to Kentucky in 1797. "He died in 1803, aged seventy-five; his wife died in 1802, aged seventy-three. His eldest daughter married the Rev. Thomas B. Craighead, of Tennessee. His eldest son, John, was three times

He says he employed Mr. Brainerd to go to Virginia, with others, to supply his place.

The state of Brainerd's mission at the time of President Davis' visit may be learned from the following letter:—

To the Preses of the Society in Scotland, dated Bethel, October 22, 1753.

Since my last to your lordship,* which bears date March 2d, 1753, I have steadily attended to the business of the mission, and have not been absent from my charge but upon some necessary occasions, and then only for a short space. I have endeavored strictly to attend to my commission and instructions, preaching the gospel, administering the sacraments, catechizing both the grown people and the children, visiting my people, praying and conversing with the sick, attending funerals, and watching all opportunities to do them good. I have constantly attended public worship three times on the Lord's day, steadily once, and sometimes more, in the rest of the week; besides, I have advised my people, especially of late, to meet at least one evening in a week at a private house, which they do in the several parts of their town, sometimes at one house, sometimes at another. This meeting I have generally attended, and carry it on by

---

elected a member of the United States Senate from Kentucky; he married the only sister of the Rev. Dr. John M. Mason, and died in 1837, aged eighty. His third son, James, was the first Secretary of State of the Commonwealth of Kentucky, a member of the United States Senate for many years from Louisiana, and for six years Minister to the Court of France. His fourth son, Samuel, was an eminent physician, and a Professor in the Transylvania Medical College."—*Webster's History of the Presbyterian Church*, p. 657.

* Gillies' "Historical Collections." Glasgow, 1754, p. 448.

prayer, singing of psalms or hymns, and religious conversation. At these meetings I address myself to particular persons, inquire into the state of their souls, warn, exhort, encourage, etc., as I see occasion; and, when I am absent, the meeting is carried on by religious conversation, together with prayer and singing of psalms as above. My endeavors, may it please your lordship, through the blessing of Heaven, have been, I hope, attended with some degree of success. I have had the satisfaction of admitting one adult person to baptism, who, I trust, is a true convert to God and savingly acquainted with Jesus Christ; and sundry children have been the subjects of that divine ordinance. I can also with pleasure inform your lordship and the Society that many of our former converts adorn their profession by a sober, virtuous life; but some, I must needs say, have grievously backslidden, which has been matter of unspeakable grief to me, and done more to exhaust my spirits and wear me out than all the bodily fatigues I have ever undergone in the prosecution of this mission.

Afterwards he writes of the great difficulties the Indians have labored under of late with regard to their lands, and of the lamented death of a promising young Indian the Society were educating for the gospel ministry, of whom he says:—

He had been a member of New Jersey College near two years, was much beloved by his classmates and the other scholars, and made a decent, handsome appearance among them. He died of a quick consumption. I had opportunity of conversing with him in the latter part of his sickness, and though he was under some darkness, yet his discourse was good and discovered much of the Christian, etc.

JOHN BRAINERD.

While Brainerd found something to cheer him in his field, he was not fully satisfied with it. The Indians were disturbed in their land-titles, and uneasy as to the future. They were few in number, and so insulated that good men among them could exert no influence on the aborigines at large; and they were both hated and corrupted by bad whites in the vicinity. It is not strange, then, that he should listen favorably to overtures for a removal to a better district.

Mr. Gideon Hawley,* long a teacher under President Edwards at Stockbridge, this year visited and planned a mission at Onohquanga (now Unadilla), on the upper waters of the Susquehanna, in New York. He desired John Brainerd to transfer his mission and Indians to the same place: President Edwards favored the plan. In a letter to the Boston correspondents,† dated Stockbridge, April 12, 1753, President Edwards says:—

"Mr. Brainerd, the pastor of the Indian congregation at Bethel, New Jersey, who is supported by the Correspondents, having met with much trouble from the enemies of religion in those parts, and his Indians being greatly disturbed with regard to the possession and im-

---

* Allen's Biographical Dictionary, p. 420.

† Edwards' Life, pp. 530, 531, 528.

provement of their lands, the Correspondents have of late had a disposition that he, with his schoolmaster and whole congregation, should remove, if a door might be opened, and take up a new settlement somewhere in the country of the Six Nations. Mr. Hawley has seen Mr. Brainerd, and conversed with him on the subject this spring. He manifests an inclination to such removal, and says his Indians will be ready for it. If such a thing as this could be brought to pass, it would probably tend greatly to the introduction of the gospel and the promotion of the interests of religion among the Six Nations, as his congregation are, I suppose, the most virtuous and religious collection of Indians in America, and some of them have now been long established in religion and virtue.

"There are several towns of the Onohquangas, and several missionaries might probably find sufficient employment in those parts. If Mr. Brainerd should settle somewhere in that country with his Christian Indians, and one or two more missionaries not at a great distance, they might be under advantage to assist one another; as they will greatly need one another's company and assistance in so difficult a work in such a strange, distant land. They might be under advantage to consult one another, to act in concert, and to help one another in any case of peculiar difficulty. Many English people would be found to go from New England and settle there, and the greatest difficulty would be, that there would be danger of too many English settlers and of such as are not fit for the place.

"But, in order to accomplish this, especially in order to such a body of new Indians coming from the Jerseys and settling in the country of the Six Nations, the consent of those nations, or at least of several of them, must be obtained. The method which Mr. Woodbridge, Mr. Hawley, and I, have thought of, which we submit to the wisdom of the Commissioners, is this: that Mr. Woodbridge and Mr. Ashley and his wife should go as speedily as possible into the country of the Conneenchees, they being the first tribe in honor, though not in numbers, and there spend some weeks, perhaps a month, among them, to get acquainted with them, and endeavor to gain their approbation of a mission for settling the gospel in the country of the Six Nations,—Mr. Hawley in the mean time to keep Mr. Woodbridge's school. Then, that Mr. Hawley and Mr. Gordon should join them there, and go with them from thence to Onohquanga; and, when they have acquainted themselves well with the people and the state of the country, and find things agreeable, and see a hopeful prospect, then for Mr. Woodbridge to return and leave Mr. Hawley and Mr. Gordon there, and forthwith send word to Mr. Brainerd, and propose to him to come up with some of his chief Indians to see the country And if, on the observations they make, and the acquaintance they get with the people and country, they believe there is an encouraging prospect, then to endeavor to gain a conference with some of the chiefs of the Five Nations at an appointed time, to know whether they will consent to their coming to settle in their territories. All this will occupy some considerable time; so that, if they can obtain their consent, Mr. Brainerd must return home, and he and his chief Indians must come again to the treaty at the time and place appointed.

* * * * * *

"Mr. Brainerd told Mr. Hawley, that if he removed with his Indians he should choose to do it speedily, and that the longer it was delayed the more difficult it would be, by reason of his building and the Indians increasing their buildings and improvements at Bethel. Probably, if the removal cannot be brought about the next year, it never will be; and, if his Indians remove the next year, it will be necessary that they remove as early as the spring, in order to plant there that year. And, if so much needs to be done this summer, it is as much as it will be possible to find time for."

In connection with this migration, Mr. Brainerd addressed the following letter to Mr. Hawley:—

BETHEL, April 19, 1753.

To Mr. G. HAWLEY:—

DEAR SIR:—Yours of the 2d instant I received last evening, which, together with some other letters from London and other parts of England which came to hand at the same time, were very refreshing and comfortable. Nothing in the world ever animates and cheers my spirits like the observation or news of something that gives a prospect of spreading the gospel among the poor Indians.

This is the object my heart has been upon for many years: when I have engaged in this desirable business, or any thing that I could think had a tendency to promote it, then only did I breathe in my own proper air,— I enjoy myself. But, alas! I have been miserably fettered and pinioned since I have been employed in this excellent undertaking.

The situation of the Indians I have had the peculiar charge of being at least one hundred and fifty miles from any considerable number of Indians elsewhere, and my annual income far short of what was necessary in order to carry on such a design, I have never been satisfied with this place since my first engaging in this business, and have been from time to time using endeavors to procure one better suited to the important design of spreading the gospel among the Indians; but as yet Providence has not opened a door for our remove. Of late, however, there seems to be a great prospect of it. Some of our principal Indians have lately disposed of a great part of the land on which they live, notwithstanding all we could do to the contrary; and it is finally gone from them, so that now they have not enough to subsist upon long. Just at this juncture there came a messenger from the Six Nations, and two or three nations more, with wampum, etc., inviting our Indians to go and live at Whawomung,* on the Susquehanna,—a place I have visited several times. They (the Six Nations) offer to give land for them and their children forever, and that they shall be abridged of none of their privileges, etc. Our Indians, after two days' consideration, thought best to accept the offer their *uncle* was pleased to make them, and accordingly agreed to remove there about this time twelvemonths. I was present at their consultations on this head, and laid every thing before them in the best manner I could, and then left them to determine for themselves.

But, notwithstanding all this, I don't see why the plan of going to Onohquanga might not be prosecuted; for, if all things suit there, I am inclined to think our Indians would be as well pleased to move to that place as Whawomung, if they had the same invitation to the former as the latter. And though they should be actually removed as above, yet, if we could be admitted to live among the Oneidas, the report of our being there would soon cause them to supplicate their *uncle* for liberty to come there too.

---

* Wyoming.

For my part, I am heartily willing to make trial, and earnestly desirous, if the Lord in his providence should open a door, to spend my life in their service. But my taking a journey with you this ensuing summer must depend very much upon the determination of the Correspondents; and whether it will be best or not, I am not able to say. The spring, I imagine, is much the best time, but it is impracticable for me to go this spring: as things appear to me at present, I am inclined to think we had best defer the journey till next spring. But time and consultation on this head may better determine what is duty in that regard. Let us in the mean time be waiting upon God, and have our eyes to him who only can make our endeavors effectual.

I was never more desirous of prosecuting the Indian affairs than now; and, though many things look discouraging, yet I cannot but hope and pray that God will yet do great and glorious things among the poor Indians: let us be instant in prayer to God for so great a blessing.

Please to present my humble regards to Mr. Edwards and his worthy consort, in which my wife joins; and accept affectionate regards from,

Sir, your humble servant,

J. BRAINERD.

Why this plan was not carried out we are not accurately informed: probably the Correspondents changed their purpose. President Edwards says: "they have altered their determination from time to time with respect to Mr. Brainerd and his Indians."* Had the project been realized, it would hardly have procrastinated the fate of the Indians,

* Edwards' Life, p. 553.

as the French War drove Hawley from the Iroquois nation in 1756, and broke up his mission. Good men planned, struggled, and prayed to avert their destiny, but the annihilation of the aborigines seemed to be what no philanthropy or piety could prevent.*

* Manuscript records of the Society in Edinburgh, January, March, and June, 1754.

CHAPTER XXVI.

ELECTED A TRUSTEE OF THE COLLEGE OF NEW JERSEY—CORRESPONDENCE BEGUN WITH THE REV. ELEAZAR WHEELOCK, OF LEBANON, CONN.

1754.

THE project for settling Brainerd's Indians on the Susquehanna, we have seen, failed. Another effort was made, by purchase, to secure for them a tract of land of above four thousand acres in the State of New Jersey; and it marks the generosity of Christians in England, that they were willing to advance the money. The Edinburgh Society in their minutes endorsed the proposition, and voted a large sum for its accomplishment; but the whole matter ultimately failed.

The Synod of New York regarded the Indian mission from the outset with great tenderness, and seemed to place an abiding confidence in Mr. Brainerd. In 1752 they "ordered the collections for Indian missions to be put into his hands, to be disposed of by the Correspondents for Indian affairs." They also directed him, in 1753, to "supply" for four weeks in Hanover, Va., but very properly, in 1754, excused his not going.

May 8th of this year, Mr. Brainerd was elected a trustee of the College of Princeton, and held the office twenty-six years, until his death in 1781. It may gratify curiosity to know that there were present at his election Governor Belcher, Hon. William Smith, Samuel Woodruff, Esq., President Aaron Burr, John Pierson, Richard Treat, William Tennent, David Cowell, John Frelinghuysen, Jacob Green, Elihu Spencer, and Caleb Smith. Most of these names are historical, and cherished by the Church.

It was during this year that a correspondence was opened with the Rev. Eleazar Wheelock, of Lebanon, Conn., afterwards President of Dartmouth College.

Rev. Mr. Wheelock had established a school in Lebanon of English boys. Sampson Occum, a Mohican Indian, solicited admission into this school in 1743, and remained some five years in the family of Dr. Wheelock. In consequence of the education of Occum, Dr. Wheelock was induced to form the plan of an Indian missionary school.

"He conceived that educated Indians would be more successful than whites as missionaries among the red men. The project was new; for the labors of Sergeant and the Brainerds, as well as those of Eliot and the Mayhews, were the labors of missionaries among the Indians, and not labors to form a band of Indian missionaries." *

Under date of December 16, 1762, in "A Nar-

* Allen's Biographical Dictionary, p. 844.

rative from Eleazar Wheelock, Pastor of a Church at Lebanon, and of the Indian Charity School," dedicated to the Marquis of Lothian, he says:—*

"With these views of the case, and from such motives as have been mentioned, above eight years ago I wrote to the Rev. John Brainerd, missionary in New Jersey, desiring him to send me two likely boys for this purpose of the Delaware tribe. He accordingly sent me John Pumshire, in the fourteenth, and Jacob Woolley, in the eleventh years of their age. They arrived here December 18, 1754, and behaved as well as could be reasonably expected. Pumshire made uncommon proficiency in writing. They continued with me until they had made considerable progress in the Latin and Greek tongues, when Pumshire began to decline, and, by the advice of physicians, I sent him back to his friends with orders, if his health would allow, to return with two more of that nation whom Mr. Brainerd had, at my desire, provided for me. Pumshire set out on his journey November 14, 1756, and got home, but soon died; and, on April 9, 1757, Joseph Woolley† and Hezekiah Calvin came on the horse which Pumshire rode."

---

* Narrative from Eleazar Wheelock, etc. (Philadelphia Library), p. 39.

† As the name of this lad will often occur, we give a little sketch of him:—

"Joseph Woolley was a Delaware. He was sent by Mr. John Brainerd to Dr. Wheelock's school, where he arrived with Hezekiah Calvin, another Delaware, April 9, 1757. He spent the winter of 1764 at Onohoghquage, for the purpose of learning the Iroquois language. He was licensed to teach in the spring of 1765, and set out shortly after with Rev. Mr. Smith on his return to his previous post at the Susquehanna River; but he fell sick at Cherry Valley, and died in the course of the same year. He is represented as of an amiable disposition and polished manners."—*Documentary History of New York*, p. 342.

We insert also the following letter, as a specimen of his style:—

The mutual concern of Dr. Wheelock and John Brainerd for the Indians, the desire of Dr. Wheelock to procure hopeful pupils, and the interest of Brainerd in those he had sent so far from home, furnish the staple of their written correspondence, which was frequent and affectionate. Dr. Wheelock's letters are not at hand; but our venerable friend, Dr. William Allen, of Northampton, who married a granddaughter of Dr. Wheelock, sen., has kindly furnished us with more than thirty original letters from John Brainerd to President Wheelock. The first of these letters accompanied the two Indian boys referred to in Dr. Wheelock's narrative.

BETHEL, November 27, 1754.

REV'D AND DEAR SIR:—

Yours of October 30th came to hand about a fortnight

"*Abstract of a Letter from Joseph Woolley, an Indian of the Delaware nation, Schoolmaster on the Mohawk, to Rev. Mr. Wheelock.*

"JOHNSON HALL, July, 1765.

"REVEREND AND HONORED SIR:—

"The language of my heart is, to contribute the little mite I have to the living God, and be in his service. My soul seems to be more and more upon the perishing pagans in these woods. I long for the conversion of their souls, that they may come to the knowledge of our Lord Jesus and be saved.

"But, oh, what reason have I to be ashamed before God, and confess my corrupt nature and lukewarmness in the things of religion that I live no nearer to him! It is worth while to go mourning all my day. Oh, it is impossible to express the things I mean! My heart feels sorry for the poor Indians, that they know no more about our crucified Saviour; and I wish I was made able to teach and instruct them. And I shall do whatsoever lies in my power to tell them of Christ, as long as I tarry: I feel ashamed that I have done no more towards it.

"I hope you enjoy your health, which I wish may long continue. I have no more to say, but that I beg leave to subscribe myself, and be esteemed,

"Your dutiful and most humble servant,

"JOSEPH WOOLLEY."*

---

* Wheelock's Narrative, pp. 40, 41.

ago: I rejoice to be informed of your welfare, both personal and relative. We also, through Divine Goodness, enjoy many comforts, and join in cordial salutations to you and Mrs. Wheelock.

I have sent the Indian boys mentioned in my last, not without some reluctance and a great deal of concern. But I heartily join with you in saying: "The Lord grant his blessing, or defeat the attempt."

John Pumshire.

The biggest boy has been with me; and I must needs say I have been somewhat disappointed in him, both as to his natural abilities and the temper of his mind. Neither his judgment nor memory is as good as I thought, before I had a particular acquaintance; and yet I cannot but hope he may do pretty well in that respect. The temper of mind he has shown also has given me much uneasiness, especially of late: I find he has never had any government. I have taken much pains with him, and thought several times that I must have given him up. Correction, it is highly probable, he will stand in absolute need of: he must by no means be humored and made much of. He is proud, very high-spirited, and has too great a conceit of himself, which must be mitigated and mortified.

Jacob Woolley.

The little one, I think, is a boy of a good natural temper: he seems to discover something of it in his countenance. But I believe he also has had his head very much; for he has had nobody to take care of him but an aged grandmother of near fourscore, and will doubtless stand in need of some discipline.

How Indian pupils should be treated.

The best way, according to my humble opinion, to manage with the Indians is to treat them with kindness, and such as shall make them see that we are their real friends and hearty well-wishers; but that we owe them nothing, are under no obligation to show them any special favors, nor (personally considered) expect any thing from them; that what we do is out of pity to them, and from a concern for their good, and that (as God's instruments) they are greatly beholden to us for it; that we do not despise them for their color, but for their heathenish temper and practices; and that when they become Christians, and behave as becomes such, *they shall have the same treatment as white people.* After such a manner these Indian boys should be treated: they must by no means be more made of than other children of their age, either by the Master or the people belonging to the town, and, if they behave well, they doubtless ought to have as kind and good treatment in all respects. Peter Tottany, who died about the end of his second year in college, had *all the privileges of other scholars;* and this point was determined in a full meeting of the Society's correspondents in New York. And his classmates *treated him with the same respect as others, eating, lodging, walking with him, etc.*

Indians likewise, whenever they go into a Christian house, should hear something that is good, something of religion, or at least something that is virtuous and savory. Nothing in the world is of so much disservice to the good design of Christianizing the Indians as the unchristian behavior and conversation of those who call themselves Christians. I hope there is little danger of this among your people, who have been celebrated for religion, and trust that these Indian boys, as they may be occasionally at any of their houses, will (on the other hand) meet with such treatment as will abundantly recommend Christianity to them. Every one should look upon it as his duty to help forward so pious and public a design. It belongs to thousands to endeavor the Christianizing of the Indians, as well as to us; it is as really their duty, and would be every way as much to their advantage, as ours. If the country in general were sensible of the obligation that lies upon them in this regard, how would they exert themselves, how freely would they disburse of their substance, and what pains would they take to accomplish this great and good work! The Lord hasten the time when this shall be universal!

But to return: a prudent care must be taken with regard to these boys, to treat them with kindness and Christian respect, and yet at the same time to keep them at a proper distance, which, to be sure, must be carefully observed. May the Lord give direction and add his blessing to the pious endeavors of you and your dear people!

With respect to clothing, I have observed your orders especially as to the little boy, who was naked and miserably l——y when I took him a day or two ago from his home. We have done the best we could to clean him, and I hope he will *carry nothing with him but what he should:* however, it may not be amiss to inspect that matter a little.

I conclude with wishing that a blessing from Heaven may attend all our attempts for the advancement of Christ's kingdom in the world, that multitudes may be brought in and the earth be filled with his glory.

Your brother and humble servant,

JOHN BRAINERD.

To the Rev'd Mr. WHEELOCK.

The paternal anxiety of the good missionary for the young Indians sent far from home, and the excellent suggestions he gives for their mental and moral training, will strike every mind. His maxims for teachers of these Indian youths apply with almost equal force to those engaged in elevating the freedmen of the South. What the degraded and ignorant require is not morbid fondness and fanatical caressing, but the substantial kindness which will inspire confidence, conjoined with the healthful restraint and dignified authority adapted to beget respect.

The year 1754 closed gloomily on the missionary and his people. They were becoming landless, homeless, and scattered, and their missionary anxious and active, but despondent. Bethel, the Indian town in New Jersey, to procure which as their permanent home David Brainerd had paid the debts of the Indians, amounting to some ninety pounds, and had aided them to clear its forests with his own labor, was now passing from their hands forever. As in the more recent case of the Cherokees in 1832, the fire on the hearthstone of the Indian cabin was to be extinguished, and its walls levelled, as a sacrifice to the cupidity of men boasting of their civilization and refinement. No wonder the Indian tribes have perished. Men like the Brainerds, the Wheelocks, and Worcesters, delayed, but could not prevent, their annihilation.

CHAPTER XXVII.

ACTION OF THE SCOTCH SOCIETY—INDIAN LANDS LOST—MR. BRAINERD DISMISSED—GOES TO NEWARK, N. J.—HIS LETTER.

1755.

THE defeat of General Braddock on the Monongahela, July 8th of this year, giving the Indians a lofty idea of French power and prowess and a corresponding contempt for English authority, roused the whole border tribes to hostility, so that it required all the skill of statesmen and the persuasion of missionaries to keep even the Delawares, the Oneidas, and other half-civilized nations from wielding the tomahawk. It is thought by able men that the missions of Bethel and Bethlehem, of Stockbridge and Oneida, prevented the tide of blood from flowing over Massachusetts, New York, Pennsylvania, and New Jersey.

"The Indian settlement of Stockbridge, though in the very road of the Indians from Canada, remained secure and unmolested, also Sheffield and New Marlboro; while other parts of New England suffered severely." *

But we are anticipating events.

* American Magazine. Philadelphia, 1757.

As a sequence to the troubled state of the country in 1755, we find the following action of the Scotch Society. We give a large extract, as the Minutes develop facts entirely new to us, and which, we think, will be new to our readers:—

Extract from Minutes, dated Edinburgh, 6th November, 1755.

"The Committee reported, that since last General Meeting they have received a letter, dated the tenth of June, from their Correspondents at New York, bearing that the Indians at Bethel, having parted with their lands, would soon be obliged to move from that place; that by reason of the present dangerous situation of the back part of the country, it would be very difficult to open a mission there this year; that therefore the Correspondents had dismissed Mr. Brainerd from his charge, and that his dismission took place from the seventh of May last; that, in order to keep the Indian congregation together, the Correspondents had agreed to give Mr. William Tennent twenty-five pounds sterling per annum for visiting that congregation once a week, catechizing their children, and sometimes on the Lord's day to administer the sacrament of the Lord's Supper to them; that, as the settlements on Indian lands are very precarious, the titles being in the chiefs, who are easily cheated out of their property, the Correspondents propose, as the most likely method of propagating the gospel there to good purpose, that the Society should either purchase a tract of land where it would be most convenient for the Indians to settle in, or apply to the government for a tract of unappropriated lands for that purpose. That the Committee, having considered the said letter, are of opinion that, in respect of the present disturbances in that corner, it is impracticable at this time to make the purchase therein proposed, and therefore delay further consideration of that part of the letter till these disturbances are settled. But, for the reasons mentioned in the said letter, the Committee approved of Mr. Brainerd being dismissed and of the Correspondents giving twenty-five pounds per annum to Mr. Tennent for his services among the Indians, and ordered that the Correspondents be made acquainted thereof, and at the same time to notify to the Society the most convenient tract of unappropriated ground for which application might be made to the government for the purpose above mentioned."

Mr. Brainerd's own account of this transaction is as follows:—

The proprietors laid claim to the land, and sued the Indians for trespass, which put an end to our schemes and threw all into confusion. We then turned our thoughts towards Susquehanna, and were attempting to provide a settlement for the Indians there, when, hostilities breaking out on the frontiers, the most barbarous murders were committed; which entirely defeated our design and put a final stop to all further attempts of that nature.

And now, things being in such a situation, the Correspondents thought proper to dismiss me from the Society's service, which they did in May, 1755. I was then in New England, and upon my return had an invitation to Newark, which, with the advice of the Presbytery, I accepted.*

* Brainerd's letter in Sprague's Annals, vol. iii. p. 151.

At this late day, the dismission of Mr. Brainerd by the Correspondents strikes us as abrupt and premature. It seems to have been the result of the panic and confusion of the times. Mr. Brainerd makes no complaint; but his language indicates surprise and wounded feeling. It probably grew out of some temporary disagreement.

President Edwards, with his accustomed calm and kind judgment, was so hurt by it that he interfered in the matter. He says, April 10, 1756:—

"With respect to Mr. Hawley and Mr. Brainerd, and their Indians, concerning which you desire to be informed, the Correspondents have altered their determination from time to time with respect to Mr. Brainerd and his Indians. They seemed inclined at first to their removal to Wawwoming, alias Wyoming, and then to Onohquanga, and then to Wyoming again; and finally, about twelve months ago, they wholly dismissed him from employ as a missionary to the Indians, and pastor to the Indian church at Bethel. I cannot say I am fully satisfied with their conduct in doing this so hastily, nor do I pretend to know so much concerning the reasons of their conduct as to have sufficient grounds positively to condemn their proceedings. However, the congregation is not wholly left as a sheep without a shepherd, and are in part committed to the care of Mr. William Tennent, who lives not far off, and is a faithful, zealous minister, who visits them and preaches to them once a week, but, I think, not often upon the Sabbath. The last fall I was in Philadelphia and New Jersey, and was present at a meeting of the Correspondents, when Mr. Tennent gave an agreeable account of the then present state of these Indians with respect to religion, and also of their being in better circumstances as to their lands than they had been. Mr. Brainerd was then at Newark with his family, where he had been preaching as a probationer for settlement ever since Mr. Burr's dismission from that place on account of his business as president of the college. But whether Mr. Brainerd is settled, or is like to settle, there, I have not heard.

"At the forementioned meeting of the Correspondents I used some arguments to induce them to re-establish Mr. Brainerd in his former employ with his Indians, and to send them to Onohquanga. But I soon found it would be fruitless to urge the matter. What was chiefly insisted as an insuperable obstacle to Mr. Brainerd's going with his family so far in the wilderness was Mrs. Brainerd's very infirm state. Whether there was indeed any sufficient objection to such a removal at that time or no, Divine Providence has, since that, so ordered the state and consequences of the war subsisting here in America that insuperable objections are laid in the way of their removal either to Onohquanga, Wawwoming, or any other parts of America that way. The French, by their indefatigable endeavors with the nation of the Delawares, so called from their ancient seat about Delaware River, though now chiefly residing on the Susquehanna and its branches, have stirred them up to make war on the English; and dreadful have been the ravages and desolations which they have made of late on the back parts of Pennsylvania and New Jersey. They are the principal nation inhabiting the parts about Susquehanna River, on which both Wyoming and Onohquanga stand. The latter, indeed, is above the bounds of their country, but yet not very far from them; and the Delaware Indians are frequently there, as they go to and fro; on which account there is great danger that Mr. Hawley's mission and ministry there will be entirely broken up. Mr. Hawley came from there about two months ago with one of my sons,* about ten years old, who had been there with him near a twelvemonth to learn the Mohawk language."†

How Brainerd regarded the whole matter is shown by the following letter to Dr. Wheelock:—

NEWARK, May 17, 1755.

REV'D AND VERY DEAR SIR:—

I received yours of April 28th by Mr. Williams, and shall endeavor to have a strict regard to your orders respecting a schoolmaster, and do my best in that affair.

I came to town last evening, and had but a few minutes with the president,‡ by reason of company and his setting out for York this morning, but expect to see him upon his return, and shall endeavor to engage him in the matter. And, oh, I wish Heaven may succeed the enterprise, and every other attempt for the conversion of the poor Indians to Christianity!

I am still in a great plunge. I hope I am desirous to know the will of God, but am at a great loss. I am told by the president that I was dismissed from my charge as missionary about the 7th instant, and that the people of Newark have since had a society meeting, and voted unanimously to give me a call upon probation; or, if

* This was Jonathan Edwards, D.D., jun., afterwards President of Union College.

† President Edwards' letter to Rev. Mr. McCulloch, Scotland.

‡ President Aaron Burr, of New Jersey (Princeton) College, which, then in its infancy, was located at Newark. It seems to have travelled with its presidents. Under the presidency of Mr. Dickinson it was located at Elizabethtown, his residence.

there were one or two that did not vote, there was not one that negatived it. This seems to look like a call in Providence, and certainly suggests duty. But, for my part, I cannot but look upon myself as very unequal to the work, and can truly say I had rather continue in the mission if any suitable provision could be made for the re-settlement of the Indians and the comfortable support of the mission; and, to be sure, I have been very far from desiring a dismission. But who can tell what the designs of Infinite Wisdom are? I hope I feel something of a disposition to say: *Lord, what wilt thou have me to do?* I intend to open my heart to the Presbytery, who are to sit in about ten days' time: perhaps I may get some light. You will, I trust, not be unmindful of me, though, indeed, I am not worthy of a thought. I need, greatly need, the prayers of the Lord's servants, though I am very undeserving.

Please to present my best regards to Mrs. Wheelock, in which my wife joins, and accept the same from,

Reverend sir,

Your very humble servant,

JOHN BRAINERD.

The spirit of this communication is most beautiful. How humble, submissive, devout, and benevolent! There is in it a tenderness, naivete, simplicity, and unselfishness, marking the writer as eminently Christian,—"a child of God." It were well if we had more of this spirit in all our hearts.

Aside from its piety, the letter is shaded with sadness. Invited as the successor of President Burr to the church in Newark, then and now one of the strongest and most influential in the land, John Brainerd is cheered by no gratified ambition, by no prospect of augmented salary, or more élite social enjoyments. His heart is with his Indians, —"with his few sheep in the wilderness."

The Synod of New York this year appointed "Messrs. Brainerd and Spencer to take a journey to North Carolina before winter, and supply vacant congregations six months, or as long as they should think necessary."* Synods of that period said "to one, Go," and he went; but in this case the dangers of the times hindered obedience.

In this year also the "Rev. Gilbert Tennent reported that he had received from Great Britain a bill for two hundred pounds sterling, generously given for the propagation of the gospel among the Indians, and to be under the direction of the Synod."† It was the interest of this sum which the Synod annually voted for the support of Mr. Brainerd, his mission and school.

---

* Records of Presbyterian Church, p. 264.

† See Records, *passim.*

CHAPTER XXVIII.

MR. BRAINERD RESUMES THE MISSION—REMOVES TO BRUNSWICK—AGAIN DISMISSED—RETURNS TO NEWARK—ACTION OF THE SCOTCH SOCIETY—BROTHERTON.

1756.

ALTHOUGH invited to Newark, and for a time having charge of the church, Mr. Brainerd was still longing for his Indian field. He says:—

I moved with my family to Newark, and continued there till June, 1756, when the Correspondents, thinking they had a prospect of procuring the land on which the Indians are now settled, requested me to resume the mission, with which I complied; and, giving up the call I had to settle at Newark, moved with my family to Brunswick, being the best place I could now fix to accommodate the Indians in their present situation, till the land for their settlement could be procured. In this situation I continued till September, 1757, when the Correspondents, being disappointed, and seeing no way to procure the land, dismissed me a second time; and the congregation at Newark, having continued all this time unsettled, renewed their call to me the next week, which I soon after accepted, moved again with my family, and settled there.*

The manuscript records of the Society in Edin-

* J. Brainerd's letter, Sprague's Annals, vol p. 151.

burgh give the best solution of these complicated and conflicting movements. We give them in full, as they show the zeal and sacrifices with which good men in Europe and America labored to protect and help the poor Indians.

Extract from Minutes, dated Edinburgh, 2d June, 1757.

"The Committee reported that there was transmitted to them from their Correspondents at London a letter, of the 30th December last, from the Rev. Mr. Burr, President of the College of New Jersey and Preses to the Society's commissioners there, bearing that the said Correspondents have again taken Mr. Brainerd into the Society's service, since the tenth of June last; that the reasons of his demitting his charge and returning to it again were communicated in a letter to the Marquis of Lothian; that the Committee have agreed to the employing Mr. Brainerd with his former salary, and have at the same time withdrawn the allowance given Mr. Tennent for visiting the congregation in Mr. Brainerd's charge during the time that he was out of the Society's service; that the letter from Mr. Burr to the Marquis of Lothian is but newly come to the Committee's hands, and, as it contains a proposal of meeting the Correspondents at New York to buy a tract of ground for the Indians, the Committee transmitted the said letter, with one from Mr. Brainerd to Mr. Burr, to the General Meeting. The General Meeting, having heard the said report, caused the aforesaid letter from Mr. Burr to the Marquis of Lothian to be read, dated the sixth August last, and bearing that the aforesaid proposal of purchasing land in the Indian country, where a mission might be settled, being become impracticable by reason of the present war there, the Correspondents have lately fixed upon a tract in the Province of New York, (?) very commodious for the Indians, where they will be free from danger, and where such as incline to hear the gospel may find a safe retreat. That the Correspondents have agreed to purchase that tract, the title to be in the Society, and to be for the use of the Indians; that this land will cost about four hundred and fifty pounds sterling, whereof the Correspondents have near one hundred and fifty pounds in hand, and know not where to get the rest, only they are in hopes this Society will do something towards it, as it will be a fast and growing estate; that they have written to Mr. Whitefield and some other friends in London to attempt getting something contributed towards so good a design; and, as all hopes of having a mission among the Indians back in their own country is at present at an end, the Correspondents think it of great importance that this should be supported, especially as there seems a door open for carrying it on to better purpose than ever.

"Which letter being read, the General Meeting caused to be read the letter from Mr. Brainerd to Mr. Burr, dated the 3d of July last, giving a more particular account of the aforesaid land, of which he had taken a particular view, and finds it every way commodious; that it contains at least three thousand acres; that the soil is very good,—near one-half of it, he imagines, would bear very good wheat, the rest rice and Indian corn, which the Indians are very fond of; that it is well watered and timbered, and that a considerable quantity of fine meadow might be made in some parts of it; that there is a fine cedar swamp in it,—a very valuable article, by which the Indians will often help themselves to a little ready cash in time of need; that it is a much better spot than ever he expected to find in that country, and that nothing could have a better effect upon the Indians than the purchase of that land at this time; for, as the Cranberry Indians have lost their land, and cannot go to Susquehanna by reason of the enemy, they will take it as a particular favor, and serve not only to attach them to our interest in a political sense, but give them a good opinion of our religion.

"The General Meeting, having considered the subject-matter of the above-recited letters, and after reasoning thereon, did approve of the design of purchasing the aforesaid tract of land for the Indians; and finding the aforesaid sum of one hundred and fifty pounds is already provided by the Correspondents, and that applications are making at London for contributions for making the aforesaid purchase, do remit this affair to their Committee, and appoint that they transmit a copy of the said two letters to the Correspondents at London; and the Committee are authorized, upon getting notice of what is contributed there, to apply as much of the Society's funds for making the said purchase as they shall think expedient."

Extract from Minutes, dated Edinburgh, 17th November, 1757.

"The General Meeting, having heard the said report, and having caused to be read the minutes of their correspondents, with the letter from Mr. Anderson, both above recited, and considering that at the last meeting they had agreed to make the said purchase, do now, in respect of the opinion of the Correspondents and the many donations received from London, agree to lay out the aforesaid sum of three hundred pounds sterling for completing the said purchase, and authorize the treasurer to pay the same; and the General Meeting remit to their Committee to see the conveyances to the aforesaid lands duly executed in the Society's name."

The place Brainerd selected to be purchased for his Indians is said in the Records to have been in New York; but the Scotch Correspondents erred in their geography. The description answers perfectly to the tract in Burlington county, New Jersey, afterwards given to the Indians by the State. This view is confirmed by a letter of Rev. William Tennent to Dr. Wheelock, in 1758. Speaking of the land donated by the State, he says:—*

"It will refresh your heart, dear sir, to know that our Province has, in consideration of all the Indian claims to lands in this part of it, purchased a tract of land containing near three thousand acres, to be a possession for them and theirs for ever. It is the same tract that our dear brother Brainerd chose for them, but could not purchase it, though he incessantly labored for it. It is now made theirs in a time and way hardly expected: it is surely the doings of our Lord, to whom be all the glory."

The purchase failed, but the generosity of the projectors is remembered before God. Mr. Brainerd, disappointed, went back the next year to Newark, where, it seems, he was gladly received.

In the mean time, the Indians were supplied once a week by Rev. William Tennent. Though he was put in Mr. Brainerd's place, there seems to

* Memoirs of Wheelock. Newburyport, 1811, p. 218.

have been no shade of jealousy between them. In the quotation above, Mr. Tennent speaks of "dear brother Brainerd."

At the Synod of New York, this year, Mr. Brainerd was an influential and active member. He was put on the Committee of Overtures,* was appointed to receive the collections for the college, and placed on the Board to examine candidates for the charity fund of the college. The interest on the charity fund for Indian missionaries was voted to assist him in laboring for the Indians. They also ordered him with others to spend "four months in supplying vacancies in the South before winter, in Virginia and North Carolina." If he had received any chill from the action of the Correspondents, this kindness of his Synod was adapted to reassure and comfort him. As the first paid missionary of the Presbyterian Church in the United States, which, we believe, was the first ecclesiastical body in the land organically to engage in missions, Brainerd was always true to his church; and to the last his Presbyterian brethren were true to him.

* Records of Presbyterian Church, p. 270.

CHAPTER XXIX.

HIS MISSION TO STOCKBRIDGE—DEATH OF HIS WIFE.

1757.

PROVIDENTIALLY, we have one of his letters, indicating the temper with which he bore the trials of the times:—

NEWARK, December 17, 1757.

REV'D AND DEAR SIR:—

I had a letter for you, written at Princeton, to go with Sr. Barnum; but he went off unbeknown to me, and left it. And I have time at present to write but a few words, being in an hour or two to set out on a journey to Stockbridge, Mass., to meet a council of ministers in behalf of the college.

You have doubtless heard the choice the trustees have made of the Rev. Mr. Edwards to succeed our late excellent President Burr, whose death occurred just a week after the most affecting breach upon my family, by which was removed the *dearest of my earthly enjoyments*. This sorrow you have heard long before, and, I doubt not, sincerely mourned with me. Let me, dear sir, have your prayers for me and my dear little offspring, who have lost a most valuable friend.

We have likewise to mourn the loss of our dear wrestling Jacob,—I mean that man of God, the Rev. Mr. Davenport. Oh, we exceedingly want such gap-men!

Little Jacob* was not fit to enter college; but the commissioners, however, took him under their pay, and at the end of the year from the last Wednesday in September, 1757, you may draw upon the commissioners for the year's expenses, and it will be paid to Mr. Pomroy's son at college. You may draw upon Mr. William Tennent, who at present has the care of the Indians. The affair has appeared so discouraging, and our late attempts proved so unsuccessful, together with the loss of about twenty of our men who enlisted in the Provincial Army and were lost at Fort William Henry, that the commissioners thought fit to dismiss me again last commencement, though, if I could have answered the end of a missionary, I should have chosen to be continued before taking the charge of any congregation in America.

I can send you another pretty Indian boy in the spring, if we live, and I doubt not but two. Please to let me know your mind.

And now I can only ask your excuse for this incorrect thing. The reason of my writing now is, because I have a direct opportunity to New Haven. I got home from Princeton last night about nine o'clock.

My best regards to Mrs. Wheelock. Love to Sr. Barnum, your family, to the little Indian boys, etc.

In the greatest haste,

Reverend and honored sir,

Yours most affectionately,

JOHN BRAINERD.

P.S.—My duty to Mr. Pomroy: his son was well yes-

---

* He means Jacob Woolley, whom Dr. Wheelock had sent to enter Princeton College. He failed to develop a good character, and was no honor to his instructors.

terday, and all the scholars. Things go on bravely; the Indian boys are well.

The Rev'd Mr. Wheelock.

From this letter we see what sorrows he had to meet, and how bravely he bore himself. The loved and cherished wife of his youth and mother of his three little children died September 17th of this year. In another letter, alluding to this event, he says:—

"My dear wife, after a long and painful sickness, departed the 17th of September, 1757,—the greatest loss I ever sustained, the most sorrowful day I ever saw. May God sanctify it to us in spiritual and divine blessings! Dust thou art, and unto dust shalt thou return. Having a desire to depart and to be with Christ, which is far better, she has exchanged a vale of tears for a crown of glory. Blessed are the dead that die in the Lord; they rest from their labors, and their works do follow them." *

The Correspondents had made her ill health a reason for detaining him from the Onohquanga mission. Did they fear that a husband's sympathy with an afflicted wife absorbed too much of his attention? or did they sympathize with her in her affliction, and feel unwilling to hazard her life in the wilderness? We know not. As there is no evidence to the contrary, we infer that this afflicted wife was herself willing to endure the

* Brainerd Genealogy, p. 286.

perils of any enterprise. She was an element of strength, not weakness, to her husband, and, with all his zeal for missionary labor, he speaks of her death as the "greatest loss" of his life. He has not told where she died (probably at Newark), and we have not been able to find her grave. The Saviour knows where the ashes of this true woman repose, who, to solace a servant of Christ, exiled herself from civilization and refinement to elevate and save degraded savages.*

Brainerd's mission to Stockbridge was a responsible one. He and the Rev. Caleb Smith, of Newark Mountains, had been appointed agents of the College of New Jersey to tender the appointment of President to Rev. Jonathan Edwards, and secure his acceptance and the consent of his brethren to his removal. The mission, as all know, was completely successful; and Mr. Brainerd must have rejoiced in having so earnest and affectionate a friend of his brother and himself in such a position, and so near at hand. But here again he was doomed to sorrow. Edwards came, was installed, presided a few weeks, and died on the 22d of March, 1758. The successive deaths of Presidents Burr

---

* We asked S. H. Congar, Esq., of Newark, N. J., for information as to her grave. In response, under date of June 10, 1861, he says:—

"Were it in my power, I would cheerfully answer your queries. We would look for her grave adjacent to those of her children. I have never seen nor heard of a monument of any kind bearing her name. In 1844, the inscriptions in our old cemetery were copied, but many stones had then been broken, destroyed, or removed. Mrs. Brainerd was doubtless buried, with her children, near the family graves of the Rev. Dr. McWhorter. Her gravestone has perished by neglect."

and Edwards with Mrs. Burr and Edwards, all in about one year, took from Brainerd his most cherished friends at a period of his own deep affliction. No wonder he reeled under it.

His mission to Stockbridge had one result he little anticipated.

"The council of ministers in Stockbridge, at the request both of the English and Indian congregations at Stockbridge, addressed a letter to the Commissioners in Boston, requesting that the Rev. John Brainerd might be appointed Mr. Edwards' successor; the Housatonnucks offering land for a settlement to the Indian congregation at Cranberry, New Jersey, if they would remove to Stockbridge; and another letter to the trustees of the college requesting that they use their collective and individual influence to procure the appointment of Mr. Brainerd and his removal to Stockbridge." *

To be invited by the council of ministers and the people to succeed Jonathan Edwards in the pulpit was a compliment sufficient to please any ordinary man; but we do not find that Mr. Brainerd makes any allusion to it in his letters. It shows what he was at that period, what impression he made at Stockbridge, and how sternly, like his brother David, he subordinated himself to duty. He came to New Jersey, to his Indians and his work, and remained in it in relative shade and dependence: his life going out in obscurity in

* Edwards' Life, pp. 576, 577.

the Jersey Pines, like the Niger dried up by the sands of Africa.

In the Synod of New York, which met at Maidenhead (now Lawrenceville, N. J.) this year, the vote of the interest on the Indian fund to Mr. Brainerd is with a proviso: "in case the Correspondents shall continue him in the mission."* We confess to some embarrassment in ascertaining precisely what was his exact position. It seems, from all we can glean, to have been this: he was dismissed from his mission, and went to Newark. The prospect of purchasing land for the Indians induced the Society to reappoint him, and him to accept, and so he removed to Brunswick. The scheme failed: he is now again at Newark, delaying to be installed, and ready to go to his Indians if the way opens. The Synod provides for this contingency.

He speaks of having been a chaplain in the army once, before his campaign in Canada in 1759. This must have occurred, we think, about 1756, at the time Mr. Beatty went as chaplain of Colonel Benjamin Franklin's regiment to protect the Moravian settlements of Pennsylvania. After one hundred years, it is not easy to make a biography strictly consecutive: it is enough to approximate truth.

---

* Records of the Presbyterian Church, p. 278.

CHAPTER XXX.

REUNION OF OLD AND NEW SIDE PRESBYTERIANS—MR. BRAINERD'S DOMESTIC SORROWS—THE GRAVES OF HIS WIFE AND HIS TWO CHILDREN—HIS REMOVAL TO BROTHERTON.

1758.

THIS year, among Presbyterians, was made memorable by the happy reunion of the Old and New Side Presbyterians, as represented by the Synods of Philadelphia and New York. After a long storm of controversy and recrimination precedent, and a sulky separation for seventeen years, they found that they had not fully understood all truth nor each other; that each side had some truth and some error, and had both excellencies and defects; that the evils of separation and conflict were more pernicious than the errors of either party: so, when the old men had become softened by time, amended by reflection, or passed to heaven, there were none to rebuke a younger generation who crept up and shook hands over the wall which had separated their fathers. A century later, "this history is likely to repeat itself."

At the meeting of the united Synods of New York and Philadelphia at this time, Mr. Brainerd is marked as absent, which no doubt he regretted, for it must have been "good to be there." During the year Mr. Brainerd seems to have quietly prosecuted his labors in Newark; but he did this under the pressure of most overwhelming afflictions. The following letter, although bearing a later date, refers to these trials of 1758:—

NEWARK, March 20, 1759.

DR. WHEELOCK:—

REV'D AND VERY DEAR SIR:—I was at New Haven last fall, with a design to have gone farther eastward; but, as I was then riding for my health, my design was prevented by that turn of extreme cold we had the beginning of November, otherwise I might perhaps have had the pleasure of seeing you at your own house. How often, and how many ways, are our expectations dashed and disappointed! Of late, I had very great and sorrowful experience of this. Death has made the world to me, what it really is in itself and ever was, *an empty nothing.* The loss of two dear lovely babes in less than a year after the death of their amiable, virtuous mother, the desire of my eyes,* has brought me very low indeed;

---

* Since our first allusion to the wife of Mr. Brainerd, we have received from the Rev. E. L. Cleaveland, D.D., of New Haven, Conn., an extract from a paper prepared by him for the Historical Society, giving some account of his church-lot. Incidentally he gives the following facts respecting the Lyon family, into which the Rev. John Brainerd married. Though out of place, we insert the extract here:—

"After the death of Matthew Gilbert, son of the governor, the north side of his old homestead was sold by his widow and children to William Lyon. This was the first William Lyon, who came to New Haven. His wife was Experience Hayward, or Howard. They had two children, William and Experience. This second William Lyon was father of Colonel William Lyon, the well-known President of New Haven Bank.

"William Lyon, the purchaser of the Gilbert place, died before the year 1743. His purchase must have been as early as 1735. His house stood near the site of Mr. Henry O. Hotchkiss' house.

and I am ready to say with the Psalmist: *Unless the Lord had been my helper, I had even perished in my afflictions; but having obtained help from him, I yet live.* I long to see you very much; but whether I shall ever have an opportunity in this world, God only knows. I have some thoughts of going into the army again, but am at a great loss what is my duty, mostly on account of my present very low state of health. I hope duty will be made plain to me one way or another; I think I desire to be absolutely at the disposal of Heaven.

I wonder who goes [to the army as chaplain] this year in Connecticut? whether dear, good Mr. Pomroy goes again? I have heard nothing.

Our Assembly [New Jersey] have bought that land for the Indians, which I attempted in vain to purchase, and Governor Bernard appears very forward to promote the mission. 'Tis not altogether improbable I shall engage in it again, if I live.

'Twas the desire of the Correspondents at a meeting last fall, if I remember, that Jacob should be sent down about this middle of April with an account in regard to what we did for Mr. Pomroy's son, and what you have done for him. I hope your school flourishes. May the time be hastened when God will send the gospel among the poor Indians and other benighted heathen.

My best regards to Mrs. Wheelock; and when you

"After the death of William Lyon, in 1743, his widow and children remained in the house on Church street.

"In 1749, they sold it to their aunt, Silence Hayward, but probably continued to live there. In 1752, Silence Hayward sold the north part of the lot, extending to Court Street, to Yale Bishop, the husband of Sybil Gilbert. In 1754, she sold the south half to Mr. John Brainerd, of Perth Amboy; and in 1758, John Brainerd, then of Newark, sold his lot to Timothy Alling.

"John Brainerd's interest in this lot was natural and legitimate. In 1752 he had married Experience, daughter of William and Experience Lyon; and he was therefore buying back his wife's former ownership in the estate."

see Mr. Pomroy and Mrs. Pomroy, please to salute them in the most affectionate manner for me: and please, sir, likewise to give love to the little boys and others of your school.

'Tis a very great favor that the British and Prussian arms are still so much smiled upon. The taking of Guadaloupe is no inconsiderable thing.

Colonel Schuyler goes this year at the head of our forces. God send them all prosperity, and make us a thankful, fruitful people. I hope, among many others, you do not wholly forget to pray for,

Reverend and honored sir,
Your humble servant,
JOHN BRAINERD.

The tombstones of the little ones mentioned in the above letter are still to be seen in the grave-yard of the First Presbyterian Church in Newark. Rev. Dr. Stearns, in his history of that church, gives the inscriptions on these stones as appended in the note below.*

While personal sorrows were pressing heavily upon Mr. Brainerd, the hopes of his Indian mission were reviving. The Legislature of New Jersey, alarmed by the hostile spirit of the Indian tribes in Pennsylvania, who had carried bloodshed

---

* "Miss Sophia Brainerd, elder daughter of the Rev. John Brainerd, died Sept. 5, 1758, in the 6th year of her age.

"David Brainerd, only son of the Rev. John Brainerd, died Sept. 14, 1758, in the 2d year of his age.

Sweet babe, so late received thy breath,
And now commanded unto death;
Thy warfare ended ere begun,
Triumphant victory is won."

along the borders, and apprehensive lest the New Jersey Indians, smarting under a sense of their wrongs, might join their brethren in the West and become dangerous, had awakened to a sense of justice.

"The first outbreak occurred in 1755, but, so soon as a hostile feeling became apparent, the Legislature appointed commissioners to examine into the causes of dissatisfaction. A convention was held at Crosswicks for the purpose in January, 1756, and in March, 1757, a bill was passed, calculated to remove the difficulties which had grown out of impositions upon the Indians when intoxicated, the destruction of deer by traps, and the occupation of lands by the whites which they had not sold.* During this year, however, and the first part of 1758, the western borders of the province were in much alarm from the hostile feeling prevalent among the Minisink and neighboring tribes,—from May, 1757, to June, 1758, twenty-seven murders having been committed by them on the West-Jersey side of the Delaware. A constant guard was kept under arms to protect the inhabitants; but it was not always able to check the predatory excursions of the savages.

"In June, 1758, Governor Bernard, of New Jersey, consulted General Forbes and Governor Denny, of Pennsylvania, as to the measures best calculated to put a stop to this unpleasant warfare, and, through Teedyescung, king of the Delawares, he obtained a conference with the Minisink and Pompon Indians,—protection being assured them.†

* Neville's Laws, vol. ii. p. 125.
† Smith's New Jersey, pp. 447, 448.

"The conference took place at Burlington, August 7, 1758. On the part of the province there were present the Governor, three Commissioners of Indian Affairs of the House of Assembly, and six Members of the Council. Two Minisink or Munsey Indians, one Cayugan, one Delaware, messenger from the Mingoians, and one Delaware who came with the Minisinks, were the delegates from the natives. The conference opened with a speech from the Governor. He sat, holding four strings of wampum, and thus addressed them: 'Brethren, as you are come from a long journey, through a wood full of briers, with this string I anoint your feet, and take away their soreness; with this string I wipe the sweat from your bodies; with this string I cleanse your eyes, ears, and mouth, that you may see, hear, and speak clearly; and I particularly anoint your throat, that every word you say may have a free passage from the heart. And with this string I bid you heartily welcome.' The four strings were then delivered to them. The result of the conference was, that a time was fixed for holding another at Easton, at the request of the Indians: that being, as they termed it, the place of the Old Council fire." *

"The Act passed in 1757 appropriated £1600 for the purchase of Indian claims; but, as the Indians living south of the Raritan preferred receiving their proportion in land specially allotted for their occupancy, three thousand and forty-four acres in the township of Evesham, Burlington county, were purchased for them. A house of worship and several dwellings were subsequently erected, forming the town of Brotherton; and, as the selling and leasing of any portion of the tract was pro-

* Historical Collections of New Jersey, p. 61.

hibited, as was also the settlement upon it of any persons other than Indians, the greatest harmony appeared to have prevailed between its inhabitants and their white neighbors." *

This treaty secured the land for which Brainerd and the Scotch Society had negotiated. As the town of Christian Indians was called Bethel, this new town was named Brotherton; long the residence of Mr. Brainerd, and from which he dates many of his letters.

The tract, as it appeared in a state of nature one hundred years ago, has been pretty accurately described by Mr. Brainerd in his Edinburgh correspondence. It comprehended three thousand acres lying in the east part of Burlington county, about twenty miles from Burlington, fifteen from Mount Holly, and twenty from the sea at Tuckerton. Led by our friend Rev. Samuel Miller, of Mount Holly, we have visited the spot and studied its surroundings, but reserve the description for another part of this book. The securing of this land for the Indians turned at once the eyes of the Government of New Jersey, of the Synod of his Church, and of the missionary Correspondents upon Mr. Brainerd, as most likely "to care for the estate of the poor Indians;" and they all set to work to draw him from Newark, which, with his martyr-spirit, was not difficult.

---

* Allinson's Laws, p. 221.

CHAPTER XXXI.

MR. BRAINERD A CHAPLAIN IN THE ARMY.

1759.

THE French War was now raging along our whole northern frontier. As the flag of France bore Romanism with it, and as the French armies were accompanied by yelling and scalping Indians, the Protestant as well as martial spirit was stirred by the war, and ministers and people gave their prayers and persons to the work of beating back the invaders and carrying the war into Canada. As with us in our present struggle with traitors and treason, all the loyal clergymen of the land (and all Presbyterian clergymen *in that day* were loyal) stood ready to make any sacrifice for their country. Their sermons and prayers, as in the case of Rev. Mr. Davis and others, breathed a warm and unequivocal Christian patriotism. So it ought always to be in our country's perils. John Brainerd would have been false to the instincts of his family and the nobleness of his heart had he failed to share in the responsibilities and spirit of the times. We might suppose that, with his church in Newark, his Southern tours, his Indian missionary interests, his college burdens and responsibilities, he had sufficient to keep him at home; but no; we find him, in the middle of this year, four hundred miles north of New Jersey, on the borders of Canada.

CROWN POINT, August 9, 1759.

REV'D AND DEAR SIR:—

I had the pleasure of seeing a letter from you to dear Mr. Pomroy, of a much later date than any thing I had heard from you before. I always rejoice to hear of your welfare, and desire to sympathize with you under any afflicting dispensation. Your son, I observe by your letter, is in a low, fading state: may the Lord prepare both him and you for his good will and pleasure.

It has pleased a sovereign God to bereave me of all but one dear little babe: I know he is just and righteous in giving me a bitter cup to drink, *for I am worthy*. But to lose such dear friends, such tender parts of ourselves, as wife and children, is hard to flesh and blood! The world can never be to me what it has been; and doubtless 'tis best it should not.

After considerable hesitation, I thought it my duty to come into the army again. But, alas! dear sir, I feel as if I did but little good. Profanity and wickedness greatly prevail, and at times my heart almost sinks within me; but I try after my poor manner to make a stand for God, and I desire to be very thankful. I never had so much courage in general as this year. Oh, what a mercy of mercies it is to have a face to speak for God! Good Mr. Pomroy is at present my near neighbor, and often strengthens my heart.

God has done wonderful things for us! 'Tis *his own right hand and his holy arm that has gotten the victory!* 'Tis pity, O 'tis infinite pity, that he should be the more dishonored, his sacred, adorable name the more profaned, and his most holy, excellent, equitable laws the more trampled upon on that account! Oh, my dear sir, there is a dreadful day a-coming for the wicked! But what our eyes have seen and your ears have heard from these parts are, I trust, but the beginning of the dawn of a glorious day to the Church of God.

The Lord's stand was most conspicuous, and very remarkable, in the reduction of Niagara as well as these two important posts. *O sing unto the Lord a new song, for he hath done marvellous things!*

I hope your school will be established upon the best foundation, in the best time, and in the best way.

I am sorry to hear of dear Mr. Buel's affliction: we know how to sympathize with him. May his great loss be made up in spiritual and divine blessings.

Mr. Beebe was very poorly when we left Carillon a few days ago. I should be glad to hear that he was so far recovered as to be gone homeward. The rest of our fraternity, I believe, are pretty well. The provincial chaplains, except Mr. Pomroy, are all at Carillon.

My best regard to Mrs. Wheelock, love to your children and the scholars, and cordial salutations to all friends. And never forget to pray for,

Reverend and dear sir,
Your affectionate friend
And humble servant,
JOHN BRAINERD.

P.S.—Mr. Pomroy's letter in answer to yours gives you the substance of what is doing here. May Heaven succeed the important business the army are engaged in. I hear Mr. Beebe is better.

Rev'd Mr. WHEELOCK.

Mr. Brainerd's account of the wickedness of the army and of his times may lead us to hope that a merciful God may still be with us, as he was with our fathers, in spite of our sins. It is touching to remember that the Indians of Bethel, the converts of David Brainerd, shared in the patriotism of their pastor, and cheerfully gave up their lives for their country and its safety.

Mr. Brainerd says:—

"The Indians have, every year since the commencement of the war, enlisted into the king's service far beyond the proportion, and generally more or less every campaign have died in the army." *

Brave and true men, fighting for a government that had denied them a place where to "lay their heads"! They helped "to save others," but their own national existence they could not save. Like our own colored soldiers, they perilled the loss of all things, with but a dim and doubtful vision of any benefit to themselves. We trust God remembered them. Their loss must have been severe in a community of less than two hundred.

The united Synod of New York and Philadelphia, in their minutes of this year, say:—

"Mr. Brainerd applied to the Synod for their advice, whether it was his duty to leave his present charge at Newark and resume his mission to the Indians.

* Letter of J. Brainerd, Sprague's Annals, pp. 151, 152.

"Arguments on both sides were fully heard.

"Though the Synod are tenderly affected with the case of Newark congregation, yet, in consideration of the great importance of the Indian mission, they do unanimously advise Mr. Brainerd to resume it.

"The Synod do farther agree to give him the interest of the Indian fund for this year, in order to his more comfortable subsistence." *

Under the same date, the minutes add:—

"Mr. Brainerd being removed from Newark, it is ordered that Messrs. Woodruff, Kettletas, Darby, and Cummings supply there, each one Sabbath."

Mr. Brainerd had not yet left Newark officially, but was absent probably in the army. His own account of matters about this time is as follows:—

"In this settled state, in Newark, I remained but a little while; for in March, 1759 (in consequence of a treaty with the Indians and this land purchased and secured to them by the government), I was requested by Mr. Bernard, the then governor of this province, and the Society's correspondents, at a joint meeting at Perth Amboy, again to resume the mission. I took their proposals under consideration, and in the May following laid the matter before the Synod at Philadelphia; and, with the unanimous advice of that venerable body, gave up my charge at Newark, and embarked once more in the cause of the poor Indians.

"About this time I made the Indians a visit at their

---

* Records of the Presbyterian Church, p 294.

new settlement, and procured some supplies for them by order of the Synod during my absence in the army; and, upon my return the November following, fixed myself down among them, where I have steadily resided ever since."

The following letter was addressed by him to Mrs. Elizabeth Smith, of Wethersfield, Conn., wife of the Hon. William Smith, and previously the wife of Colonel Elisha Williams,* once Rector of Yale College:—

BROTHERTON in NEW JERSEY, August 24, 1761.

MADAM:—

According to my promise, I here send an account of the Indian mission in this province, which for some years has been the object of my care.

In 1757 we lost near twenty, taken captive at Fort William Henry,† and but three or four have ever returned to this day; so that our number is greatly reduced.

---

* Colonel Elisha Williams graduated at Harvard College in 1711; was a minister of the gospel in Wethersfield, Conn., in 1726; inaugurated President of Yale College,—resigned from ill health, 1739; and went as chaplain in the expedition against Cape Breton in 1745. The next year he was appointed colonel of a regiment in the proposed expedition against Canada. Dr. Doddridge, who was intimately acquainted with him, says: "He had a nobleness of soul capable of contriving and acting the greatest things without seeming to be conscious of his having done them." He went to England, where he married a lady of superior accomplishments, the daughter of the Rev. Thomas Scott, of Norwich: to her the above letter was addressed. He died July 24, 1765, aged sixty.—*Allen's Biographical Dictionary*, p. 862.

† Fort William Henry, at the south end of Lake George, Warren county N. Y. Erected in 1753; captured by the French in 1756.

On this spot, which is a fine, large tract of land, and very commodiously situated for their settlement, there are something upward of an hundred, old and young.

About twelve miles distant there is a small settlement of them, perhaps near forty. About seventeen miles farther there is a third, containing possibly near as many more; and there are yet some few scattering ones still about Crossweeksung. And if all were collected, they might possibly make two hundred.

I spend something more than half my Sabbaths here at Brotherton; the rest are divided. At this place I have but few white people: the reason is, because this is near central between Delaware and the sea, and the English settlements are chiefly on them. The other places are in the midst of the inhabitants, and, whenever I preach there, I have a large number of white people that meet to attend divine service. But, besides these, I have preached at eight different places on Lord's days, and near twenty on other days of the week, and never fail of a considerable congregation,—so large and extensive is this vacancy.

Two large counties, and a considerable part of two more, almost wholly destitute of a preached gospel (except what the Quakers do in their way), and many of the people but one remove from a state of heathenism.

As to the success that has attended my labors, I can say but little: it is a time wherein the influences of the Divine Spirit are mournfully withheld. I think, however, I have ground to hope that some good has been done among both Indians and white people, and the prospects of further usefulness are very considerable if proper means could be used. But such is the state of this country, there is such a mixture of Quakers and other denominations, and so many that have no concern about religion in any shape, that very little can at present be expected towards the support of the gospel. On my own part, I have never thought proper to take one single farthing yet in all my excursions, fearing that it might prejudice the minds of some and so, in a measure, frustrate the design.

At this place, where most of the Indians are settled, we greatly want a school for the children. When I built the meeting-house last year, I provided some materials also for a schoolhouse, and in the fall addressed the legislature of this province for some assistance, not only for the support of a school, but for the erecting of a small grist-mill, a blacksmith's shop, and a small trading store to furnish the Indians with necessaries in exchange for their produce, and so prevent their running twelve or fifteen miles to the inhabitants for every thing they want; whereby they not only consume much time, but often fall into the temptation of calling at dram-houses (too frequent in the country), where they intoxicate themselves with spirituous liquors, and after some days, perhaps, instead of hours, return home wholly unfit for any thing relating either to this or a future world.

The Governor, the Council, the Speaker of the House of Assembly, and several of the other members, thought well of the motion, and recommended it; but the Quakers, and others in that interest, made opposition, and, being the greater part of the house, it finally went against us. If the same could be done some other way, it would be the best step towards the end proposed, and be the most likely to invite not only the Indians at these other small settlements above mentioned, but those also who live in more distant parts of the country.

Thus I have touched upon the most material things relative to this mission, and, I fear, tired your patience with my long epistle. And now, that all needed provision may be made for the promotion and perfecting of this good work among the Indians, and you, among others, be made an happy instrument of the same; that many faithful laborers may be thrust forth, and all vacant parts of the harvest be supplied; that this wilderness in particular may be turned into a fruitful field, and even the whole earth be filled with the knowledge of the Lord, is the fervent prayer of,

Madam, your most obedient, humble servant,

JOHN BRAINERD.

P.S.—Since my settlement here, I have been obliged to advance above £200 for the building of the meeting-house, for some necessary repairs of an old piece of an house that was on the spot, and for my support and other necessary expenses.

This letter somewhat anticipates our narrative; alluding to his labors in the field which he was just entering in 1759. But, as it includes also facts occurring at an earlier period, it is relevant here.

CHAPTER XXXII.

ACTION OF SYNOD—WAS HE PASTOR AT NEWARK?—HIS LETTERS.

1760.

THE Synod of New York and Philadelphia this year adopted the following minute, alike considerate in them and honorable to Mr. Brainerd:—

"It is known to many in the bounds of this Synod that some ministers, moved with an holy zeal to promote the kingdom of Christ among the Indian tribes, applied to the Society in Scotland for Propagating Christian Knowledge, and obtained a grant of a certain sum of money yearly to support two missionaries to promote the conversion of the savage nations. They employed Mr. David Brainerd, whose praise is in the churches of Christ, and whose endeavors were blessed with success in this great work of bringing the Indians to a knowledge of Christ.

"It pleased God soon to remove him from his useful labor on earth to the joys of his heavenly kingdom. As the name of Brainerd was dear to these poor tribes, his brother was chosen to succeed him in the mission, in which station he continued for seven or eight years; but, as the prospect of a troublesome war made the mission dangerous and disagreeable, the Commissioners, who employed him, dismissed him from his care of the

Indians, and he was employed to preach the gospel at Newark.

"At an Indian treaty, the province of New Jersey bought all the small tracts of land that the Indians claimed in different parts of the government; and, that they might still encourage the native inhabitants to reside among them in their own country, they bought and bestowed on the remnant of these people about four thousand acres of land, which they gladly accepted, and, as many of them were converted to Christianity, they earnestly requested that Mr. Brainerd might be granted to them again as a gospel minister.

"The annuity which the Society in Scotland had allowed to the missionary was stopped upon Mr. Brainerd's dismission, though there was and is hope of procuring it again: Mr. Brainerd was requested by the Governor and Commissioners of Jersey to undertake the Indian mission. He applied to the Synod for advice; and, though he had a very comfortable settlement at Newark, yet the Synod, through an earnest desire to promote the kingdom of Christ among these poor Indians, advised him to give up these temporal advantages and settle as a missionary among those poor Indians, with which advice he readily and generously complied. But, as there is no provision yet made to support him, and to answer many and various expenses in preaching to and settling schools among those people, the Synod think themselves obliged to use all lawful endeavors to support said mission, and have now, at their Synodical meeting, agreed to contribute themselves and to make application to the congregations in the bounds of this Synod for a general collection to promote this pious and good design; and do order that a collection for this purpose be made in every congregation under the care of this Synod, and the respective collections be sent by the Moderators of the Presbyteries before the beginning of September to Mr. Jonathan Sergeant, near Princeton, who is to receive it and pay it to the Correspondents of the Indian mission, to be by them used for this purpose.

"Ordered, that a copy of this minute be taken by the Moderators of such Presbyteries as are present, and sent to such as are absent." *

The question has been raised, whether Mr. Brainerd was in fact settled as a pastor in Newark, inasmuch as the Rev. Dr. McWhorter fails to mention him in his "Century Sermon." The Synod, speaking deliberately and of its own knowledge, seems to conclude the matter: it says "he was comfortably settled in Newark." Why Dr. McWhorter totally ignored his pious and self-sacrificing predecessor is a mystery difficult of explanation or apology. As he succeeded Mr. Brainerd, there may have been personal relations of the parties to explain this strange omission.

Probably Mr. Brainerd was never installed officially; but all the ecclesiastical writers recognize him as pastor in Newark, and he claims the same for himself. He says he had "some encouragement as a preacher there;" and, though his name is not in the catalogue of its ministers, we trust the influence of his teaching and prayers had a place in forming the character of a congregation so blessed of God and so wide-spread in its useful-

* Records of Presbyterian Church, pp. 299, 300.

ness to the Church and the world during the century gone by.

Let us now hear from Mr. Brainerd at his new home at Brotherton:—

BROTHERTON, NEW JERSEY, November 24, 1760.

REV'D AND DEAR SIR:—

Yours to Mr. William Tennent by Mr. Whitaker he received at the Commencement, and immediately delivered it to me. I thought with an answer to have sent two little Indian girls to the care of Mr. Whitaker, at Norwich; but the fever and ague has so prevailed among the Indians, and continued so long, it is now become too late for this season: I hope to send them as early in the spring as will do. Both parents and children are pleased with the offer; and I am much pleased to hear that your school flourishes. I hope God will make it a distinguished blessing.

I likewise rejoice to hear that more provision is made for the support of missionaries to the Indians: I could not tell you of one for Onohquanga. It is hoped such a person may present after a while: I shall make all the inquiry I can.

My best regards to Mrs. Wheelock, etc.; love to the little boys.

And please to accept the most respectful and affectionate salutations from,

Reverend and honored sir,

Your very humble servant,

JOHN BRAINERD.

To the Rev'd Mr. WHEELOCK (LEBANON.)

We find Mr. Brainerd the next month still seeking a missionary for another field.

NEW HAVEN, December 9, 1760.

REV'D AND VERY DEAR SIR:—

After I wrote the inclosed, I set out on a journey to the northward, not without some hopes of reaching as far as Lebanon; but the season is so far advanced, and I am under some necessity to be home by such a time, that I think I must deny myself that pleasure.

I waited on Mr. President Davis in my way, and advised with him about a young gentleman for Onohquanga. After maturely considering, he thought of one who took his degree at Princeton last Commencement, Amos Thompson by name. With him we conversed on the head, who told us "it was new to him; but, if it should appear that he could serve his generation better in that capacity than any other, he had no objections to it." The president thinks him well qualified.

Sir, I write in the utmost haste, in a cold morning, and without fire. I know you are a good reader, otherwise I should fear this would not answer the end; I likewise know you are kind and good, and therefore need add no more but my very affectionate regard to you and Mrs. Wheelock, and subscribe myself,

Reverend and dear sir,

Your very humble servant,

JOHN BRAINERD.

Rev'd Dr. WHEELOCK.

CHAPTER XXXIII.

THE SYNOD EARNEST IN ITS CARE OF THE MISSION—ACTION OF THE SCOTCH SOCIETY—THE GOVERNMENT OF NEW JERSEY NOT FULFILLING ITS PLEDGES.

1761.

THE Synod of New York and Philadelphia still exhibited a care for their missionary. They say:—

"The Synod, taking this matter into serious consideration, judge that, though the mission among the Oneida Indians overtured by Mr. Kirkpatrick is a matter of great importance, and which we would gladly favor were it in our power, yet, inasmuch as after all the inquiry we can make no person can be found to undertake said mission, nor can we in present circumstances raise a sufficient supply for its support, it is agreed *that we will, to the utmost of our power*, support Mr. Brainerd; and for this purpose agree that another collection shall be raised in all our congregations,—one hundred and fifty pounds of which shall be allowed to Mr. Brainerd for the ensuing year; and that those who have not yet collected shall be included in this order, besides their fulfilling the order of the last year's Synod on this subject." *

This language, so cordial and strong, indicates

* Presbyterian Record, p. 311.

their missionary zeal, and makes us proud of our venerable Church. The minute of the Scotch Society is interesting:—

Minute dated Edinburgh, 5th March, 1761.

"Upon letters from America, Mr. Brainerd's salary is paid, and he continued as formerly."

Extract from Minutes dated Edinburgh, 4th March, 1762.

"The Committee reported that there was given in to them a letter of the 23d September last, from the Rev'd Mr. David Bostwick, President of the Society's Correspondents at New York, in answer to that sent them by order of the Committee on the 7th of March last, which letter bears that the Government of New Jersey, in a contract with the Indians, on condition of their quitting all right to any other lands in the province, had purchased for them and settled on them and their successors, by a legislative act, that whole tract of land which the Correspondents were endeavoring to procure for them; that the Correspondents had inadvertently, without acquainting the Society, assumed the following gentlemen to be joint with them, and now propose the Society would send them commissions for that purpose, viz.: the Rev'd Messieurs Richard Treat, Timothy Johnes, David Bostwick, Elihu Spencer, Caleb Smith, John Brainerd, Abraham Kettletas, ministers of the gospel in New York and New Jersey; William Livingston, Esq., attorney-at-law, Messieurs Peter Vanbrugh Livingston and David Vanhorn, merchants in New York, the Hon. Samuel Woodruff and William Peartree Smith, Esquires, Messrs. Robert Cuming and Jonathan Sergeant, of New York.

"The Committee agreed to transmit to the General Meeting, with the opinion that Commission of Correspondence be given to the gentlemen above proposed."

Same date as above.

"The General Meeting having heard the said report and opinion of their Committee, and the foresaid letters being now read, the General Meeting agreed that letters of commission be sent to the gentlemen above proposed."

The names in the above designate the persons who at that time represented the Scotch Society in America.

Mr. Brainerd speaks gloomily of his new home and his prospects at Brotherton. He says:—

"I had repeated promises from Governor Bernard of a comfortable, decent house for the place of my residence, as also a house for the public worship of God. But promises were all I could get towards either; and, when I came to think of moving here, was obliged to sell almost all my household furniture, because I had no place to put it in. And the loss I hereby sustained, together with the losses and expenses in my several removes, was about £150 damage to my estate, besides all the fatigue and trouble that attended the same." *

When the Governor and Council of New Jersey induced Mr. Brainerd to make his home in the forests and among the swamps of Brotherton, the

* J. Brainerd's letter, Sprague's Annals, vol. iii. p. 152.

least they could do properly was to give him the means of carrying out the very object of his residence there. It seems they abandoned him to his own resources. His Scotch salary appears to have failed, so that his only certain dependence was on the twenty pounds from his Synod. He certainly was not

"Passing rich with twenty pounds a year,"

if he had to build a dwelling-house, a church, a schoolhouse, a store, and a mill for his people. His friends in the Synod and elsewhere stood by him; and all these buildings, of a sort, were set up. A mill on the old site, called the "Indian mill," exists to this day.

We have hitherto regarded him as a missionary to the Indians only: the following letter to Rev. Enoch Green shows how apostolically he carried the gospel to the destitute whites. He is directing a Synodical supply on his field:—

TRENTON, June 21, 1761.

REV. AND DEAR SIR:—

It has not been in my power, by any means, to make a visit to the shore since the session of the Synod, and consequently could not make appointments for you; your plans of preaching, however, will be as follows: *Tom's River*, the most northerly place; then southward, *Goodluck*, either at Thomas Potter's or David Woodmonsee's; *Barnegat*, at Mr. Rulon's; *Manuhocking*, at Mr. Haywood's or Mr. Randal's; *Wading River*, at Charles Loveman's or John Leak's; *Great Egg Harbor*, at Captain Davis', Wm. Reed's, Benjamin Ingersoll's, And'w Blackman's, John English's, Philip Schull's, George May's, Elijah Clark's; *Cape May*, either at Captain Sillwill's or John Golden's, and at *Tuckahoe* meeting-house; and any other places you may think proper when you come on the spot. And some of those mentioned possibly you may not think best to preach at: that will be as you judge best; but these are the houses where meetings are generally held.

If you could begin with Tom's River, and be there a day or two before Sabbath to notify the people, then you might make the rest of your appointments and send them seasonably before you. The proportion will be: two Sabbaths to the northward of Little Egg Harbor River, three in Great Egg Harbor, one at the Cape or Tuckahoe, and as many weekly lectures at all as you can.

Thus, dear sir, in a minute or two, as I pass through town, I have given you these hints, which perhaps may be of some use to your tour on the shore; in which I hope the blessing of God will attend your labors, and am, with all respect,

Reverend and dear sir,

Your affectionate brother,

J. BRAINERD.

P.S.—If you could consult with Mr. Thomas Smith and Mr. McKnight, who will succeed you, and make their appointments for them, it would be of use. I hope you will be kind enough to call and see me on your return.

To the Rev. ENOCH GREEN.*

---

* Rev. Enoch Green was licensed, in 1761, by the New Brunswick Presbytery, in company with Rev. William Tennent. He was Mr. Brainerd's predecessor at Deerfield, N. J., and died there about 1776.

We have seen that Mr. Brainerd had sent several Indian boys (John Pumshire, Jacob Woolley, Hezekiah Calvin, Joseph Woolley, etc.), at Dr. Wheelock's request, to be educated in his Indian school in Lebanon, Conn. Dr. Wheelock was disposed to try the same experiment with little Indian girls. Our young friends will have great interest in the following letters of Mr. Brainerd's, introducing those girls to their new home at Dr. Wheelock's:—

NASSAU HALL, May 30, 1761.

REV'D AND VERY DEAR SIR:—

Yours of the 18th instant met me here the day before yesterday; at the same time I received a letter from Mr. Andrew Oliver, of Boston.

I rejoice that your school is so prosperous: I shall always esteem it a favor to have it in my power to do any thing for its promotion. I communicated your letter to Mr. Wm. Tennent; but we have had the affairs of college, in its present melancholy circumstances, under consideration, and are hardly in a capacity to think maturely of what you proposed respecting an incorporation.

I hardly know what you mean "*by advising you with respect to taking three Indian boys at the expense of the Commissioners, and three more at your own risk.*" I am highly pleased with every thing of that kind; and doubtless it would be best to get them from remote tribes, if they can be had.

I am glad to hear our little boys are well: their parents are, too.

One of the girls proposed to be sent has been in a poor state all winter; I hoped she might be well enough in the spring, but have now no hopes. Several others I have tried, whose parents are not willing to let them go so far off; but I hope, nevertheless, to send two by the first vessel that sails,—either to Captain Coit, of New London, according to Mr. Whittaker's direction, or by Captain Loveman, of Middletown, who will take care of the children till you can leave word and they can be conveyed to Lebanon.

Mr. Samuel Finley is chosen president of this college in the room of the dear and much lamented Mr. Davies.

You will easily guess I have not much time at command. Please to excuse incorrectness, etc. etc., and present affectionate regards to your spouse.

I am, in the tenderest bonds,
Reverend and honored sir,
Your very humble servant,
JOHN BRAINERD.

To the Rev'd Mr. WHEELOCK.

BROTHERTON, ON MOUNT CARMEL, September 14, 1761.

REV'D AND VERY DEAR SIR:—

With this I have at last sent the little Indian girls to Middletown, having no direct way to convey them to Norwich. It has given me no small uneasiness that I could not send them before. I have sent the two I at first proposed; not being able to prevail with the parents of any other to let their child go so far.

She that was sick last fall, and for that reason could not be sent, continued so all winter, and until the summer, but seems now to be fully recovered and quite well. But her mother for some time past has been in a very poor way, and is now so low that she does not expect ever to see the child again in this world after she parts with her,—which is an affecting circumstance.

The name of the elder child is Miriam Store. She is a very amiable child, and I have much reason to think was savingly converted when she was about three years old. Her life, however, has hitherto no way contradicted such a marvellous work as seemed then to be wrought upon her, of which I had the pleasure and satisfaction to be an eye-witness. I could not then determine what it was, but thought *multitude of days would speak.*

The name of the younger is Elizabeth Quela; has been a pretty-behaved child as far as I have known, but nothing respecting her any ways remarkable. They were both baptized in their infancy; the father of the elder and the mother of the younger being members of this church. Miriam will be twelve years old if she lives till December; Betty will be ten some time next spring.

They have had very little schooling; and the younger, I believe, has near or quite lost what little she was taught.

We have had no school since the Indians were settled on this land, nor have we yet any thing to support such an expense. I have thought sometimes of trying to do something at it myself; but the country round about me is so large, and so destitute of the means of grace, that I know not how to think of spending my time with a few little children. I am in hopes that, by some means or other, we shall be able after a while to set up a school again.

I feel tenderly concerned for these little girls; and, as it is a very considerable thing for them to go so far from their parents and all their relations and acquaintances, I hope they will meet with the kindest and best treatment; and may Heaven succeed the design.

I have had the favor of two letters from you this summer, and when I received them was somewhat at a loss to know why you had not received my answer. I sent it by Mr. Thompson, and at the same time an answer to one I received from Mr. Oliver, of Boston. I have wanted very much to hear from Mr. Thompson, but have heard nothing from the day he left Nassau Hall.

Mr. Occum * has done bravely. I heard of him after his arrival among the Oneidas, and that he was well re-

---

* As the name of Mr. Occum often occurs, some account of him may be pertinent. Sampson Occum, an Indian clergyman, was born at Mohegan, near Norwich, Conn., in the year 1733. He was the first Indian pupil educated at Lebanon by the Rev. Mr. Wheelock, with whom he entered in 1742, at the age of nine, and remained with him four years. In 1748 he taught school in New London, and about the year 1755 went to the east end of Long Island, where he opened a school for the Shenecock Indians. He was ordained by the Suffolk Presbytery in August, 1759. In January, 1761, he visited the Oneidas, and in 1766 was sent by Mr. Wheelock to England with Mr. Whittaker, the minister of Norwich, in order to promote the interest of Moor's school, as Mr. Wheelock's institution at Lebanon was called.

As Occum was the first Indian preacher that visited England, he attracted large audiences, and preached between three and four hundred sermons. About ten thousand pounds were collected for establishing schools among the American aborigines. This was placed in the hands of trustees, of whom the Earl of Dartmouth was the principal, and Dr. Wheelock's school was removed to Hanover, N. H. On Occum's return he labored among his countrymen, and removed eventually, in 1786, to Brotherton, near Utica, N. Y., whither many Mohegans and Montauks accompanied him, where he died in July, 1792, aged fifty-nine. He was accompanied to the grave by upwards of three hundred Indians.

An account of the Indians of Montauk, by Occum, is published in the *Massachusetts Historical Collections.* He published a sermon at the execution of Moses Paul, at New Haven, September 2, 1772, and much of his correspondence is among the papers of the Historical Society of Hartford, Conn. A portrait of him was published in one of the early volumes of the *Evangelical Magazine.—McClure's Life of Wheelock; Memoirs of the Countess of Huntington; New York Historical Collections; Allen's Biographical Dictionary.*

ceived: I suppose you have had later advices. Oh, may Heaven succeed the laudable design!

I am very glad to hear of the encouragement your school meets with, and the blessing that seems to attend your endeavors; particularly the visitation it has met with from Heaven, the notice taken of it by the Marquis of Lothian and the Commissioners in Boston. We do not write to the marquis now: they have directed us to write to the Preses of the Committee of Directors, by whom all the Society's business is transacted. I propose soon to write to that gentleman (Mr. Smollett), and shall take occasion to mention your school, by which means it will probably come before the whole Society. I would be most heartily willing to promote that laudable design in every possible way, but doubt whether I can be of any use in the *suit of an Incorporation for Indian affairs:* I should be very glad, however, to converse with you a few hours on the head. For that and other reasons I want very much to take a journey into New England; and would go as far eastward as Boston, but I know not how to spare the time.

I supply at more than *half a dozen places* on Lord's days besides this, and preach lectures on other days of the week at near *twenty*,—so large is this destitute country; and never had people greater need of ministerial help. When it will please the Lord of the harvest to send laborers here I know not; there is no provision for their support.

I am glad to hear so well of the little boys: their parents were well lately. Jacob Woolley is like to make a good scholar, and behaves well.

My *little daughter* is lately returned from Cohansey, where she has been all summer, and has a great desire to go to Mr. Wheelock's with the Indian children, to learn *good things.* May-be, sir, you may sometimes think of her in your retired moments: she is just turned of six.

Accept of all duty and affection from,

Reverend and honored sir,

Your very humble servant,

JOHN BRAINERD.

NASSAU HALL, December 9, 1761.

REV'D AND VERY DEAR SIR:—

Yesterday I had the pleasure of receiving your favor of the 6th ultimo, and conversing several hours with your son.*

Am much pleased with his account of your school, and more than ever confirmed in my hopes that God designs something *great* by it.

It gives me pleasure to hear of the safe arrival of the Indian child I sent last, of the comfortable situation of her and the rest of the children, and particularly what you inform me of about Hezekiah.

Please to give my love to them: their parents and friends were all well a few days ago.

Your son may expect every thing from me that he might from a father, so far as my ability reaches; but whether the Commissioners can take Joseph [Woolley] under their care depends upon our hearing from the Society, and what we hear. We have had nothing yet from that quarter for Jacob's support, and his expenses have for some time been borne by the college fund: we hope to hear from the Society some time this winter, or in the spring at farthest. You may depend upon every

* Dr. Wheelock's son was subject to nervous spasms, and his health broke down in Princeton College. He was put in charge of Brainerd.

thing in my power in favor of your proposal, if your son is suited with his situation and inclines to continue at the college.

I am very unfortunate in not seeing dear good Mr. Pomroy.* I heard of his being gone southward, but could not learn when he expected to return. Hoped to meet him here at this time, but find he is not expected till next week, and uncertain whether then.

My best regard to Mrs. Wheelock. I write in haste, and feel so aguish this morning that I think I don't do quite so well as common. You have goodness enough to excuse all, and to believe that I am

Your most affectionate
And very humble servant,
JOHN BRAINERD.

To the Rev'd Mr. WHEELOCK.

---

* The Rev. Benjamin Pomroy, D.D., minister of Hebron, Conn., died December 22, 1784. His wife was a sister of Dr. Wheelock, and his daughter married Rev. David McClure. As a friend of the Revival and of Whitefield, he was once arrested and deprived by government of his salary seven years. Dr. Trumbull describes him as a real genius, and among the best of preachers in his day.

CHAPTER XXXIV.

MR. BRAINERD ELECTED MODERATOR OF THE SYNOD OF NEW YORK AND PHILADELPHIA—HIS SERMON—REV. SAMPSON OCCUM—WESTERN MISSION—HIS LETTER FROM GREAT EGG HARBOR.

1762.

MR. BRAINERD was this year elected Moderator of the Synod of New York and Philadelphia, at its annual meeting in Philadelphia, May 19. For the first time he is entered as a member of the Philadelphia Presbytery, instead of New York. Why his relation was changed he does not tell us; but probably the accession of new elements had made the Presbytery of Philadelphia more accordant to his taste. Fifty-nine members were present in the Synod, and fifty-three absent. Mr. George Duffield was made clerk. After one hundred years a Duffield and Brainerd have been often associated in Philadelphia ecclesiastical bodies in a friendship as cordial as that cherished by their namesakes of old.* The Synod† this year, threatened with a storm about "the examination

* At the General Assembly of the Presbyterian Church held in May, 1864, at Dayton, Ohio, Thomas Brainerd was elected Moderator, and George Duffield, Clerk,—a singular coincidence.

† Records of the Presbyterian Church, pp. 317, 224.

of the experiences of candidates," went into a committee of the whole, with Mr. Brainerd in the chair, and finally reached a compromise, which did not satisfy all, but to which all submitted. Mr. Brainerd seems to have honored his office: unless a Moderator can do this, the office of Moderator never honors him.

We have no report of Mr. Brainerd's missionary labors this year.

1763.

Mr. Brainerd opened the meeting of the Synod of New York and Philadelphia with a sermon from John ix. 4: "*I must work the works of him that sent me, while it is day: the night cometh, when no man can work.*" A characteristic text, marking the practical, energetic, martyr-like spirit of the preacher.

No theological hair-splitting, no rancorous controversy, no transcendental dreamings, no rhetorical flourishes, no parade of great learning, no egotistic sentimentalism, we will venture to affirm, had a place in that sermon. It was the voice of John "crying in the wilderness," that men should repent and do works meet for repentance. Synod directed that:—

"The members who have made collections for the Indian mission are ordered to pay the same to Mr. Ewing before to-morrow morning.

"Ordered, that there be a collection made in all the

congregations under the care of this Synod, both in those who have and who have not ministers settled among them, for the Indian mission and the Indian school; and that every Presbytery take care that the collections in their vacancies be made in due time; and that thirty pounds be given to a schoolmaster for the ensuing year; and that Messrs. John Meas, John Wallace, George Bryans, John Bayard, Isaac Snowdon, be requested to assist Mr. Brainerd to build a schoolhouse, and to dispose of the money collected for the use of said school, and lay the accounts before the next Synod; and that Mr. George Bryan be appointed treasurer of the committee.

"Ordered, also, that Mr. Ewing procure a state of the accounts of Mr. Sergeant, relating to the Indian mission under the care of Mr. Brainerd, and lay them, with an account of the money received by himself, before the Synod at their next meeting.

"A request from the corporation for the relief of poor and distressed Presbyterian ministers, etc., was brought in and read, which is as follows:—

"'*Nov.* 16, 1762. At a meeting of the corporation in this city it was agreed, that this board appoint some of their members to wait on the Synod at their next meeting, and in their name request that some missionaries be sent to preach to the distressed frontier inhabitants, and to report their distresses, and to let us know where new congregations are forming, and what is necessary to be done to promote the spread of the gospel among them, and that they inform us what opportunities there may be of preaching the gospel to the Indian nations in their neighborhood.

"'And it is agreed that the necessary expenses of these missionaries be paid by this board, and that Messrs. John

Meas, Dr. Redman, William Humphreys, George Bryans, Treat, Ewing, and the secretary, wait on the Synod, and earnestly press them to grant this request.'

"In consequence of the above request, the Synod appoint Messrs. Beatty and Brainerd to go on the aforesaid mission, as soon as they can conveniently, so as to be able to return to make a report to the corporation at their next general meeting in October; and that Messrs. William Tennent, sen., McKnight, and Hunter supply Mr. Brainerd's pulpit and take care of his concerns among the Indians, and that Mr. Treat supply Mr. Beatty's pulpit once every three Sabbaths. Mr. Chestnut is to supply at Barnegate and Manchockin the first Sabbath of September."

This mission failed; the Synod, next year, say:—

"The Moderator and Mr. Brainerd were prevented from fulfilling the order of the Synod in their mission to the frontiers, and the whole design of the mission was entirely prostrated by the breaking out of the Indian war." *

Messrs. Duffield and Beatty afterwards accomplished this work.

We have only one letter of Mr. Brainerd's this year: it is mainly devoted to Dr. Wheelock's affairs. We give a brief extract:—

GREAT EGG HARBOR, June 6, 1763.

REV'D AND DEAR SIR:—

I thank you for the letter by your son, and your kind

* Records of the Presbyterian Church, p. 335.

present of the pamphlet giving account of the rise and progress of your school.

I spoke to Dr. Alison in favor of it: found he was fur nished with one of your books. He seemed cordial, but was afraid nothing could be obtained at present from the fund.

I expect to set out some time next month, in company with the Rev'd Mr. Beatty, on a journey to the remote Indians. We propose to go up the branches of the Sus quehanna, from thence to Alleghany, down to Pittsburgh and parts adjacent, and endeavor to learn the state and temper of the Indians. I hope it may have some good effects.

My best regards to Mrs. Wheelock: love to the children in the school. The parents of those belonging to us were well lately. I am more encouraged with our Indians than some time ago: they are more sober and industrious.

The Synod of New York and Philadelphia at their last session determined to support a school among them, and voted Mr. Occum £65 for the current year to assist him in his mission. I hope God intends some good to the poor Indians: may the time haste when the earth shall be filled with his glory.

I am yours, etc.,

JOHN BRAINERD.

To the Rev'd Mr. WHEELOCK.

CHAPTER XXXV.

SYNODICAL ACTION—JACOB WOOLLEY—WHITEFIELD'S SUCCESS IN COLLECTING MONEY—A REVIVAL NEEDED—SICKNESS OF GILBERT TENNENT—SENDING OCCUM TO EUROPE.

1764.

THIS was one of the most important years in Mr. Brainerd's life. In the Synod he must have been a most influential member. He was put on the Committee "to appropriate the money for pious youths in Princeton College," made one of the members of the "Commission" for the year, and one of the "Committee of Correspondence with the American and Foreign Churches," which comprehended delegates from New England.

The Synod say:—

"The Indian affairs come under consideration, and Mr. Brainerd reports that there has been paid into his hands the sum of twenty-eight pounds, nineteen shillings, and four-pence, provincial currency, which money, with other collections that are or may be put into his hands, the Synod order to be laid out, as in manner ordered last year, for the support of the Indian school; and that the money allowed for the support of the master shall not exceed fifty pounds provincial currency; and further appoint that a collection be made this year also, through their bounds, for the support of said school, and that each Presbytery take care that said collection be duly made through their bounds, and that they lay their accounts, regularly adjusted, before our next Synod.

"And Mr. Brainerd further reports, that there appears to have been paid to Mr. Occum about the sum of thirty-four pounds, provincial currency." *

Mr. Brainerd's letters furnish a glimpse of his manner of life.

BROTHERTON, March 31, 1764.

REV'D AND DEAR SIR:—

Yours of December 1763, came last evening by your son, who is now with me, and Mr. Kirkland,† a very

* Presbyterian Records, p. 336.

† Mr. Kirkland, "the pretty, agreeable youth," was afterwards the Rev. Samuel Kirkland, a missionary among the Indians, who died March 28, 1808, aged sixty-six. He donated the land for Hamilton College; and it may be said that through him and Dr. Wheelock both Hamilton and Dartmouth Colleges rose up, indirectly but really, as a result of Indian missions.

"Mr. Kirkland was the son of Daniel Kirkland, minister of Norwich. After enjoying for some time the advantages of Wheelock's school, he finished his education at the College in New Jersey, where he graduated in 1765. While at school he had learned the language of the Mohawks, and he commenced a journey to the Seneca Indians, in order to acquire their language, November 20, 1764, and did not return till May, 1766. June 19 he was ordained at Lebanon as a missionary to the Indians. He removed his wife to Oneida Castle in 1769. She was Jerusha Bingham, whose mother was a sister of President E. Wheelock, in whose family she long lived. In the spring he went to the house of his friend General Herkimer, at Little Falls, and there his twin children were born, August 17, 1770, of whom one was President Kirkland, of Harvard College. His daughter Jerusha married John H. Lothrop, of Utica, the father of Rev. S. K. Lothrop, of Boston. About 1772 he removed to Connecticut, and afterwards lived for a time at Stockbridge. For more than forty years his attention was directed to the Oneida tribe in New York, and he died at pretty, agreeable youth: I hope the Lord designs to make him a blessing to his church. Your son is tolerably well.

I am very sorry to have such a melancholy account of Jacob Woolley; but he is in the hand of God, and we must pray for him. His grandmother and aunts were very much affected when we told them to-day, which was done in the most prudent manner. I am likewise pained for poor Enoch Class; am afraid he will be wicked. But what your son tells me of Josey and the rest is comfortable: may the Lord perfect what is lacking.

With pleasure I heard of the collection at New York for your school, by the instrumentality of our dear and very worthy Mr. Whitefield. The Lord makes him a blessing wherever he goes: may he long be continued such to the Church of God.

New York and the churches in these parts have met with a very great loss in the death of dear Mr. Bostwick. I know not how the vacancy will be filled up; but the great Lord of the harvest lives.

Our valuable young brother Mr. C. J. Smith has been faithfully laboring in these frozen parts all winter, and is, I trust, an helpmeet of very considerable good in this uncultivated world. He is a good young man: he will tarry five or six Sabbaths longer with us.

I have greatly to mourn my unsuccessfulness among the Indians, and yet (I thank God!) some good is done. I have had three persons under examination some time for baptism, two of whom have evidently been wrought upon of late, and one or two great backsliders give some hopes of returning. The prospects among the white

---

Clinton, in that State, the place of his residence in the neighborhood of Oneida."—*Allen's Biographical Dictionary.*

h——n appear something encouraging in several instances. All glory to Him who *does all things well!*

My kind salutations to the children: their parents are all well.

I redeem a few moments to write this from my sleep: It is between eleven and twelve, and my pen writes very badly. Adieu.

Honored and dear sir,

I am yours till death,

JOHN BRAINERD.

Rev'd Mr. WHEELOCK.

The hopes of both Dr. Wheelock and Brainerd to make their educated Indians useful begin to shake.

BROTHERTON, June 17, 1764.

REV'D AND VERY DEAR SIR:—

This incloses a line to poor Jacob Woolley: I wish it may have some good effect on his mind. His awful apostasy is truly affecting, and very distressing: the Lord, in great mercy, bring him again to the exercise of his reason and make him yet a vessel of honor.

I have sent the letter open (written in some haste), that, if you judge it not best to send, you may suppress it, or alter, or add, as you think proper. Oh that the Lord would reclaim other apostates too, awaken sinners, comfort saints, and build up Zion! Blessed be his holy name for the good news we have from Long Island and some other parts: may this glorious work overspread the land and become a praise in the whole earth! There is little of it in these parts: I hope our infinitely gracious God will hear prayer and revive his work. We kept a fast, by Synodical appointment, the day before yesterday, principally on that account. Oh, when shall we

"see his tribes rejoice,
And aid the triumph with our voice"?

It is certainly a mournful time now; yet, alas! how few mourners! may the number be multiplied by thousands!

In my neighborhood there is little more than some distant prospects, such as people becoming disposed to exert themselves to build meeting-houses, propose for the settlement of ministers, etc., which yet has something encouraging in it; and I would hope the time draws near when a glorious shower will fall upon us. Oh, may it be plenteous and extensive! Dear Mr. C. J. Smith has been very helpful in the winter past.

I am in a poor, low state of body, scarce able to go on with my work anyhow. I thought sometimes last winter I must have wholly desisted; but was considerably better in the spring; otherwise I believe I should have attempted a journey into New England. Now for about three or four weeks I have been down again, very weak and languid: nevertheless, I do officiate in several places as well as I can. Ministerial help is greatly needed in this neighborhood: half a dozen ministers might be well employed here every Sabbath. How afflicting to have the faithful laborers so disproportioned to the harvest: may the Lord greatly increase their number!

Mr. Gilbert Tennent is far gone with a kind of feverish habit; he has not been able to preach for some time, and in all probability will not continue long. He has been, you know, a laborious servant in the Lord's vineyard, and we know not how to spare such; but the residue of the Spirit is with Christ.

My best regards to Mrs. Wheelock. I have not heard whether your son is come to college: my love to him if he is at home, and Mr. Kirkland. My little daughter sends duty to Mr. Wheelock and Mrs. Wheelock, and desires in the best manner she can to express her grateful sense of your son's kindness in the present he sent her after he was here last spring, and Mr. Kirkland for his.

The [Indian] children's parents and relations are all well. I send my love to them, and a solemn charge to behave well and be good children.

I humbly ask the continuance of your prayers for me and mine, and am, with greatest respect

Reverend and dear sir,

Your very humble servant,

JOHN BRAINERD.

P.S.—My little daughter comes in while I am folding up this, and says that Mr. Wheelock has two little daughters, whom she desires to be remembered to in the kindest and most respectful manner, which, she says, is the least she can do: she would write to them if she had time. The little monitor has freshened my memory and reminded me of my duty, in consequence of which I send my affectionate regards to your family.

Did the Rev. George Whitefield originate the idea of which Dartmouth College was the final result? It would seem from the following letter that Whitefield, through John Brainerd, first proposed to Dr. Wheelock the plan of removing his school from Lebanon to the Indian Border, up the Connecticut, and to send Occum to England to beg for it. These two ideas, whoever originated them, founded Dartmouth College.

BROTHERTON, October 9, 1764.

REV'D AND DEAR SIR:—

Yours of 7th August I received at Commencement, but could not possibly get a moment to write then. Am greatly afflicted that my miserable, wretched creatures are such a trouble to you, and like to turn out so poorly after all. The Lord pity and help us! Alas! I am greatly distressed at home too: some of the Indians behave inconceivably bad!

I know not what the Lord designs with these distressed creatures: oh that His infinite mercy may reach our deplorable case! We have had several days of fasting and prayer of late, besides what have been of public appointment, and the Lord is gracious to us in many respects, forever adored be his sacred name! Some Christians are considerably enlivened, and some are lately added, of such as, I hope, shall be saved.

I had an interview last week with Mr. Whitefield, at Philadelphia. He was indeed at Princeton, and preached Commencement-morning half-after eight; but I could get no time with him that day, and next morning early he went off westward. He says he will do all in his power to raise a fund for Indian service in Great Britain, etc., if a good plan can be laid, and that he thinks I must go with *Messrs. Occum and Fowler to transact the affair*. But how can my extensive, extremely necessitous charge be taken care of? I also alleged my unfitness for such an important undertaking with real sincerity and, I think, much propriety. But he said, "I was Mr. David Brainerd's brother," etc. I mentioned Mr. C. J. Smith. He objected to his youth, want of experience and acquaintance with mankind. I said then, Mr. Smith must supply my place; but Mr. Smith is up the North River, and could not hear a word of what we said,—and thus the matter stands.

Mr. Whitefield has written to him to be in Philadelphia some time this month: perhaps he will be the man, after all, to cross the Atlantic. For my part, I feel just at the disposal of Heaven. I should be glad of the advantage of a year in Great Britain, not to mention the agreeableness of such a tour and how much it would gratify my curiosity: I have also tender connections here, and it is likely it would be with loss to my outward circumstances, etc. But all these I entirely set aside, and feel myself wholly at the disposal of Divine Providence. Where I can be the instrument of most good and best serve the interest of our dear Divine Master, that is the spot, and no other: may Heaven direct and order for the best!

But what plan will you lay? Mr. Whitefield thinks a tract of land should be procured and a house built, and he would be glad as near as might be to the Indian settlements; that the boys should be taught all sorts of plantation-work, to read and write English, arithmetic, etc.; but that it would be quite lost to teach them the dead languages, etc., as I suppose he told you at your interview.

I am glad you have a Commission for Correspondents in Connecticut: cannot you and we correspond as bodies? We have written, desiring the Society to send Letters of Commission to the Trustees of New Jersey College, and make that board, for the time being, their Correspondents and Commissioners for propagating the gospel among the Indians; but have no return yet. It is likely the Society will grant our request.

I am sorry for your poor, dear son: the Lord grant him the grace of patience and resignation to his will, and send him help in the best time! I cannot, as a friend, advise him to apply for a degree unless he is at least tolerably well qualified with learning. The trustees, as such, cannot think of showing favor, how much soever they would be desirous to oblige as private friends.

My best regards to Mrs. Wheelock; kind love to your son, Kirkland, and the Indian children,—their parents are generally well.

My humble, affectionate salutations to the reverend Commissioners, particularly dear Mr. Pomroy; my little daughter sends duty to Mrs. Wheelock, and love to dear little misses. Pray do not at any time forget,

Reverend and dear sir,

Your affectionate, unworthy

JOHN BRAINERD.

Mr. Brainerd seemed to acquiesce in his proposed visit to Europe with Mr. Occum. The following letter is on the subject, though some parts are unintelligible at this day. Precisely what he expected of Mr. Livingston he does not tell us.

NEW YORK, December 19, 1764.

REV'D AND DEAR SIR:—

I arrived here yesterday in the forenoon; after dinner waited on Mr. Wm. Livingston. Delivered your letter, and he read the copies: thinks highly of your school, as also Mr. P. V. B., his brother, who read them before dinner. Afterwards I waited on Mr. David Vanhorn, who says Mr. Whitefield is friendly to your school and desirous to promote it, but did not think well of Mr. Occum's tour: I set the matter in as good a light as I could. Then I waited on the Hon. Mr. Smith and his lady, and did as you bid me. His three eldest sons were there,—the third, a doctor, lately from England, France, and Holland, where he has spent several years. They read the copies, seemed much pleased, and the doctor begged that he might copy that from Onohquanga, at least. They expressed great satisfaction respecting your school, and seem to think it will be best to have it continued where it is, and particularly Mr. Wm., the eldest son, was very full in that opinion. They doubt of Mr. Occum's capacity,—say he preached very poorly here; but Mrs. Smith thinks he would do, and they say he might, if he could get more acquaintance with men and things, carefully study a number of sermons and commit them to memory, etc. Mrs. Smith can think of no man that would do to go with him but Mr. Rodgers: your humble servant, you may be sure, was not mentioned. I am satisfied, and still feel as I did at your house; but more than ever think it necessary that the matter should be agitated and determined soon, that I may know what to depend upon; for it must take me a good while to settle my affairs and make necessary provision. I would go as strong as possible.

Mr. P. V. B. Livingston mentioned Mr. Occum's incapacity,—that on the whole he hopes he might do; he would have another with him, and, if possible, a Mohawk. They all say it would be of great advantage at least, if not necessary, that those who go, especially the Indians, should be well acquainted with the interior parts of this land, Canada, the lakes, forts, Indian towns, castles, etc. I am sensible it would be a good thing; but every thing cannot be obtained. However, as there is now peace with the Indians, it might be worthy of thought whether it would not be best to spend a year in getting such acquaintance. I propose, if the weather will permit, to set out this afternoon for New Jersey. Hope to hear from you by your son: forgot to ask you to let him come and tarry with me as many days as he can when he comes to Princeton.

My best regards to Mrs. Wheelock; compliments to the young ladies, Mr. Lothrop, and Mr. Smith; love to the children, etc. Please to correct inaccuracies,—I write in haste,—and accept most cordial salutations from,

Reverend sir,

Your affectionate servant,

JOHN BRAINERD.

To the Rev'd Mr. WHEELOCK.

Dr. Wheelock, a shrewd and statesmanlike man in the Church, eagerly caught at Whitefield's idea, as may be inferred from the following appeal which he made to the Correspondents:—

"*To the Honorable Board of Correspondents in the Province of New York and New Jersey, commissioned by the Honorable Society in Scotland for Propagating Christian Knowledge.*

"The Memorial of Eleazar Wheelock, of Lebanon, in the Colony of Connecticut, humbly showeth:—

"That, by the blessing of God upon endeavors used, the Indian Charity School, which he has for several years last past had under his immediate care, is now increased to the number twenty-six; and the prospect both of the increase of their number and the usefulness of the undertaking, as well as the expense of it, is yet growing; that several of this number are young gentlemen whom he apprehends to be well accomplished for a mission among the Indians, and ten others of them are Indian youth, whom he esteems well qualified for schoolmasters, excepting that some of them yet want age, which difficulty, he supposes, may be well accommodated by their being under the inspection, direction, and conduct of the missionaries, and such of the schoolmasters as are of ripe age and judgment are ready to be authorized and sent with them.

"These are, therefore, to pray your Honorable Board to take it into consideration, and grant the concurrence of your endeavors with ours in these parts for the furtherance and speedy accomplishment of the design in view; and particularly that you would grant liberty to the Rev. John Brainerd, your missionary, to go to Europe in company with an Indian from these parts, to solicit the charity of such as are of ability for the support of this school, and such missionaries and schoolmasters as Divine Providence shall enable us to send; and that you would commissionate, authorize, and suitably recommend him, said Brainerd, for that purpose, and also recommend the design itself to the charity of God's people abroad, etc.

"All which is, with much respect, honorable gentlemen, humbly submitted to your consideration and determination by

"Your most obedient
"And most humble servant,
"ELEAZAR WHEELOCK.

"Dated at Lebanon, in Connecticut,
"January 14, 1765." *

Dr. Wheelock accompanied his petition with the following letter to the President of the Board of Correspondents:—

"LEBANON, January 14, 1765.

"SIR:—

"I am informed that the calling your Board of Commissioners together is committed to you, which occasions

* Manuscript of Dr. Wheelock, furnished by Dr. Allen.

you the present trouble. You will see by the prayer inclosed what is designed, and the difficulty of proceeding in any other manner at present.

"If your Board shall see fit to return answer in favor of my request, I pray you would not fail to make as speedy return to me as may be; for I would not fail to have every thing done that is necessary and suitable, to put Mr. Brainerd under all advantages possible to serve the design in the proposed tour.

"Please, sir, to accept sincere respects
"From your unknown friend,
"And very humble servant,
"ELEAZAR WHEELOCK.

"WM. PEARTREE SMITH, Esq."

Why Mr. Brainerd failed to carry out the suggestion of Whitefield and the desire of Dr. Wheelock, that he should go with Occum to Europe, and why the Rev. Nathaniel Whitaker, of Norwich, Conn., took his place, we are left to conjecture. The mission realized fifty thousand dollars; and, though the Indian school finally died out, Dartmouth College arose as the result of the mission. We are sorry, on his own account, that Mr. Brainerd lost the personal benefits of the contemplated European tour. The modesty that declined notoriety and despised intrigue and spiritual ambition made it more desirable that his friends should give him position and prominence. It was hard to find one willing to labor in the wilderness for the poor Indians, but easy to select a man ready to travel for them in Great Britain. Desirable posts in

Church and State never "go a-begging." The Rev. Mr. Whitaker performed his duties with energy and success in Europe. He went recommended by Sir William Johnson, Lord Sterling, and General Thomas Gage, by six royal Governors, many eminent judges, senators, lawyers, and merchants, and by fifty-eight of the leading clergymen of all denominations in America. This gave the mission weight in England, while the novelty of the Indian Occum's preaching drew crowds to hear the appeals of the mission. The Rev. Mr. Whitaker also published his appeals in a little book, issued in London, 1765. He was the right man in the right place.

CHAPTER XXXVI.

MR. BRAINERD DECLINES TO GO TO NEW YORK—HIS LETTER OF CONDOLENCE—HIS SALARY—DISAPPOINTMENTS IN HIS INDIAN YOUTH.

1765.

THE Synodical "Commission," of which Mr. Brainerd was for several years a member, was a "committee *ad interim*" borrowed from the Scotch judicatories. It had, during the year, the authority of the Synod itself, and its sessions were as formally opened with a sermon.* Mr. Brainerd's continued membership of this committee marks his status among his brethren.

The Synod, as usual, granted Mr. Brainerd the interest on the Indian fund "as an addition to his salary." They also

"Ordered, that a collection be made for propagating the gospel among the Indians, and for teaching their children; and that the several Presbyteries take care it be made in all their congregations, as well in those that want as in those that have settled ministers; and that

* "I have before me, in a pamphlet, a sermon preached before the Commission of the Synod at Philadelphia, April 20, 1735, by E. Pemberton, pastor of the Presbyterian Church in the city of New York. The dedication 'to the Reverend Commission of the Synod' refers to its having been 'preached in obedience to your commands.'"—*Dr. Hall's History of the First Presbyterian Church, Trenton*, p. 94.

each Presbytery appoint some member to bring into next Synod a particular account how every congregation in their bounds has complied with this order." *

New appeals from aggrieved parties were given entirely into the hands of two committees, to meet at the residence of the parties "to issue and determine both those matters." As a peace-maker, Mr. Brainerd had a place on each of these committees.

The Rev. Dr. Wheelock, writing to Sir William Johnson, says:—

"The Board of Correspondents in New Jersey have been applied to for Mr. Brainerd for the Oneida mission; but, for several reasons, he cannot be obtained." †

The following letter of condolence to an afflicted friend presents the writer in a very amiable light. The lady addressed we have already described:—‡

NEWARK, September 16, 1765.

MADAM:—

I have lately had the mournful news of the much lamented death of Colonel Williams, your honored and very worthy consort. I heartily condole with you in this great and public loss,—great to many, but greatest of all to you. But, whoever is the loser, he is doubtless an infinite gainer. He has exchanged darkness for light, and a vale of tears for a crown of glory; left a world of sin and sorrow for the perfection of holiness and everlasting

---

* Presbyterian Records, p. 350.

† Documentary History of New York, vol. iv. p. 357.

‡ See p. 316.

joys, where he has the beautiful sight of Christ and the blissful enjoyment of him, and out of all danger of ever losing the glorious vision and blessed fruition while time and eternity endure. This, madam, must needs be matter of unspeakable comfort to you under the afflicting hand of God, in the sore bereavement you have lately been exercised with, and especially as you expect shortly, through Infinite Grace, to ascend *yourself* and join the same glorious company,—I mean the general assembly, consisting of angels, archangels, and the spirits of the just made perfect,—there to spend a blessed eternity; not in the company of your dearest earthly friend only, but in the enjoyment of God and Jesus Christ, the common friend of lost and perishing man. May these and the like considerations support you under the heavy stroke; and may you sensibly have the comfort of that blessed promise: "All things shall work together for good to them that love God." That the Lord may favor you with much of his divine and gracious presence, much more than make up the loss you sustain in the death of a most valuable man and the dearest of earthly relations, and after many profitable and comfortable days on earth admit you to join the adoring hosts above, and spend a blessed eternity in the rapturous vision and fruition of God and the Lamb, is the unfeigned desire and prayer of, madam,

Your obliged, humble servant,

JOHN BRAINERD.

To Mrs. WILLIAMS, widow and relict of
Colonel Elisha Williams, late of Wethersfield, Conn.

We ought, perhaps, here to remind the reader that, though we have hitherto regarded Mr. Brainerd mainly as a laborer among the Indians of Brotherton, he in fact, from his first advent there, assumed the responsibility of a domestic missionary among the destitute whites of the New Jersey Pines and along a coast of nearly one hundred miles, from near Cape May to Shrewsbury and Shark River. His position as an Indian missionary was very trying: he loved his Indians too well to leave them. But they were too few to justify the entire appropriation of his time and energies. He clings to them, but at the same time, with apostolic fervor and benevolence, travels far and wide along the coast and among the Pines to give the gospel, gratuitously almost, to the destitute whites. How much they needed reformation, those who have read the history of the "*Piners*" in New Jersey will understand.

1766.

We glean from the minutes of the Synod this year a pretty definite idea of Mr. Brainerd's salary at this period of his hardest and most self-denying labor. The Synod say:—

"Mr. Brainerd is appointed to receive the money in the hands of the Trustees of New Jersey College for Indian affairs for the current year, as an addition to his salary."

And again:—

"From last year's minutes, some affairs respecting Mr. Brainerd's mission to the Indians, with some papers now received from him, were taken under consideration; and it is ordered that what moneys have been collected last year for this mission be put into the hands of Mr. Treat, jun., an account of which he is desired to give the Synod to-morrow."

Once more:—

"The Synod resolves to support the Indian school under Mr. Brainerd's care, and for that purpose order such members as have not this last year made collections immediately to collect, and transmit to the hands of Mr. Joseph Treat or Mr. Ewing, to be paid to Mr. Brainerd; and that the money now in Mr. Treat's hands be paid to Mr. Brainerd as soon as possible, which sum appears to be twenty-one pounds, sixteen shillings, and one penny."

According to this, the salary of Mr. Brainerd consisted of twenty pounds from the interest at Princeton, and twenty-one pounds, sixteen shillings, and one penny,—making in all a little over forty pounds, with two or three pounds' addition by Mr. Ewing; and this, with all his extra expenses for his Indians, all his journeys to meet missionaries, and all his domestic missionary labors in a field so obscure, so wide, and so poor that when he died his churches decayed, and no Presbyterian minister rose to follow him for near a hundred years. Truly he waged a warfare at his own charges. The Synod had some sympathy for him, as they this year say:—

"Mr. Brush is appointed to assist Mr. Brainerd in supplying the vacancy in his neighborhood."

The following letter to Dr. Wheelock shows that Mr. Brainerd's anxiety in sending his young Indians to a distant school was not groundless. We read such a letter with sorrow:—

FORKS OF EGG HARBOR, February 26, 1766.

REV'D AND VERY DEAR SIR:—

I received a letter from you some time this winter which I had not opportunity to answer, and so, as is too common in more important matters, deferred preparing until an opportunity should present to reply; and now I hear of a vessel designed for New London in about a fortnight, but am on a journey and can say but a few things.

I was grieved to hear such an account about poor, unhappy Enoch. His mother, who is a calm, Christian woman, was, indeed, very much hurt, but behaved under it as became her character; but his father used me ill, and charged me with what had befallen his son. I was obliged to give him a good setting down, and soon quieted him, so that in a few minutes he was very humble, and begged me to write, and he would go to New England and look for his son. I discouraged that, as it was a bad season in the year and he a drunken fellow, telling him I would write to Mr. Wheelock. If therefore, dear sir, you can be any way instrumental in getting him home to his parents, it will, I think, be the best thing that can now be done. I am very much grieved for the trouble you have already had with him; I could wish a hundred times he had never gone a step that way. Pray, sir, if you can hear any thing of him at Rhode Island or elsewhere, let him know that his parents would have him come home, and the sooner the better.

Where is Jacob Woolley? I have not heard a word of him since I was at your house. I wish I could get a sight of him,—poor, unhappy youth!

Some of our Indians behave better of late than they did.

Where is Josey Woolley? and how does he manage? Where is Mr. Smith? and what encouragement has he?

And, above all, how does your poor school live? I am sorry from my heart I can do nothing but say: "*Be ye warmed.*"

Where is Mr. Whitaker? I never heard whether he went to England.

In haste.

Reverend and honored sir,
Yours most cordially,
JOHN BRAINERD.

CHAPTER XXXVII.

SCHOOLMASTER PAID—BEATTY AND DUFFIELD'S TOUR AND JOURNAL—CONGREGATIONS TROUBLED BY SNAKES—FORT PITT, AND LABORS THERE—SUCCESS AMONG THE INDIANS—MR. BRAINERD AND HIS INDIANS URGED TO MIGRATE TO OHIO—THE INDIANS REPLY IN THE NEGATIVE.

1767–68.

THE Synod of New York and New Jersey begins to be more considerate of its first foreign and domestic missionary. It says:—

"The affairs of Mr. Brainerd's school came to be considered, and the Synod agree to allow Mr. Brainerd the sum of thirty pounds per year for the last three years for defraying the expenses of the Indian school, which sum he acknowledges he has already in his hands.

"And it is further agreed to allow Mr. Brainerd the sum of thirty pounds for the support of the Indian school for the current year, and the sum of twenty pounds as an addition to *his salary for his extraordinary services* in forming societies and laboring among *the white people in that large and uncultivated country*." *

As if his labors were not sufficient, they impose, no doubt with his consent, new responsibilities.

In 1766, the Synod had appointed Messrs. Duf-

* Records of Presbyterian Church, pp. 371, 275.

field and Beatty to go together the first of August, and preach at least two months among the destitute on the frontiers of the province. These gentlemen went accordingly, and a report of their tour was published in 1768, drawn up mainly by Dr. Beatty.* In their report to Synod in 1767, they say:—

"That they performed their mission to the frontiers and among the Indians. That they found on the frontiers numbers of people earnestly desirous of forming themselves into congregations, and declaring their willingness to exert their utmost in order to have the gospel among them, but in circumstances exceedingly distressing and necessitous from the late calamities of the war in these parts; and, also, that they visited the Indians at the chief town of the Delaware nation on the Muskingum, about one hundred and thirty miles beyond Fort Pitt, and were received much more cheerfully than they could have expected. That a considerable number of them waited on the preaching of the gospel with peculiar attention,—many of them appearing solemnly concerned about the great matters of religion; that they expressed an ardent desire of having further opportunities of hearing those things; that they informed them that several other tribes of Indians around them were ready to join them in receiving the gospel, and earnestly desiring an opportunity. Upon the whole, that there does appear a very agreeable prospect of a door opening for

* "The Journal of a Two Months' Tour with a View of Promoting Religion among the Frontier Inhabitants of Pennsylvania, and of Introducing Christianity among the Indians to the westward of the Alleghgeny Mountains. By Charles Beatty, A.M. London, 1768."

the gospel being spread among those poor, benighted, savage tribes."

The Synod in 1767 appointed

"The Rev. Messrs. Brainerd and Cooper to pay a visit to our frontier settlements and Indians on Muskingum and other places, and tarry with them at least three months this summer, provided the report brought back by the Indian interpreter Joseph from them, and delivered to the Rev. Dr. Alison and Messrs. Treat, Beatty, and Ewing, proves encouraging; which gentlemen are hereby appointed a committee to receive and judge of said report.

"Ordered, also, that Messrs. Brainerd and Cooper take no money from the frontier settlements for their ministerial labors among them.

"Ordered, that Mr. McKnight supply Mr. Brainerd's place among the Indians and at Mount Holly the second, third, and fourth Sabbaths of July, and that Mr. William Tennent serve Mr. McKnight with a copy of this minute."

We have procured Mr. Beatty's journal from London. In their journey outward, leaving Carlisle August 16, they threaded the water-courses among the mountains, and preached wherever they found straggling settlers in the valleys. It is somewhat difficult to follow them on the Juniata, and fix their stations.* All was rude and

* Above the present Lewistown on the Juniata, Mr. Beatty records the following scene: "While the people were convening, it began to rain, and the rain continuing obliged as many as could to crowd into

wild in their way. They reached Fort Pitt on September 6, in twenty-five days from Carlisle.

"The Rev. Mr. McLagan, chaplain of the garrison, with other gentlemen of the place, furnished them with *blankets* to sleep in, and some other necessaries, so that they fared as well as they could expect."

Their expectations from Pittsburgh at that time seem to have been very moderate. They preached on the Sabbath "to the garrison, and the people, who live in some kind of a town without the fort," *the first sermons ever preached in Pittsburgh, except by army chaplains.*

September 10, they left for Keahlampaga, the residence of the King of the Delawares, one hundred and thirty miles distant, and reached his place, near Zanesville, on the 18th. Being cordially received by the king, they delivered an address. Among other things, they gave him:—

"First, a message from the commanding officer at *Fort Pitt*, informing that their fathers, the *English*, concerned for them and pitying their state of ignorance, sent now two ministers to ask them whether they would embrace the Christian religion, that they might see clearly as we

---

a small house. While I was preaching, and the people were very attentive, we were alarmed by a rattlesnake creeping into the house, it being pretty open; but this venomous creature was happily discovered and killed before it did any damage. Scarcely were the people well composed again, before we were alarmed anew by a snake of another kind being discovered among the people, which was also killed without any detriment besides disturbing us."

do, and that the evil spirit might not tempt them any more to what is wrong; that he expected they would treat these men, sent them on such a good errand, well, and send their young men to hunt for them and bring them back safe to the fort, and that he wished they would put in execution what their agent and he at the last treaty had invited them to do, namely, to return back to their old towns and there live, that they might be nearer their brethren the *English*, who might more easily send ministers to teach them. Secondly, we told them that, some years ago, our *Great Council* (for such we called our Synod), who met from different provinces once a year to consult about religion, did appoint two of their number to come out to speak to them about the great things of religion;* but that the war breaking out stopped up the path and thereby prevented their coming, for which we were very sorry, and therefore prayed earnestly to the *great God* that the war, so hurtful to them and us, might come to an end and peace again be restored; that now the *great God* had granted our request."

They gave a string of wampum with their message. Mr. Beatty continues:—

"In the evening, Tepis-cow-a-hang and his sister, both advanced in years, came to our house, who both had formerly been in New Jersey at the time of the revival of

---

* "Referring to Mr. John Brainerd and myself [Beatty], who were appointed by the Synod to visit them; but as we were preparing for our journey, the last war broke out. Had we been among the Indians at that juncture, we had probably either suffered death or captivity; and therefore it appears a very kind interposition of Providence that we were not set out on our mission."—*Beatty's Journal*, pp. 45, 46, 47, 49.

religion among the Indians there, and had received some good impressions under the ministry of Mr. David Brainerd. They desired us to talk to them about religion, which I did some time by the interpreter, particularly concerning backsliding, and pointed out to them in the plainest manner I could how they should come to God again through the Lord Jesus Christ." *

The next day the Indians responded to the address; they said:—

"Our dear brothers, what you have said we are very well pleased with, as far as we can understand it; but, dear brothers, when William Johnson spoke with us some time ago, and made a peace which is to be strong and forever, he told us we must not regard what any other might say to us; that though a great many people all round about might be speaking a great many things, yet we must look upon all these things only as when a *dog sleeps, and he dreams of something*, or something disturbs him, and he rises hastily and gives a bark or two, but does not know any thing or any proper reason why he barks: and just so the people all round that may be saying some one thing, and some another, are to be no more regarded, and therefore they cannot understand or hear any in any other way."

Messrs. Beatty and Duffield stayed ten days, and thought that nearly forty-seven Indians had some "considerable impression made on their minds by their preaching." They left with light hearts and

* Beatty's Journal, pp. 45, 46, 52.

their hopes elevated by the success of their mission.*

One incident of their mission had a special reference to Mr. Brainerd and his Indians at Brotherton. On the Sabbath, September 21:—

"About four o'clock two of the council returned, and gave our interpreter *Joseph* a belt of wampum with a speech, the purport of which was to invite the Christian *Indians* in *New Jersey*, under the care of the Rev. Mr. John Brainerd, to come to Qui-a-ha-ga,† a town the king and some of his people here had lived in, about seventy miles northwest of this place, where, as they said, there was good hunting, and where they might have a *minister* with them; and all the Indians who desired to hear the gospel, as they gave us to understand there was a number of such, might then go and settle with them."

This invitation Messrs. Beatty and Duffield reported to Mr. Brainerd's Indian congregation. Their response was as follows, reported by Mr. Beatty:—‡

* Mr. Beatty was credulous. He records with confidence the statement of a white man found among the Indians, "that he had visited a tribe who spoke Welsh, and had a book in that language." Mr. Beatty also tells a story of a captive Welshman about to be put to death by the Indians, who saved his life by praying in Welsh at the stake. The Indians understood him, and let him go.—See *Beatty's Journal*, p. 24.

† Probably an Indian town on Cuyahoga River, near the present villages of Alton or Cuyahoga Falls, or at the mouth of the river where Cleveland is built.

‡ Beatty's Journal, p. 93.

"*A copy of a Letter from the Christian Indians under the care of the Rev. John Brainerd, in New Jersey, to their brethren the Delaware tribes to the westward of Alleghgeny River, in answer to a message and invitation sent by Joseph, our interpreter, to go back and settle among them (dated February,* 1767), *which message, etc. is mentioned in this journal.*

"To the Chief of the Delaware Tribes of Indians, and all that reside at Ke-la-mip-pa-ching, on the other side of Alleghgeny.

"BROTHERS:—

"You sent us a message by our friend Joseph Peepy, with a belt of wampum, which we have returned by him, according to your order, with these strings, which he will deliver to you at a proper time.

"Brothers, you tell us we sit near a great water, where we are in danger of being drowned; and you take us by the hand and lead us, and set us down at Qui-a-ha-ga, where we may have good land, hunting and fishing, and where we may sit down quietly and worship God.

"Brothers, we thank you in our hearts that you take so much care of us, and so kindly invite us to come to you; but we are obliged to tell you that we do not see at present how we can remove with our old people, our wives, and our children, because we are not able to be at the expense of moving so far, and our brothers, the English, have taken us into their arms as fathers take their children, and we do not think we ought to go without their consent, and indeed we cannot go without their assistance and protection. We have here a good house for the worship of God, another for our children to go to school in, besides our dwelling-houses and many comfortable accommodations,—all which we shall lose if we remove.

"We have also a minister of Christ to instruct us in all our spiritual concerns and lead us to heaven and happiness, which are of more worth to us than all the rest. Now, whenever these difficulties can be taken out of our way, we shall cheerfully embrace your kind, friendly offer; in the mean time we desire the path between you and us may be kept open, and hope that some of us shall be able soon to make you a visit.

"Brothers, you tell us you behold us from a great distance at our devotions, and desire to join us.

"Brothers, we are very glad you have such good desires: certainly the Great Spirit above has given you these desires. We also should be very glad to have you with us in our holy devotions; but our land *here* is so narrow that we cannot expect you will leave your wide, rich country and come to us, but we rather think that, after some time, we may be able to order things so *here* as that a number of us may come to you, if not all.

"Brothers, you tell us you wonder none of us have been so kind as to make you a visit and inform you what we have met with, and desire we would now tell you.

"Brothers, we have not been altogether negligent in this matter. Some of us have gone several times to Wyoming and other parts of Susquehanna to inform our brothers there of the good things which the Lord has made known to us; and some of us who were at Lancaster with our minister, when the last Council-fire was kindled there, would gladly have informed all the Indians thereof what we had learned about the Christian way, and now also we are cheerfully willing, with all our hearts, to let you know what we have found and met with.

"Brothers, we have learned the whole of our duty.

We know what will please God, and what will displease him; what will bring us to happiness, and what will make us miserable; and so now, if we are not forever happy, it will be our own faults. But, alas! though we know all this, we are not so good as we should be. We have also learned to pray, sing psalms, and some of us can read and write.

"Brothers, what we have now told you of is the substance of what we have learned; but we cannot on this little piece of paper tell you every thing particularly.

"Brothers, you tell us you desire we should come, that we might teach you the Christian way, and how you also may come to be happy.

"Brothers, we wish to do this with all our hearts, so far as it is in our power, and are sorry you are so far from us.

"Brothers, we have learned many good things, it is true, and should be very glad to see you and talk with you as brethren; and some of us might teach you to sing psalms, and to read and to write, but are not fit to be ministers, nor are we called to that high office. Ministers are men that the great God calls to preach the gospel, and to teach mankind what they must do to be saved. And when they preach, they speak in God's name: from such we received the gospel, and all other heathen people that have been made Christians have been made so by the preaching of God's ministers. Two such men, we are informed, you had with you last summer; and we do not doubt that, if you desire it, they or some others will visit you again, at which we shall very much rejoice.

"Brothers, we have heard our minister say he has a great concern for you; and though we always want him at home, yet we should be willing to part with him a while that he might teach you and do you good, as he has done us. He has lived with us many years, and we know him to be a good friend to the Indians and that he seeks their best good.

"Brothers, we wish you all good; that you may have good ministers to take you gently by the hand, and lead you safe to heaven and happiness. And, that you might obtain this great good, we think it might be well for you to speak to Sir William Johnson, who, you know, is the person the great king George has appointed to speak to the Indians, and we do not doubt he would be willing to help you. He might also, perhaps, so order matters that we, after some time, might remove to you and be very happy in your country.

"Brothers, we desire to commit you and all that concerns you and us to the great God, who made all things.

"We pray that he would take you under his particular care, and that you and we may so know him and his Son Jesus Christ as that we may meet in heaven and be happy with him for evermore.

"We are your sincere friends
and loving brothers,

"(Signed) THOMAS STORE,
JOSEPH MEECHY,
STEPHEN CALVIN,
ISAAC STILL,
JACOB STAKET."

Who can read this letter without emotion? Thomas Store and Stephen Calvin were the fathers of children sent to Dr. Wheelock. This mission of Messrs. Duffield and Beatty to the Muskingum, and the invitation of the Indians to Mr. Brainerd's congregation, no doubt led to the appointment of Messrs. Brainerd and Cooper to go West in 1767. They failed to go. The Synod, in 1768, says:—

"The Synod proceeded to consider the affair of the Indian school under the inspection of the Rev. Mr. Brainerd, and it appears from Mr. Brainerd's report that there is still a school existing among the Indians under his care; and this Synod do agree to continue to support said school, and do appoint the usual salary of thirty pounds to be paid to Mr. Brainerd for the ensuing year; and do order the clerk of the Synod to give an order for that sum on the Synodical treasurer. It is further agreed to allow Mr. Brainerd twenty pounds as an addition to his salary for his extensive services and labor in those uncultivated parts, and that the clerk also give an order to Mr. Brainerd on the Synodical treasurer for this purpose.

"The Synod do also appoint Mr. Brainerd to receive for the current year the sum of eighteen pounds, being the interest of the money in the hands of the Treasurer of New Jersey College, appointed to support an Indian mission.

"Messrs. Brainerd and Cooper report, that they did not execute their mission among the Indians on the Muskingum and other parts, as ordered at Synod, by reason of the discouraging accounts brought in by the interpreter Joseph, sent out as mentioned in our last year's minutes, and other discouraging circumstances; and, as it appears that Mr. Brainerd had occasion to be at the expense of sending an Indian to prepare the way for his intended mission, therefore the Synod do agree to pay the sum of five pounds to discharge said expense.

"Ordered, that the Synodical treasurer pay said sum." *

* Records of the Presbyterian Church, p. 380.

Dissatisfied with the hitherto loose manner of conducting missions, the Synod this year appointed a committee, of which Mr. Brainerd was one, "to draw up a plan" and report next year. This was a prelude to those modern mission boards and societies which have long been the order of the day. As a Church, Presbyterians were early in the field of missions.

It is believed that about this period Mr. Brainerd left his Indian home in Brotherton, and removed to Bridgetown (now Mount Holly), a village seven miles from Burlington and fifteen from his former residence.

The Synod in 1767 appointed Mr. McKnight to supply Mr. Brainerd's place among the Indians and at Mount Holly. It seems that he then had, in addition to his great domestic missionary field along the shore and his Indian charge, a congregation at Mount Holly (or Bridgetown); and thither he removed in 1768.

His reasons he does not give for the removal; perhaps he was driven there by pecuniary necessity or failing health. At Mount Holly he was near two of his stations, Rancocas and Quakertown, now Vincenttown.

Located at Mount Holly, where he gathered a congregation and built a church, he purchased property near his church-edifice, and erected a dwelling and a schoolhouse. We have seen the deeds of this property, which is now the site of a modern church in Mount Holly, situated on "Brainerd" Street. The late venerable John McDowell, D.D., of this city, in the reorganization of the Presbyterian Church at Mount Holly, October 27, 1839, alluded feelingly to the early church planted there by John Brainerd, but which had been left to die out. From the doctor's manuscript, kindly furnished us by him shortly before his death, we make an extract. He said:—

"Brethren, this was anciently Presbyterian ground, and we are about to-day not to introduce something before unknown in this place, but to restore that which long since existed and probably flourished among you, but which has fallen into decay. A Presbyterian church existed in this place for many years in the last century, and for a time enjoyed the ministerial and pastoral labors of that eminently pious and devoted servant of God, the Rev. John Brainerd, as I have learned from a respectable and aged citizen of this place, of another denomination, since my arrival here. Mr. Brainerd preached between twenty and thirty years, and was much beloved, and was instrumental in doing much good among the inhabitants of the place, and also among a tribe of Indians in the neighborhood.

"Mr. Brainerd died about sixty years since, in 1781, in Deerfield, in Cumberland county, whither he removed. During the Revolutionary War, the house of worship, which was then situated on your graveyard, was torn down by the British soldiers. After that, I understand, for some time the congregation had occasional preaching in private houses; but by degrees the church declined, until it became extinct."

We shall again have occasion to refer to this early church at Mount Holly; we only allude to it now to explain the date of the following letter:

BRIDGETOWN (MOUNT HOLLY), February 12, 1768.

REV'D AND DEAR SIR:—

The reason of my inability to answer your letter was, I could not tell what assistance I should want of you for the journey to the Western Indians. The provision to be made here was uncertain, and depended upon a meeting of the Corporation for the *Widows' Fund*, who have moneys for propagating the gospel. That corporation sat some time after, but did nothing in the affair. The reason assigned was, "the present prospect of an Indian War."

This melancholy prospect has since increased. Ten of the Indians have been cruelly murdered by a white man, the man apprehended and confined with irons, but soon after forcibly taken out of Carlisle jail; all which and much more you doubtless have seen or will see in the public papers.

Besides satisfaction for this barbarous outrage, the Indians, I am told, demand three things:—

1. That all the white people be removed off their unpurchased lands.

2. That there be a line drawn and settled between them and the English.

3. That the blood shed by the murder of the Indians some years ago in Lancaster jail be wiped off.

I am also informed that Sir William Johnson has written to some of our governors, particularly of Pennsylvania, of aggrievances and disturbances among the Indians in those parts.

While things are in this sad situation, you doubtless will be of opinion with us that to attempt any thing of the kind before proposed would be very imprudent.

We must no doubt wait a more favorable opportunity, which may the Lord hasten, though I something scruple my ever embarking in it again: my state of body is too weak and slender for such fatigues.

We are all tolerably well, through Divine goodness, and the Indian children's parents, etc., were so lately.

The Lord smile on all our attempts to enlarge the kingdom of his dear Son, and hasten the blissful period when he shall reign from the rising to the setting sun.

When you feel well, try to remember us, and particularly,

Reverend and dear sir,
Your very affectionate
JOHN BRAINERD.

P.S.—It won't do for Hezekiah* to be anywhere near his father.

To the Rev'd Dr. WHEELOCK.

---

* Hezekiah Calvin, the son of Stephen Calvin, one of Mr. Brainerd's Indian elders at Brotherton. We shall see that he disappointed the hopes of his excellent father: when at home, he was unreliable.

CHAPTER XXXVIII.

MR. BRAINERD'S SCHOOL—WHEELOCK'S INDIAN PUPILS VERY IMPERFECT—MR. BRAINERD ASKS A COMMITTEE OF SYNOD ON HIS MISSIONARY AFFAIRS—"FIFTY-NINE POUNDS FOR FIVE HUNDRED SERMONS."

1769.

THOUGH Mr. Brainerd had only reached the age of forty-nine, the "shadows of the evening" seemed to be gathering over his life. He complains more of ill health; he is less prominent in the Synod; he is sent on fewer missions. All his health and time and energies were demanded by the great field of his personal labor. As his hopes failed in regard to giving permanent character and prosperity to his Indian mission, he seems to have devoted himself entirely to founding churches among the scattered whites.

The Synod this year appointed a committee, consisting of Drs. Alison, Witherspoon, Rogers, and Mr. Brainerd, to see if a *plan of missions* could be reported next year. They also say:—

"From Mr. Brainerd's report respecting the school under his inspection, which the Synod agreed to support, we find it hath not been kept up more than half the last year, for which we therefore allow him fifteen pounds, which is half of what was voted last year. But, as he expects he shall be able to continue that school the current year, having provided a master for that purpose, voted that he be allowed thirty pounds for the support of it.

"Ordered, also, that Mr. Brainerd shall receive for the current year the sum of eighteen pounds, being the interest of the money in the hands of the Treasurer of the College of New Jersey for the support of an Indian mission, and that he also have twenty pounds from the Synodical treasurer for the continuance of his labors in the year past in those desolate parts where he has been usefully employed, and the Synod desire Mr. Brainerd to supply in these parts as formerly." *

They continued him on the Great Committee to meet, on the 14th September, at New Haven, in the Convention of Presbyterians and Congregationalists, assembled for the purpose of devising measures to resist the inroads of Episcopal authority. He was in an obscure field, but still honored by his brethren.† They appointed him to supply vacancies at Burlington, Gloucester, and Cape May counties.

---

* Records of Presbyterian Church, p. 270.

† Sir Walter Scott, in one of his novels, makes an old gray-haired butler, who had been in the family forty years, affirm that his gray head was an emblem of both his and his master's honors,—*i.e.*, he thought it honorable to himself that he had been so long employed, and honorable to his master that he had the discrimination to appreciate him.

Mr. Brainerd might have said this to the members of the New York and Philadelphia Synod.

BRIDGETOWN (MOUNT HOLLY), February 3, 1769.

REV. AND DEAR SIR:—

It is true I am not a good correspondent,—I have neither inclination nor facility to write letters; but I think I have a friendly heart, and sincerely wish prosperity to Zion and your Indian academy.

Two of your kind letters are now before me: one by Miriam Store,* which came the last of November, the other bearing date the 4th of July last, which I came across in a journey a few days before. Much of the contents of both are very afflictive to me. Is it so, then, that all our painful labors and long-continued expense must be unspeakably worse than lost? I could give you a long detail of baseness and ingratitude, such as I did not think could exist even in Indians till of late. I know of no other way than to bear every thing or quit the service.

Dr. Whitaker gave me a sad account of Hezekiah,† which was grievous. I was glad, however, of an interview with him: shall always think myself well employed when attempting any thing for the promotion of your school. Pray draw upon me often that way, if there be occasion; I shall always most readily answer your bills in the best manner I can, though I am sensible it is little I can do.

I yet sometimes feel a very strong bias towards Indian affairs, notwithstanding I have been so pitiably used by them. Should be very glad of an interview with you, and the more so if it could be any degree of comfort to you in your worn-out state.

---

* The Indian girl mentioned already as sent to Dr. Wheelock's school.

† Hezekiah Calvin.

Miriam came to Bridgetown with a heavy heart; was there some time before my return from a journey. Told Mrs. Brainerd* she was on the point of turning back when she came to New London, and even after she got to New York. Speaks very well of Dr. Wheelock and all his family, etc.

After the receipt of your letter, I took an opportunity to talk with her; she appeared to be considerably affected, but, upon the whole, did not discover so good a temper as I could have desired. Her behavior since her return, as far as I know, has been unexceptionable.

I have not been able yet to get her into a tailor's shop as a journeywoman, to perfect her trade. She at present does house-work with a serious, religious woman in this town, and is well liked. I return you very many thanks for your faithful and painful care of her and the rest. Her poor old parents were overjoyed to see her: I wish she might be a blessing to them.†

I told Stephen Calvin about his son, the watch, etc. I know not what he intends to do: he did not desire me to write any thing about it.

The account from Oneida is very comfortable: may the work spread far and wide, and Jesus reign in all that barbarous world. By the first opportunity please to give my kindest regards to Mr. Kirkland, and congratulate him

---

* About nine years after the death of his first wife (during which time his only companion was his little daughter Mary), Mr. Brainerd married Mrs. Elizabeth Price, of Philadelphia, who survived him, and died in 1783. She was a woman of great excellence of character,—not only a good wife to Mr. Brainerd, but a most affectionate and beloved mother to his only daughter. Of her family relations we have no knowledge.

† We infer that Miriam had run away from Dr. Wheelock's school and returned home. She seems to have been not much worse than other girls of her age.

for me. The Lord comfort his heart and strengthen his hand abundantly.

My best salutations to Mrs. Wheelock, in which Mrs. Brainerd joins: kind love to your son and family.

Reverend and dear sir,
Your very humble servant,
JOHN BRAINERD.

BRIDGETOWN (MOUNT HOLLY), June 22, 1769.

REV'D AND DEAR SIR:—

Hezekiah Calvin* is this minute come into my house, on his way to New England, and finds me just returned from a journey into Pennsylvania. He has behaved pretty well, for any thing I know, since he has been in these parts. I have given him the offer of the school if he could behave steady and well: he talks of accepting the offer after his return from New England. Miriam Store is not the thing I want her to be, by any means.

She has, however, behaved better of late than last winter. I am greatly distressed often. There is too much truth in that common saying: "Indians will be Indians." I am at present very poorly, almost worn out; have neither time nor strength to write. Send the most cordial salutations, in which Mrs. Brainerd joins with,

Reverend and honored sir,
Your affectionate
JOHN BRAINERD.

---

* Hezekiah Calvin had become unsteady. In 1766, three years before, Dr. Wheelock said of him, "he is a sober, well-behaved youth, and teaches a school among the Mohawks. He is a good scholar in English, Latin, and Greek, and writes a good hand."—*Wheelock's Narrative*, London, 1766.

BROTHERTON, August 25, 1769.

REV'D AND DEAR SIR:—

I have been some years attempting to send the gospel to Muskingum, and met with repeated disappointments; some of which you have not been unacquainted with.

Two years ago I furnished out an Indian to go into their country and carry a letter to Natotrohalament, chief king of the Delawares, who resides at Kalamapahung, an Indian town five days' journey from Fort Pitt westward, and containing, I am told, about one hundred huts. The Indian wholly deceived me, spent my money another way; afterwards was taken sick, and never went, nor ever returned me a copper of the expense.

Some time last month there was one to visit me and the Indians here from those parts. He appeared to be one of the most sincere, modest Indians I have met with for a long time, and, to all appearances, was indeed a pretty fellow. He appeared likewise to be a man of note among the Indians, much inclined to embrace Christianity, and bid fair to be an instrument of introducing it among his neighbors. By him I sent another letter to the king, attended with wampum as before, but have lately had the afflicting news of his being murdered by the white people on his way thither. It is also said that murders are committed by the Indians on some of the frontiers. Sad, indeed! Alas! that there should be so many afflictions to that which is of so much importance.

I expected the above Indian here again next spring, and intended in the mean time to exert myself to the uttermost that a minister and schoolmaster should be provided to go back with him, and had some thoughts, if my state of body should permit, to go myself; but now I know not what to do. I do not intend, however, to give out so, and beg you would have your eye out for some proper persons to go in both those characters, and let me know. It is beyond doubt that the above-mentioned king and a number more in that town are friendly to Christianity.

I have had thoughts of attending the Convention at New Haven, where my principal business would have been to lay some foundation, if possible, for erecting a mission at Kalamapahung; but my state of health is low, and I have other obstacles in the way, too: this late news is also very discouraging. I hope you will be at New Haven, and, if so, every thing that can be done will be.

I want to hear very much from Mr. Kirkland, and what prospects there still are in that part of the world.

Miriam Store has been gone several months from us: I hear of late that she is in East Jersey, not far from where the Indians formerly lived.

I wish I could write more comfortably about her. Hezekiah is gone into New England: I send you a few lines by him. If he returns and behaves well, I shall employ him in the school here.

My best salutations wait on Mrs. Wheelock.

I am, reverend and honored sir,

Your ever affectionate

JOHN BRAINERD.

Rev'd Dr. WHEELOCK.

We give, to fill up the history of this year, the following from the Scotch Society:—

Extract from Minutes dated Edinburgh, February 16, 1769.

"Letters from Mr. Brainerd, with a journal of his proceedings, and from the Society's Correspondents at New York, being read, representing Mr. Brainerd's diligence in his mission, his misfortune in having expended money for erecting and furnishing a house for worship and for the residence of a missionary upon the tract of land purchased by the Government for the Indians, on the faith of being reimbursed by the Government, of which he was and is likely to be disappointed. The letters further propose that the Trustees of the College of New Jersey be appointed Correspondents, and they send a belt of wampum in a present to the Society from the Oneida Indians.

"Ordered, that letters be wrote acquainting the Correspondents that as to Mr. Brainerd, though the Society are very much pleased with the diligence shown in his journal of his proceedings, and sincerely regret the expense of money he has been at, yet their funds cannot admit to reimburse him at this time. They wish he would represent the matter either to Governor Bernard himself, who pledged his faith for his reimbursement, or to the present Governor of the Province; and are hopeful in that way he may still obtain redress." *

1770–71.

The Synod appointed a committee to visit Mr. Brainerd's school, with power to draw on the treasurer "for such moneys as the exigencies of the school might require, and report to the next Synod;" and voted "twenty pounds for the con-

* "The Minutes of the *General Meeting* of the Society for Propagating Christian Knowledge, so far as concerns their proceedings with regard to their Foreign affairs, *end here.*

"David W. Morris,

"*Librarian p. t. to United Presbyterian Church.*

"Edinburgh, 1862."

tinuance of his labors the ensuing year *in those desolate parts where he has been so successfully employed.*" Twenty pounds for supplying seven or eight stations!—all they had to give; but how much less than he required!

He was again sent to the "Convention" at Elizabethtown, but otherwise is not mentioned in the records of 1770. We have no details of the year's trials and labors.

May 20, 1771, the records say:—

"Mr. Brainerd reports that he has under his care an Indian school since the 24th of December, which he expects to continue through the summer, and possibly through the winter also.

"Ordered, that the Treasurer for the Synod pay Mr. Brainerd fifteen pounds for the half-year which shall end the 24th of June. And Dr. Alison, Dr. Witherspoon, Messrs. Ewing, Sproat, Treat, and Beatty, are appointed a committee, who are to meet the last Wednesday of August at ten o'clock, who shall visit the school and judge whether it shall be continued the winter half-year; and, if it appears to them that the school has been continued through the summer, that they may draw upon the treasurer for fifteen pounds more, and then determine whether it is expedient to continue the school through the winter, and to engage with Mr. Brainerd in behalf of the Synod to allow him fifteen pounds also for that term, in case it be continued.

"It also appears to this Synod that Mr. Brainerd has labored very diligently in the numerous destitute vacancies to which he was appointed the last Synod; the treasurer is therefore ordered to pay Mr. Brainerd the twenty pounds voted him last year for the said service; and it is also agreed to allow Mr. Brainerd twenty pounds for the ensuing year, provided it shall appear at the next Synod that he continues to preach the gospel in the numerous and destitute vacancies in his neighborhood.

"Mr. Brainerd requested that some members of this body should be appointed to inspect the journal of his last year's labors in the destitute places in his neighborhood, and to report the state of his accounts with respect to that service; and Messrs. Hunter and Spencer are ordered a committee for that purpose."

On the 22d, this committee reported; they say:

"The Committee appointed to examine Mr. Brainerd's accounts from the year 1760 to the year 1770 inclusive, report that Mr. Brainerd had received from the several congregations he hath from time to time supplied in the neighborhood of Monohawkin and Egg Harbor only the sum of fifty-nine pounds nineteen shillings, though he had preached *upwards of five hundred times among them*, and that his accounts respecting the Indian school stand fair." *

Fifty-nine pounds nineteen shillings for five hundred sermons! He had been engaged for years; he had travelled in all weathers, and on all roads but smooth and well-beaten ones; he had erected some half-dozen churches; and all this outside of his main work; and, as a return for this labor, he had received for five hundred sermons less than sixty pounds, or about two shil-

* Records of the Presbyterian Church, pp. 415, 416, 418.

lings a sermon. This is the grasping avarice of the Presbyterian clergy! This man was doubtless called by some, in contempt, *a hireling preacher!* If men must live by the gospel, it is little wonder that when Mr. Brainerd died, so far as Presbyterian ministers are concerned, his field lay desolate for near a hundred years.

We have a single letter from Mr. Brainerd in 1771. It has little of interest, except that it shows the warmth of his heart.

New Haven, October 16, 1771.

Reverend Sir:—

I thank you for your favor of the 7th instant by Mr. Davenport, and desire very sincerely and affectionately to condole with you and the public on the death of your dear son, the Rev'd Mr. Maltby. The Lord take care of his dear fatherless and motherless children, and send to the people of his late charge *a pastor after his own heart.*

And may Heaven's blessings in abundance rest on you, your dear family, and charge. I long to see you, your college, etc., but cannot now: what may be hereafter I know not.

Can say nothing farther respecting the intended mission on the Muskingum.

I send all respectful salutations to Mrs. Wheelock and your family.

I am, most affectionately,

John Brainerd.

CHAPTER XXXIX.

MISSION OF MESSRS. MCCLURE AND FRISBIE TO MUSKINGUM—MR. BRAINERD'S LETTERS ON HIS OWN EMBARRASSMENTS.

1772.

THE Synod say:—

"Mr. Brainerd's Indian school appears to have been successfully continued since our last Synod six months, for which it is agreed to give him fifteen pounds; and we farther desire him to continue the school this year at the expense of the Synod, and we appoint Messrs. Spencer, Hunter, and Green to visit the school twice before next Synod, or oftener, if convenient.

"It appeared also to the Synod that Mr. Brainerd had very fully complied with the order of last Synod, in supplying the numerous vacancies in his neighborhood: therefore the treasurer, agreeably to the order of last year, is directed to pay him twenty pounds. Ordered, also, that Mr. Brainerd receive for the ensuing year the sum of eighteen pounds, being the interest of the money in the hands of the Treasurer of the College of New Jersey for the support of an Indian mission." *

The correspondence of Mr. Brainerd with the Rev. Dr. Wheelock this year is unusually full,

* Records of the Presbyterian Church, p. 427.

suggesting facts bearing on his character and history. We have hesitated in spreading some of these facts before our readers; but it would be impossible rightly to represent this missionary if we failed to allow him to speak for himself in regard to difficulties which burdened and embarrassed his life and labors.

We have seen what he received for his services, his school, and his mission,—about fifty-five pounds a year from the Synod, and a few pounds additional, say five or six a year, from his white churches. He had expended much of his little estate in his mission, expecting that Governor Bernard and the Government of New Jersey, who had drawn him to the field, would see him through in the matter. He was disappointed. With advancing years and enfeebled health, he naturally became anxious to recover for his support and comfort what he had expended in good faith for the benefit of his mission. Having no relief at home, he turned to his old friends in Scotland, and appealed to the Society for Propagating Christian Knowledge. He supposes Dr. Wheelock's European acquaintance and influence would avail to bring him relief. This explains the long letter among those that follow.

TRENTON, June 19, 1772.

REV'D AND DEAR SIR:—

We have of late some things that appear very unfriendly to our design of opening a mission on the Muskingum, or anywhere in these parts. There have been, if we are not misinformed, several murders committed between the Indians and white people on both sides, and a prospect of war between the Senecas and Delawares; nevertheless, it appears to me best to prosecute the design as far as we can, and, by consulting Dr. Witherspoon and Mr. Spencer, I find they are of the same opinion: the doctor (Witherspoon) will write you on this head.

If it be so that we cannot make a tour this year, perhaps the door may be open early in the spring.

In the mean time, the young gentlemen* may be employed in my boundaries; but, after all, the matter will be submitted wholly to your judgment and at your direction.

My best regards to Mrs. Wheelock, and kind salutations to your son and family. I write in haste, and almost without pen and ink, but am, more than ever,

Reverend and honored sir,

Your affectionate friend,

JOHN BRAINERD.

BRIDGETOWN (MOUNT HOLLY), August 27, 1772.

REV'D AND DEAR SIR:—

Yours by Messrs. McClure and Frisbie† claims my thankful acknowledgments. It is not now before me.

* Young men designing to enter on missions.

† Rev. David McClure, D.D., spent some time with Mr. Kirkland at Oneida, afterwards graduated at Yale College in 1769, became a teacher in Dr. Wheelock's school, and in 1772 set out, in company with Mr. Frisbie, to visit the Delaware Indians on the Muskingum River, and made this call on Mr. Brainerd on his way. The mission was fruitless. His wife was the daughter of Dr. Pomroy, and niece of Dr. Wheelock. He died at East Windsor, Conn., in 1820, aged seventy-one. In 1811, in connection with Dr. Parish, he published the "Memoirs of Dr. Wheelock," in which there seems to be an ambitious effort to connect him with great personages in England and

After the young gentlemen had been with me some days, as long as we thought best, and both preached in my borders, I attended them to Philadelphia, spent some days with them there preparing for the tour-work among the remote Indians.

If the road had been open, I was to have gone with them to Muskingum; but, as the Board of Correspondents thought that not advisable at this time, it was concluded they should make a visit up the Susquehanna, especially the west branch, which puts out toward the Ohio; and, as no great things were expected this season, my place here important, the summer far advanced, and my state of body very frail, I could not think it duty to accompany them on that tour. But, by a letter a few days ago from Mr. Sproat, I find that, as they proceeded westward, they had intelligence by the Indian traders that the ruptures and disturbances among the Indians, especially in the parts where we first proposed to make trial, had happily subsided, and they determined to make their way for Muskingum. May Heaven prosper their way!

Their letter to Mr. Sproat was from Carlisle, about one hundred and twenty miles from Philadelphia, on the road to Fort Pitt, bearing date the 10th instant. I hope they may meet with good acceptance among the Indians. I would have gone with all my heart, and given them the best introduction in my power; but Divine Providence,

America, and to ignore Dr. Wheelock's earliest and warmest friends. When it mentions Brainerd, which it does but once or twice, it calls him Rev. Mr. B——d. No wonder the book never reached a second edition. It was false to the heart and memory of Dr. Wheelock.

The Rev. Levi Frisbie, a pupil of Dr. Wheelock, graduated in the first class at Dartmouth College, in 1771. After some years of faithful missionary labor, he was settled at Ipswich, Mass., in 1776, and died there, in 1806, aged fifty-seven. He was a most devoted and useful minister.

if I mistake not, has ordered it otherwise, and, I trust, all for the best.

Appearances here among the white people are more encouraging; among the poor, poor Indians less; nevertheless, I cannot help having a warm side towards the cause and nation, and would gladly penetrate far into their country, would my state of body permit.

My best regards wait on Mrs. Wheelock: kind salutations to your family, particularly your eldest son.

I greatly rejoice at the prosperity of your college, and am, with unfeigned regard,

Reverend and honored sir,
Yours most affectionately,
JOHN BRAINERD.

BRIDGETOWN (MOUNT HOLLY), October 5, 1772.

REV'D AND DEAR SIR:—

My last, dated some time in August, if I mistake not, gave you an account that Messrs. McClure and Frisbie were on their way to Fort Pitt, what obstructions the mission had met with, and the reasons why I did not accompany them as was proposed and as I expected.

The young gentlemen set out by themselves, if I mistake not, the 25th of July; but when they had proceeded about one hundred miles, hearing that those obstructions were in a great measure removed, they bent their course towards Fort Pitt, where, I hear, they are safely arrived, and expected soon to go for Muskingum. Frisbie was not very well; but Mr. McClure was determined to go alone if he should prove unable to accompany him.

The state of things here respecting the white people wears a more hopeful aspect than for some time past: the Indians are in *statu quo*.

I write in haste. My very kind regards to Mrs. Wheelock and your family, and please to accept the same yourself from,

Reverend and honored sir,
Your very affectionate
JOHN BRAINERD.

BRIDGETOWN (MOUNT HOLLY), December 25, 1772.

REV'D AND DEAR SIR:—

I have long expected to hear something from Messrs. McClure and Frisbie, but nothing since I wrote you last. I can hardly think they have omitted writing, but nothing has come to hand since the day I parted with them at Philadelphia. I cannot but be much concerned about them and the important embassy they went upon, and exceedingly want to hear and know something.

You remember I informed you they took a different route from what we all expected when they set out. Had we apprehended the way clear to Muskingum, I could have gone with great cheerfulness at a proper season of the year, which the last of July was not. I had an inward inclination to go up the Susquehanna, the country they expected to visit when they went from us, but could not see a prospect of being so useful there as at home; and, besides, the Board of Correspondents at their last meeting did not appoint or advise my going.

I hope, or at least most sincerely wish, that an effectual door may be opened in these parts and others for the propagation of the gospel among the poor savages.

Prospects here among the whites are rather more encouraging than heretofore. Most of the Indians manage but poorly. Hezekiah Calvin is capable enough, but will not be any thing: he seems to choose to be a useless creature after all the encouragements I can give him. Miriam Store has had a most dreadful spell of rheumatism, is not able to go or stand, and has but poor use of her hands: she has been grievously afflicted for more than a year: I hope it may be for the good of her soul. The old man, her father, is yet living. There has been one remarkable instance of conversion or recovery in a great and grievous backslider: I hope it may be permanent, and be followed with many other instances.

In November, 1763, the Correspondents appointed two of their members to examine my account, in consequence of which the following minute was drawn up:—

Mr. Brainerd's Pecuniary Statement.

"We, the under-written, appointed by the Correspondents of the Society in Scotland for Propagating Christian Knowledge as a committee to inspect and examine the Rev'd Mr. John Brainerd's accounts of disbursements in the said Society's service as their missionary among the Indians, do hereby report and certify that we have gone through and minutely examined his said accounts, article by article, and do clearly find that from the beginning of his said mission he hath expended in the said Society's service and for the benefit of the same the sum of three hundred and twenty pounds, New-Jersey proclamation-money, over and above his annual allowances from the said Society, and over and above the public collections and private donations received by him for the purposes of the said mission.

"Witness our hand, this 5th of November, 1763.

"Wm. P. Smith, *Secretary*,
"Sam'l Woodruff."

In December, 1763, I received toward the above £49 13*s.* 6*d.*: the remainder of the principal, with the interest, yet remains, together with more than £159 spent in the same way since the above settlement.

I do not know that it will be in your power, in any degree, to relieve me in the above premises; and I must beg your pardon for giving you the trouble of such a disagreeable detail. Was I a person of fortune, no one, I think, should ever hear of it. The Correspondents have written repeatedly to the Society on the head, and no help is to be expected there. In their last letter they expressed themselves well satisfied with my conduct, and were sorry for my disbursements, but pleaded inability to refund; nor have I any hopes, unless from your instrumentality or some other friend in New England. I wrote to Mrs. Smith, alias Williams, on the head some time in the fall, but have yet heard nothing. If the Correspondents could anyhow get it, they would; for I offered to give £50 of it to the College at least, if not £100. And, besides what the secretary of that board wrote, Dr. Witherspoon used his influence, and, I believe, Mr. Horton, who has lately been in Edinburgh, and was a person of so much note there as to have the freedom of the city presented him by the Lord-Provost and Corporation; but all their attempts proved fruitless, so that I have no hopes of having any part of it refunded in these parts. If Mr. Thornton of London, who, I am told, makes it a rule to give away three thousand guineas annually, or some other such able and charitable person, could know my situation, possibly he might afford me some relief.

Those disbursements above mentioned have arisen partly from attempts to promote the great design of the mission, such as clothing and schooling the children, particularly sending them to New England, which at one particular time cost me eight pounds our currency, and so more or less, according to the number sent and what clothes they stood in need of; building a meeting-house; repairing a glebe-house; clearing and fencing the parsonage-land at Brotherton, etc., so as to be able at all to live there; some church expenses, which, indeed, I am loth to mention.

But the above sums have arisen chiefly from the medium of my support being too small to subsist upon in the midst of such a very poor, needy, distressed people; so that I have been obliged to take of my own little pittance for my necessary support. No household furniture or any thing of that nature ever came into the account; but such things as were constantly consuming and consumed in the family.

I should be very sorry to give you any trouble on this head, sensible you have a great deal on your hands; but I also know you have great pleasure in doing good and affording, indeed, relief to any of your friends; and, if none can be obtained, I shall be but where I am, and have the pleasure to think that I made an honest attempt to have my aggrievances redressed, and be put into a situation in which I may be able to be of more use to mankind than now I can.

So, wishing you all prosperity in your great and very laudable undertakings, presenting my best regards to your worthy yoke-fellow and kind respects to your family, I subscribe myself,

Reverend and honored sir,
Your ever affectionate friend
and humble servant,
JOHN BRAINERD.

P.S.—The simple interest upon £295 10*s*. 6*d*., the remaining principal after the subtraction of the above £49 13*s*. 6*d*., to the 21st instant, is £44 14*s*., which, added to the above principal, is £340 3*s*. 6*d*.,—errors excepted.

Rev'd Dr. WHEELOCK.

CHAPTER XL.

MR. BRAINERD BECOMES SCHOOLMASTER—LETTERS TO DR. WHEELOCK AND REV. DAVID McCLURE—STUDENT-LIFE AT DARTMOUTH COLLEGE —THE REV. MR. RANKIN'S VISIT AND CRITICISM—CLOSE OF MR. BRAINERD'S CORRESPONDENCE—WAR SERMON—REMARKS OF THE EDINBURGH COMMITTEE—BROTHERTON.

1773–4.

THE relation of Mr. Brainerd to the Synod of New York and Philadelphia constituted one of the most impressive aspects of his life. Year after year he comes up from the wilderness with his story of hard labor and patient endurance, and year after year his brethren commend his fidelity, bless his work, and vote him his pittance for support. We could have desired them to have shared a portion of his labors, or more liberally to have rewarded his toils; but, for the times in which they lived, they showed not only the germ of that missionary spirit in the Presbyterian Church which has since expanded and filled the land, but also an adhesiveness, a tenderness, and generosity to the solitary missionary adapted to comfort his heart. This year, the records say:—

"Mr. Brainerd reports the Indian school under his care has not been continued the last year, he not being able to obtain a proper master; but that he had, as often as consistent with his other business, attended to the instruction of the children.

"And he further reports, that he preaches in seven places besides the two Indian societies under his special care. For these services, the Synod allow Mr. Brainerd twenty-five pounds: ordered, that the treasurer pay the same.

"Mr. Brainerd is also allowed the eighteen pounds, interest of money in the hands of the Trustees of New Jersey College for an Indian mission.

Mr. Brainerd has turned schoolmaster! Returning from his long journeys among the sands and along the coast, when he has preached in seven places, he *rests* himself in his forest-home at Brotherton by teaching ignorant Indian children to read and spell. Here is a man of all work for Christ and souls: he is bearing fruit, too, in advanced years!

The following brief note alludes to his long letter of December 25, 1772. While overwhelmed with labor on his own field, how steadily his heart yearns for distant Indian tribes, and sympathizes in all good done anywhere!

BRIDGETOWN (MOUNT HOLLY), February 3, 1773.

REV'D AND DEAR SIR:—

When I wrote the above, I intended soon to write it over in a finer hand and send it; but no opportunity presenting, and my time much taken up in journeying, etc.,

---

* Records of Presbyterian Church, p. 439.

I could not well get leave till now; when, glancing over it, I thought it might be read, and, time being precious with me, ventured to send it as it is: know your goodness can excuse all.

The day before yesterday I received a long, kind, agreeable letter from Mr. McClure, in which he tells me he had written to me before; but it has not come to hand.

His letter is dated December 19, in which he informs me he has sent the most "important parts of his journal to Dr. Wheelock," so that it is not likely I could communicate any thing new. Mr. Frisbie and he are preaching in the neighborhood of Fort Pitt this winter. I am sorry there is so little prospect of the designs taking effect among the Indians of Muskingum; a future day, it is hopeful, may give us more encouragement.

So, wishing you a happy new year and all prosperity, I conclude with subscribing myself,

Reverend and honored sir,
Your ever affectionate
JOHN BRAINERD.

Rev'd Dr. WHEELOCK.

The following letter from Mr. Brainerd to Mr. David McClure, with whom the reader is already acquainted, speaks for itself:—

BRIDGETOWN, February 10, 1773.

DEAR SIR:—

Your favor of the 19th December came to hand a few days ago: that you mention, sent to the care of Mr. Bayard, I have not received. I often thought of you and Mr. Frisbie, and greatly wanted to hear from you; at length I began to think you had struck through the country to Onohquanga, etc., and so to Dartmouth College.*

It gives me great pleasure to hear that you are returned well from the Indian country: I pretty well know how you

---

* In 1770, Rev. Dr. Wheelock had removed from Lebanon, Conn., to Hanover, N. H., and there set up in the forest Dartmouth College and his Indian school, which Brainerd calls the Academy, in distinction from the college. The college has had a progressive and glorious life. The Indian school, which gave birth to the college, has been long dead, like the Indian nations it was designed to elevate.

In Mr. Brainerd's letters to President Wheelock, allusion is often made to the prosperity of Dartmouth College, which was then just founded in the wilderness. We have in hand the diary of a student there, from 1780 to 1784. This young man—Elijah Brainerd, a relative of David and John—served in the Revolutionary War, was a prisoner in Jersey prison-ship, received a wound that crippled him for life, and then went to study for the ministry in Dartmouth College, where he graduated, and was afterwards settled at Royalton, Vt., and Pelham, Mass. His diary, at that early day, is suggestive and amusing. He says:—

"*October* 1, 1780.—We were alarmed by the Indians, who came to Royalton, Vt., and burnt it. I went out after them, and we overtook them in the twilight; but they escaped. We pursued them to Brookfield: I was out three days."

"*Dartmouth, March* 1, 1781.—This day an alarm was given that the Indians had taken five prisoners, not far from Coos, N. H., and were approaching Newbury. We made towards them: the enemy retreated, and our men returned back."

John Brainerd's young Indians at Dartmouth had around them rough scenes in 1770, not very favorable to their civilization or refinement.

But even then Dartmouth had revivals. Our student says:—

"*January* 2, 1782.—This day we held a fast in college, and renewed covenant, and *signed it*, at evening, at Captain Store's. Eleven were added to the Church."

"*January* 13, 1782.—This week we have had eight good sermons preached: the happy work still continues. Happy times, indeed!"

"*February* 10, 1782.—This day was a very solemn one in the church at Dresden. The Sacrament administered, and fifty admitted, by which this church has doubled its members."

"*April* 26, 1782.—This day Dartmouth students set apart *three hours* for secret devotion to our God, who has shown us great favors the winter past in visiting many of us with his Holy Spirit. O Dartmouth! may thy sons long remember this signal mercy, and always live devoted to the fear of the unchanging Jehovah!"

To this prayer of the young Sophomore of 1782 all good men of 1865 will say, with the writer, "Amen, and Amen!"

must have felt when you arrived at Christian habitations. But it is grievous to think these poor, benighted savages must still remain under the tyranny of the Prince of Darkness: a future day, I hope, will give us more encouragement and comfort.

I am glad to find you are so well employed this winter season: I hope you may have much more fruit of your labors than in your summer tour. Shall be glad to see you in the spring, if the Lord spare us.

Am quite obliged to you for writing so largely and being so particular in your letter. I have, since the receipt of yours, written to Dr. Wheelock, but have no direct opportunity to send at present; and I am not so anxious, as I suppose it probable he has by this time, if not before, the most important contents of your journal.

We have nothing very special here, unless a very great change in two Indians,—one especially, which is of some months' standing, and, I hope, may continue; the other, more recent.

Please to give very kind regards to Mr. Frisbie. My family, through Divine goodness, is now pretty well: we shall all be glad to see you both.

That a Divine blessing may ever attend you and your ministry wherever the holy Providence of God may call you, is the unfeigned desire and fervent prayer of,

Reverend and dear sir,

Yours most affectionately,

JOHN BRAINERD.

MR. DAVID MCCLURE.

The Rev. Thomas Rankin, one of the Rev. John Wesley's laborers, spent five years—from 1773 to 1778—in mission-work in America, and left probably from sympathy with the mother-country at the Revolution. He died, in 1810, in London. He kept a journal, from which we make the following extracts:—

"*Thursday, Sept.* 1, 1774.—I rode to New Mills, and preached to a large number in the Baptist meeting-house. Here, also, is the beginning of good days. On Friday I rode to Mount Holly, and preached in the Presbyterian meeting-house to an attentive congregation: I found profit and pleasure at this opportunity.

"Here I met with Mr. John Brainerd, brother and successor to that great and good man Mr. David Brainerd, missionary to the Indians. I spent an agreeable hour with him after preaching. But, alas! what an unpleasing account did he give me of the remains of his most excellent brother's labors, as well as his own, among the Indians! When his brother died (a little above twenty years ago), he succeeded him in the mission. At that time there was a large company of Indians who regularly attended the preaching of the word, and above sixty who were communicants. They were now reduced to a small number who attended his ministry, and not above ten or twelve who were proper to be admitted to the Lord's table. I asked him the reason of this declension. Some, he observed, were dead, and died happy in the Lord; others had grown careless and lukewarm; and many had wandered back among the unawakened Indians, some of whom had turned again to their heathenish customs. There were also some who had given way to the love of spirituous liquors (from which they had once been wholly delivered), so that the gold was become dim, and the most fine gold changed."

"*Wednesday, June* 7, 1775.—I spent an agreeable hour with Mr. John Brainerd, at Mount Holly. He gave me a fuller account than he had done before of the Indians under his care; and from what he said I am more fully convinced of what I have thought before, that none can do good among those outcasts of men (comparatively speaking) but those alone who are peculiarly raised up and called of God to that work. His brother David Brainerd was such an one; and such must all be who will be of use in the conversion of the Indians." *

The above is tinged with the peculiar views of the Wesleyans of his day, and perhaps colored also by the prejudices of an itinerant introducing a new sect; but still had much truth in it. Probably Mr. Rankin failed to understand Mr. Brainerd fully. About this time it was stated officially that the number of Indians, instead of being very small comparatively, amounted in all, including scattered families on Quakeson Creek, Rancocas, Crossweeksung, Cranberry, and Brotherton, to "a hundred and fifty or sixty;" and that as to their morals "they were in general rather improved, and many of them sustained an unblemished character." But Mr. Rankin's statement is confirmed to some extent by all Mr. Brainerd's letters to Dr. Wheelock. When we remember that nearly thirty years had elapsed since the Crossweeksung revival, that twice the Indians had been robbed of their lands and their families rooted up, that war had carried off a large number, twenty-two falling at Fort William Henry, that they were girded by

* Methodist Magazine. London, 1811, vol. xxxiv. pp. 885, 887.

corrupt whites tempting them to intemperance and the other vices which have ruined so many Indian nations, and that the mission itself was left to struggle with poverty in its resources,*—when we bear this in mind, we shall be rather surprised that ten or twelve, with Mr. Brainerd's high standard, were "deemed qualified for the Lord's Supper." As to the *special call* referred to by Mr. Rankin, we may ask whether the best-appointed man and means may not fail of converting sinners, and whether the best missionary may not have his usefulness hindered by causes which he cannot control. Unless we admit this, it seems that the responsibility of failure is not in any lack of holiness or industry in the preacher, nor in the stubbornness of sinners, nor in the absence of the Spirit, but in God's failing to give the "special call" to the minister. It would seem, also, that Enoch, Noah, Elijah, and even Christ himself, lacked the call of God to their work, as they failed to convert the sinners to whom they preached. Could Mr. Rankin imagine a higher fidelity than Mr. Brainerd had exhibited in his work?

The Synod this year made the salary of Mr. Brainerd forty-five pounds. We suppose the five pounds were given him as the schoolmaster: he is ready for any service of his Master.

The following letter is dated Brotherton, instead of Bridgetown or Mount Holly. We are inclined,

* Scotch American Correspondents' MSS., vol. ii. p. 48.

from various hints in his history, to believe that about this time he left Mount Holly, as a residence, and went back to Brotherton, and remained with his Indians there, or at Great Egg Harbor, in their neighborhood, about two years, until his call to Deerfield, in 1777. We copy this letter, as we have copied many others, not from any marked value in its contents, but because it furnishes hints of the times, and illustrates the beautifully kind and Christian spirit of the writer himself. It is the last letter of Mr. Brainerd's which we have been able to procure, probably the last from his pen in existence, and, so far as this volume is concerned, closes his correspondence.

BROTHERTON, May 9, 1775.

REV'D AND DEAR SIR:—

This gratefully acknowledges yours of April 1, by the Rev. Mr. Frisbie. It gives me great pleasure to hear of your welfare; that you are personally in so good a state of health, and your family so comfortable; that your college and academy are so flourishing; and especially for the late happy revival of religion and outpouring of Divine influences on the students. May the Lord's goodness be continued, and his grace abundantly manifested to that school of the prophets to the latest ages!

While the Lord is so divinely gracious to you, while we are offering up our unfeigned praises for the shower of his grace on your field, permit us to request your fervent prayers in behalf of our poor, dry, barren wilderness. It may be the Lord will hear, and send us a day of his power.

I hope Mr. Frisbie will meet with no obstruction in

the design he is come upon. My present weak and very frail state of body does in a manner forbid my making a journey of more than one hundred and seventy miles to attend a Board of the Correspondents: nevertheless, if I thought my presence really necessary, I would exert myself to the utmost.

I have much cause of thankfulness for some comfortable degree of health in my family, and for many other undeserved favors. Please to present my best regards to Mrs. Wheelock, my kind respects to your son R—— and your other children, and assure yourself that I am, with all cordial affection and esteem,

Reverend and honored sir,
Your true friend
and very humble servant,
JOHN BRAINERD.

To the Rev'd Dr. WHEELOCK.

In closing the series of Mr. Brainerd's letters, it is due to his memory to bear in mind that, if they lack variety of incidents and finish of style, it is accounted for by the fact that they were nearly all addressed to one individual, and he rather a professional than a personal friend; that they are confined mainly to one class of subjects, in which the parties had a common interest; that they were penned as opportunity of sending them offered, frequently in great haste and among distracting influences; and that they were all private, and some of them strictly confidential epistles. Considering all this, we are prepared to challenge for them, as a whole, the approbation of all lovers of true piety, unselfish benevolence, earnest religious zeal, and warm-hearted social friendship. Had we Dr. Wheelock's responses, it would add interest to the letters; but alone they will be cherished as mementos of a devout and affectionate friend of God and man.

1775–76.

We have little information of Mr. Brainerd's labors during 1775 and 1776. It was a season of public turmoil. The battles of Lexington and Bunker Hill had been fought, the Declaration of Independence made, and the Presbyterian clergy of the country, sympathizing most heartily in the principles involved in the contest, were greatly engaged in stimulating the courage and animating the hopes of their fellow-countrymen. The same zeal which led Mr. Brainerd to offer himself as a chaplain in the Old French War doubtless burned in his heart in this hour of peril. He belonged to a family not likely to stand neutral in the shock of conflicting principles, nor to be insensible of their obligations to their native land.* The State of

---

* The Rev. Allen H. Brown, of New Jersey, has furnished us with the following facts. He says, under date of August, 1864:—

"I have before me a sermon preached by Rev. B. S. Everett, pastor, at the dedication of the church of Blackwoodtown, and make this extract:—

"'The inhabitants of West Jersey were from the first strongly opposed to the crown, and at the outbreak flocked to their country's defence. Their patriotism, too, was stirred up and guided by their ministers in those days.

"'In 1776, John Brainerd preached in the church here a sermon glowing with patriotism. His text was (Psalm cxliv. 1), "Blessed be the Lord my strength, which teacheth

New Jersey, lying between the great cities of Philadelphia and New York, was in the direct track of advancing and retreating armies: sometimes it was in the possession of one side, sometimes the other. And there were not wanting then, as now, men of easy principles, whose patriotism and courage rose and fell with their interest and convenience. The Indian population, instinctively tending to "smell the battle afar off," and loosely compacted in habits of civilization, would naturally become more intractable and religiously unimpressible in these circumstances.

The motive which led Mr. Brainerd from Mount Holly to Brotherton, and from Brotherton finally to Deerfield, was, doubtless, to escape the agitations of the period, so that his influence as a minister of the gospel could be made still effective.

As his pecuniary condition had been straitened by his sacrifices for his mission, he made a final effort, as we have seen, to secure relief from his old friends in Scotland. The Society for Propagating Christian Knowledge seemed still to regard him as in some sense their missionary, and no doubt would have aided him had not their funds failed. In spite of the bitterness rising between the two countries, they still regarded him with great interest, and in the year 1776 itself, the

---

my hands to war, and my fingers to fight." He appealed to the people to enlist and fight for their country.

"'The audience was deeply impressed. Tears flowed freely: stout hearts and strong wills resolved to join the army. Randal Morgan and his two sons, Lazarus Pine and his sons, John Hedger, David Morgan, Richard Cheeseman and son, served in the war.'"

General Meeting of the Society adopted the following minute:—

Extract from Minutes, Edinburgh, June 5, 1776.

"There was read a letter, of date the 23d February last, from Mr. John Brainerd, the Society's missionary, then at Bridgetown, together with a journal of his labors, commencing December, 1770, and ending in December, 1774: he further mentions that he had not had time to transcribe the journal of last year, but had proceeded and carried it on as heretofore. Mr. Brainerd further transmitted a report, signed by two correspondent members in 1763, bearing that from the beginning of his mission in the Society's service £320 New-Jersey proclamation-money, over and above his annual allowance from the Society, and over and above the public collections and private donations received by him for the support of the mission; some small part of which sum Mr. Brainerd writes he has received, but the remainder with lawful interest amounts to above £450, Spanish dollars at 7*s*. 6*d*. He has likewise expended considerable sums since the above time in the same manner as before; all which he entreats the Society to take into consideration, and allow him to draw for the whole or part.

"The Clerk is to examine the Society's minutes and account relative to the above claim made by Mr. Brainerd, and report to next ordinary meeting of the Committee."

Before the Committee could meet, the Declaration of Independence and the prevalence of war terminated all intercourse between England and America; but we cannot record this final minute of the Society in regard to Mr. Brainerd without testifying our approbation of the Christian benevolence in which their Society was founded, our admiration of their perseverance in the great idea of converting the pagans of this continent, and our gratitude for the sympathy, encouragement, prayer, and pecuniary aid which for a quarter of a century they gave to the brothers David and John Brainerd.

The Synod of 1775 continued Mr. Brainerd on the "Commission," and appointed him a delegate to the Convention at Greenfield, Conn., the first Wednesday of September, and up to the year of his death considered him as their missionary to the Indians, allowing him the interest of the three hundred pounds in the hands of the Treasurer of New Jersey College. His pastorship at Deerfield from 1777 to 1781 was not allowed to interfere with this arrangement of Brainerd's general care of the Indian mission.

The history of Mr. Brainerd's labors as a domestic missionary among the whites of New Jersey we shall present hereafter. Outside of his mission at Brotherton there was a settlement of Indians, about a mile west of Vincenttown, where stood a log church, erected by his influence, in which he often preached. Its vicinity to Mount Holly, when that place was invaded, interrupted his labors at that station.

CHAPTER XLI.

SKETCH OF BROTHERTON—MR. BRAINERD SETTLES AT DEERFIELD—INDIANS NEGLECTED—REV. DANIEL SIMON—FINAL EXIT OF THE INDIANS FROM NEW JERSEY—BARTHOLOMEW S. CALVIN'S RETURN—DELAWARE INDIANS IN NEW YORK AND MICHIGAN—MR. BRAINERD'S LABORS NOT LOST.

IN the year 1777, at fifty-seven years of age, Mr. Brainerd removed from Brotherton to Deerfield, in Cumberland county, N. J., and took charge of the church there. He still seems to have retained some oversight of the mission. In 1778, 1779, and 1780, up to the year of his death, the Synod of New York and Philadelphia voted that "the interest on the Indian fund be paid to Mr. Brainerd for his services among the Indians." To the last of life he seems to have clung to his little flock,—his first love,—and his brethren did their best in a time of war to sustain him.

Brotherton, the Indian settlement which he had aided to build up, and where for fifteen years he had resided, was situated in what is now a prosperous and pleasant rural neighborhood, near the present Shamong station, on the Delaware-Bay and Raritan Railroad, about forty miles from Philadelphia. The "Historical Collections of New Jersey" give the following description:—

"Edgepelick (or Indian Mills) is the name of a locality about three miles north of Atsion, where was the last Indian settlement in the State. The remnant of the tribe, consisting of about one hundred souls, emigrated to the West nearly half a century since. There is, however, a single family, but of mixed breed, residing in the vicinity, in a log hut. Brainerd, the missionary, for a time resided among the Indians at this place. His dwelling-house stood about eight rods south of the saw-mill of Godfrey Hancock, on rising ground, the site of which is still marked by depression, showing the precise spot where the cellar was. Within a few rods is the spring from which the family obtained water. The natives had a saw-mill on the site of Nicholas S. Thompson's mill, a quarter of a mile northeast of Brainerd's house. Their burying-ground was on the edge of the pond about forty rods northwest of the same dwelling. In the vicinity stood their church, built of logs, and destroyed about thirty-five years since. After the Indians left, it was used by the whites for public worship."

Gordon, in his "History of New Jersey," gives a still more detailed account of this place. He says:—

"This property was vested in trustees for the use of the Indians resident south of the Raritan, so that they could neither sell nor lease any part thereof; and all persons other than Indians were forbidden to settle thereon. Soon after the purchase, they were assisted by the Government to remove to this spot and to erect commodious buildings.* In 1765, there were about sixty persons

* The readers of this book will receive this statement with due limitations. Government *promised* assistance, but failed to give it.

settled here, and twenty-nine at Weekpink, on a tract secured by an English right to the family of King Charles, an Indian sachem. But no measure has yet been devised to avert the fiat which has gone forth against this devoted race. This feeble remnant having obtained permission to sell their lands in November, 1801, between seventy and eighty removed, in 1802, to a settlement on the Oneida Lake, belonging to the Stockbridge (Oneida) Indians, who had invited their 'grandfathers to eat of their dish,' saying, 'it was large enough for both;' and adding, with characteristic earnestness, that 'they had stretched their necks in looking towards the fireside of their grandfathers until they were as long as cranes.' The united tribes remained here until 1824, when the encroachments of the whites induced them, with the Six Nations and the Munceys, to quit New Stockbridge, and to purchase from the Menomees a large tract of land on the Fox River, between Winnebago Lake and Green Bay, and extending to Lake Michigan. In 1832, the New Jersey tribe, reduced to less than forty, applied by memorial to the Legislature of the State, setting forth that they never conveyed their reserved rights of hunting and fishing on unenclosed lands, and had appointed an agent to transfer them on receipt of a compensation. This agent, a venerable chief of seventy-six years of age, bore the name of Bartholomew S. Calvin.* He had been selected by Rev. J. Brainerd, brother

* This Bartholomew S. Calvin was the son of Stephen Calvin, and brother of Hezekiah. He had another educated brother, reared on the Calvin Farm, near Brotherton. In his petition to the Legislature of New Jersey, in 1832, he said:—

"MY BRETHREN:—

"I am old, and weak, and poor, and therefore a fit representative of my people. You are young, and strong, and rich, and therefore fit representatives of your people. But let me beg you for a moment to lay aside the recollections of your strength and of our weakness, that your minds may be prepared to examine with candor the subject of our claims.

of the celebrated Indian missionary, and placed at Princeton College in 1770, where he continued until the Revolutionary War cut off the funds of the Scotch Missionary Society, by whom he was supported. He afterwards taught school at Edgepeling, where he had as many white as In-

---

"Our tradition informs us, and, I believe, it corresponds with your records, that the right of fishing in all the rivers and bays south of the Raritan, and of hunting on all unenclosed lands, was never relinquished; but, on the contrary, was expressly reserved in our last treaty, held at Crossweeks in 1758.

"Having myself been one of the parties to the sale, I believe, in 1801, I know that these rights were not sold or parted with.

"We now offer to sell these privileges to the State of New Jersey. They were once of great value to us; and we apprehend that neither time nor distance, nor the non-use of our rights, has at all affected them, but the Courts here would consider our claims valid were we to exercise them ourselves or delegate them to others. It is not, however, our wish to excite litigation. We consider the State Legislature the proper purchaser, and throw ourselves upon its benevolence and magnanimity; trusting that feelings of justice and liberality will induce you to give us what you deem a compensation.

"BARTHOLOMEW S. CALVIN,

"In behalf of himself and his red brethren."

Calvin was seventy-six years old, white-haired, venerable in appearance, and dignified in manner. As the solitary representative of his tribe, he must have seemed

"Like one who trod alone
Some banquet-hall deserted."

The Legislature of New Jersey granted him two thousand dollars on his petition. He made the following response. It does full justice to New Jersey; perhaps a little more.

"TRENTON, March 12, 1832.

"Bartholomew S. Calvin takes this method to return his thanks to both Houses of the State Legislature, and especially to their Committees, for their very respectful attention to, and candid examination of, the Indian claims which he was delegated to present.

"The final act of official intercourse between the State of New Jersey and the Delaware Indians, who once owned nearly the whole of its territory, has now been consummated, and in a manner which must redound to the honor of this growing State and, in all probability, to the prolongation of the existence of a wasted, yet grateful, people. Upon this parting occasion, I feel it to be an incumbent duty to bear the feeble tribute of my praise to the high-toned justice which in this instance and, so far as I am acquainted, in all former times has actuated the Councils of this Commonwealth in dealing with the aboriginal inhabitants.

"Not a drop of our blood have you spilled in battle,—not an acre of our land have you taken but by our consent. These facts speak for themselves, and need no comment: they place the character of New Jersey in bold relief and bright example to those States within whose territorial limits our brethren still remain. Nothing save benisons can fall upon her from the lips of Leni Lennapi."

dian pupils. As all legal claim of the tribe was, even by its own members, considered barred by voluntary abandonment, the Legislature consented to grant remuneration as an act of voluntary justice, or rather as a memorial of kindness and compassion to the remnant of a once powerful and friendly people, occupants and natives of the State, and as a consummation of a proud fact in the history of New Jersey, that every Indian claim to her soil and its franchises had been acquired by fair and voluntary transfer. By the Act of 12th March, 1832, the treasurer was directed to pay the agent two thousand dollars for a full relinquishment of the rights of his tribe." *

After Mr. Brainerd ceased his labors, in 1781, neither the Scotch Society nor the Synod seemed longer to assume responsibility for the welfare of the Indian congregation at Brotherton. The Rev. Daniel Simon (an Indian who had been ordained to the ministry) preached at Brotherton in 1783, but was soon suspended for immorality, and no missionary was ever appointed to succeed him. The Indians were left as sheep without a shepherd. Gradually sinking in moral character, and still dwindling in numbers, in July, 1802, but eighty-five Indians remained at Brotherton.

In June, 1861, in company with Rev. Samuel Miller,† of Mount Holly, we paid a visit to Brotherton, now called in the neighborhood Shamung, or Indian Mills. A morning drive of fifteen miles,

---

* Gordon's History of New Jersey, p. 64.

† Son of the late Rev. Samuel Miller, D.D., of Princeton, and a faithful missionary in the field once occupied by John Brainerd.

with a light buggy and two horses, through a well-cultivated country and on a good road, brought us to the ancient farm of Stephen Calvin, father of Hezekiah and Bartholomew Calvin (Brainerd's pupils), about noon. Stephen Calvin was a substantial farmer, and an elder in Brainerd's church. One hundred years ago his dwelling was the home of genuine Indian hospitality; but dwarf pines and scrub oaks have so reclaimed their occupancy of the soil, that Mr. Miller and myself found only an open orchard of ancient trees to indicate the existence of former cultivation. We measured some of these apple-trees, and found them more than six feet in circumference. Having taken our field repast under the most ancient tree, and possessed ourselves of a living limb as a relic, we proceeded to Brotherton, one mile distant. There the stump of a mammoth oak indicated the spot where stood the ancient Indian sanctuary: a depression in the earth, the remains of a former cellar, told us the spot of Brainerd's own dwelling. A modern mill occupies the very place and bears the name of the mill erected by Brainerd's Indians a century gone by. We found traditions rife there of the piety and labors of the good missionary; and aged persons told us that they remembered the final departure of the Indians for their new home in Western New York.

One venerable lady said she remembered well the morning of their exit. Her father was em-

"The Old Parsonage, Cranberry, N. J., near the Indian Town of Bethel."—P. 419.

ployed, among others, to transport them in his wagon to Amboy or Brunswick. Their scanty furniture, their rude Indian relics and treasures, the aged, the sick, and the little ones, were packed in the vehicles, and the healthy marched on foot. Perhaps "whistling aloud to keep their courage up," or in defiance of their painful destiny, the cavalcade moved off with the music of violins. Whatever their purpose or spirit in this mode of departure, the thoughtful would recognize in their music the requiem of a dead nation, the dirge of a Christian congregation, and the funeral rites of a noble scheme of Christian philanthropy.

By a singular providence, the cavalcade tarried a night on the Indian field at Cranberry, on the precise land occupied by Bethel, their former home; and we cannot but believe that this incident reveals in their memories a lingering recollection of their better days under the ministry of their sainted pastors David and John Brainerd.*

The Hon. Pomroy Jones, of Westmoreland, Oneida county, N. Y., in a letter to us, says:—

"When the Delawares emigrated to Oneida in 1802 or 1804, they passed my residence in Westmoreland. They had twelve wagons for their baggage and those too feeble to journey on foot. The wagons the next day, when on their return to New Jersey, again passed my house. I presume they had been hired for the occasion.

* See letter of Rev. Joseph G. Symmes, pastor of the Presbyterian Church in Cranberry, Appendix C.

The Delawares were completely amalgamated with the Oneidas and inducted into their habits, and soon were around amongst the white inhabitants selling their commodities, split brooms and baskets. In 1830 I was appointed, by the Commission of the Land Office, one of the Commissioners to appraise seventeen hundred acres of land sold by the Oneidas the previous winter to the State. As the land was partially settled, a number of families residing on it, it led to quite an intimacy with them; and I found a portion of them were of the Delaware tribe, but possessed of all the rights of Oneidas to the soil they occupied."

From this period we must regard Brainerd's Delaware Indians as identified with the Oneidas, the Stockbridges, and the Brothertons of Oneida county, N. Y.*

---

* The birthplace of the author was in Lewis county, N. Y., about thirty miles northeast from the chief settlement of the Oneida Indians. His father's house, one mile west of the Black River and three hundred feet above it, overlooked a vast expanse of the great Adirondack forest, now so famous as a resort in summer. This great wilderness, then and now one hundred and twenty miles in length by one hundred in breadth, with its mysterious and profound solitudes, its towering mountains, its wild cataracts, its myriad of beautiful lakes, and its abundant game, naturally attracted the attention of the Oneida Indians, and in the winter season they were accustomed to come in scores, leave their wives and *pappooses* in some neglected and abandoned house or barn, where the women made baskets and brought in the deer, moose, bears, etc., which the men had killed by hunting in the great Adirondack. The men, unless excited by drink, were honest and peaceful. Their wives were modest, industrious, temperate, and, many of them, pious. I was much bantered in childhood by being often told that my excellent mother once allowed me to share in the repast of an Indian infant at its mother's breast.

The coming of these Indians was always hailed with joy by the

Though many individual Indians still linger on Oneida Reservation, yet about 1832, most of these tribes migrated to Green Bay, Michigan, where the Rev. Cutting Marsh* labored among them, with patience and some success, for many years. They have since gone still farther west: their present numbers and condition we are unable to state.

For the sake of justice and humanity, for the sake of the good men who gave their lives and labors in the gospel to these Indians, as well as for the interest of this narrative, we could have hoped a better fate for the Indians of New Jersey. Superficial thinkers might regard the labors of the Brainerds, the Eliots, the Mayhews, the Kirklands, as but a bubble on the sea, broken and perished forever; but this would be a grand mistake. God educates present generations by the experiments of the past, and disciplines his servants for final victory by the example and martyrdom of good men in other ages. David, Elijah, Isaiah, Daniel, Matthew, Mark, Luke, Paul, and even Christ him-

---

young among us, for it held out the promise of beautiful baskets, tiny snow-shoes, cross-bows and arrows, and venison, without stint. I have doubtless seen some aged Indians at my father's fireside whom John Brainerd had instructed, but was too young to inquire about the matter. I may say that these Indian visits to my early home, which my father and mother always welcomed, left on my mind a pleasant impression of Indian character, and have disposed me through life to lament and resent their wrongs. We hope this volume, if it does nothing higher, will help to freshen the memory of the good man who gave his life-labors and patrimony to bless and save a degraded and wronged people.

* See letter of Rev. Cutting Marsh, Appendix D.

self, labored for the conversion and salvation of cities and nations which have long since perished from the earth. Shall we hence infer that their labors, prayers, and tears were impertinent and thrown away? No: they still live; not in the organized existence of the churches they planted or the nations they taught, but in the educated minds, the abiding faith, the purified hearts of other men, of later times, Christianized by their influence. They will thus live in the final faith and hope and holiness of the entire race, when God shall subdue the world to himself.

Crossweeks, Bethel, and Brotherton, like Ephesus, Antioch, and Thyatira, have lost the praying men and women who once dwelt there; but these places still constitute sacred shrines in the memory of the Church, and, by the recorded history of the holy men who labored in them, will to the end of time radiate light upon the world. Henry Martyn, Carey, and many other missionaries, Robert Hall, Thomas Chalmers, and other great minds of earth, have borrowed inspiration and models of holy living from the lives and labors of the Brainerds among the pines of New Jersey. We say this on the assumption that the religious influence exerted by the Brainerds on the Delaware Indians has been effaced by time and changes; but we are not obliged to concede all this. There may be still lingering among the posterity of these Indians in the far West a tradition of truth and holiness from the teaching of the Brainerds which, like "the handful of corn in the earth upon the top of the mountains," shall finally produce fruit "to shake like Lebanon" and fill the whole earth.*

---

* See Appendix D.

CHAPTER XLII.

MR. BRAINERD AS A DOMESTIC MISSIONARY AMONG THE WHITES—HIS LABORS ABUNDANT—HIS CHURCHES AFTER HIS DEATH ALLOWED TO DECAY—HE IS STILL REMEMBERED IN TRADITION—REV. ALLEN H. BROWN—MR. BRAINERD AS A TRUSTEE OF PRINCETON COLLEGE—HIS ACTIVITY AND USEFULNESS.

OUR readers have seen that, in all the latter years of his life, Mr. Brainerd, with an apostolic zeal and self-denial, preached the gospel among the whites over a vast neglected region of New Jersey. In his letter to Mrs. Smith, he says he gave every alternate Sabbath to his Indians, and devoted the remainder of his time to missionary labors among the Pines and along the sea-shore. When he died, his labors were not followed up by the Presbyterians. The churches he built fell into decay, or passed into the hands of the Methodists, who began to occupy the ground by their circuits and travelling preachers. Early settlers, elevated by the gospel and prospering in their affairs, partly as a result of their moral improvement through Mr. Brainerd's labors, sold out to strangers of a more straitened class, and sought for themselves a more fertile soil and higher social privileges.

As a result of these causes, little comparatively remains to tell of the martyr-labors of John Brainerd, save the forest graves of his church-yards, the title-deeds of the sites where he erected church-buildings, the congregations of other denominations built up on his foundations, and the traditionary recollections of him as a holy, benevolent, untiring servant of God.

Our acquaintance with the ancient places and names of New Jersey is too imperfect to follow him in his journeyings as an evangelist. He says he had seven stated preaching-stations, or fixed congregations. In his letter from Trenton to Rev. Enoch Green, he mentions twenty places where he occasionally preached. True, his brethren of that day in the Synod shared in his spirit, and sometimes came to his aid in supplying his field. With all our claims for modern times, it is still true that the spirit of missions never glowed more warmly than in the hearts of Brainerd's companions. They did what they could for his relief, but still left on his shoulders the final responsibility of supplying his seven congregations in addition to his Indian church at Brotherton. A hundred years ago a solitary horseback traveller, grave, prayerful, and benevolent, was often seen among the Pines hurrying to some preaching-place, or coming back from the funeral of the recent dead. He was for a time the only minister of Jesus, and for years and years the only missionary of his church, in that wild and extended region. No wonder that even now, when for a long time competence, education, and refinement have taken the place of the poverty, ignorance, and semi-barbarism of a past century,—no wonder that to this day there lives in tradition among those who gather around village-hearths in New Jersey the memory of the sainted man of God who came unasked, and often unpaid, to solemnize their marriages, to sanctify by religious services the burial of their dead, to set up their family altars, to baptize and aid in the training of their children, and who, by teaching and holy example,

"Allured to brighter worlds, and led the way."*

Any life of John Brainerd would be imperfect which did not allude to his official connection with Princeton College. As we have shown elsewhere, the college originated from sympathy with the wrongs of his beloved brother, and to sustain principles common to the brothers and the theological party with which they were identified. He looked to it to train the ministers whom he approved and the Indian missionaries to carry out his work. He

* The Rev. Allen H. Brown, of the Presbytery of West Jersey, has for the last eighteen years been employed as a domestic missionary on the very field where John Brainerd once labored, with a zeal, activity, and self-denial almost equal to his predecessor of a past generation. He has explored vacant districts, hunted up the sites of ancient churches, planted new congregations on the old foundations, and affectionately and reverently recorded what he could gather of the history of the Rev. John Brainerd. He has kindly sent us a communication, which embraces almost all which can be known of the labors of the early missionary in New Jersey. To this letter we refer our readers: it will richly repay perusal. See Appendix E.

was identified with it from the outset. The men that sustained the college sustained him. The first class graduated in his presence in 1748, and he took his own Master's degree from it in 1749. He was the personal and intimate friend of Jonathan Dickinson, Aaron Burr, Jonathan Edwards, Samuel Davis, Samuel Finley, and John Witherspoon,—all its early presidents from its infancy to its full maturity: he speaks of its Commencements as his holidays or chief festivals. He always alludes to it with respectful affection, and reposes in it his brightest hopes. These hopes time has realized. His Indians are scattered and his white churches decayed; but his favorite literary institution has grown stronger and stronger through a hundred years, and has a bright future still in prospect. It is, then, with great satisfaction that we say of Mr. Brainerd, as a trustee of the College of New Jersey, that he was eminently zealous for its prosperity and faithful in the discharge of his duties. His place in the Board was seldom vacant, and his influence apparently great. At an early day he was on a committee to draft certain by-laws; in 1757, a member of the committee to superintend all matters connected with the college buildings; in 1758, he was a successful delegate from the trustees to secure the accession of President Edwards; in 1759, he was a member of the committee to wait on the Synod of New York and Philadelphia to invite the Rev. Mr. Davis to become president of the college; and in 1763, a member of the committee to arrange the terms for the purchase of land. From this it would seem that his brethren had great confidence in the soundness of his judgment, and that he may be regarded as one among the far-seeing and philanthropic Christian men who aided in laying the foundation and consolidating the prosperity of that noble institution. We are not without hope that the present volume, imperfect as it is, will nevertheless in all time to come find a welcome place on the shelves of Princeton Library, and be cherished by an institution which enjoyed in its infancy the benefit of the counsels and prayers of the New Jersey missionary, John Brainerd.

Mr. Brainerd's office as trustee terminated only with his life. His successor, Mr. James Boggs, was chosen to fill the place after Mr. Brainerd's death, May 1, 1781. The popularity of the Indian mission in New Jersey, and the sympathy of the churches with David Brainerd and his brother, had great influence in Scotland and elsewhere in securing the pecuniary aid essential to the foundation and early usefulness of the college.

CHAPTER XLIII.

MR. BRAINERD AS PASTOR IN DEERFIELD—WHY HE WENT THERE—HIS PREDECESSORS—TRADITIONS OF HIS LABORS—A CASE OF DISCIPLINE—HIS INDIAN WOMAN BECKY—HIS DEATH AND TOMBSTONE.

1777–81.

WE have now followed John Brainerd to the closing years of his ministry, and of his toil-spent life. He had schemed and planned to open a wider and more promising missionary field in New York or Ohio, at Onohquanga or Muskingum. Baffled and shut up to his limited flock at Brotherton, he had carefully and prayerfully done all that could be done to protect, elevate, and save his Indian congregation, in spite of the evil influences around them. He had magnified his office by using the time spared from his Indian church in founding some seven white churches, and preaching at twenty out-stations among the whites in the destitute districts of New Jersey.

He would have died with his people, but war came, and a British army, reckless and cruel, broke in upon the field of his labors. They captured Mount Holly; and, to mark their special vengeance on the outspoken and active patriotism of the pastor, they burnt down his church, and, it is said, also his dwelling. As Brotherton was but fifteen miles distant, and he could expect no mercy at the hands of British or Tories, he felt justified in retiring, until the storm was past, some forty miles, to Deerfield,* in Cumberland county. He went not to rest there, but to labor; and hence he took charge of the Presbyterian church. It was his final field: he found there a home and a grave.

Anxious to avail ourselves of all the traditionary facts concerning Mr. Brainerd which could be collected in Deerfield, we addressed a letter of inquiry to the Rev. R. Hamill Davis, the present pastor of the Presbyterian church. Among other kindnesses shown us in the preparation of this work, is the following letter from Mr. Davis:—

"DEERFIELD, March 15, 1861.

"REV'D AND DEAR SIR:—

"I have made inquiry of a number of aged persons here and in Bridgeton, and have also called upon two

---

* Deerfield, in Cumberland county, is a pleasant village, about thirty miles southeast of Philadelphia. His predecessor, Rev. Andrew Hunter, was ordained September 4, 1746, and resigned in 1760. Rev. Enoch Green was installed June 9, 1767, and died in 1776. Rev. John Brainerd began to officiate in 1777. The sessional minute of him is this: "The Rev. John Brainerd took charge of this congregation in 1777, and during his ministry several additions were made to the church. Mr. Brainerd departed this life March 18, 1781, much lamented."

During his entire ministry war was raging. Mr. Hunter in fourteen years had added five to the church; Mr. Green, in nine years, thirteen only: we shall not be, therefore, surprised that during the four years of Mr. Brainerd's ministry his additions to the church were but ten.

antiquarians in Bridgeton, but am sorry that my efforts have been so fruitless. Mrs. Hood, of Bridgeton, used to recite her catechism to Mr. Brainerd. He would sometimes hear the children recite the catechism in the church, and when he would visit the families he would catechize them there. There is one old lady, a Mrs. Thompson, living in Bridgeton, who bears the reputation of having a very retentive memory, who has given me a few facts that may be of some little service to you. I give them, as near as I can, verbatim, as they fell from her lips, either as her own voluntary remarks or in reply to inquiries which I proposed. I think you may rely upon the truthfulness and accuracy of her statements. She is a native of Deerfield, and has frequently heard her parents speak of Mr. Brainerd. Her remarks were substantially as follows. I give them in the order in which I received them, though they may be a little incoherent.

"Rev. John Brainerd was declining in health when he came to Deerfield. He left a widow and one daughter, Mary (by a former wife), who afterwards married a gentleman in Burlington, and the widow Brainerd went to live there with her. He was a man of amiable disposition, and a solemn preacher. Mrs. Thompson thinks that he was never installed as pastor over the Deerfield church.

"Mr. Alfred Davis, descendant from one of the oldest families here, confirms the statement that he was never installed, and says the reason was the unsettled state of the country (it being in Revolutionary times). There was a great simplicity in Mr. Brainerd's style, which it was supposed he had acquired by giving the truth in a simple way to the Indians. He lived and died in the old brick parsonage, opposite the site of the present parsonage. He died, Mrs. Thompson thinks, of a pulmonary affection.

"He was very retiring in his habits. He came to Deerfield from Egg Harbor, the same place from which his immediate predecessor, Rev. Enoch Green, came. He was considered a very godly man. A witty woman of Deerfield, hearing that he was about to come thither, made the remark that she supposed he would think they would need to be taught as he had been accustomed to teach the Indians; and that, pointing downwards, he would say, 'Hell down there!' and, upwards, 'Heaven up there!' He brought an Indian woman with him, a very pious woman, who washed, helped in the house, and would spend her leisure hours in making baskets.

"The remains of John Brainerd repose under the church. A marble slab on the church-floor marks the spot, from which I copy the following inscription:—

" 'Beneath mouldereth the dust of the Rev. John Brainerd. Died March, 1781.'

"Truly and respectfully,
"R. Hamill Davis."

We have little to add to this letter of Rev. Mr. Davis. Family tradition says he carried to Deerfield with him an Indian servant-woman, named Becky, who had lived in his family many years. She was a pious, godly woman, whose sympathy and prayers cheered the depression of his declining health. When occasionally her female friends from Brotherton came to see her, they were greatly distressed by being obliged to sleep on a featherbed. Becky was energetic, tidy, and skilful as a housekeeper, and much respected by her employer and the community in general.

The session-book of Deerfield church furnishes no record of Mr. Brainerd's baptisms or marriages. Several cases of discipline are recorded, and among these one so characteristic of the pastor that we give it in a note.*

In the year 1840, we had a brief interview with the widow of the Rev. Enoch Green, Mr. Brainerd's predecessor at Deerfield. She was very aged, but intelligent and communicative. The author's name

---

* *March* 10, 1779.—Mrs. R., apparently in a fit of passion, and for some slight reason, had accused Mr. S. of cheating, abuse of her relations, hypocrisy, falsehood, &c. Mr. S. brought Mrs. R. before the session for slander. She denied that she had uttered some of the statements, but justified herself as to the truth of the others. After a long trial, the session (doubtless at the suggestion of Mr. Brainerd) came to the following decision, which all will regard as frank, wise, and characteristic:—

"1. That Mr. S. does not appear to be guilty of the first and second charges in every particular; but we think he ought to have conducted himself with more prudence and tenderness towards his aged mother, and is really guilty."

In respect to the rest of the charges, of which the session generally acquit Mrs. R., they, nevertheless, say:—

"Although the session wish to make all proper allowance for human frailty, and although Mrs. R. seems to have believed that the particulars with which she charged Mr. S. were true, yet we think she has spoken imprudently, and too much under the influence of passion and prejudice, against the reputation of her brother. The session think it incumbent on them to express their entire disapprobation of her conduct in this regard.

"Upon a review of the whole case, we cannot but think that both parties are, in some respects, censurable. We would therefore recommend to them to cultivate peace and harmony, as becomes Christians, and especially those who sustain so near a relation to each other."—*Deerfield Session-Book.*

This is a pretty fair specimen of ordinary family quarrels, where both parties are partly right and partly wrong and about equally need admonition from church authority. The whole proceedings in Deerfield are marked by an impartiality and faithfulness creditable to Mr. Brainerd and his elders.

and profession induced her at once to call up her early acquaintance with John Brainerd. She related many facts concerning him; but, as I had then no thought of ever writing his life, her statements have mainly passed from my recollection. I distinctly remember, however, that she spoke of him as an able preacher, a most faithful pastor, as a man of warm affections and eminent personal holiness. She seemed to have cherished his memory with tenderness and reverence for half a century. At the same time, she gave me an intimation that his efficiency in Deerfield was hindered by his feeble health and a tendency to mental depression, for which the constitution of his family, as well as the burdens and sorrows of his life, fully account. In Deerfield, as in every other place where he labored, John Brainerd not only won the hearts of the people, but enstamped them with a holy influence. His ashes rest in the aisle of the same old church in which he preached the gospel at Deerfield.

He died, aged sixty-one, in the dark and stormy days of revolution and bloodshed. He was not permitted to see his country emerge from its perils and take a place among the nations of the earth. He died, remote from cities and crowds, in a quiet village and among plain people, and at a period when society, struggling for national life, took little account of the fate of individuals. No gazette heralded his departure, no orator gave him

"Presbyterian Church, Deerfield, N. J., in which John Brainerd ministered and was buried."—P. 434.

an eulogy, and no generous appreciation raised him a monument. For nearly seventy years his grave was unmarked even by a stone; but recently a friendly and generous hand has placed over his ashes a little slab, about twenty inches by thirty, on which are inscribed his name and the date of his death. He was of the number of Christ's "hidden ones." His modesty led him to shrink from prominence in society; his field of labor buried him for years in the forest. His death was in a secluded neighborhood; and the Church, for half a century, failed to mark even his grave.

Believing that the Church and the world cannot afford to lose the radiance of his example and the record of his holy purposes and prayers, we have drawn aside the veil thrown over him by his humility and the world's indifference, and through this volume he stands once more before a living generation. May we hope "that, like an old prophet risen from the dead," some good "works may show forth themselves in him"? It would be presumptuous in us, perhaps, to hope, though we may earnestly desire it, that, "dead in Christ, he shall yet live," not alone in the resurrection of the just, but a sainted example on earth, before rising and fading generations, to the end of time. He lives in tradition by the wigwam-fires of the Far-West Indians; he is worthy also to live in the literature of the Church.

CHAPTER XLIV.

MR. BRAINERD'S LAST WILL AND TESTAMENT—HIS DESCENDANTS—HIS PERSON AND MANNERS.

MR. BRAINERD'S last "will and testament," which we have transcribed from the Clerk's Office at Trenton, N. J., was prepared at Deerfield in March, 1780, just one year before his death. As he seems to have written it himself, and as it throws light on his state of mind and health, his worldly circumstances, and his domestic relations, we insert it entire.

John Brainerd's Will and Testament.

In the fear of the Lord, and as one that must give an account,

I, John Brainerd, Minister of the Gospel of Christ, at present laboring under some bodily indisposition, but, through the grace of God, blest with the fullest use of reason, for which I bless and praise God, think it my indispensable duty to Christ and my family to signify my will in writing.

And, first of all, I give and recommend my soul into the hands of God in and through Jesus Christ, firmly relying on his name, merits, and righteousness for pardon, justification, and eternal life.

The body I commit to the ground, to be decently interred only at the discretion of my executor hereinafter named, fully expecting to receive the same in the morning of the resurrection, glorified only through the rich grace of Jesus Christ.

As to what *worldly substance* God has seen fit to intrust me with, I think it my duty to dispose of it in the following manner:—

1st. I give and bequeath to my dear, well-beloved, and faithful wife, Elizabeth Brainerd, all that part of my estate that was hers before we were married, and that she brought with her in consequence of our marriage, as also my silver watch.

2d. I put all the rest of my estate into her hands, as money or cash, bills, bonds, certificates, cattle, horses, and every other part and parcel of my estate, except what will by-and-by be mentioned, not to be aliened or given away, but which may be sold for her comfortable support during her state of widowhood; then to become the property of my dear, well-beloved, and dutiful daughter Mary Ross, wife of Maj. John Ross.

3d. I do now give and bequeath unto this my only daughter and child all and every individual thing that came to me by her mother, as also the bed I had before I was married, all the plate marked E. L., together with a mustard-pot and pepper-box not marked at all, as also a three-year-old heifer and yearling heifer. My books I leave with my wife and daughter, to be disposed of as they shall agree and think proper; and they have free liberty to sell any number of them as they shall choose. My annuity in the Widows' Fund at Philadelphia I desire may be paid only to my wife, that she may enjoy the whole benefit of the same.

4th. I denominate and ordain my well-beloved son-in-law, Maj. John Ross, to be my sole executor of this my last will and testament; and do hereby empower him to sell any part of my estate at vendue, or otherwise, with the advice and full consent of my above-mentioned dear wife, who will then be my widow; but not without.

This I ratify and confirm as my last will and testament, disannulling all others by me at any time made or done.

In testimony whereof, I set my hand and affix my seal, this 21st day of March, 1780.

JOHN BRAINERD.

In presence of
EZEKIEL FOSTER,
EPHRAIM FOSTER,
JEREMIAH FOSTER.

From this "will" we draw the inference that Mr. Brainerd, while he had been willing to labor hard for little compensation in his Master's service, and while his charities to his Indians had drawn heavily on his resources, had, nevertheless, managed his pecuniary affairs with care and skill, so that he had always been able, with his own patrimony and what he received by his marriage connections, to live genteelly and comfortably. All received by his first marriage he leaves to his only daughter and child by his first wife; he leaves to the second wife all he had received by her; and to both he makes such addition as his own personal estate would allow. According to the standard of the day, he seems to have been neither rich nor poor,—the allotment for which Agur prayed, and which best befits a minister of the gospel.

His wife, Elizabeth (Price) Brainerd, survived

him several years, residing alternately with her step-daughter at Mount Holly and with her own relatives in Philadelphia. Between her and her step-daughter Mary, the only surviving child of John Brainerd, there seems to have subsisted a most tender, delicate, and permanent affection, which found expression in constant intimacy and correspondence. The letters of the daughter to her step-mother are marked by so much filial love, piety, taste, and refinement of feeling as to indicate on the part of her father great care in her training and an excellent parental example: they do credit alike to the father, mother, and daughter.*

Major John Ross, who married the only daughter of John Brainerd, was born in Mount Holly, N. J., 1752, and died there in 1796. March 13, 1776, he was commissioned a captain in the Third Regiment of New Jersey troops of the Revolutionary Army. He received a major's commission April 7, 1779, and the same year was united in marriage to Mary Brainerd, two years before the death of her father. He was one of the original members of the Society of Cincinnati, and, under Washington, Collector of the Revenue for Burlington county. His wife died at Mount Holly in 1792, leaving three children. Only one of these —the eldest, Sophia Marion—left descendants.

---

* We give a few of these familiar epistles as a specimen. See Appendix F.

Sophia Marion Ross, granddaughter of John Brainerd, married John Lardner Clark, Esq., August 1, 1797. He was the youngest son of Hon. Elijah Clark, of Egg Harbor, the warm personal friend of the Rev. John Brainerd, and elder in one of Brainerd's churches. He was also a member of the Provincial Congress, and a colonel in the militia of New Jersey during the Revolutionary War.*

Mrs. Clark, granddaughter of John Brainerd, had six children, only two of whom survive. These are Mrs. Louisa Vanuxem Peacock, widow of James Peacock, Esq., late of Harrisburg, and Mrs. Emeline Marion Sims, wife of John Clark Sims, an original proprietor of the Philadelphia Evening Bulletin, and now Actuary of the American Insurance Company. The only brother of these ladies, Brainerd Clark, Esq., of Mount Holly, N. J., died several years since, leaving a family. These three families comprehend the entire descendants of the subject of this memoir. We have named them

---

* During the war, Elijah Clark and Richard Westcott, Esqs., built at their own expense a small fort at the Fox Burrows, on Chestnut Neck, near the port of Little Egg Harbor, and bought a number of cannon for the defence of said fort. While the Revolutionary Legislature was in session at Haddonfield, in September, 1777, the two branches passed a resolution for paying Clark and Westcott four hundred and thirty pounds one shilling and three pence for this fort, which, we are told, was at one time defended by fifteen hundred of the Shore-men, who, upon the enemy ascending the river in great force in barges, evacuated it. The good people of Chestnut Neck ought to mark the site of this old redoubt, that future ages may know it.—*Mickle's History of Gloucester County, New Jersey*, p. 80.

freely, for they are of a character and position to imply no discredit to their ancestor. Happily, they need no letters of commendation from us; but, in justice to the memory of John Brainerd, we must express our satisfaction that his religious faith and purity of life have so richly adorned his children and his children's children.

We may also add, that our personal regard for these living descendants has mingled with our reverence for the dead in cheering the preparation of this volume.*

From all we can learn by tradition concerning Mr. Brainerd's person, we infer that he was tall in stature, large in frame, and active in his movements.

Rev. Dr. Field, who was for many years minister of the parish in which Brainerd's parents resided, says, "In person, John Brainerd was rather tall."

Mrs. Hood says she recollects something about his person: he was a large-boned man, not fleshy, a little above the medium size. From our knowledge of his family, we incline to believe that the tradition in his native town was correct. We set him before us as a tall, dark-haired, gray-eyed, heavy-browed, grave, sensitive, sanguine, and rather

* From Mrs. J. C. Sims and her intelligent son, Clifford Stanley Sims, Assistant Paymaster in the United States Army, we have received assistance indispensable to the completion of this book. At our earnest request, Mrs. Sims has kindly sent us a sketch of her great-grandfather's family. See Appendix G.

timid and formal man. His personal manners and habits may be inferred from his journal and correspondence. He was "a man always conscious of his awful charge." A little more flexibility, cheerfulness, and unrestraint would have left a more radiant halo over his memory; but these were not consistent with his views of ministerial holiness and propriety.

A connection of Major Ross' family, an excellent member of the Episcopal Church, has addressed us the following note:—

"DEAR DR. BRAINERD:—

"Of the beautifully-good pictures that hang 'on memory's wall,' I could not say that your kinsman John Brainerd exceeds them all. The impression left on my mind is, he was far too good. Letters are said to be characteristic; and here, perhaps, we have them in sentences of good words crowded together in such a mass, that you have to wait until they become ancient documents to appreciate them.

"How big these letters were with thoughts I cannot say; but we distinctly remember in early youth to have heard his name always pronounced with reverence, even while perhaps passing one or another of his epistles from an older hand to the blazing hearth.* It seems there

---

* It was the office of the lady writer of the above, innocently, but in our view most disastrously, to aid in consigning the manuscripts of David and John Brainerd, which had long reposed in a garret at Mount Holly, to the flames, about forty years ago. *Hinc illæ lacrymæ!* Sir Isaac Newton said of the innocent pet, whose gambols had upset his ink to the ruin of his great mathematical researches and jottings, "O Diamond! thou little knowest the mischief thou hast done."

must have been a pent-up sort of goodness in him, so that you would never find out while he lived how good he was. His only daughter was very dear to him, but she was not familiar with him; and you know it will be so, when one can only look to see how awful goodness is."

This is not flattering, but doubtless expresses an impression prevailing among the young of his generation concerning not only him, but other dignified clergymen of his day. We think her picture is too deeply shaded. John Brainerd's frequent messages from his little daughter to Dr. Wheelock's children, and the fact that he held a pen in the hand of his infant granddaughter to announce her own birth to the grandmother, show that he had warm affections, and *some* playfulness in his disposition.

Mrs. Hood, now living at Bridgeton, ninety-one years old, says she resided in Deerfield until her twentieth year, and remembers Mr. Brainerd as a pastor.

"He was much given to speaking to children, and would take much notice of them when he visited. I thought a great deal of him when I was a little girl, because he used to speak to me when he met me."

Whatever might have been the personal manners of Mr. Brainerd,—and we believe they were not only dignified, but attractive,—there can be no doubt that he bore with him everywhere a tender, affectionate, and benevolent heart. By his brethren he was called the "good missionary" and "dear Mr. Brainerd." His Indians clung to him with affectionate attachment to the last; and among the aged in all the region from Mount Holly to the seashore his name is still familiar, and his memory cherished with love and reverence.

CHAPTER XLV.

CONCLUDING OBSERVATIONS ON MR. BRAINERD'S LIFE AND LABORS.

AS, from the nature of the case, the writer could have no personal knowledge of Mr. Brainerd, and as this volume embraces almost every item of information concerning him which time has spared, the author has little advantage of his readers in forming a true estimate of Mr. Brainerd, and of the value of his services to the Church and the world. Those who read the book will draw their own conclusions.

Was his life a success or a failure? He had great obstacles to encounter. Not alone was his little Indian flock always invaded by an evil influence from without, but his pecuniary means for doing good were always limited. In New York and Virginia, collections for missions were obstructed by law.*

* The Rev. Epher Whitaker, of Southhold, L. I., under date of January 18, 1865, gives us the following extract from the records of Suffolk Presbytery, L. I.:—

"SMITHTOWN, L. I., October 29, 1761.

"This Presbytery being acquainted with an order of Synod (by a letter from the Rev. Mr. Simon Horton, of New Town), enjoining all their Presbyteries to make a publick collection for the support of the Rev. Mr. Brainerd, missionary among the Indians,—concluded that we cannot safely comply with that order of Synod in promoting such a contribution, it being (as we are informed) *contrary to the Constitution of the civil Government of New York, unless a License or Brief be first obtain'd from the Governour of* the Province for *the purpose.*"

As the first foreign and domestic missionary sustained by the Presbyterian Church in this land, he had to strike out a new path, with no opportunity to avail himself of the observations or experience of others. The arrangements for his support were inchoate, unreliable, and stinted. He lived in a time of public turmoil and revolution. He was alone as a foreign and domestic missionary in a field which required the united and steady exertions of half a dozen preachers of the gospel. That, in spite of all this, he was able to found a colony of Indians at Brotherton, give them the appointments, comforts, and religious privileges of a Christian town, without government aid, to shelter a Christian church there to his death, and at the same time hold up seven churches among the destitute whites, marks a life of eminent success as well as piety.

Despairing of his ability to elevate a small Indian community, surrounded by a broad waste of practical heathenism among the whites, he bravely undertook to grasp all in the arms of Christian love, and lift them—as Peter saw the sheet raised by its four corners—towards heaven. It was a noble idea, well essayed, and successful to a marvel. He did not accomplish all he desired and

---

"HUNTINGDON, L. I., October 27, 1762.

"Another letter received from the Clerk of the Synod, bearing date May 21, 1762, enjoyning us by Synodical authority to propose collections for the support of the Indian missions. We cannot think it safe to comply with the enjunction, for the reasons given in the minutes of October 27, 1761."

attempted; but he evangelized a field so broad, so difficult, and so poor, that when he ascended to heaven there was no one bold enough and benevolent enough to assume his mantle.

In the result of his labors for the poor Indians is there aught to discourage the Church? Nothing whatever. Notwithstanding the ravages of war and sinful temptation, the Indian church at Brotherton, at the death of John Brainerd, embraced by one account one-seventh, by another one-third, of the entire population.* This is, probably, as large a proportion as is found to-day in Princeton or Rahway, N. J., or Northampton, Mass. His people had farms, dwellings, orchards, a mill, a schoolhouse, and a church. They had, it is true, among them idleness, intemperance, and profligacy; but these are not peculiar to Indian neighborhoods.

It is time an avowal should be made, to the credit of the Indians and for the encouragement of their friends, that our aborigines have always shown a readiness to receive the gospel and adopt habits of civilization when they were understood and proper agents employed. It is known that Eliot and his companions in Massachusetts, Horton on Long Island, Stewart among the Mohawks, Kirkland among the Oneidas, the Brainerds with the Delawares, the Moravians in New York, Ohio, and Canada; Blackburn, Byington, and Worcester among the Choctaws and Cherokees, and Gleason

* See remarks on Rankin's Journal, pp. 405, 406.

and Wright among the Tuscaroras, have all and everywhere met with encouragement in their labors. Indian schools have been generally well filled by young sons of the forest. At Lebanon and Cornwall, Conn., Fort Hunter and Oneida, N. Y., Great Crossings, Ky., Brainerd, Tenn., in former days Indian youth gathered by hundreds, all eager to study. The same may be said of modern mission-schools among the Indian tribes of New York and the far West. The Rev. Mr. Bissell, who has a seminary at Twinsburgh, Ohio, was invaded by scores of young Indians, who came voluntarily from the forest to ask an education.*

Dr. Wheelock and John Brainerd, indeed, complain of the conduct of their educated pupils with much feeling; but we must remember that hitherto an educated Indian has had no status in society. He has been a kind of hermaphrodite,—too elevated for his forest companions, and excluded by his caste from good society among the whites. What else could we expect but the ruin of the majority? And yet among Wheelock's and Brainerd's pupils we find Occum preaching in London; Brandt a royal officer with epaulets; Woolley, Fowler, and H. Calvin instructors; and B. S. Calvin training a Christian family in the West, and coming, at seventy-six years of age, a venerable chief, to negotiate successfully for the rights of his people with the government of New Jersey.

* See Rev. Mr. Bissell's letter, Appendix H.

More cases might be cited; but these are enough to show that, in proportion to the number educated, as many Indian pupils became prominent as among white students in our academies. The Indians, we affirm, have readily received the gospel and improved opportunities for literary instruction. Why, then, have the Indian nations perished and their churches died out? We answer, briefly, it has been found impossible to nourish the virtues which cluster around a fixed home and neighborhood while men are frequently rooted up and forced from state to state.* It is difficult to impart industry; economy, and a disposition to lay up wealth to a people whom the violent can outrage without punishment, and the cunning defraud without compunction or infamy. It is not easy to persuade a feeble minority to adopt the religion and modes of a superior race and at the same time avoid the contagion of their vices. It is hopeless to endeavor to create an ambition for education, taste, refinement, and elevated character among a people when they perceive that the possession of all these fails to shelter them from our indifference, injustice, and social contempt. If this has been the allotment of the poor Indian in the presence of a proud and grasping race, we must not wonder that missionary effort has failed to protect Indian nations and churches.†

---

* See Appendix I.

† See Appendix (I), Doc. Hist. of New York, pp. 397, 398.

If Mr. Brainerd, by the grace of God, was enabled to protect his Indian church in its integrity until he was driven from it; if, besides this, for a score of years he was permitted to keep a wild region of country under the influence of the gospel, and, dying, to bequeath to posterity a reputation which has stimulated the faith and activity of the Church for a hundred years, then his life was not a failure.

If human life in its real value is properly measured by its holy and generous impulses and emotions; if virtue is to be estimated by what it will sacrifice and endure for the right; if rewards are finally imparted according to aims and endeavors of usefulness; if the beatitudes of Christ rest on such as hunger and thirst after righteousness; if charity is rated by the depth of its condescension to the low, the patience of its toleration of the ignorant, and its adhesiveness to the well-being of the unthankful and unworthy; then few men have ever transcended John Brainerd in worth or usefulness. All his intercourse with his brethren and society at large seems to have been regulated by a sense of duty and self-respect; and his letters indicate, on his part, a careful compliance with the customs of good society and the obligations and courtesy of a true gentleman. The proprieties of place, persons, position, and circumstances, no inattention nor rudeness ever allow him to forget or neglect.

His writings, in style and finish, compare favorably with those of his cotemporaries one hundred years ago. He aimed at no display of talent or learning. He seems to have been too busy to meddle with mere metaphysical theories, and too conscientious to absorb time and thought on belle-lettres diversions in the regions of imagination and taste. Governed himself by truth and duty, he may have erred in supposing that these alone would govern others; and he may thus have failed in reaching and moulding certain classes of minds. We think he was defective in this respect.

In addition to this, we see some evidence that his caution and prudence bordered on indecision; his modesty on timidity. His tendency in this direction may have been confirmed by his insulation in the wilderness, his labors with the ignorant, and his dependence on church-charities for his salary. Thus, his keen sensibility and high moral standard, joined with imperfect success in his work, made him dissatisfied with himself, and left bolder, more obtuse and reckless, but less worthy men to execute schemes which his piety had planned and his prayers sanctified.

We have sought in vain, in his life, the traces of unkindness towards a human being: he was involved in no contentions; he mixed in no controversies; he is carried away by no fanatical delusions; he rides no theological nor ecclesiastical hobbies; he gives no token of exasperated feeling, permanent or transient; he develops no emotions of jealousy nor envy towards his brethren who basked in sunshine, nor contempt for those in the shade: he was a lover of all good men and good objects, and seems to have hated nothing but sin. He was a holy man of God; and his whole life bears testimony to his sympathy with suffering humanity.

> "And, lo! that withering race, who fade as dew 'neath summer's ray,
> Who, like the rootless weed, are tossed from their own earth away;
> Who trusted to a nation's vow, but found that faith was vain,
> And to their fathers' sepulchres return no more again:
> Long did thine image freshly dwell beside their ancient streams,
> Or mid their wanderings, far and wide, did gild their alien dreams;
> For Heaven to their sequestered haunts thine early steps did guide,
> And the Delaware hath blessed thy prayer his cabin-hearth beside;
> The Indian orphan meekly breathed his sorrows to thine ear,
> And the lofty warrior knelt him down with strange, repentant tear."

In reviewing what can be known of his life, we are unable to fix our eye on a prominent moral defect. He seems to have made duty his standard, and Christ his model; and, though he doubtless fell short in many things, we are unable to see in what, and when, and where he failed. The spirit of all he wrote, as well as the record of all his words and acts, confirm the tradition in his native town, that "*he was as holy a man as his brother David;*" and to have equalled in holiness his eminent brother implied an excellence seldom found on earth.

The holiness of his character, rather than an admiration of his greatness, induced the preparation of this volume; and, in closing it, we have a solid satisfaction in having recalled such an example of moral purity and worth to the gaze and the imitation of present and, we trust, future generations. We can hardly hope by this book to make bad men good, for they will see little beauty or attraction in such a man and such a life; but we shall be greatly disappointed if the *example of John Brainerd fail to make good men better.*

APPENDIX.

A.

Letter of Rev. Joseph G. Symmes, of Cranberry, N. J., concerning Bethel, the former Indian town in his neighborhood (see pp. 107, 419):—

CRANBERRY, N. J., August 27, 1864.

REV. THOMAS BRAINERD, D.D.:—

DEAR SIR:—You came thirty years too late to collect accurate information from the people with reference to the labors of the Brainerds among the Indians in this vicinity. Those who possessed such information have passed away; and all that remains consists of the traditions of a former generation, always inaccurate in some points. But such traditions abound among us; and perhaps it would be well to put some of them upon record. Some of them assert very definitely that under an old elm-tree, now standing at the north end of our village, Brainerd was accustomed to gather his Indians for the worship of God. It is not stated which one of the Brainerds it was; but, as it was probably before the Indian settlement at Bethel, it would seem to have been David.

Concerning the location of the Indian town of Bethel there can be no doubt. It lies to the northeast of the village of Cranberry, a little more than two miles away in a straight line, which is the Indian line. It is about one mile to the west of Old King George's Road. You remarked, once, that your only doubt about this being the location was in its distance from a stream of water. But the Indian Field, as it has long been called, lies on a small stream of never-failing water, supplied by two or three springs; and at the lower end of the Field there is a dam that has been from two to six feet high, and wide enough to permit a wagon to pass. It is still in existence, and is called Beaver Dam, but was probably built by the Indians. This would have given them a large pond of clear water. The space once occupied by the pond was long mowed for hay, but is now a waste. Besides this dam, there are a few old apple-trees to mark the locality; they are said to be the remains of an orchard planted by the Indians. They stand scattered over the ground in such a manner as indicates that they were never planted in regular order. They seem to be natural fruit; but some of them still yield a very good apple. Some of the oldest people around say there was a large orchard there when they were young, which was a great resort of the school-children. The grounds are now under cultivation, and the soil is such as could be made very productive.

There are old burial-grounds in various localities around; but they are falling into neglect, and the traces of them will soon disappear altogether. There are still some mementos preserved of those who were once possessors of this soil; but, as they were crowded out of their possessions by their greedy white brethren, they disappeared from the face of the earth, and their memory is rapidly fading away from the minds of the living. We should rejoice in every effort, such as yours, to rescue that memory from oblivion, and especially such as record the labors made to save the sons of the forest from the march of our civilization,—labors which, though their direct fruits have perished, will yet be had in everlasting remembrance.

Yours very truly,
JOSEPH G. SYMMES.

B.

David and John Brainerd's Journeys in Pennsylvania (see p. 195).

REV. THOS. BRAINERD, D.D.

DEAR SIR:—In compliance with your wish, I will endeavor to give you all the information I possess relative to localities, in order to discriminate the travels of the Rev. David Brainerd when, in 1743 or 1744, he visited the Forks of Delaware, with the view of preaching to a number of Indians residing there. In his journal he mentions but very few places, and such as are mentioned cannot be recognized by the general reader. In the year 1849, I commenced forming a collection of historical facts of Northampton county, Pa., and Mr. Brainerd's stay in the Forks consequently had the requisite attention paid to it which it deserved. We learn from his journal that on the 10th of May, 1743, he left Kanaumeek; after travelling one hundred and forty miles, he arrived at the Minnisinks. This name implies the country belonging to and inhabited by the Monsey or Minsi Indians, who were one of three nations of Indians that formed the so-called Delaware Indians. This country was northward of the Blue or Kittatinny Mountains, and included within its limits the country adjoining that mountain on the north side of it, near one hundred miles northeastward and southwestwardly. The town of Stroudsburg, in Monroe county, is in the Minnisink country; and it was about twenty miles above this town that Mr. Brainerd met with the Indians and conversed with them on the subject of religion. The path or road over which Mr. Brainerd passed was the general thoroughfare from Philadelphia to Albany, the nearest route between those cities, and much frequented by travellers. The path commenced at or near the Hudson River, at Kingston, thence up the Esopus Creek, and down the Machemack Creek to the river Delaware, which it crossed seven miles above Mitford, in Pike county, and continued westwardly along the Blue Mountain to near the Delaware Water Gap, thence to near Bethlehem, where it crossed the Lehigh River, and then in a nearly southwardly course to Philadelphia. Mr. Brainerd continues, and says:—

"On May 13, 1743, I arrived at a place called by the Indians 'Sakauwatung,' within the Forks of Delaware;" the meaning of this Indian name is "the mouth of a creek, where some one resides." This creek is now called Allegheny Creek. It was here where Alexander Hunter lived: he had a farm of three hundred acres of land, and a ferry across the Delaware River. The farm and ferry at present are owned and occupied by a member of the Aten family. It is in Upper Mount Bethel township, Northampton county, about three miles east of the town of Richmond. Mr. Hunter was one of the first settlers of this part of the country,—he, with about thirty other families, arriving here from the north of Ireland in 1730. For many years it was called Hunter's Settlement. There was another Irish settlement near the Lehigh River, fifteen to eighteen miles westward, which was known as Craig's Settlement. These two named persons were the leaders or most prominent amongst them, and both of them appointed justices of the peace in 1748. It appears from Mr. Brainerd's journal that he had his home with Mr. Hunter until November 23, 1744, when he took possession of a cottage mentioned thus: "He [Brainerd], with the help of others, made a little cottage to live in by himself." This cottage was within about one-fourth of a mile of an Indian town, the Indian name of which, as Count Zinzendorf, the Moravian bishop, informs, was Clistowacki, meaning "fine land." The count visited those Indians in August, 1741. Mr. Brainerd alludes to this Indian village very frequently, as being three miles down the river from Mr. Hunter's. In the year 1849, I visited the place where the cottage of Mr. Brainerd had stood: the land then belonged to an old gentleman named Baker, whose wife was the daughter of Abraham Hubler, the purchaser of this land in 1790. Mrs. Baker informed me that her father for many years had kept in good repair a fence around the Indian burying-ground, near to where the Indian cabins had been, about a quarter of a mile from Brainerd's cabin, and that he never would permit the grounds to be ploughed, or otherwise made use of. She pointed out to me the spot where the cabin or cottage had stood; and a well that Brainerd had dug near the cabin, she said, had remained open until a few years ago, when it was filled up with stones. The cabin was about two hundred yards from the Delaware River, and about one mile above the junction of the Martin's Creek with the river Delaware: there is a beautiful level tract of about three hundred acres of land here, and of an excellent quality. Mr. Brainerd frequently visited at Craig's Irish settlement, distant fifteen miles. The road to this settlement passed very near to the Moravian town, called Nazareth. At Craig's Settlement they had a small church, and a preacher, who was also the schoolmaster. On the 9th of September, 1744, Mr. Brainerd set out on his second journey towards Susquehanna River; and he informs us in his journal that he directed his course towards the Indian town more than one hundred and twenty miles westward from the Forks. This Indian town was called Shamokin, and was situated at the junction of the north and west branches of the Susquehanna, where Sunbury now is, about fifty or sixty miles above Harrisburg, and near one hundred and seventy-five miles from his cabin in Lower Mount Bethel township. The path over which he passed (accompanied by his interpreter, Moses Fonda Tetamy) was very bad, and, in passing over the numerous mountains in the present Schuylkill county, actually dangerous. They passed over the Blue Mountain in Bethel township, Berks county, on the Indian path that led direct from Philadelphia, passing near to Reading in that county. Upon his return, Mr. Brainerd proceeded down the Susquehanna River to the junction of the Juniata River, a distance of about forty-five miles. Here, upon an island called Duncan's Island, he met with a large number of Indians. He passed Craig's Settlement fifteen miles westward of his house in Mount Bethel, on his homeward journey.

In 1749, Rev. John Brainerd visited the Moravian Indian town, called Gnadenhutten (meaning "Tents of Grace"). It was situated three miles below the present county town of Carbon county, called Mauch Chunk, about half a mile from the river Lehigh, on the Mahoning Creek. This Moravian town was laid out in 1746, and in 1749 had near four hundred Indians living in it. In proceeding there, Mr. Brainerd passed the Blue Mountain at a small gap, called Smith's Gap, seven miles westward of the Wind Gap. About two or three miles from the foot of the mountain, on the north side, was an Indian town, called Menislagamikessuk; the Moravians preached here regularly, and in 1755, when the Indian wars commenced, these inhabitant Indians removed to Gnadenhutten.

Gnadenhutten was destroyed by hostile Indians on the 24th of November, 1755, and eleven of the missionaries and their wives murdered. In January, 1756, Benjamin Franklin, by order of the Governor of Pennsylvania, erected a fort, called Fort Allen, upon the spot where the town had stood. The well in the fort is yet to be seen.

M. S. Henry,
Historian of Lehigh Valley.

C.

Letter of Rev. Cutting Marsh, on the present condition of the Delaware Indians and their traditions of the Brainerd brothers (see p. 421).

Waupaca, Waupaca County, Wis., July 1, 1864.

Thomas Brainerd, D.D.

Rev'd and dear Sir:—Yours of May 22d, together with one from the Rev. David Greene on the same subject, were duly received. I was glad to see the handwriting of the Rev. D. Greene, my former kind and faithful correspondent whilst laboring amongst the Stockbridge Indians; and I distinctly remember your countenance when you alluded to our student-days, in 1828, at Andover. Oh, how do years dwindle to a mere point in the retrospect! But I did not know, previous to the receipt of your letter, that you were a relative of the missionary Brainerds. Their names are still engraved upon the memories of the living, notwithstanding the ravages of time and death.

Upon the receipt of your letter I wrote to a Delaware woman, who lives with a small remainder of the Stockbridges in an adjoining county, as I knew that she could furnish me with more information upon the subject you desired than any other person living with whom I am acquainted. But my letter was detained a long time in some post-office, which is the reason you have not had an answer sooner: hers has just come to hand. The mention of the names of the missionary Brainerds, and that they had relatives still living, seemed to touch a slumbering chord, which sweetly vibrated in her bosom. That woman was hopefully converted under my preaching, and, although beset with many trials and surrounded by numerous discouragements, still gives evidence of being a new creature in Christ Jesus. Her father, it seems, had told his children much about the Brainerds; and I remember that he used to speak of them with lively interest and great respect.

He was converted under the preaching of the Rev. Jesse Miner, my predecessor amongst the Stockbridges, when an old man, perhaps sixty or seventy years old. I lent him the Memoirs of David Brainerd to read; and one morning early he called upon me in much distress of mind. "Yesterday," said he, "I was reading of his frames of mind before his conversion, and I thought it possible that I might be in the same condition; and, as his preaching was the means of converting my mother, I thought now he was preaching to me." His name was Bartholomew S. Calvin.* He was, at the solicitation of the Society in Scotland, selected by John Brainerd to receive a liberal education. His natural talents were above mediocrity; but in his Sophomore year in college the funds failed in consequence of the Revolutionary War with England, and he was obliged to leave college. Afterwards it appears that he was employed as a school-teacher amongst the Indians for some years.

His daughter, who has only one surviving sister of quite a family of children, says that her great-grandfather, who resided in New Jersey, was a king amongst his people; and although he lived and died a pagan, yet he was said to be a very upright and honest man. He was rich, and owned a great deal of land and many horses; that his name was We-queh-a-lak.

A wicked white man living amongst his people would from time to time get him intoxicated, and then extort from him large tracts of land. At a certain time, after he became sober, having been made drunk in this manner, the white man told him how many miles of land he had sold to him. This so exasperated him, that he drew his gun and shot him through the heart. Previously he had been very intimate with the Governor, and they were accustomed to dine at each other's houses.

The old king then gave himself up to the white people, who not only took him, but all of his horses and all of his silver-ware which they could find, of which he had a good deal. His subjects offered to go and release him from jail and the white people, and let him go West. But no; he told them it would not be right for a king to run

* The man who came as delegate to New Jersey in 1832.

away, and, moreover, he exhorted them to live in peace with their pale-faced brethren. He told the white people that he wanted to have them shoot him like a man, as he did, and not hang him; but they disregarded his entreaty, and hung him before the time. The Governor sent him a reprieve, but it was not received until after he was dead. He exhorted his people before he died to go West, where there were no pale-faces; "for," said he, "they will sell you rum and cheat you out of your land. It I suffer the white people to hang me, the Great Spirit will receive me to the good hunting-ground; but if I run away, he will not suffer me to go there."

After the death of the old king, the white people went and took every thing which his wife had left—not only his property, but his land—from her, and turned her out of doors with four or five small children, one of them being only a few days old. But she died soon after her husband, and all of her children, except an only daughter three years old; but, before she grew up, she saw her aunt killed by a white man, and she suffered almost every thing but death. This orphan was the mother of Mr. Calvin, and the *first convert to Christianity* under David Brainerd's preaching after he went amongst the Indians; and her husband was his teacher or interpreter. She said that he was the first white man she could ever love, having suffered so much from them, for she had always been afraid of them; but now God had sent this man to pay her for all the wrongs which she had suffered, and now she could pray for everybody.

She loved David Brainerd very much, because he loved his heavenly Father so much that he was willing to endure hardships, travelling over mountains, suffering hunger, and lying on the ground, that he might do her people good; and she did every thing she could for his comfort.

After his death, his brother John succeeded him, and died much lamented by the Indians. Her father said, when David Brainerd first explained to the Indians what sin was, and how Jesus Christ came into the world and died to save them from everlasting punishment, it affected them so much to hear that Christ suffered to save such wicked Indians as they were, that they threw themselves upon the ground and sobbed aloud. Several hundreds were hopefully converted under his preaching, and he had two or three large churches in different parts of the country, as the Delawares were quite numerous at that time. Before David came amongst them, his people commenced going West in small bands; but, after the Brainerds closed their labors amongst them, they followed on after their brethren in small bands, and many of them carried the good seed which had been sown in their hearts to the far West. But the last company which was left in New Jersey her father brought to New Stockbridge, in the State of New York. Some of these went to Kansas; but they are dead, and nearly all which he brought with him.

Says that she never heard her father say much about David's labors amongst the Stockbridges, as he knew but little respecting them; but that she had heard old Mr. Metoxen, who was a head man amongst them, and lived and died a devoted Christian, say that David did a great deal of good amongst his people, and had a large church, but that he did not stay long.

Old Mr. Metoxen has been dead a number of years.

When John Brainerd died, he left the *conch-shell* which his brother and himself also used to call the people together for public worship. It bears evident marks of age by its smoothness; and I obtained it of his daughter, and preserve it as a precious memento of such devoted missionaries.

Whilst I labored amongst the Stockbridges, it was composed of remnants of two other tribes besides them, namely, Delawares and Munsies. My church at one time, I think, numbered about seventy members, and generally they gave as good evidence of personal piety as a church of the same number amongst white people. But political dissension was their ruin. A part wished to become citizens of the United States, and another was determined to remain in the Indian state. This, together with another cause, beyond my control or the control of the American Board, seemed to render my labors well nigh nugatory. I was succeeded by an excellent brother in the ministry, though not a missionary of the Board; and, after laboring for a considerable time, he gave up, for the same reasons, I believe, that I did.

Since I left them they have been in a deplorable condition, very much divided and distracted. They sold out the Reservation which they owned when I labored with them, and have part of them removed to one in an adjoining county; but it is so poor and frosty that they cannot live there, and they are about to sell out to go West, perhaps to Nebraska. There are only thirty-four families in this latter place, with a church of about twenty members in connection with the Methodists; but there are only ten of the old members. Some thirty of the Stockbridges have enlisted in the United States service, but some are already dead.

Yours very truly,

CUTTING MARSH.

[The Indian woman's story, if it misstates some facts, is generally truthful, and confirms our statement, that the religious influence exerted by the Brainerds still lives, and is energizing on the Indian tribes of the West. Our old friend, the Rev. Mr. Marsh, will have from our readers many thanks for his interesting communication.—EDITOR.]

D.

[The following, from the *Missionary Herald* of 1834, is confirmatory of the letter of Rev. Mr. Marsh, as to the interest still felt by Indian wanderers in the missionaries of New Jersey. The extract is long, but we could not withhold it from our readers. The scene occurred some six hundred miles beyond the Mississippi (see p. 423).]

David Brainerd not Forgotten.

On the subject of converting the Indians to Christ, the question is often asked, "Where are the fruits of the labors of Eliot, the Mayhews, Brainerd, and other eminently holy and successful missionaries among them?"

The churches must charge to the account of their own negligence or abandonment of the work, that they have seen so little fruit from the labors of those missionaries of apostolic spirit, just referred to. Successors were not sent to carry forward and finish the work which they began; to instruct, enlarge, and perpetuate the churches which they gathered; or to prepare books, establish schools, and use other means for promoting their intellectual improvement. A vine was planted, a choice vine; but it was overtopped and choked by thorns; and while no man dug about it or watered it, or even visited it to see whether it bore fruit or not, it withered and died.

The following interesting account of a single family descended from David Brainerd's church was addressed to a Christian friend, and has been kindly forwarded for the *Herald*:—

"I have here, in this part of the world, found some of the children of David Brainerd's church-members. My heart has been so full ever since I found them, that I have hardly thought of any thing else; and this morning I resolved to return to the house, and sit down and give some account of them.

"Last Saturday I went to a missionary-station in the Shawnee nation, situated a little above the mouth of the Kansas River, and about a mile and a half from the river on the south side. A two-days' meeting among the Shawnee and Delaware Indians commenced on this day. Full an hundred Indians assembled. They were well dressed, and they behaved well; many of them appeared to be serious Mr. Kingsbury and Mr. Pixley, late of the Osage mission, were there with the people at the first meeting. At the second meeting, Mr. Kingsbury and myself addressed the Indians through interpreters. We told them about the Choctaws, and our labors among them: they were quite attentive.

"After the meeting closed, I walked a few steps and spoke to an Indian woman, who spoke good English. I inquired of her concerning her origin. She said she belonged to David Brainerd's people. This at once roused up my heart to make many inquiries. At her side sat her sister, also a member of the church: both could read in the Bible, and both kept their Bibles through all their wanderings. Their father and mother and grandmother were members of David Brainerd's church.

"These two women became pious about twenty years since, under the preaching of Isaac Wab-e, who was a disciple of Sampson Occum, at Brotherton, in the State of New York. When they were quite young, their father, Jacob Skiket,* left the State of New Jersey, and removed to New York. The children yet remember how he prayed in his family. They spoke much of their grandmother, who often prayed with them, and, when she prayed, Catharine, one of the sisters, said, 'I would look to see if I could see anybody; but I could not see any one.'

"I asked Catharine if she had ever seen any trouble.

"'Oh, yes!' she replied.

"'Have you ever seen the time when your children have cried for something to eat, and you had nothing to give them?'

"'Oh, yes! When we lived down on James River (which is a branch of White River, which empties into the Mississippi), we had hard times: we had to go one hundred and fifty miles to buy corn, and we had no preaching.'

"'Did not you almost forget the things of religion, and your hearts become cold?'

"'Oh, yes! my heart died;' and here she spoke at length.

"Elizabeth then spoke of her troubles, when she was on a journey of nine hundred miles from the State of New York, and, while passing along on the south shore of Lake Erie, her husband died of the lake fever, leaving her with six small children, and the youngest two days

* His real name was Stakit, not "Skiket." He was one of John Brainerd's principal men who signed the answer to the Muskingum invitation, before recorded.—ED.

old. 'I thought I never should get through my troubles; but the Lord helped me; I did not forsake him.' *She now has a son who is pious, and prays in his family;* his mother lives with him. These two old women were well dressed, spoke good English, and seemed to be very happy, as now they live where they can attend religious meetings. They sustain a good religious character among their acquaintance; their children have attended our mission-school at Harmony. Think of this, and see how the Lord provides for his people, for their children and their children's children! A school was established at Harmony, in the Osage nation, to educate the grandchildren of David Brainerd's church-members. Several of the children are hopefully pious.

"I also inquired about David Brainerd. 'What did your grandmother say about him?'

"'He was a young man,—he was a lovely man; he was a staff,—he was a staff to walk with. He went about from house to house to talk about religion: that was his way. He slept on a deer-skin or a bear-skin. He ate bear-meat and samp: then we knew he was not proud. He would come to my grandmother's and say, "I am hungry,—make haste!" Then she would take down the kettle, and he would eat. But some of the people did not like him, and said, "What has this white man come here for? we don't want him here?" and they told him to go off. When the Indians assembled to dance and have a feast, he would go there also, and go away in the bushes and pray for them; and then some said, "We do not want this white man here; let us make away with him." But others said, "No; we will not kill him." After a while they found that he was an honest man, and then they would do any thing he said.'

"I then asked her why Brainerd died so soon, as he was a young man.

"'My grandmother said he was not used to our way of living,—so cold in the winter, sleeping on skins and on the ground. He went to New England, and died of the consumption.'

"I then told her where and how he died.

"'After his death, his brother John came to our people: he died in Deerfield, in New Jersey. He was in doubt* when he was about to die, and one Indian woman went and talked to him.'

"I could tell you much more, and must add what a girl, residing

* We see in this painful evidence that John Brainerd shared in the peculiarities of his family, many of whom, first and last, have had a tendency to religious despondency. My own pious father, a most conscientious man, was thus afflicted.—Ed.

in a missionary's family, said of these women one day to her mistress: 'I think these old Indian women have meetings enough now. When they lived on James River, they were always talking about how much they wanted meetings; and, when the Sabbath came, they would gather up all their children and have a meeting by themselves. No one ever went to see what kind of meeting it was; but they always had their meetings on Sundays.'

"I give you, as near as I can, a literal statement of what I have heard. I spent Saturday and the Sabbath at the meeting, and had several opportunities to converse with the women. I seemed to be nearer at least to Brainerd, as a laborer, than I ever expected to be. I had often inquired for the remnants of his flock, and now I saw them. Truly my heart was full: I saw the goodness and faithfulness of God. These two were the only persons belonging to Brainerd's people in the place; there are others at Green Bay."

E.

Letter of Rev. Allen H. Brown, of Absecom, N. J., on John Brainerd's Domestic Missionary Labors (see p. 126).

Rev. Thomas Brainerd, D.D.

Dear Sir:—Upon a subject of such mutual interest as the life and labors of the Rev. John Brainerd, I extend to you the right hand of coöperation. For seventeen years I have travelled more or less extensively over the same ground which he trod, and during this period have discovered some facts respecting the churches planted by him, which had passed into oblivion and were entirely unknown to the Presbyteries of the present day. Like a traveller among ancient ruins, we felt a sadness, which was relieved somewhat by the hope that these ruins shall be built again.

From the second volume of the Minutes of the Presbytery of Philadelphia, commencing with 1759, it appears that frequent supplications for supplies were presented, and that appointments were made, for Great Egg Harbor and Little Egg Harbor, and in 1762 supplies were requested for Barnegat Shore. During the time of the Revolutionary War, and subsequently, these places are mentioned with less frequency.

First in time and importance here belongs Mr. Brainerd's letter to Enoch Green (published originally in Dr. Van Rensselaer's Presbyterian Magazine for 1852, p. 471).

The attentive reader, comparing the *private houses* herein mentioned with the *meeting-houses* of Mr. Fithian's later journal, will notice the progress made in the erection of houses of worship from 1761 to 1775. For purposes of reference the following letter is re-inserted:—

TRENTON, June 21, 1761.

REV'D AND DEAR SIR:—

It has not been in my power, by any means, to make a visit to the Shore since the session of Synod, and consequently could not make appointments for you. Your places of preaching, however, will be as follows: Tom's River, the most northerly place; then southward, Goodluck, either at Thomas Potter's or David Woodmansee's; Barnegat, at Mr. Rulon's; Manuhocking, Mr. Haywood's or Mr. Randal's; Wading River, at Charles Loveman's or John Leak's; Great Egg Harbor, Captain Davis', Wm. Reed's, Benjamin Ingersoll's, Andrew Blackman's, John English's, Philip Scull's, George May's, and Elijah Clark's; Cape May, either at Captain Stillwill's or John Golden's, and at Tuckahoe meeting-house; and at any other places you may think proper when you come on the spot. And some of those mentioned, possibly, you may not think best to preach at; that will be as you judge best; but these are the houses where meetings are generally held.

If you could begin with Tom's River, and be there a day or two before Sabbath to notify the people, then you might make the rest of your appointments and send them seasonably before you. The proportion will be two Sabbaths to the northward of Little Egg Harbor, three in Great Egg Harbor, one at the Cape or Tuckahoe, and as many weekly lectures at all as you can.

Thus, dear sir, in a minute or two, as I pass through town, I have given you these hints, which, perhaps, may be of some use to your tour on the Shore: in which I hope the blessing of God will attend your labors, and am, with all respect,

Reverend and dear sir,

Your affectionate brother,

JOHN BRAINERD.

To the Rev. ENOCH GREEN.

P.S.—If you could consult with Mr. Thomas Smith and Mr. McKnight, who will succeed you, and make their appointments for them, it would be of use. I hope you will be kind enough to call and see me on your return.

Tom's River is now the flourishing county seat of Ocean county. Its old, dilapidated, free church has been succeeded by substantial

Methodist and Presbyterian churches: the latter was dedicated in September, 1858.

Here for several years has been a Mormon house of worship. If the labors begun by Brainerd and his cotemporaries had not been suspended for three-quarters of a century, whether Mormonism would have found this only home in New Jersey is a question which we submit to the consideration of the thoughtful reader.

At Goodluck is a tombstone, with this inscription: "In memory of Thomas Potter, the Friend and Patron of John Murray, an early advocate of Universalism in America."

The curious autobiography of Murray, published in Boston in 1853, gives an account of eccentric Thomas Potter, and illustrates the times and scenes during which our missionaries labored.

Murray, taking passage in a vessel from Philadelphia to New York, was driven ashore, during a fog, near Cranberry Inlet. In quest of fish, he met Potter, who surprised him by his abrupt refusal to sell, and free offer to give what he needed. Potter gives this account of himself and the country:—

"I am a poor, ignorant man; I know neither how to read nor write. I was born in these woods, and my father did not think proper to teach me my letters. I went on coasting-voyages to New York, and was pressed on board a man-of-war; I ran away, and returned. I entered into navigation, constructed a saw-mill, and have got together a large estate. I opened my house to the stranger, and especially if a travelling minister passed this way he always received an invitation to put up at my house and hold his meetings here. I continued this practice for seven years, and was fond of asking them questions. My wife became weary of having meetings held in her house; and I determined to build a house for the worship of God. My neighbors offered assistance; but I declined it, and said that God will send me a preacher, and of a very different stamp from those who have heretofore preached at my house and are perpetually contradicting themselves."

The Baptists first applied for the house; but Potter replied that all should be equally welcome to preach in it. The Quakers and Presbyterians received similar answers. He continues:—

"I engaged the first year with a man whom I exceedingly disliked. We parted; and for some years we have had no stated minister."

Potter claimed a vivid impression, almost a supernatural intimation, that the vessel cast away contained the long-looked-for preacher after his own heart, and that Murray was the man.

Murray, seeing only thick woods (the tavern across the field excepted), requested to know what he meant by neighbors.

"Oh, sir, we assemble a large congregation whenever the meeting-house is opened. Indeed, when my father first settled here, he was obliged to go twenty miles to grind a bushel of corn; but there are now more than seven hundred inhabitants within that distance."

The wind continuing unfavorable for Murray's departure, he on Saturday afternoon consented to preach, and servants were sent on horseback to give notice, far and wide, until ten in the evening.

It was in September, 1770, when John Murray consented to accept Potter's invitation, and remain a few years preaching universal salvation. He says:—

"Our Sundays were indeed blessed, holy days! People began to throng from all quarters on horseback; some from the distance of twenty miles."

This may seem too extended a digression from John Brainerd's letter to Enoch Green; and we will return to it, after giving Murray's account of Potter's dwelling and meeting-house:—

"I returned to the cabin. The house was neat, the situation enchanting: it was on the margin of the deep, on the side of an extensive bay, which abounded with fish of every description and a great variety of water-fowl. On the other side of this dwelling, after passing over a few fields (which at this time stood thick with corn), venerable woods, that seemed the coevals of time, presented a 'scene for contemplation fit, towering majestic, and filling the devotional mind with a religious awe.'

"I entered the meeting-house. It was neat and convenient, expressive of the character of the builder. There were no pews: the pulpit was rather in the Quaker mode; the seats were constructed with backs, roomy, and even elegant. I said there were no pews: there was one large square pew just before the pulpit; in this sat the venerable man and his family, particular friends, and visiting strangers. In this pew sat upon this occasion this happy man; and surely no man upon this side of heaven was ever more completely happy."

Potter, in his last will, gave the meeting-house and one acre of ground to John Murray. Subsequently the executor sold the adjoining property, and, no reservation being made of the meeting-house, this passed into the hands of the Methodists, by whom it is still held. A Conference of Universalists was held there in 1833, and by them the tombstone was erected to the memory of Thomas Potter.

In another burial-ground at Goodluck is an old brown head-stone, with this inscription:—

David Woodmansee,
Born Nov. 14, 1719,
Died July 13, 1799,
In his 80th year.

From Tom's River to Tuckerton is a distance, from north to south, of thirty miles. In this district lived the Potters, the Woodmansees, the Rulons, the Haywoods, and the Randals. Only recently has the Presbyterian Church cultivated this important district, and appointed an itinerant for the pleasant and populous villages of Forked River, Weir Town, Barnegat, and Manuhocking. Webster's History (page 568) says: "There was in 1767 a new Presbyterian meeting-house at Barnegat, and probably as early was one at Manahawken;" but I have not yet found the oldest inhabitant who can give any traditional confirmation of this statement.

Coming from Tuckerton and the ocean, about six or nine miles in a northwesterly course, and keeping on the north side of the Little Egg Harbor or Mullica River, in Burlington county, we find Bass River and Wading River, where lived the Lovemans and the Leaks. A small church at Bass River, and a more costly edifice at Tuckerton, with its school and parsonage and settled pastor, are among the results of many visits of the Rev. Samuel Miller and others, and of the one visit of Rev. Dr. C. Van Rensselaer, who gave not only his living but his dying testimony to the importance of the field by his legacy of one thousand dollars to the Church of Tuckerton.

We must continue the same course wearily through the sand to find a bridge at the head of navigation whereby we cross into the Great Egg Harbor country, between the Little and Great Egg Harbor Rivers, now belonging to Atlantic county. In this district lived the next eight families, to whom Mr. Brainerd introduced Mr. Green. Here, too, fourteen years afterwards, Mr. Fithian found three houses of worship; and at the present day the traveller will find four edifices and five Presbyterian organizations, viz., May's Landing, Leed's Point, Absecom, Brainerd, and Hammonton.

On the borders of Atlantic, Cumberland, and Cape May counties is Tuckahoe, with a Presbyterian church of recent origin.

We cannot positively decide what or where was the only meeting-house which Mr. Green could occupy in his long ride: long indeed, for he could not visit all the places mentioned *between* the two extremes, Tom's River and Tuckahoe meeting-house, even by the *most direct route*, without riding at least one hundred miles; and while searching out the families he probably travelled much more.

The following statements are drawn chiefly from permanent records; while some of the connecting links of history are furnished by living witnesses.

They were published in the Woodbury "Constitution" in 1850.

We now present some extracts from the journal of Mr. Philip V. Fithian, who was licensed to preach by the Presbytery of Philadelphia, November 6, 1774, and who visited Egg Harbor in February, 1775. The original journal is in the possession of Dr. E. Fithian, of Greenwich, to whose kindness we are indebted for a copy of this interesting document.

"*Friday, February* 3, 1775.—Early in the morning, in company with Dr. Elmer, I left Cohansie for Egg Harbor. We arrived at Mr. Thomas Stites', at Great Egg Harbor, about 4 P.M. Sermon was appointed for Sunday at Mr. Champion's, in the neighborhood, a half-brother in the cause.

"*Sunday, 5th.*—Many straggling, impertinent, vociferous swamp-men accompanied me this morning; they, however, used me with great civility. At 12 began service. There were present between forty and fifty persons, who were attentive without any impropriety of behavior, and seemed to have some solemnity. I spoke with great freedom of spirit, yet, I hope, with a real reverence of the universal presence and awful majesty of the great God.

"*Monday, 6th.*—I rode to the Forks at Little Egg Harbor, and put up, according to direction, at Elijah Clark's, Esq. Mr. Clark is a man of fortune and taste: he appears also to be a man of integrity and piety, an Israelite indeed; and, O religion, thou hast one warm and unfeigned advocate in good and useful Mrs. Clark! I had rather have her spirit with the condition of a starving beggar, than destitute of it to have the wealth of worlds: she has more than the form, she has the spirit, of religion. This peaceful, friendly, heaven-like spirit is breathing from her in every sentence.

"*Wednesday, 8th.*—According to appointment, I preached in Mr. Clark's little log meeting-house; present about forty. I understand the people in this wild and thinly-settled country are extremely nice and difficult to be suited in preaching; one would think that scarcely any but a clamorous person, who has assurance enough to make a rumpus and bluster in the pulpit, would have admirers here. It is, however, otherwise. They must have, before they can be entertained, good speaking, good sense, *sound divinity*, and neatness and cleanliness in the person and dress of the preacher: this I found from the remarks which several of them freely made upon gentlemen who had formerly preached here.

"*Sunday*, 12*th*.—We had at the small log house a large assembly. The day snowy. I preached but once.

"*Monday*, 13*th*.—I rode by appointment up to Brotherton, and preached to Mr. Brainerd's Indians. Present about thirty, and as many white people."

Mr. Fithian then proceeded to Greenwich, and, returning on the 21st to Egg Harbor, writes thus:—

"*Saturday*, 25*th*.—From the Forks of Little Egg Harbor I rode to the seashore, to Mr. Price's, an English young gentleman of fortune and breeding, with a design to preach still lower down.

"*Sunday*, 26*th*.—I preached to a thin assembly at Cedar Bridge meeting-house. At 2 P.M. I preached at Absecom, at one Mr. Steelman's; a full house.

"*Monday*, 27*th*.—At 11 I preached at Clark's Mill meeting-house; the assembly very attentive. Here they gave me a dollar. Afternoon, I returned to the Forks; found Mr. and Mrs. Brainerd there.

"*Sunday, March* 12*th*.—Our little meeting-house almost filled. Most of the people from the Furnace, almost every one from Mr. Clark's little settlement and Mr. Wescott's; and, blessed be God! all seemed attentive. I preached twice.

"*Monday*, 13*th*.—After dinner I rode over to the Furnace" at Batsto, "and visited friendly and agreeable Mrs. Richards. Toward evening, with Mr. and Mrs. R. and Mrs. B., called to see Mrs. P., where we had some useful conversation. In the evening, rode from the Furnace to the singing-school: we had not, however, the greatest harmony. On our return, at my lodgings was pious Mr. Brainerd arrived for the serious exercises appointed for to-morrow. I sat with him and listened to his pious and useful discourse till 11, when I went reluctantly to bed.

"*Tuesday*, 14*th*.—A solemn fast. The day rainy: we have yet a good number. At Mr. Brainerd's request, I preached first from Lamentations iii. 40, composed for the occasion. Mr. B. afterwards preached an excellent discourse on the happiness of a strong and special reliance on the merits of the Redeemer.

"I have said that the people here are nice in their taste concerning preaching. It is not without reason: they have had subjects for comparison. Mr. Brainerd and Mr. Clark enumerated the following gentlemen who have occasionally, and some of them *very often*, preached here as supplies: Messrs. Brainerd, Tennent, Smith, Benj. Chestnut, Hunter, Spencer, Dr. James Sproat, Charles Beatty, Wm. Ramsey, Nehemiah Greenman, Green, J. Clark, S. Clark, McKnight, McCracken, Mitchell, Watt, Boyd, Gravis, Brockway, Van Artsdalen, Hollinshead McClure, Frisby, Keith, and Andrew Hunter, jr."

Here are the names of twenty-six Presbyterian ministers besides Mr. Fithian, who left their flocks in Cape May, Philadelphia, and other places, and travelled long distances on horseback that they might seek and feed the few scattered sheep in the wilderness. Mr. Greenman at one time left his congregation at Pilesgrove, now Pittsgrove, and spent six months on the shore, and almost made an engagement to settle there.

What conclusion shall we draw? Did those servants of God esteem this region more important, or had they any more of the spirit of self-sacrifice than their successors, that until recently, and with a vastly increased population, the existence and situation of these churches were actually unknown to the two Presbyteries within, or rather between, whose bounds this Egg Harbor country is situated? May a double portion of their spirit fall upon *us*, and may their God raise up and qualify many to walk in their footsteps!

We proceed to show the situation of the places which Rev. P. V. Fithian mentions in his journal. "Champion's," to whose place he first came, was probably near Tuckahoe, as one part of the village is now called Champion's Landing. The waters of the Atsion and Batsto Creeks unite near the present villages of Pleasant Mills and Batsto, and form the Little Egg Harbor or Mullica River. At or near these Forks stood "Mr. Clark's little log meeting-house," built of cedar logs and about twenty-five feet square, ceiled throughout with cedar. Upon nearly the same site stands a commodious house of worship, in which the Methodist Episcopal Church has the preference: yet it is free to all denominations, and for nearly three years has been occupied by a Presbyterian minister once in two weeks.

Brotherton, or Indian Town, or Edge Billock, where some of Mr. Brainerd's Indians were settled, was ten miles north of Batsto, in Burlington county; and that district is now commonly called Shamong.

Mr. Fithian next proceeded to the shore of the present Atlantic county, and on his way called on Mr. Price, who lived on the estate now occupied by Enoch Doughty, Esq.

"Steelman's" house was a large two-story dwelling, standing until recently, about a mile north of Absecom, and on the eastern side of the shore road. The lower story was divided into three rooms, but the upper story was undivided, having a large chimney in the centre, and afforded a convenient place for any minister to preach the gospel.

"Clark's Mill meeting-house" was in the northeastern part of Atlantic county, nearly one mile from Unionville. The old burying-ground near the residence of the late Sherman Clark marks its true position. An aged member of the same family, who remembers in his boyhood to have seen John Brainerd, has informed us that this house was about twenty-five feet broad and thirty feet long, and was covered with shingles, and, having been neglected for a long time, was blown down thirty or more years ago. Here was an organized Presbyterian church, and Robert Doughty and Thomas Clark were the ruling elders.

"Cedar Bridge meeting-house," called also Blackman's meeting-house, was near the village of Bargaintown, and about ten miles southeast of May's Landing. It was built of planks nailed perpendicularly.

The following extracts from a deed recorded in Trenton, liber X., folios 407, 408, a copy being certified by James D. Westcott, Secretary of State, will prove the existence of a Presbyterian church and to whom the property of right belongs:—

"This Indenture, made the nineteenth day of March, in the year of our Lord one thousand seven hundred and sixty-four, between Andrew Blackman, Cordwainer, of Egg Harbor, in the county of Gloucester and Province of New Jersey, of the one party, and Joseph Ingersoll, John Scull, Joseph Scull, and Return Babcock, of the aforesaid township, county, and province, of the other party, Witnesseth, that the said Andrew Blackman, for and in consideration of the sum of two pounds, proclamation-money, to him in hand paid before the ensealing hereof, by Joseph Ingersoll, &c., * * * hath granted, sold, &c., * * * ; containing one acre, more or less, together with the mines, &c., * * * ; for the erecting, building, and standing of a Presbyterian Meeting-House, for the carrying on of Publick Religious worship for all that shall incline to meet and assemble in it; together with a publick Burying-yard, for the interment of the deceased of all denominations." * * *

Three years afterward, June 2, 1767, a memorandum was written on the back of the deed, explaining the views of the persons named, and proving that the house had then been erected. It reads as follows:—

"We, the within Grantees, * * * having been chosen Trustees to carry on and manage the building of a Presbyterian meeting-house upon the lands within granted and sold for that purpose, do hereby acknowledge that the said land and meeting-house is not our own personal property, but is bought and built by a subscription of many persons; neither do we claim any other interest in it but what we have in common with all who have subscribed hereto; and, though the legal title is vested in us, yet we hold it only in behalf of our constituents, and do promise that it shall be kept as a house of publick worship and the land for a free Burying-yard, in which all may have equal privileges with ourselves, without monopolizing it or engrossing and applying it to any private use of our own. A memorandum whereof we leave on the back of this instrument, that posterity may not be defrauded of their right or mistaken about the intent hereof, which is to secure a House of Public Worship, as before mentioned. In testimony whereof, we have hereunto subscribed our names, hands, and seals." * * *

Respecting the subsequent history of this house, we content ourselves with adding that, before it was decayed, the materials were removed, and upon a portion of the very site of the old building stands now a brick edifice, bearing on its front this inscription:—

METHODIST CHURCH, 1822.

Let us now visit the remains of another Brainerd church, which have been discovered near Bridgeport, on the Wading River, in Burlington county. There John Brainerd preached under a wide-spreading oak, until a cedar log house was erected. The oak still casts its shade, and a few of the foundation-stones of the building and the crumbling monuments of the burial-ground mark the consecrated spot. Our chief information in reference to it is drawn from the copy of a will which James Linn, Register of the Prerogative Court in 1817, certified to be a true transcript from liber No. 19 of Wills, page 214, &c., remaining in his office. The portion which is interesting to our ecclesiastical history is the following:—

"In the name of God, Amen, I, John Leak, of Little Egg Harbor, in the County of Burlington, in the Western Division of New Jersey, yeoman. I do, this fifth day of May, in the year of our Lord one thousand seven hundred and seventy-seven, &c. &c., * * * Item. I give and bequeath unto the several inhabitants of Wading River and Bass River, in Little Egg Harbor, and to their heirs forever, they being Presbyterians, for the use of the Presbyterian Meeting-House and burial-ground, one certain lot of land, containing sixty-five perches, butted and bounded as followeth: * * * All which said sixty-five perches of land and meeting-house and burial-ground for the use of a Meeting-House for Presbyterians to carry on the worship of God in. But in case it should so happen in process of time that there should be a vacancy when there is no Presbyterian minister or other person set apart to carry on the worship of God in said meeting-house by said Presbyterians, in that case it is my will that any Protestant minister of any Society, that is well recommended by the Society they belong to, to have the liberty to preach in said meeting-house until the Presbyterians can be enabled to carry on the worship of God in said meeting-house themselves; and it is my desire that the Presbyterians belonging to said meeting-house, when there is a vacancy as aforesaid, that they lovingly receive those of other societies that come to minister in said house with Christian love and forbearance as much as possible."

[The Rev. Mr. Brown here gives a detail of Mr. Brainerd's labors among the Indians, but, as he adds no facts to those stated before in this volume, we omit this portion of his letter.]

We propose yet to consider two questions, which are often suggested to the minds of different persons.

Presbyterians, upon hearing the statements contained in this series of letters, with wonder inquire, How is it possible that our Church has so neglected the region in which it was so much esteemed by the first settlers? And some of the descendants of those settlers, many of whom never heard a minister of the Presbyterian Church until very recently, demand, By what right or authority do these intrude into a country where other denominations have so long held undisputed possession?

In reference to the first question, we can present some reasons which have no connection with the doctrine or government of our Church, and which—without admitting her inferiority, or conceding that she was ever driven out, or deliberately determined to abandon that territory—naturally and sufficiently answer the question.

1. Some assign the connection of the churches of West Jersey with the Presbytery and Synod of Philadelphia as an important cause. As they were remote, and attention was called to the more important churches, this thinly-settled region did not receive its due attention.

2. But there is another reason, to which allusion has just been

made. We refer to the *modern* exclusive adherence to the policy of establishing a pastor within a very contracted sphere of usefulness, to the neglect of the work of the evangelist. The first ought ye to have done, and not to leave the other undone.

3. There is another reason, which appears to the writer to have been the occasion and immediate cause of the first neglect of those ancient churches, and to this the other two reasons have been accessory, and account for their subsequent neglect until they have been forgotten. This reason, which is offered with deference to the opinion of older men, is drawn from the circumstances of the times. It was a time of trouble and of war. It is perfectly plain that, up to the days of the Revolution, those churches were nourished constantly by the Presbytery of Philadelphia; and it is equally evident that during and after the noble struggle of our fathers for national independence they began to be neglected. Whatever may be the ultimate benefits resulting from war, there can be no question that it is attended by many immediate evils, and that the religious interests of any community cannot escape its desolating influence.

Leaving out of view the decay of vital piety, the changes of residence, the interruption of business and loss of property, all of which would more or less affect the prosperity of churches, and especially the weaker, what was the direct effect upon the ministry? Some pastors were called from their pulpits to attend to national affairs; others, like the Rev. P. V. Fithian, whose journal has been noticed, served as chaplains in the army or navy. The career of this man of God was short; and, while ministering to the sick and dying soldiers, he himself sickened of the camp-fever, and died. What was the natural consequence when such instances multiplied,—at a time, too, when there were no educational societies nor theological seminaries to raise up young men for the ministry, and, owing to the death of some ministers and the unfaithfulness of others, important churches were found destitute of pastors? What, then, more natural than that these vacant churches should first be supplied,—as, for example, John Brainerd was called, in 1777, to be the pastor at Deerfield, where he died, in 1781,—and thus laborers were withdrawn from the frontier to the centre? About the same period the Methodist ministers, who had retired from our country during the Revolutionary War from conscientious convictions of duty (we would believe), returned again; and, with the zeal for which they have ever been celebrated, entered into places which Presbyterians, *in consequence of the circumstances of the times*, could not cultivate; and we presume that the scattered Presbyterians, seeing no prospect of having a church of their own order, and esteeming their Methodist brethren as pious and devoted men, did act upon the advice of that good Presbyterian, John Leak, and did "receive them with Christian love and forbearance as much as possible."

A. H. B.

F.

Letters from Mrs. Ross to her step-mother, Mrs. Brainerd (see p. 439).

MOUNT HOLLY, April 18, 1788.

MY DEAR MAMMA:—

I have never been able to learn as yet where you are, or whether you have yet arrived in the city or not; but I do assure you I am very anxious to hear from you. My house seems to have a vacancy that nothing temporal will supply, though my friends have been very kind,—especially Mrs. Brumley and Mrs. Spraggs.

Doctor [Ross, her husband] and the children are well; Betsey [her daughter] sends her duty to grandma, and three kisses to Sophia [Mrs. Ross' oldest child]; please to give a dozen from me to my precious lamb. My dear mamma, do not be forgetful of me at the throne of grace; and, oh, how unwearied a wrestler have I need to be to reach His hands who formed all things, through the interceding blood of a dear Redeemer! I commit my guilty soul to him, but not, I trust, without strict watchfulness and prayer. Please to remember me to all who think me worthy of their notice. Doctor [Ross] desires to be remembered affectionately to you and our dear Sophia. Adieu, my dear mamma.

Believe me ever your affectionate,
dutiful daughter,
M. ROSS.

MOUNT HOLLY, June, 1788.

MY DEAR MAMMA:—

I was very happy in hearing from you, but shall be much happier in seeing you as soon as is agreeable to you and dear aunt Seliunus. We have got the house completely and beautifully clean; you will hardly know us when you return: the partition is down. By advice of my friends I have finally dismissed Bidde, as I could no longer put up with her impudence, and have got one of the neatest little creatures to do my whitewashing: I believe that you never saw walls in your life so smooth and white; all that is now wanting is your dear, good company to make me happy.

Doctor has been very ill these two days, but is now something better. I feel myself very much fatigued; but rest will, I hope, restore me to myself. You are never absent from my mind: your counsels and advice are ever present with me. Oh, how happy shall I be in your return! Please to remember me to all inquiring friends. I have sent you the things you wrote for.

Adieu, my dear mamma.

Believe me,
Ever yours dutifully,
M. Ross.

Mount Holly, Thursday evening.

September, 1788.

My dear Mamma:—

I was very happy to hear of your safe arrival in town: I thank you for the biscuits and radishes: they have been a great comfort to me. I think I am something better than I was when you left me, but am still weak. We all long much to see you return; but I hope a kind and gracious Providence will be all our preserver until that moment arrives that shall reunite us. We are, through Divine favor, pretty well; nothing remarkable has happened since your departure.

I hope, my dear mamma, you will not forget your promise next Saturday. The doctor and children join in affectionate love to you and all inquiring friends. Sophia is writing to you, and she has been a pretty good girl; she incloses in her letter the measure of her hat, which pleases her much. Remember me affectionately to all who think me worth inquiring after, but particularly Mrs. Annis; and that a kind and gracious Providence may restore you soon to us again is the sincere prayer of,

Dear mamma,
Your ever affectionate,
dutiful daughter,
Mary Ross.

Mount Holly, Thursday evening.

My dear Mamma:—

I hope this will meet you on its arrival at the city. I should not wish to disturb the pleasure you enjoy, were not our family visited by sickness. I have been myself very poorly this two weeks, but enabled, I trust, to commit all into better hands, from which springs a peace passing understanding indeed; but my body has been much racked with pain.

My dear little Alexander was and still is very sick; it seems he has got some hurt on the left side, so that he screams out every time he is touched, and daily and hourly cries for grandma. While I am writing, he is much pleased at the thought of your coming home. I need not attempt to describe the joy it will be to all our family, though to none more than,

My dear mamma,

Your affectionate, dutiful daughter,

M. Ross.

November 4, 1788.

G.

Letter from Mrs. E. M. Sims (see p. 441).

PHILADELPHIA, **December 27, 1864.**

MY DEAR DR. BRAINERD:—

You have given me a task that I scarcely know how to fulfil,—to give you some account of my paternal and maternal grandfathers and grandmothers: they had passed away many years before I was born. My father was an uncommunicative man, though a very superior one; and I should have known but little of his parents but from the fact of my being a very inquisitive child. I asked many questions, and the answers received comprehend my whole store of knowledge.

My mother (John Brainerd's granddaughter) died before I was old enough to estimate or feel her loss; but an aunt of hers, a sister of Dr. John Ross, who lived till she was an aged woman, and who, from being extremely deaf, dwelt far more in thought with the dead than the living, loved to discourse by the hour on the deceased members of her family, and gave me many little particulars concerning them.

Mr. Elijah Clark, my paternal grandfather, was born in Connecticut (I forget his native town), in 1732,—I think I have heard my father say, in the same year and month as General Washington. His father was a man of property, and held responsible offices. My grandfather was sent to Yale College, and educated. After completing his course, at a later period, he came into New Jersey, and purchased a large tract of land near Egg Harbor, and built upon it, and settled there. He married Miss Jane Lardner, both a godly and beautiful woman, who was born in Ireland, though belonging to an English family.

My father told me that the Lardners had been among the Dissenters from an early period. During the wars of the Commonwealth they were firm adherents of Cromwell's, and served him faithfully.

On the accession of Charles II., their position being an uncomfortable one in England, they removed to the north of Ireland, and came from thence to this country. My father's name was John Lardner Clark. My grandparents on this side of the house were very godly people. Elijah Clark, I have always been told, was a man of mind, taste, and cultivation. He possessed a fine library, and was an extensive reader. He owned many slaves, whom he instructed and cared for as his children: he was quite a wealthy man. He erected a small meeting-house on his plantation, and, when unable to procure the services of an ordained minister, held services in this building every Sunday himself for the benefit of his children and dependents. He had quite a large family of children,—eleven, I think; some died in infancy, but seven reached maturity. My father was one of the younger children. He was a very superior and cultivated man, possessing uncommon force and decision of character.

He had not the advantage of a classical training, owing, as he told me, to the very unsettled and disturbed condition of the country when he was a youth. His elder brothers were educated at Princeton. He was born on his father's plantation about the year 1769, and when quite young came to Philadelphia to reside, entering the counting-house of his brother-in-law, Mr. James Vanuxem (Mrs. Chas. S. Wurts' father), where he continued, afterwards becoming his partner. They were shipping and commission merchants, and held constant correspondence with Italy, France, and England.

Mr. Vanuxem was a Fleming by birth, but was wholly educated in France, and entirely lost his knowledge of his native tongue. My father, from constant intercourse with his brother-in-law as well as with most of the French society of this city, acquired a perfect knowledge of the French tongue, and both wrote and spoke it with exactly the same fluency as he did the English. In 1797 he married Sophia Marion Ross, eldest daughter of Dr. John Ross, and granddaughter of the Rev. John Brainerd. He was about twenty-eight years of age when he married, and my mother only seventeen. I have often heard him say he thought he was marrying a woman, but found he had married a child. My mother died at the age of thirty-one: out of a family of seven children, four died in infancy. My brother Brainerd died in 1837; my sister Louisa (Mrs. James Peacock) and myself are now alone remaining.

My maternal grandfather, Dr. John Ross, was the son of Dr. Alexander Ross, who was born in Scotland, and, after completing his course at Edinburgh University, came to this country and settled in Mount Holly. He married a Miss Becket, whose mother, a Miss De

Normandie, belonged to a French Protestant family who fled from France after the revocation of the Edict of Nantes.

My grandfather was born in Mount Holly about the year 1752. I think he was educated at Princeton, and afterwards adopted his father's profession. He was in the army during the Revolutionary struggle, as an officer. I believe it was in the year 1779 that he married Mary Brainerd, only surviving child of the Rev. John Brainerd, who died, I think, in 1792, at the age of thirty-five, leaving three children; Sophia Marion (my mother) the eldest, Elizabeth, afterwards married to Dr. John Brown, of Swedesborough, N. J., and Alexander, who went to Italy at the age of twenty-one, and died there of some sudden disease. Dr. John Ross was a totally different man from Mr. Elijah Clark,—far more gay and worldly, and, I imagine, with much less dignity and weight of character. I have understood that he was a tall, fine-looking man, and had a great reputation as a singer, being able to entrance an audience with the sweetness and power of his voice.

My mother's early death prevented my getting many little particulars concerning her parents which I might, and no doubt would, have procured had she lived till I was old enough to ask her questions. But I have scarcely any recollection of her at all, excepting the sad one of seeing her in her coffin, which so startled and impressed my childish mind that I have never forgotten it.

Most respectfully and truly yours,

E. M. Sims.

H.

[Old Pine Street Church, to which the author ministers in Philadelphia, have aided the Rev. Mr. Bissell, the writer of the following letter, to the amount of fifteen hundred or two thousand dollars. He did a noble work, with a most generous spirit, but, like John Brainerd and others, was but feebly sustained in his endeavors. His experience is instructive (see p. 448).]

A Modern Experiment in the Education of young Indians.

Twinsburgh, Lake Co., Ohio, July 11, 1864.

Dr. Brainerd.

Dear Sir:—Having a few days since received a note from you by the hand of Mr. Upson, requesting me to give the history of Indian youth who have been educated by me; after some delay, created by the closing of the spring term and other peculiar things, I most cheerfully comply with your request. Suffer me first to premise that, owing to the wide distance which separates these youth from each other and from me, and never having been able to visit their respective localities, I shall be unable to give you many particulars which I have no doubt would equally interest you and myself. Some of them are in the State of New York, some in Central Michigan, some in Northwestern Michigan at Mackinac and at the outlet of Lake Superior, and some in Central Wisconsin and at the head of Lake Superior.

Their whole number will not differ much from one hundred and twenty-five, who have been with us from a single term to three years; perhaps, on an average, one year each.

Let it be further stated that every one of them came of their own free will, and without, in most instances, any certificate of character or circumstances respecting them. Many of them came ignorant of all science, and with none or very little knowledge of our language. Under such circumstances, all sensible people would be ready to conclude that great allowances must be made for them in the matter of high expectations. More than a dozen of them were girls.

Under all these disabilities, and separated as they are widely apart and from me, yet I have been quite as much gratified to learn well of them, and of quite as large proportion of them, as of any class of youth I have educated. A. J. Blackbird is at present the national interpreter of the Ottawas; and, from the last information, instructing and promoting education among his people. Two others, Wakaroo and Allen, have been much employed as interpreters of missionaries laboring among them.

Others are enterprising farmers; encouraging education, temperance, and industrious habits, among the Ottawas and Chippewas.

One of the young ladies, soon after she left us, was employed as principal in an academy at the west end of Lake Superior, among the Ojibways. Of the New York Indian youth, one of them, by the name of Prince, became the principal of the chief high school among the Senecas, and fully maintained his reputation as a teacher of youth; and at least from three to four of the young ladies have become teachers of common schools. Six, I know, and probably several others, have enlisted in the army, and, as officers and privates, are baring their bosoms to the bullets of the rebels for our sakes. I have just received a letter from one, wounded, in Alexandria, saying that another of our scholars was there, also wounded, belonging to the First Michigan regiment of Sharpshooters. In the winter past I received a Michigan newspaper containing two columns written by one of these young men on the state of the country, that would have done honor to the head and heart of some of our best lawyers: I would inclose it to you, but had sent it, previous to the receipt of your note, to a friend of the Indian in Massachusetts. These are the facts I now have on hand, and am persuaded they are but a few only that might be given were I so situated as to get what is now transpiring in regard to them. When we reflect that these youth were so destitute of education and of the habit of studying, I feel that our highest expectations have been realized thus far, and that the amount of good that will finally result from these scanty efforts will be very great.

Some of your excellent people have been interested in aiding your unworthy servant in affording the means of educating these youth, and they would certainly be glad to know that their benefactions have not been in vain: I wish I could gratify these good people much more. If I had had the means of travelling, I should have visited these people and learned all particulars; as it is, I must content myself with the above statements.

Since I saw you last in Philadelphia, I have not been from home to ask a single benefaction; and yet our number of Indian youth has been very considerable.

We had three during the last fall and winter terms; we now have two applications from the West, and have said *yea* to them; one we expect this month. As to the general character and conduct of these youth while with us, I think they will compare well for desirableness with an equal number of white youth. Such is the disposition among our people, even among many professing Christians, to cavil with any thing done for the Indian, I have but little heart to ask them for aid. One exception, as that of Dr. Wilson, is enough to dry up every fountain of benevolence; while a dozen of such examples among our race would do but little damage.

Suffer me here to add, in conclusion, that four years ago, when my excellent companion, who had been a true helpmeet in our efforts and self-denials to help the poor Indian, was gradually sinking into the grave and left me to mourn her loss, I found myself so embarrassed with debt, I sat down and wept, and for the moment resolved to make an assignment of all I had, and content myself with abject poverty. My debts amounted to about six thousand dollars, and no part of it had accrued from extravagance or a single luxury. As I remarked in the above statement, our number of Indians was not less than one hundred and twenty-five, averaging one year each, with board, books, stationery, etc., say at the moderate rate of one hundred dollars per year, making at least twelve thousand dollars, of which we may have received six thousand dollars in every thing: this sacrifice, together with many favors to poor white youth, building, repairing, and losses, thus involved me. Poverty I could endure; but to have it said that I failed in a cause of benevolence so important in my estimation, I could not endure. Upon second thought, I determined, God helping me, I would make every effort to sustain myself and maintain my cause. The war began. My patronage was lessened; my creditors became frightened, and demand upon demand was made for dues; I was distressed on every hand, and had to submit to legal exactions, and that without mercy. We parted with every thing we could spare, denied ourselves all comforts, and, by the blessing of God, we still retain the Institution, and have never as yet omitted our regular terms, or suffered a debt to pass by in default beyond the legal time, nor have we turned the poor Indian away.

How long we may be permitted to struggle thus, I cannot tell. I have felt, sometimes, such are the high rates of living that we must yield the matter; but I pray God that we may go on with our object. More than six thousand youth have gone out from under our hands, and are scattered in every part of our country, acting as governors of States, members of legislatures, ministers, physicians, attorneys, officers in the army, and great numbers of privates. I feel that such a cause should not, must not, fail. I could desire to be free from debt, that I might the more cheerfully endure the necessary cares and labors of the Institution; but God knows what is best, and, I am persuaded, will order all things wisely.

I fear I have already wearied your patience, and will close, asking an interest in your prayers. Give my best respects to Mr. Alexander Whilldin and family, Mr. William Clark, and any others who may be interested in my object.

Yours most affectionately,

SAMUEL BISSELL.

The young Indians came of their own will from the forest to the Seminary of Mr. Bissell, and he could not turn them away. Those who have seconded his efforts rejoice with him that his labors were not in vain. He has coveted neither notoriety nor praise, but, we hope, will not be offended that, by inserting his letter in full, we have linked his name with the memory of David and John Brainerd, whose example of sacrifice he has imitated.—ED.

I.

Indian Wrongs.

[The author believes that the great reason why Indian missions, churches, and nations have so often perished, will be found in the practical adoption towards Indians of the unchristian and inhuman principle applied by Chief-Justice Taney to the negroes, to wit:— "*That they had no rights which white men were bound to respect.*" Hence treaties and covenants with Indians have been regarded about as much as we would regard treaties with apes and monkeys. To inspire semi-civilized communities with a profound regard for the right, while they saw every principle of right trampled upon for their oppression and ruin, has been above the power of ordinary Christian teaching.

In 1768, a great Indian Council was convened by royal authority, as represented by Sir William Johnson, at Fort Stanwix, now Rome, Oneïda county, N. Y., to procure a cession of the lands held by the Mohawks and Oneidas. As early as 1745, the Rev. Mr. Barclay, an Episcopal missionary, had at Fort Hunter, on the Mohawk River, "five hundred converts among the Mohawks, eighty of whom were communicants."

The Rev. Mr. Kirkland and others had made a prosperous beginning among the Oneidas and Senecas. The Six Nations seemed to be in a favorable condition to receive Christianity. But this Council was gathered to root up those Christian communities, through bargains consummated by an appeal to Indian fears, poverty, and recklessness. To their credit be it recorded, two clergymen, Rev. Messrs. Johnson and Avery, attended as delegates from the clergy of New England, to ask that the Indians might not be removed. We give a portion of their remonstrance:—]

*Caveat of two New-England Missionaries against His Majesty's Orders to Sir William Johnson.**

To the Honorable Sir William Johnson, Superintendent of the Six Nations, &c.

Your Excellency having received a letter lately from the Rev. Dr. E. Wheelock, as also seen his instructions for propagating the gospel among the Indians, etc., pursuant whereunto these are humbly to desire and importune your Excellency that, as a tender father to these perishing Indians, your Excellency would be pleased, of your most generous and benevolent disposition, so to befriend their cause

* Documentary History of New York, vol. iv. p. 390.

as to prevent their setting themselves off from their lands, thereby to frustrate the aforesaid design of propagating the gospel among them, which undoubtedly will be the sad consequence of their so doing. That this effect may not happen, your Excellency is humbly desired to restrict the bounds of the respective provinces, that they may not be extended so far north and west as to cut off the lands and inheritance of the natives; but that they possess and enjoy them for their own private temporal use, and that more sacred benefit of propagating the knowledge of the great Saviour of the world among them, that so, by the grace of God, they may have a further opportunity of a more general offer of the gospel to them.

(Signed) JACOB W. JOHNSON,
DAVID AVERY, *Missionaries.*

Dated FORT STANWIX,
October 17, 1768.

*Rev. Mr. Johnson to the Commissioners.**

To Sir Wm. Johnson, Governor Franklin, Colonel Graham, Colonel Butler, and other respectable gentlemen interested and concerned at this Congress.

HONORABLE AND RESPECTABLE:—

As I am here in behalf of Dr. Wheelock, in the cause of propagating the gospel among the Indians of these nations, I must be faithful to let you know that, whereas the Doctor especially, and some others with him, have laid out much labor and cost with a view to spread the gospel among the Indians, we are extremely loth to see the cause die under our hands, and a fund at home of above twelve thousand pounds sterling, that was raised by noble, generous, and charitable benefactors, and additions thereunto in this country, be lost or diverted from the design of the donors; which, we imagine, must be in whole or in great part, if the Indians, and especially these Oneidas, yield up their lands: we therefore ask that a door may be kept open to them where the gospel has been preached and schools set up, that we may know where to find them, and not have to ramble all over the world after them or find them vassals on other men's land.

We therefore pray you, most honorable gentlemen, duly and deeply to consider and weigh the cause, not for man, but for God, to whom you and I must soon give an account.

With all due respect, yours,
JACOB W. JOHNSON.

FORT STANWIX, October 30, 1768.

* Documentary History of New York, vol. iv. p. 394.

[This appeal of these good men was treated as a grand impertinence. In writing to General Gage, under date of November 24, 1768, Sir William Johnson says:—*]

"I have now the pleasure to enclose you a copy of the Indian deed of cession to his Majesty, &c. It will be impossible for you to judge of the difficulties I had to overcome. Added to all the rest, two New-England missionaries came up,—the one of whom was strongly recommended to me by Dr. Wheelock, of Connecticut,—and did all in their power to prevent the Oneidas from agreeing to any line that might be deemed reasonable. They had even the face, in opposition to his Majesty's commands and the desire of the Colonies, to memorial me, praying that the Indians might not be allowed to give up far to the north or west, but to reserve it for the purposes of religion. The New-Englanders have had missionaries for some time amongst the Oneidas and Oqhquagaes, and I was not ignorant that their old pretensions to the Susquehanna lands was their *real*, though religion was their assumed, object; but, knowing that any steps I could take with these missionaries would, from the Indian's conceptions, be deemed violent, *I treated them with silent contempt!*"

[Sir William Johnson's language is a fair specimen of the spirit in which appeals for justice to the red men have been treated by public authority. When the United States Government was induced by Georgia bluster to sacrifice the national honor in violating its treaties with the Cherokee nation in 1832, the climax of injustice to the Indians was reached. "*Finis coronat opus.*" The Indian and negro have been avenged. Sanctioning wrong, our government has in turn felt the sting of wrong, and from the very parties whose cruelties it had silently indorsed.

"The mills of the gods grind slowly;
But they grind exceeding small."]

* Documentary History of New York, vol. iv. pp. 397, 398.

INDEX.

www.ingramcontent.com/pod-product-compliance
Lightning Source LLC
LaVergne TN
LVHW020911110826
845150LV00004B/645

* 9 7 8 1 4 2 5 5 5 6 5 2 5 *